Verses of Life
Through the Chapters of Love
by
Malcolm Alexander Neal

Verses of Life: Through the Chapters of Love
by Malcolm Alexander Neal

Copyright © 2024 by Malcolm Alexander Neal
All rights reserved.

No part of this book may be reproduced, distributed, or transmitted in any form or by any means, including photocopying, recording, or other electronic or mechanical methods, without the prior written permission of the publisher, except in the case of brief quotations embodied in critical reviews and certain other noncommercial uses permitted by copyright law.

For permission requests, please contact the publisher at:
Mac Neal LLC
308 S Jefferson #169, Chicago, IL 60661
Email: malcolm@macnealllc.com

ISBN: 979-8-218-65387-3

Printed in the United States of America

First Edition

Table of Contents

Preface
Emotion: Introspection

Before we embark on this journey through my life's verses, I want to acknowledge those who have played pivotal roles in its creation. While this is not the dedication itself, I want to introduce the **Dedication Section** you'll find within the book, where I've written personal dedications and poems for the individuals who have inspired and supported me along the way.

In that section, you'll find heartfelt acknowledgments to my family and friends, whose love and encouragement have been my bedrock. There is a special dedication to Rafa, my future spouse, whose unwavering love guides me forward. I have also dedicated a poem to my photographer, whose visual artistry parallels the emotions captured in these poems, and to my graphic book artist, whose creativity has brought this collection to life in a tangible way. My editor also have a place in that section, as their insights helped shape this book into its final form. Lastly, there is a dedication to Robert Plutchik, whose work on emotional labels deeply influenced how I assigned and understood the emotions woven throughout each poem in this collection.

"Verses of Life" is a unique biographical poetry collection where each poem serves as a window into significant moments and emotions of my life. More than a collection of poems, "Verses of Life" is a deeply personal narrative of joy, heartbreak, growth, and introspection. My goal through these verses is to normalize the range of emotions we all experience, embracing them as part of the rich tapestry of our existence.

Each chapter will begin with a summary that offers an overview of the themes and emotions explored within the chapter. These summaries guide the reader through the central ideas, preparing them for the emotional landscape they are about to enter. With 10 chapters in total, each one builds upon the last.

The book begins by **introducing** myself, giving you an idea of who I am—my values, interests, the outline of the book, poems that set the tone, my writing process, my love for travel, my horoscope, my stance on therapy, and more. After these introductory poems that set the stage and provide an understanding of the book's framework, you will journey through my **childhood**, middle school, and high school years, which lay the foundation for how I developed my viewpoint on love.

The journey of significant loves starts with **Jace** , a leo, my first love during high school, whose tender friendship blossomed into something deeper. Though our love was significant, we both needed to grow in our own ways. **Kyle**, a Gemini and my first significant relationship, brought intensity and chaos, but ultimately, we realized we were better as friends. **Mark**, a Taurus, came into my life after Jace , and while our connection was passionate, it was a fleeting love that couldn't sustain a long-term relationship. **Darren**, a leo, my ex-husband, and I shared eight years together, but his struggle with alcoholism eventually marred our powerful connection. **Brandon (Bax),** a Libra, entered my life during my divorce; our relationship, while filled with fun and deep conversations, became overwhelming due to his mental health struggles. **Nico**, a Capricorn, brought a profound cultural exchange into my life, but our differences made it impossible to remain friends. Finally, **Rafa**, a Libra, my current love, is a relationship characterized by health, positivity, and deep mutual respect. I know without a doubt that he is my future husband.

The **Perspectives on a Shared World** chapter is a mix of poems—many political, but also a blend of various thoughts that I had while writing this book from May 2024 until September 2024. During this period, there were significant political events, along with impactful moments in my personal life and the lives of those around me. This chapter reflects on a range of topics, not just this period in time, but also birthdays, my ideas about travel, what a relationship should be like, and more. It offers you an insight into my thoughts during these times.

As my story unfolds, especially in the later chapters such as **Nico** and **Rafa**, and also within some of the poems in the **Perspectives on a Shared World** chapter, you will notice a mix of Spanglish. As I began learning Spanish, influenced by my significant relationships with Mexican partners, Spanish became an integral part of my identity and growth. These chapters pay homage to my language journey, reflecting how this learning process has woven into the fabric of my life and my writing. By incorporating both English and Spanish, I aim to honor not only my personal journey but also the rich Mexican culture that has become part of my story. My goal is to show respect for my adopted home and the love I've introduced you to, recognizing that language is not just a tool of communication but also a reflection of growth, identity, and cultural connection.

Each poem in this collection is paired with a narrative that provides context and insight into the personal significance behind the verses. Many of these poems were written in the moment, reflecting the constantly shifting nature of politics, while others, particularly those about significant loves, are reflections on the past. These explanations, much like short stories, enrich the reader's understanding and connection to the poetic expressions. The purpose of this book is to encourage readers to find the silver linings in their experiences, particularly the challenging ones, and to recognize that emotions, whether in love, loss, or longing, are integral to our growth and self-awareness.

Each poem in this collection is paired not only with a narrative explanation but also labeled with an emotion that captures the primary feeling or emotional state behind the writing of the poem. Assigning an emotion to each poem allows readers to connect on a deeper level, understanding the emotional landscape that shaped each verse. These emotion labels are not only a reflection of what I was feeling when the poem was conceived, but also an acknowledgment of how those feelings transformed into the art you see on the page.

At the end of the book, I have included an **index** where I delve into the details of each emotion, offering further clarity on its role in shaping the poetry. For instance, the emotion label for 'Turning Thoughts to Gold' would be creativity, celebrating the transformative process of turning raw thoughts and emotions into meaningful art. This system of labeling helps to guide the reader through the varied emotional journeys contained in this collection, providing a fuller understanding of the poems' essence.

As Carl Jung observed, "I am not what happened to me, I am what I choose to become." By sharing my journey, I hope to demonstrate that even in the face of adversity, there is always a path to growth and enlightenment. The therapeutic process has taught me that feelings are not inherently good or bad; rather, it is our response to them that shapes our lives.

"Verses of Life Through the Chapters of Love" is a heartfelt exploration of love in all its forms. It offers readers a mirror to their own experiences and a guide to navigating the complexities of life and relationships. Through my personal growth and therapeutic insights, I hope to inspire others to embrace their emotions, find their own paths to healing, and ultimately, to fulfillment. As Maya Angelou wisely said, "We delight in the beauty of the butterfly, but rarely admit the changes it has gone through to achieve that beauty." It is my sincere wish that this book helps others see the beauty in their own transformation.

Disclaimer: The views, experiences, and interpretations presented in this book are my own, shaped by how I have lived, processed, and understood them. This book reflects my personal perspective, influenced by my lived experiences, reflection, and the therapeutic process. The situations depicted are as I see them now, with the wisdom and clarity gained over time.

Dedication

To the dreamers, the believers, and the ones who never gave up. May this work remind you that the journey is worth every step, and that with courage and persistence, anything is possible.

This dedication is my personal acknowledgment to individuals who have played a significant role in my life and the creation of this book. It serves as a heartfelt expression of gratitude, recognizing the impact each person dedicated has had on my journey. My personal motto, "Lift as We Climb," borrowed from the National Association of Black Accountants, a club I was a part of in college, reminds me to always pay homage to those who have poured into me. It's important to honor my support system and influences, and I hope these dedication poems create a bridge between my work and the people who have helped me—just as they may help you in your own journey.

For the Hands That Held the Pen

This book is dedicated to Aunt Bernadine, my first muse, who opened my eyes to the beauty of poetry. It was with you, Auntie, that I discovered the magic of words and the creativity of the pen. In middle school, we wrote a poem called "I Like Me," and that piece became a foundation for my love of writing. I remember entering it into a contest with the Detroit Free Press, and to my surprise, I won $500. That was a pivotal moment, but it was more about what we created together that fueled me. You've always been my inspiration, Auntie. I hoped one day I would help you write your own poetry book. Now, here I am, dedicating my first book to you.

To Julie Berg-Einhorn, my therapist since the summer of 2019, whose insights and guidance have been instrumental in my growth. Through our sessions, I've learned to view my life, my relationships, and myself through a therapeutic lens, constantly reflecting, healing, and evolving. Julie, you've helped me mature my outlook on past situations, navigate complex emotions, and build a healthy, thriving relationship—one where the work continues every day. I hope that through this book, readers not only enjoy my storytelling and perspectives but also learn from my lived experiences and the growth I've achieved, much of which I owe to therapy. Thank you for your wisdom, patience, and unwavering support, which have been key to the breakthroughs that shape the pages of this book.

To my family and loved ones. To my grandparents, who have been my rock, my guiding light, and my unwavering support. To my mother, who is my biggest cheerleader, always by my side, and the one I turn to whenever I need. And to my father—though absent as a traditional father figure—we've forged a relationship that fulfills me. I see so much of myself in you, especially the best parts. This book has come together partly because of you, through our conversations, and your encouragement to set deadlines.

To each of my significant loves—you've shaped my history of love, and your stories are threaded through the pages of this book. And to my future spouse, my vida, mi Cielo, Rafa—I love you to the moon, stars, galaxies beyond, and back. With you, I know we will take on the world together. You complete and complement me, and the life we are planning feels like a beautiful dream coming true. Thank you to each of my friends and family members, whether directly mentioned or not. Each of you has supported me, listened, and played a part in this journey. I am eternally grateful for every soul I have touched and that has touched me.

For the Hands That Held the Pen

The first spark of the pen was lit by you,
My Auntie, who taught me to see it through.
Words poured like rivers, flowing in sync,
And now this book is the bridge, our link.

And to Julie, who helped my soul unfold,
Through sessions of truth, where stories are told.
With each breakthrough, you lit the way,
Healing my past, guiding my steps today.

To family who shaped the soil I stand,
Your love was the ink in my hand.
Guiding me, showing me how to be,
A writer, a thinker, fully and free.

And now to you, my life, my love, my guide,
We walk together, side by side.
In this book are the whispers of our dreams,
A future as bright as moonlit beams.

To Aja, the Editor with a Pen of Grace

In the margins of dreams, where stories reside,
Aja, you stood as my compass and guide.
With your pen poised, like a wand in hand,
You turned my jumbled thoughts into a grand plan.

A fellow Pisces, with wit so keen,
Your calm made the chaos feel serene.
You smoothed the edges, sharpened the prose,
Turning raw words into art that glows.

From Baltimore's heart, with three by your side,
You balanced my vision, with grace as your guide.
You held each chapter, like your own creation,
Treated my words with tender dedication.

Through edits and notes, through drafts and revisions,
You nurtured my book with your sharp precision.
An artist of words, a spirit so bright,
You made me trust the process—turning fear into flight.

So here's to your craft, to your gentle might,
For being the light that made this journey feel right.
Aja, with gratitude, I raise this verse,
For you've made this book better, page by page, word by word.

Inspiration Behind "To Aja, the Editor with a Pen of Grace"

The dedication to Aja Dorsey Jackson, who edited **Verses of Life: Through Chapters of Love**, was born out of immense gratitude for her guidance, precision, and artistry throughout the editing process. Aja has been more than just an editor; she has been a partner in shaping this book, turning the vision I had in my head into a tangible reality. Her attention to detail, her sharp wit, and her calm, nurturing spirit made me feel supported every step of the way.

As a fellow Pisces, Aja understands the depth and fluidity of storytelling, and she used her intuitive talents to enhance the flow of my words without ever altering my voice. She gave me the confidence to trust the process, and her dedication ensured this book became everything I dreamed it would be. I wanted to pay homage to her work, her spirit, and her craft in the form of this dedication poem because, without her, this project wouldn't have been the same.

Contact Aja Dorsey Jackson

If you're an aspiring author, writer, or entrepreneur looking for a talented editor to help bring your ideas to life, Aja is the professional you need. Her expertise in writing, editing, and book coaching makes her an invaluable resource for anyone navigating the self-publishing world. You can contact Aja for her services through the links below:

- **Website:**   https://ajadorseyjackson.com

- **Email:**   aja@charmcitypress.com

- **Instagram:**   @ajadjackson

- **LinkedIn:**   https://www.linkedin.com/in/ajadjackson

To the Architects of Vision: My Book Cover Designers

In the world of pixels, lines, and code,
You've crafted brilliance, a vision bestowed.
From Mississauga to Karachi's streets,
Your artistry and skill—oh, nothing competes.

Years of friendship, a bond so true,
You've designed for Mac Neal, helping dreams come
through.
Now my book wears your creative flair,
With each graphic touch, you've shown such care.

Not just a cover, but a story you've framed,
A piece of my heart, through design you've claimed.
Your team, a force of innovation and pride,
Turning ideas to magic, with every guide.

Web, mobile, software too,
There's nothing your hands cannot pursue.
From campaigns you've helped craft and plan,
To covers that embody this author's stand.

Reliable, brilliant, with talent so vast,
You've shaped my journey from first to last.
This dedication's more than just a line,
It's homage to your genius, timeless and fine.

So here's to the work, the bond we hold tight,
Your design shines brilliantly in every light.
For those seeking art, tech, and heart combined,
Look no further—here true talent you'll find.

Inspiration Behind "To the Architects of Vision: My Book Cover Designers"

The inspiration for this dedication poem stems from my long-standing relationship with Systechlogic, a company I first came across years ago through PeoplePerHour. They've been instrumental in the success of my accounting firm, Mac Neal LLC, helping with various graphics and always delivering exceptional service with speed and care.

Over the years, their quick response times and professional work ethic have made every collaboration not just easy, but a pleasure. When it came time to design the cover for my book, **Verses of Life: Through Chapters of Love,** it felt natural to trust them with this important task. Their creativity and technical expertise shone through, and I'm honored that they not only designed my book cover but also took over the marketing campaign for social media and Amazon.

This dedication is a tribute to their incredible work and the ease of our partnership over the years. Their commitment to quality and customer service has helped me bring my vision to life, and I'm grateful for the role they've played in this journey.

Contact Systechlogic for world-class design and digital solutions:

- **Phone**: +(92) 346-3324491
- **Email**: info@systechlogic.com
- **Address** (Pakistan): 403, Building, 45-C Lane No. 10, Phase 6, Khayaban-e-Bukhari Commercial Area, D.H.A Karachi, Pakistan
- **Address (Canada):** 1-3395 Cliff Road North, Mississauga, Ontario, Canada L5A 3C6
- **Website**: *[Systechlogic]* https://www.systechlogic.com

To Ron and Lisa, Love Through Every Frame

In the light of your lens, mi historia tomó forma,
Ron and Lisa, your talent, una obra de norma.
From Mexico City's heart to my book's own core,
You captured more than moments, you gave me much more.

Aquarius y Cáncer, con el destino en la mano,
Desde el cine hasta la vida, juntos, mano a mano.
Una pareja tan dulce, su amor brilla fuerte,
Y ahora su historia, en mi libro tiene suerte.

With Rafa unaware, you snapped engagement smiles,
In secret, you crafted our future for miles.
Those portraits you made, mi amor y mi vida,
They wove into my book, como una historia compartida.

Desde los taqueros hasta el arte que hacen,
Their love, their bond, forever, nunca se deshacen.
Panquecito, Bebé, y Negrita roam free,
As their love creates magic, just wait and see.

Cada frame, cada shot, with a touch so fine,
You took my vision y la hiciste brillar.
Ron y Lisa, your craft, una obra del corazón,
This book, in part, es su dedicación.

So here's to your love, to the stories you show,
May your éxito grow, y su luz siempre glow.
Their vibes, their passion, their cuteness untold,
Ron y Lisa, mis amigos, your talents are gold.

Inspiration Behind "To Ron and Lisa, Love Through Every Frame"

The dedication to Ron and Lisa was born from the incredible bond we shared during the creation of my book portraits and, secretly, my engagement photos. Their talent as photographers is only surpassed by their connection as a couple, and it's an honor to have them be a part of this journey. Their story, full of love, friendship, and creative passion, resonated deeply with me, and I wanted to ensure their role in my book was recognized. Their vibes, their cuteness as a couple, and their remarkable skill behind the camera made this experience unforgettable.

As two talented individuals who met at cinematography school, their friendship blossomed into a beautiful love story that continues to thrive. Ron, who grew up in a family of taqueros, and Lisa, a free-spirited Aquarius who navigated life between Mexico and the U.S., are the embodiment of support, love, and creativity. Their connection has grown since their transformative experience in 2020, where they realized their love for each other. Now married and sharing their lives with three adorable cats, they've built a creative life and career together.

Their artistic eye and attention to detail transformed not only the portraits for this book but also the secret engagement photos that captured one of the most special moments in my life. It's impossible not to love and appreciate their work, their journey, and the beautiful partnership they share. I dedicate this book, in part, to them, in gratitude for their friendship, their story, and their incredible craft.

Contact Ron and Lisa

For anyone seeking to capture moments of their own with love, creativity, and heart, I highly recommend working with Ron and Lisa. Their photography services are unparalleled, and their passion for their craft shines in every image. You can explore their work and get in touch with them through the following links:

Instagram: @lisa__dmr

Instagram: @ron_ron_neo

Website: ronronneo.com

Website: mediocielostudio.com

Turning the Wheel

In a world of words, I sought to know,
What each poem meant, and how to show
The feelings that slipped through the seams—
The truth beneath my hidden dreams.

I turned to Plutchik, his wheel so grand,
A map of emotions, a guiding hand,
Eight primary forces, spinning round,
In every poem, their echoes found.

Joy burst forth in **serenity's** light,
A flicker of peace, a lover's delight,
But in **ecstasy's** rush, I felt it peak,
From tranquil warmth to something unique.

Sadness lingered in a lover's sigh,
Not just **pensiveness**—a heavy cry.
Through **grief**, I wrote of sorrow's weight,
Tracing the lines where love turns late.

And **anger**—how it burned and grew,
From **annoyance** to a **rage** I knew,
As I penned those battles deep inside,
Where fire and fury would collide.

Fear played its part, in **terror's** height,
Yet started in **apprehension's** light,
A whisper of worry, a cautious glance,
That transformed through every stanza's dance.

And oh, **trust**—its quiet start,
From **acceptance**, it warmed the heart,
To **admiration**, where love takes flight,
A steadfast bond that felt so right.

With **disgust**, I found a subtle truth,
From **boredom's** quiet, to **loathing's** proof—
The taste of words I couldn't digest,

In lines where bitterness expressed.

Then came **surprise**, a **distraction** slight,
To **amazement**, when the world shone bright,
A sudden turn, a twist in the tale,
Where wonder blooms, where reason fails.
And **anticipation**—how it grew,
From **interest's** spark to **vigilance** true,
I held my breath as moments passed,
Expecting futures to unfold at last.

With each poem, I spun the wheel,
To find the essence, raw and real.
I let emotions blend and fuse,
To paint with words, the shades of blues—
And reds, and golds, and every hue,
Of life's full spectrum, bold and true.

I learned that **joy** and **fear** may meet,
And birth **optimism's** steady beat.
That anger twinned with disgust's sharp sting,
Could form contempt, a bitter thing.

Each combination, each unique,
A blend of heartbeats, soft or bleak.
From **serenity** to **grief's** deep well,
From **terror's** rise to **trust's** sweet spell.

Plutchik's wheel, it spun for me,
A guide to help my soul feel free.
I labeled every poem's core,
So I could name what lived before—
Before the words, before the ink,
The swirling feelings made me think.

And now, as I read back each page,
I see the wheel in every stage.
In every line, a twist, a turn,
Emotions waiting there to burn,
Or calm, or soothe, or break, or heal—
And all because I turned the wheel.

Inspiration Behind "Turning the Wheel"

The poem **"Turning the Wheel"** was inspired by a deep exploration of how emotions weave through my writing and how the nuances of each feeling affect the stories and experiences I convey through poetry. While working on my book, I realized that every poem held a core emotional essence, sometimes obvious and sometimes hidden beneath layers of thoughts and metaphors. I needed a way to better understand, categorize, and even enhance these emotional undertones. That's when I came across **Robert Plutchik's Wheel of Emotions.**

Plutchik's work provided me with a clear, structured understanding of emotions—not just in isolation, but in how they interact, intensify, and evolve. His **Wheel of Emotions** became a guiding framework for me to assign emotional labels to each of my poems. Whether I was expressing joy, sadness, anger, or trust, Plutchik's wheel helped me identify the root emotion and its variations in intensity. For instance, a simple feeling of **serenity** could evolve into **ecstasy**, while **annoyance** could flare into **rage**. Understanding these emotional gradations and combinations enriched my writing process and helped me offer more depth to the emotional experiences I share in my poems.

In **"Turning the Wheel,"** I aimed to capture not only how emotions evolve but also how they blend and interact, forming complex feelings like **optimism** (a mix of anticipation and joy) or **contempt** (a blend of anger and disgust). Plutchik's wheel showed me that emotions are not static, but fluid and dynamic, which is reflected in how each poem in my book holds different shades and intensities of emotional truth.

The Wheel of Emotions: Understanding Emotional Complexity

The **Wheel of Emotions** created by Robert Plutchik is more than just a visual tool; it's a window into the complexity of human emotions. The wheel maps out eight core emotions: **joy, trust, fear, surprise, sadness, disgust, anger, and anticipation**, and illustrates how these emotions intensify or diminish. Emotions moving inward on the wheel become more intense like **fear** turning into **terror** or **joy** evolving into **ecstasy**. Moving outward, emotions lose intensity, like **anger** softening into **annoyance** or **disgust** fading into **boredom**.

What's truly fascinating about Plutchik's wheel is how it highlights the connections between emotions. For instance, **fear** and **anger** may seem like opposites, but when blended with **surprise**, they create the feeling of **alarm**. Understanding these emotional combinations allowed me to break down complex feelings in my poems and give them names, transforming vague emotional currents into defined and relatable experiences.

Here is a placeholder for an image of **Robert Plutchik's Wheel of Emotions**, which has been invaluable to my writing process.

A Shout-Out to Robert Plutchik

I want to take a moment to give a heartfelt shout-out to **Robert Plutchik**. His groundbreaking work on emotions has not only influenced the field of psychology but also helped writers, artists, and thinkers like me dive deeper into the human experience. Through his **Wheel of Emotions**, Plutchik showed us that emotions are not just singular, static experiences but multi-dimensional and ever-evolving. Through his insights, I have been able to better articulate the emotional essence of each poem in my book.

Dedication

I am dedicating the emotion-label part of my book to
Robert Plutchik and his work on the Wheel of Emotions.
Without his framework, I could not have explored my
emotional depths with such clarity. His wheel helped me
think critically about which emotions to highlight and how
to label the emotional tone of each poem. As you move
through my book, you will find that each poem has an
emotional label inspired by Plutchik's wheel, capturing the
precise intensity and variation of feelings that shaped each
piece. Whether it's the warmth of **serenity**, the rush of
ecstasy, or the sting of **contempt**, Plutchik's influence can
be found throughout the pages of my work.

This dedication is a small token of appreciation for
the immense impact his work has had on me and countless
others. Thank you, Robert Plutchik, for helping us all
better understand the emotional landscapes that define our
lives.

Introduction
Emotion: Anticipation

In this introductory chapter, I invite you to journey with me through the vastness of my experiences, embracing the freedom of exploration and the lessons I learned along the way. As I delve into the internal realms of self-discovery, examining the many facets of my identity and growth, you are invited to reflect on your own journey. This chapter sets the stage for an emotional and reflective exploration of my life—filled with moments of joy, love, and discovery. An undercurrent of strength and optimism runs through these verses, embracing life's imperfections and finding beauty in the journey. This introduction serves as a prelude, preparing you for the deeply personal yet universally relatable themes unfolding throughout the book.

Verses of Life: An Emotional Prelude

In the chapters of love, where hearts dare to tread,
A tapestry of emotions, both whispered and said.
From the depths of grief, where shadows reside,
To the peaks of joy, where our spirits confide.

Love blooms in pages, both tender and fierce,
Through passion's embrace and the sting of a tear.
It's the warmth of nostalgia, the ache of regret,
A dance with the past we'll never forget.

Grief weaves through the lines, a solemn refrain,
Mourning lost moments, the echoes of pain.
Yet hope finds its way, like light through the cracks,
Promising dawn where the night turns its back.

Anger burns bright in the battles we've fought,
Against injustices, against all we've sought.
Resilience stands tall, like a tree in the storm,
Rooted in strength, through heartache reborn.

In the quest for self, in the mirrors we face,
Reflection gives way to a deeper embrace.
Forgiveness unfolds, like petals in bloom,
Releasing old ghosts from the corners of gloom.

Loneliness whispers in the silence of night,
Yet comfort comes softly, in love's gentle light.
Curiosity sparks, igniting the flame,
Of growth and discovery, no two paths are the same.

Disappointment may linger, in promises broken,
But gratitude rises, in words unspoken.
Pride fills the heart in the steps that we take,
In the victories earned, in the risks that we stake.

Insecurity looms, like clouds overhead,
Yet vulnerability leads where courage has fled.
Freedom is found in the truths that we bear,

In the choices we make, in the lives that we share.

Peace rests within, a calm after strife,
A quiet acceptance, a harmony in life.
Determination fuels the dreams that we chase,
Fulfillment awaits at the end of the race.

Confusion will pass, as clarity shines,
In the love that we give, in the ties that we bind.
Admiration stands for the souls that inspire,
For the heroes among us who light the fire.

Fear may creep in, as we walk into the night,
But the dawn of new beginnings is always in sight.
Politics shape the world we embrace,
Yet love, in its essence, will always find it's place.

In these verses of life, through chapters of love,
We journey together, below and above.
Expect every tear, every laugh, every sigh,
For emotions are the wings on which we fly.

This is the journey, the path that we take,
Through shadows and light, through every heartache.
In this book, in these words, you'll find the key,
To the soul of love, to the essence of me.

Inspiration behind "Verses of Life: An Emotional Prelude"
Emotion: Introspection

This book is a deeply personal exploration of love, relationships, politics, and the myriad of emotions that shape our lives. This prelude sets the stage for the journey ahead, guiding readers through the emotional landscapes they will encounter in the verses that follow.

The inspiration for this prelude stems from the desire to encapsulate the full spectrum of human emotions within the context of love and life's experiences. Emotions, by definition, are complex psychological states that involve a subjective experience, a physiological response, and a behavioral or expressive component. They are the very essence of what makes us human, driving our actions, shaping our perceptions, and influencing our relationships.

Therapists often emphasize the importance of acknowledging and expressing emotions as a pathway to healing and personal growth. Emotions are not just fleeting feelings but are deeply connected to our thoughts, memories, and experiences. Expressing these emotions, particularly through writing, allows us to process and understand our internal world, making sense of our experiences and how they shape who we are.

Philosophers have long explored the nature of emotions, considering them as fundamental to our understanding of the self and our place in the world. Plato, for example, viewed emotions as integral to the soul's journey toward truth and wisdom. Similarly, modern psychology recognizes the importance of emotions in shaping our mental and emotional well-being. Emotions are seen as signals that provide valuable information about our needs, desires, and boundaries. By paying attention to these signals, we can navigate our lives with greater clarity and purpose.

The act of writing, especially poetry, is a powerful tool for expressing and exploring emotions. The pen becomes a conduit through which we can articulate the unspoken, giving form to feelings that might otherwise remain hidden or suppressed. Writing allows us to externalize our emotions, to see them on the page, and to engage with them in a way that can lead to deeper understanding and healing.

In this book, emotions are not just themes but are the very fabric of the narrative. Each poem delves into different emotional experiences—love, grief, joy, sadness, hope, and more—creating a rich tapestry that reflects the complexity of human relationships and the journey of self-discovery. This poem serves as an invitation to the reader to embark on this journey, to explore their own emotions, and to find resonance in the shared human experience.

This poem is a celebration of the power of emotions and the transformative potential of expressing them through writing. It acknowledges that our emotions are what make us unique, what connect us to others, and what ultimately guide us on our path through life. Whether we are navigating the joy of love, the pain of loss, or the challenges of personal growth, our emotions are the compass that leads us forward.

Through the verses in this book, I hope to offer a space where readers can reflect on their own emotional journeys, find solace in shared experiences, and be inspired to express their own truths. Verses of Life Through Chapters of Love is not just a collection of poems; it is a testament to the resilience, depth, and beauty of the human spirit, captured through the lens of emotional expression.

Meet Malcolm

They call me Malcolm, a name that holds weight,
Born in Detroit, where the streets dictate fate.
But my story isn't the typical Motor City grind,
Raised by love, by wisdom, and by a different kind.

Grandparents stepped in, took the reins tight,
Pulled me from a life that wasn't right.
Mitchell and Sonia, they showed me the ropes,
Taught me to hustle, dream, and to cope.

Private school polish, Catholic-educated mind,
Yet the world's complexities, I struggled to find.
High school loomed large, public or private?
Would I thrive, or would I fight it?

In a city where MSU and U of M reign,
I didn't quite fit in, I didn't follow the train.
No grand visions, just a kid full of nerves,
In a big ol' apartment with spiral stairs and curves.

A sheltered life, with cousins and kin,
Talking with grown-ups, never lost in the din.
I played cards, watched stories, learned the ways,
But the world outside? Just a distant haze.

Yet through it all, one thing stayed true,
A worry-free vibe, I carry it through.
Nonchalant about life, about what's next,
But don't mistake it, I'm still complex.

So here I stand, Malcolm Alexander-Neal,
From the east side to the world, ready to reveal.
I'm more than my past, more than what's seen,
A low-key hustler with a Detroit sheen.

Ready or not, here I come,
I'm just getting started; this is just the drum.

Inspiration behind "Meet Malcolm"
Emotion: Resilience

This poem stems from my journey of self-discovery and reflection on the path that has shaped me into who I am today. Growing up in Detroit, Michigan, under the care of my grandparents, I experienced a unique blend of love, discipline, and wisdom that guided me through a childhood marked by both protection and independence.

This poem captures the essence of my upbringing in a city where resilience is a way of life. It delves into my experiences of moving from an abusive environment into the safety of my grandparents' home, where I learned the value of hard work, even if I didn't fully grasp its meaning at the time. The transition from private to public education, the fears and uncertainties of adolescence, and the feeling of being out of sync with the expectations around me all contributed to my sense of identity.

I wanted to express the dichotomy of growing up sheltered in some ways while being exposed to the complexities of life in others. The apartment where I spent my formative years symbolized both my comfort zone and the limits of my social world, shaping my mature outlook and my laid-back attitude toward life's challenges.

Ultimately, this poem is a declaration of who I am—an acknowledgment of my roots, my growth, and the experiences that have molded me into the person I am today. It's an introduction to the world, filled with pride, humor, and a nod to the journey that continues to unfold.

My Name Is Malcolm Elajuwon, Alexander Neal

My name is Malcolm—
A follower of Columba, a defender of faith,
Born of Scottish kings and ancient lands,
A name that speaks of leadership and grace.
In its syllables, I hear the whispers of my past,
A lineage of resilience, a path forged to last.

Elajuwon—
A name that dances with the rhythm of Yoruba roots,
Where honor returns, and wealth is anew,
A nod to ancestors who knew the value of truth.
In its letters, I find the echo of tradition,
A rich history, a name with a noble mission.

Alexander—
Protector of mankind, defender of men,
A name that carries the weight of warriors' swords,
Greek in origin, yet universal in its pen.
Through its sound, I feel the strength of purpose,
A guardian spirit, a beacon in the darkness.
Neal—
A son of Niall, descended from champions,
With clouds that gather but never stay,
A name of Gaelic pride, enduring through generations.
In its simplicity, there lies a quiet might,
A name that holds my roots, steady in the night.

My name is Malcolm Elajuwon, Alexander Neal—
Each name a gift from parents, a heritage revealed,
A tapestry of cultures, a story to tell,
A nod to the book where my name first swelled.
"My Name Is"—I recall that lesson well,
A high school poem, where meaning began to dwell.

Through these names, I honor those who came before,
My parents' choice, an ancestral lore,
In every sound, a legacy unfurled,
My name is a bridge between me and the world.

Inspiration behind "My Name Is Malcolm Elajuwon, Alexander Neal"

Emotion: Pride

When I think about the significance of my name, it's not just about the sounds or the letters that form it—it's about the story it tells, the heritage it carries, and the love that was poured into it by my parents. Each part of my name—Malcolm Elajuwon, Alexander Neal—holds a deep meaning, woven together by the threads of ancestry, culture, and the people who have shaped me.

Malcolm—This name connects me to the Scottish roots of strength, faith, and leadership. It's a name that has seen kings and warriors, a name that stands tall in history. For me, Malcolm represents resilience and the power to lead, a nod to the past and a guide for the future. Malcolm also has a special origin, rooted in a moment of shared love and connection between my parents. Late at night, while watching The Cosby Show together, they saw the name Malcolm-Jamal Warner roll across the screen. My parents loved the show for what it represented—a celebration of African American excellence, diversity, and success during a time when such representations were rare. They saw something in that name, something that spoke to them about the kind of world they wanted for me, a world where our stories, our excellence, and our diversity were celebrated.

Elajuwon— I was named from my mom's crush on a famous basketball player, Hakeem Olajuwon. A quick look back into history, and I found out who he was—Hakeem Olajuwon, a dominant force in the NBA during the 80s and 90s, widely regarded as one of the greatest centers to ever play the game. It tracks with my mom's type—he was tall, talented, and had that charismatic presence. But beyond the crush, the name Elajuwon ties me to the Yoruba heritage of Nigeria, where honor and wealth are deeply valued, and where tradition and modernity meet. It's a name that connects me to a rich cultural history, a reminder of where I come from and the values that shape me.

Alexander—This is my mother's family name, a name that speaks of protection, leadership, and strength. It's a name that has traveled through time, from ancient Greece to my own lineage, carrying with it the legacy of warriors and protectors. Alexander is a reminder that I am part of something greater, that my name carries with it the strength of those who came before me.

Neal—This is my father's family name, a name with deep roots in Gaelic tradition. It's a name that connects me to Scotland, to the history of my ancestors who lived and thrived in those lands. Neal represents a lineage of champions, people who stood strong through life's challenges. It's a name that grounds me, reminding me of the strength and resilience that flows through my veins.

But my story doesn't stop with my name. My DNA tells an even richer tale, one that spans continents and cultures. My heritage is a tapestry woven from Nigeria (42%), Cameroon, Congo & Western Bantu Peoples (19%), Ivory Coast & Ghana (10%), Mali (7%), England & Northwestern Europe (6%), Senegal (3%), Scotland (3%), Benin & Togo (2%), Eastern Bantu Peoples (2%), Southern Bantu Peoples (1%), Northern Philippines (1%), Indigenous Americas—North (1%), Finland (1%), Norway (1%), and Wales (1%). Each of these regions contributes to who I am, to the way I see the world and my place in it.

This diverse heritage shapes not only my identity but also my connectivity to lands, people, and cultures across the globe. It's a reminder that I am a product of many stories, many histories, and that each part of my DNA carries with it a piece of the world. This complex mix of heritage, combined with the meanings of my names, creates a unique narrative—one that speaks of resilience, strength, and the importance of knowing where you come from.

So as you read my story, as you journey through the poems of my life, you're not just reading about me. You're reading about a legacy passed down through names and blood, a story that connects me to lands far and wide, to cultures rich and diverse. My name holds weight; it's how the world sees me, how I see myself, and I am proud to share not just the meaning of my name, but the story behind it—a story that is as much about my parents, my ancestors, and my heritage as it is about me.

This book is a window into my life, viewed through the lens of significant loves. It begins with how I grew up, how I came to understand love, and how I formed my identity and values. As you delve deeper, you'll learn about each significant love, and gain insight into my thoughts on politics, grief, and various experiences that shaped my life from May 2024 until August 2024. This narrative parallels one part of my life—mostly through the prism of love. Future books will offer different perspectives on my story, my heritage, and my deep connection to lands and travels.

I think my love for travel isn't just about the excitement or fulfillment it brings. Deep down, I believe I've been on a journey not just to explore new places but to reconnect with my ancestral homes. I vividly remember the feeling of connectivity when I was in Nigeria, a place where I felt an inexplicable bond—a sense that I was in search of something beyond the present, something rooted in my

past. This exploration is part of what makes up Malcolm, a
journey that I invite you to experience through the pages
of my life.

I Am a Pisces

I am a Pisces, born from the sea,
A soul that swims in mystery.
I seek my peace, my quiet space,
Where no confusion dares to chase.

I love you deep, yet I can leave,
A sudden silence, hard to believe.
My words may cut, my tone direct,
But harm's not what I intend to reflect.

I give my all, but once I'm through,
You'll fade away like morning dew.
I cherish actions more than speech,
And once you're gone, you're out of reach.

I trust the stars to guide my way,
But know I'm more than what they say.
A mix of values, pain, and grace,
Therapy, culture, all in place.

I stand alone when storms arise,
A strength that often hides the cries.
I sense your games, I see your mask,
Charming, yes, but I don't ask.

I'm honest, private, deep in thought,
I solve my puzzles, tight in knot.
I cut the ties that bring me pain,
For peace and sanity I'll reclaim.

I fall for souls, not just the face,
And once I love, it's with full grace.

But don't mistake my quiet stride,
For I have oceans left inside.

I'm Pisces strong, and that's my truth,
A mix of dreams and solid proof.
A being of contrasts, highs and lows,
I swim through life, where the current flows.

So when you think of who I am,
Know I'm more than just a sign's plan.
I'm guided by stars, but never bound,
A Pisces, true, in depth profound.

Inspiration behind "I am a Pisces"

Emotion: Contemplation

This poem stems from a deep connection to the traits often associated with Pisces, the twelfth sign of the zodiac. As a Pisces, I identify with the complexity, duality, and emotional depth that this sign embodies. The poem reflects the inherent contradictions and strengths that define a Pisces: the ability to love deeply yet detach when necessary, the preference for solitude despite a strong need for connection, and the use of intuition as a guiding force in life.

In crafting this poem, I aimed to capture the essence of these traits in a way that resonates with both those who understand astrology and those who might see it as just a guide rather than an absolute. The poem weaves together the idea that, while horoscopes can offer insights, they do not define the entirety of a person. It acknowledges the influence of therapy, life experiences, and cultural values in shaping who we are.

The rhyming structure and metaphorical language were chosen to intensify the impact of each line, making the poem not only a reflection of Pisces traits but also a declaration of my unique identity. The poem is meant to evoke a nod of recognition from those familiar with Pisces and to offer a window into the complexities of being born under this sign. Ultimately, it's a celebration of my self-awareness, emotional intelligence, and the deep, flowing currents of my inner world.

My Chart

In the depth of Pisces, my Sun does shine,
Dreamy, ethereal, where the divine aligns.
I swim in oceans where logic is sparse,
My world of emotion, a chaotic art.
Yet here I stand, with my head held high,
A soul searching the stars, questioning why.

Aquarius rises, the mask I wear,
A cloak of intellect, a mind laid bare.
Detached, broad-minded, I dance in thought,
Ideas eccentric, in abstractions caught.
But the first impression isn't always true,
For beneath the surface, my depth ensues.

My Moon in Scorpio, intense and deep,
Where emotions churn and secrets I keep.
Passion and power, in shadows I trust,
Yet faith and philosophy are my anchor and must.
A heart guarded, with walls built high,
But through wisdom and knowledge, I learn to fly.

Mercury in Aquarius, a mind so free,
Insightful thoughts, in layers of me.
Communication, abstract and bold,
I challenge norms, let new stories unfold.
But my words can cut, my ideas can burn,
In the quest for truth, many lessons I learn.

Venus in Taurus, slow and steady I go,
In love, I crave what's simple, what's known.
Comfort and warmth, in the familiar I find,
But timidity hides the passions entwined.
For love to me is a delicate art,
One that speaks softly, yet touches the heart.

Mars in Capricorn, where ambition reigns,
I push forward, through struggles and pains.
Calculated, deliberate, I conquer the climb,
In the eleventh house, my dreams align.
Social status and hopes, a fire within,
Driven by the need to achieve, to win.

Jupiter in Taurus, where growth takes root,
In security and wealth, I find my pursuit.
Success through patience, in the tangible I trust,
Building foundations, strong and robust.
Yet in this comfort, my spirit may roam,
Seeking the balance between wealth and home.

Saturn in Capricorn, where discipline lies,
Boundaries and fears in my social ties.
Responsibility weighs, ambition drives,
Yet in the eleventh house, my struggles strive.
Learning through trials, I rise above,
With wisdom gained, I redefine love.

Uranus in Capricorn, a rebel with cause,
Breaking the mold, defying old laws.
In the tenth house, I redefine success,
Pushing past limits, I won't settle for less.
Generational tides, I swim against the flow,
Creating a legacy, where freedom can grow.

Neptune in Capricorn, dreams grounded in grit,
Ambition fuels the fires I lit.
In the eleventh house, ideals take flight,
Yet the weight of reality holds them tight.
Balancing dreams with what's practical and real,
A journey of compromise, where I learn to feel.

Pluto in Scorpio, where power resides,
In the ninth house, my soul confides.
Transforming meaning, through faith and thought,
A seeker of truth, in battles fought.
Intensity marks the path I tread,
But through this journey, my soul is fed.

So here I stand, a complex blend,
Of signs and planets that twist and bend.
Each part of me, a different light,
Guiding my journey through day and night.
The Sun, the Moon, the Rising too,
Each holds a truth, a piece of the view.
In this chart, my story's told,
A dance of stars, both new and old.

For I am more than just one sign,
A constellation where truths align.
The complexity of life, a cosmic art,
And in these stars, I find my heart.

Inspiration Behind "My Chart"

Emotion: Self-awareness

This poem was born out of a deep reflection on the complexities and layers within my astrological natal chart. Each element in my chart—the Sun, Moon, Ascendant, and the various planetary placements—represents a different facet of who I am, and together, they create a nuanced portrait of my personality and life experiences. This poem was my attempt to weave these astrological influences into a cohesive narrative that captures the essence of my inner and outer worlds.

Pisces Sun:

The Sun in astrology represents the core of our identity, the essence of who we are. My Sun is in Pisces, a sign known for its dreamy, intuitive, and deeply emotional nature. This placement in my first house makes these qualities hyper-present in my personality. I wanted to convey the idea that I often navigate life on a plane that's more spiritual than material, immersed in my imagination and emotions. The imagery of swimming in oceans of emotion and existing on a chaotic divine plane reflects how I perceive the world around me.

Aquarius Ascendant:

The Ascendant, or rising sign, is often described as the "mask" we wear—the first impression we give to others. My Aquarius Ascendant gives me an outward appearance of being broad-minded, intellectual, and perhaps a bit detached or eccentric. This placement can make me seem somewhat aloof or abstract in my thinking. However, as the poem suggests, there's more beneath the surface. The Aquarius rising influences how I approach new situations and interact with people, adding a layer of complexity to how I'm perceived versus who I truly am inside.

Scorpio Moon:

The Moon governs our emotions, moods, and the way we feel most comfortable. My Moon in Scorpio is intense, passionate, and secretive. It represents the depth of my emotional world, which I often keep hidden. This placement means that I experience emotions powerfully, and trust is something I don't give easily. In the poem, I wanted to express how this intensity shapes my inner life, especially how I seek security and meaning through philosophy, faith, and intellectual pursuits. The Scorpio Moon adds a layer of depth and introspection to my personality, influencing how I handle my emotions and relationships.

The Complexity of My Chart:

Astrology reveals that we are more than just our Sun sign. The different signs and planetary placements in my chart create a complex and sometimes contradictory personality. For example, while my Pisces Sun makes me dreamy and intuitive, my Mars in Capricorn drives me to be ambitious, disciplined, and focused on social status and long-term goals. These different energies can sometimes pull me in opposite directions, but they also blend together to create a unique and multifaceted individual.

The Role of the Houses:

In astrology, the houses represent different areas of life where these planetary energies manifest. My Sun and Ascendant are in the first house, emphasizing self-expression and identity. My Mars, Saturn, and Neptune in the eleventh house highlight my focus on social status, friendships, and long-term aspirations. Each house placement in my chart adds another layer to my life story, influencing where and how these astrological traits play out.

Constructing the Poem:

The structure of the poem mirrors the complexity of my chart. Each verse is dedicated to a different astrological element, highlighting its influence on my personality and life journey. By using rich imagery and metaphors, I wanted to capture the mystical and often contradictory nature of astrology—how different aspects of ourselves can sometimes seem at odds, yet together they form a complete picture. I hope this poem conveys the beauty and depth of understanding that astrology can offer, and how it can help us appreciate the many layers of our own selves.

Love and Legacy

I hope to leave a legacy, a wealth that's truly mine,
Not just in coin but in words that echo through time.
Pieces of me, etched in verse, for others to see,
A guide through my journey, a map to set them free.

"Verses of Life" in every hand, a number one to be,
A beacon of hope for those who come after me.
In every line, a lesson, in every word, a spark,
To break the chains of silence that keep us in the dark.

Therapy's not taboo, it's a lifeline we all need,
A chance to heal the wounds, to plant a better seed.
In Black and Brown communities, the stigma still remains,
But through my story, I hope to ease those chains.

I've learned the terms, the themes, the truths we often
hide,
And I pray my words inspire someone to turn the tide.
To see themselves in my tale, and feel the urge to seek,
A path to healing, a strength when they feel weak.

As an accountant, I've balanced books, but never life or
death,
The numbers fall in place, they never steal my breath.
But in my union work, I've found a deeper call,
To fight for rights, for justice, for the workers, one and all.

Sometimes I'm a therapist, in the office halls,
Listening, advising, catching those who fall.
This purpose fills my soul, it gives my work a light,
A sense of fulfillment that carries me through the night.

Yet in all these roles, in all the work I do,
Love's the thread that binds them, the purpose that rings
true.
For what is wealth, what is legacy, without someone to
share?
Someone to love, to cherish, someone to show you care.

Love's the reason, the drive behind my quest,
The force that pushes me to be my very best.
To build a future, to carve a path, to leave a mark so clear,
That those who follow after know that love was here.

So, as I write, as I work, as I love and give,
I hope my legacy's a testament to how I lived.
A life of purpose, of passion, of love that never fades,
A boundless becoming, in every choice I've made.

Inspiration behind "Love and Legacy"

Emotion: Purpose

I wrote this poem with the mindset of having a deep desire to leave a lasting impact on the world—an impact that goes beyond material wealth and reaches the hearts and minds of future generations. This poem reflects my commitment to building a legacy that is rooted not just in financial success but in the words I leave behind, the stories I tell, and the lessons I share. Through this autobiographical poetry collection, I hope to create a beacon of hope for those who come after me, offering them guidance, inspiration, and a map through my journey.

A significant part of this legacy involves breaking down cultural and societal barriers, particularly within Black and Brown communities, around the importance of therapy. I've seen firsthand the stigma that still exists, the belief that we don't need therapy, but I'm here to challenge that. My own experiences with therapy have been transformative, and I hope that through my poetry, others will feel compelled to seek healing and strength in their own lives.

As an accountant, I've always balanced books, but my true sense of purpose came when I transitioned into my role as union president. In this position, I found fulfillment in helping others, advocating for workers' rights, and being a voice for those who needed support. Sometimes, I feel like a therapist at work, listening, advising, and catching those who fall. This role fills my soul with a sense of purpose that extends beyond numbers and spreadsheets.

Yet, in all the work I do, love has always been the thread that binds everything together. Love is the force that drives me, the motivation behind my quest to build a future and leave a mark. Whether it's the love I share with my partner, my friends, or my family, it's love that gives my life meaning and shapes the legacy I hope to leave.

This poem is a testament to that journey—a reflection of my life's purpose, passion, and the love that has guided me through every choice I've made. It's a reminder that true wealth isn't just measured in coins but in the impact we have on others, the love we give, and the legacy we leave behind.

Boundless Becoming

I'm a wanderer, a soul set free,
A traveler with sights yet to see.
Happy in the heart, though I sometimes hide,
It takes time for the full me to come outside.

I dance around conflict, I step to the side,
But love? I dive in with a powerful tide.
Sometimes too strong, sometimes to a fault,
But I treasure every bond, every heart I exalt.

I'm a lover of cultures, of food, and the Earth,
I cherish the learning each journey gives birth.
A family person, bound by love's tight cord,
Every morning, I send out words to be adored.

Optimism's my shield, in this world so wide,
I seek the bright side where hope can reside.
65 lands have felt my feet tread,
But 200+ is the dream that lies ahead.

I once wore the ring, and I'll wear it again,
True love is the vow, the journey with him.
I believe in evolving, in shaping the self,
Constantly learning, like a book on the shelf.

Early retirement is the dream I chase,
To roam with my man, finding every hidden place.
Living on the joys that my past left behind,
A life full of love, with no ties to bind.

I am all these things, and still I grow,
A soul on a journey, with much left to know.
I am who I am, yet I'm more than I see,
A reflection of life's endless possibility.

Inspiration behind "Boundless Becoming"

Emotion: Optimism

This poem is a reflection of my journey through life—a continuous evolution that mirrors the endless horizons I seek to explore. It's a celebration of the different facets of my identity, woven together by my love for travel, culture, and human connection. This poem captures the essence of who I am: a wanderer at heart, a lover with depth, and a seeker of joy in every corner of the world. It's a tribute to the optimism I hold dear, the relationships I cherish, and the lifelong commitment to growth and self-discovery. Each verse is a step along the path of my boundless journey, a reminder that I am constantly becoming, ever-evolving, and always embracing the infinite possibilities that life offers.

Wanderlust Symphony

Sixty-five nations, stories untold,
Each passport stamp, a memory to hold.
My spirit roamed through South America's embrace,
Three months of wandering, a thrilling chase.

From Guatemala's heart to Peru's ancient might,
Bolivia's heights bathed in golden light.
Brazil's lush dance, Uruguay's serene coasts,
Paraguay's whispers, Argentina's boasts.

Chile's long spine, stretching to the stars,
Then southward bound beyond earthly bars.
Antarctica's cold, a pristine frontier,
Aboard Hurtigruten, amidst penguins' cheer.

A detour spun through Madrid's lively streets,
Where history and modernity uniquely meets.
Languages flowing, my Spanish found wings,
In cafes and plazas, life's simple things.

On this voyage, I learned to just be,
To exist in moments, wildly free.
No work to tether, nor home to bind,
Just earth's vast wonders, and peace of mind.

This journey, a glimpse of a life I crave,
A nomadic pulse with each wave I brave.
Dreams of retiring early, roaming the sphere,
To live as I did those three months, without fear.

Travel has sculpted me, refined and whole,
Gifting perspectives that nourish my soul.
For in every land's embrace, I find
A better version of myself, unconfined.

Inspiration Behind "Wanderlust Symphony"

Emotion: Freedom

This poem was inspired by a particularly transformative three-month journey across South America and Antarctica, which stands out among the 65 countries I've explored. This poem reflects the profound sense of freedom I experienced, as I immersed myself in diverse cultures, improved my Spanish, and enjoyed a life unburdened by work.

Traveling has always been a way for me to expand my mind and soul. This trip reinforced my love for the nomadic lifestyle, highlighting my desire to possibly retire early and dedicate my life to global exploration. This poem captures the essence of what travel means to me: a continuous discovery process that enriches my understanding of the world and myself, celebrating a life filled with adventure and the freedom to roam.

Breaking the Silence

In shadows we've lived, in silence we've stayed,
A legacy of strength, but with costs unpaid.
The whispers of pain, brushed off as weak,
A burden we carry, but seldom speak.

In Black communities, the struggle is real,
A mistrust of the system, a wound that won't heal.
History's scars run deep in our veins,
Misdiagnosed, mistreated, bound in invisible chains.

They say we're strong, that we've survived it all,
But strength doesn't mean we don't stumble or fall.
Prayer's been our anchor, faith our shield,
But sometimes, even warriors need to yield.

Therapy's seen as a taboo, a flaw,
A threat to the image of strength we all draw.
But beneath that armor, the pain still grows,
A silent battle that nobody knows.

We've been criminalized for the way we feel,
Judged, not helped, when our wounds won't heal.
Fear of the law, fear of the blame,
Keeps us from speaking, from naming our pain.

But now's the time to shatter the glass,
To break the silence, let the stigma pass.
Mental health isn't a curse or a shame,
It's a journey to healing, a reclaiming of name.

We need to shift the stories we tell,
From suffering in silence to living well.
Celebrities speak, their voices loud,
But it's in our communities where change is most proud.

Culturally competent care, that's the key,
Led by those who understand, who see.
Therapy for Black Girls, Henry Health, Ayana's light,

Guiding us forward, making wrongs right.

We need more than just words, we need change in the law,
Access to care, without the fear or the flaw.
Education for the young, awareness from the start,
To break the cycle, to heal the heart.

So here's to the day we all stand tall,
Breaking the silence, tearing down walls.
A future where mental health's not a fight,
But a right to be honored, in every Black life.

Inspiration behind "Breaking the Silence"

Emotion: Empowerment

This poem is a deeply personal piece inspired by my lived experience as an African American male in the USA, where therapy is often stigmatized within the Black community. Growing up, I constantly heard people dismiss the idea of seeking mental health care, reinforcing the belief that therapy was unnecessary or even a sign of weakness. This poem is my attempt to shed light on that stigma, to challenge it, and to encourage others in my community—and beyond—to embrace the healing that therapy can provide.

The poem draws heavily from the research of Clinical Associate Professor Ruth White, who explores the complex social dynamics that create barriers to mental health care within Black communities. Her work highlights how the psychological stress of systemic racism, combined with a deep mistrust of the medical establishment, has led to a significant mental health crisis among African Americans. Despite these challenges, the stigma around mental health care remains pervasive, with many in our community viewing therapy as a weakness rather than a necessary tool for healing.

But this issue isn't just confined to the Black community; it resonates across other Brown and minority communities as well. The stigmatization of mental health care is a common thread that unites us, regardless of our specific backgrounds. In many cultures, the survivalist mentality born from enduring systemic oppression creates a reluctance to seek help, as doing so can be perceived as admitting defeat. Moreover, the phenomenon of religiosity, prevalent in many of our communities, often leads people to turn to faith and prayer as the sole solutions for mental health issues, rather than considering therapy as a viable option.

Research shows that this stigmatization is not unique to African Americans. For example, studies have found that within the Latino community, mental health issues are often dismissed or attributed to spiritual weakness, leading to underutilization of mental health services. Similarly, in Asian American communities, the concept of "saving face" often discourages individuals from seeking help, as mental health struggles are seen as bringing shame upon the family. These cultural barriers further compound the challenges faced by minority groups in accessing the care they need.

This poem is a call to action for all of us—Black, Brown, and minority communities alike—to confront these stigmas head-on. We must shift our cultural narratives, challenge the harmful stereotypes that keep us from seeking help, and embrace mental health care as an essential part of our overall well-being. This poem is not just about highlighting the problem; it's about offering hope and a path forward. By sharing my story, and by referencing the work of researchers like Professor White, I hope to inspire others to see therapy not as a weakness, but as a powerful tool for healing and growth.

Ultimately, this poem is about reclaiming our right to be healthy in mind, body, and soul. It's about acknowledging the pain and trauma that many of us carry, and taking the necessary steps to heal, both individually and as a community. We owe it to ourselves, and to future generations, to break the chains of stigma and create a new legacy—one where mental health is valued, supported, and accessible to all.

Three Truths Inspired by Oprah

First, know your essence, your soul's true flame,
The purpose that whispers, that calls out your name.
For in this vast world, it's not chance or mere fate,
But the reason you're here, the role you'll create.

Second, be grateful, each breath is a gift,
A chance to rise up, to soar and to lift.
To stand in your power, to live and to do,
With grace in your heart, let gratitude guide you.

Third, share this journey, with love as your guide,
With those who uplift, who stand by your side.
For what is success if it's held all alone?
It's the joy in the sharing where true wealth is grown.

As Oprah spoke, in her wisdom so true,
I saw in her words what I am meant to do.
To tell stories that matter, to light up the dark,
To share with the world, my own unique spark.

So, here I stand, with a tale to impart,
Inspired by Oprah, with fire in my heart.
To know who I am, to be grateful and share,
This is my purpose, my truth laid bare.

Inspiration behind "Three Truths Inspired by Oprah"
Emotion: Gratitude

The inspiration for this poem comes from a place of deep admiration and respect for Oprah Winfrey. Growing up, Oprah was the one person I saw on television who resembled me, someone who told stories that mattered, stories that resonated with the lives of people who looked like me. As a child, she was more than just a talk show host; she was a beacon, an example of what it meant to use your voice and platform to uplift others. She wasn't just sharing stories; she was creating a space for Black talent, for storytellers, and for voices that often went unheard.

When I heard Oprah speak at the 2024 DVF Awards, her words struck a chord deep within me. She spoke about three things that are most important to her: understanding who you are and what you're meant to do in the world, being grateful for the ability to do what you do, and sharing that journey with the people you love. These words echoed the values that have guided my own path, and I knew I had to include them in a way that reflects my own purpose.

Oprah's influence on me as a storyteller is profound. She is the reason I believe in the power of stories to change lives, to connect us, and to bring light to the world. Her journey and her truth have been a guiding force for me, reminding me of the importance of knowing who I am, being grateful for my gifts, and sharing those gifts with others.

So, Oprah, thank you for sharing your truths and your gift with the world. You've shown me, and countless others, the power of storytelling, the importance of lifting others up, and the beauty of living a life of purpose. This poem is my way of honoring your influence, of acknowledging the impact you've had on my life, and of continuing the legacy of storytelling that you've so powerfully championed.

Echoes of Open and Close

Beginnings are sweet, like a dawn's first light,
A new day rising, full of hope and might.
Middle school came with its share of fear,
But it was just the start, the way wasn't clear.

I stumbled through halls, unsure of my pace,
Each ending a push, a new starting race.
High school loomed, a serious leap,
From childhood's dreams to goals I'd keep.

High school's end, a door gently closed,
College ahead, where ambition rose.
No longer the boy unsure of his stride,
But a young man ready, with fire inside.

Beginnings are bright, they often deceive,
They promise the world, make you believe.
But endings come too, as they always must,
Teaching us to navigate, to adapt, to trust.

Love too follows this cyclical thread,
Sweet in the start, but bittersweet when it's dead.
I've loved and lost, more than I'd care,
But each ending taught me, made me aware.

Recently, another chapter closed,
A relationship ended, though it decomposed.
The break wasn't easy, the healing is slow,
But life's about learning to let go.

Not every end is wrapped up neat,
Some are messy, some incomplete.
But each one's a step, a lesson, a guide,
To navigate the ebb and flow of life's tide.

In love, I've had beginnings so sweet,
Like the first taste of honey, a tempting treat.
But many have ended, save one I hold dear,

This love, I claim, will not disappear.

Life's a cycle, a book of chapters and lines,
Each verse tells a story, each ending defines.
So as you read through my verses of life,
Know that beginnings and endings are part of the strife.

But they also bring growth, they shape who we are,
Each end is a sunset, each start a new star.
So turn the page, embrace what's ahead,
For life's a book where all must be read.

Inspiration behind "Echoes of Open and Close"

Emotion: Reflection

This poem was born from my reflection on the many beginnings and endings that have shaped my life, particularly as I prepared parts of my life in this book. This poem captures the cyclical nature of life—the way each chapter opens with promise and ends with lessons that guide us into the next phase.

As an African American male, I've navigated these cycles with the weight of cultural expectations and personal aspirations. Growing up, each transition felt monumental. The shift from middle school to high school was not just an academic progression but a rite of passage into adulthood. High school was serious business for me— the jumping point to a future I was determined to shape. I knew it was the tool I needed to get into college, the foundation for a career that would secure my success. The uncertainty I felt at the end of middle school pushed me to focus intensely on where I would go next, ensuring I wouldn't feel that lost again. When high school ended, I entered college more confident, having learned that each beginning, while daunting, was just a step toward something greater.

But life isn't just about academic and professional milestones. As I became more accustomed to the ebb and flow of beginnings and endings in school and work, I faced new challenges in the realm of love. This is where the lessons became more complex, where the stakes felt higher. Relationships, with all their beauty and pain, taught me that not all endings are clean or easy. My recent breakup, even though the romantic aspect had ended long before, brought me face-to-face with the reality that endings often require more navigation, more healing, and more growth than we expect. Love, unlike school or work, involves another person's journey, maturity, and willingness to let go, which adds layers to the process of moving on.

Throughout this book, you'll see how these cycles of beginnings and endings have played out in my relationships—from my first love, Jace, whose friendship turned into something deeper, to my current love, Rafa, whom I claim now as my future husband. Each relationship has had its own beautiful beginning, marked by the honeymoon phase that we all cherish. But except for my relationship with Rafa, all of them have also come to an end, leaving me with lessons that have shaped who I am today.

This poem explores these themes with the understanding that life is a constant flow of starting anew and letting go. It's about recognizing that every ending is not a failure but a necessary part of the journey. Each beginning brings hope, and each ending brings wisdom. This poem serves as a bridge in my book, connecting you from the broader themes of life's cycles to the intimate details of my personal experiences. It's a reminder that while we may not have control over when things begin or end, we do have the power to grow from each chapter and carry those lessons into the next.

Turning Thoughts to Gold

It started with a bed, a phone, a sigh,
Texts from suitors—sweet, but why?
They buzzed like bees around my head,
Addicted, I thought, to words unsaid.

And there, in that moment, a seed took root,
A poem was born from the noise and pursuit.
"Sweet Addiction," my very first line,
From a fleeting thought to a crafted rhyme.

My process? Oh, it's messy, it's raw,
I jot down thoughts, every single flaw.
Spill my emotions, let them flow,
On paper they land, like scattered snow.

Then comes the alchemy, the poet's grind,
Taking those thoughts and shaping the mind.
I turn the raw into something that sings,
With rhythm, with rhyme, and all the right rings.

Thesaurus in hand, I polish and prime,
Every word chosen to dance in time.
English and I, we wrestle, we fight,
But with intention, I get it just right.

Union life taught me the power of the pen,
Communicating plans, time and again.
A struggle at first, but then it clicked,
Writing became a tool, not a trick.

It's like journaling, but with a twist,
Turning private thoughts into a public list.
There's fear in the sharing, it's raw, it's real,

But catharsis comes with each reveal.

Sometimes, a chat with family or friends,
Leads to a poem where their wisdom blends.
I jot down themes, their words take flight,
And what I create feels powerful, bright.

It's in these moments, more than the rest,
That writing feels like I'm at my best.
Words hold power, they capture the soul,
Turning life into art, making stories whole.

So here's to the process, the struggle, the gold,
To the poems that emerge from the thoughts I hold.
It's a journey, a joy, a task so fulfilling,
Turning life into verse, with every willing.

Inspiration behind "Turning Thoughts to Gold"

Emotion: Creativity

This poem captures the essence of my creative process—the way a fleeting thought, an emotion, or even a conversation can ignite the spark that leads to a piece of art. The journey of writing this autobiographical poetry collection began with a single moment of frustration, lying in bed, overwhelmed by the constant buzz of messages from admirers. That raw emotion led to my first poem, "Sweet Addiction," and it became the template for how I approach my writing: capturing thoughts as they come, unfiltered, and then refining them into something poetic.

Writing has always been a challenge for me—grammar, spelling, and structure don't come easily unless I'm deliberate and intentional. This became especially clear when I took on the role of union president, where communicating clearly and effectively was not just a skill but a necessity. It was through this role that I realized the power of words, and how, with effort, I could wield them to express complex ideas and emotions.

This poem also reflects the cathartic nature of writing for me. It's like journaling, but with the added element of sharing my inner world with others. There's vulnerability in that—exposing my thoughts and experiences to the world—but it's also deeply fulfilling. The process of turning raw emotions into polished poetry feels like alchemy, transforming the mundane into something valuable, something that resonates.

One of my favorite aspects of writing is drawing inspiration from conversations with family and friends. Their words often carry a profound wisdom that I feel compelled to capture and amplify. These moments remind me of the power of language, how it connects us, how it records our history, and how it can make us feel seen and understood.

Ultimately, this poem is a celebration of the creative process itself—the struggle, the joy, the fear, and the fulfillment that comes from turning life into art. It's a testament to the idea that every thought, every emotion, no matter how small, can be transformed into something beautiful and meaningful.

Journey's Verse

In Michigan's quaint arms, youth's journey began,
A Gemini's whirl, Kyle first led the clan.
Freshman year's spark, soon a tempest unfurled,
A prelude to heartache in a too-vivid world.
His vibrant chaos, a tempest in play,
Jace's calm next, a contrasting array.

Jace's love blossomed, then waned in pain,
A closet of fears, a love undisclosed,
To Chicago's arms my heart then proposed.
But between these chapters, Mark' allure,
St. Martin's voice, passions mature.
Miami's sunsets, Chicago's breeze,
A backdrop of love that seemed to ease.

An ex-husband's love, in cheers drowned deep,
Our vows eroded where secrets seep.
A Zoom-screen divorce as the world stood still,
Pandemic echoes of a personal will.
Freed, I roamed to corners untold,
Yet Brandon's shadows caught me in cold.
Italian sunsets, a birthday's end,
Solo journeys, time to mend.

Nico's love, a different hue,
Languages of the heart, but views askew.
Two years of searching, paths diverge,
Love's lessons, onward, I urge.

Now, Mexico City, under vast skies,
Rafa's presence questions old heart ties.
In therapy's echo, I find my beat,
Interdependence laid at my feet.

Each chapter's close opens anew,
A self, unmasked, authentic, true.
My story—woven through men, it seems—
Is but a vessel for my own dreams

Inspiration behind "Journey's Verse"

Emotion: Evolution

This poem was written from a detailed narrative that spans several significant relationships and geographical moves, encapsulating a personal journey from Detroit, Michigan to Mexico City. This poem serves as a reflective summary of life experiences, presented through the lens of relationships that have played pivotal roles at different stages.

The narrative begins with Kyle Grayson, the first significant relationship at Michigan State University, which was marked by vibrancy and turbulence. Following Kyle, the journey introduces Jace, whose personal struggles with identity deeply impacted the dynamics of our relationship. Between these chapters, Mark from St. Martin brings a period of passion and excitement, illustrating the thrill of love that was both long-distance and intensely present during visits to Miami and Chicago.

Darren, my ex-husband, met in Chicago, brought the promise of something stable yet turned turbulent in the end. Our relationship became increasingly strained due to Darren's struggle with alcoholism, which led to significant emotional challenges. Despite our deep connection, the pressures of his addiction caused the relationship to unravel, ending in a drama fueled divorce.

The relationship with Brandon, who met in Chicago and later accompanied in a move to San Diego during the pandemic, adds a layer of complexity as it unfolds against the backdrop of global upheaval. The break-up with Brandon led to a transformative period marked by frequent travels to Mexico City, where the next chapter with Nico unfolded. Those visits became a backdrop for deep emotional connection and the eventual realization of our diverging personal paths

After ending the relationship with Nico, the encounter with Rafa in Mexico City marks the current phase of hopeful exploration. This relationship, characterized by mutual understanding and the pursuit of an interdependent partnership, signifies a mature approach to love, influenced by past experiences.

Each relationship not only narrates a specific time and interaction but also weaves in broader life themes such as identity, freedom, and the continuous quest for emotional fulfillment. The poem highlights how each relationship, with its unique challenges and joys, contributes to an evolving sense of self and place in the world, guiding the pursuit of authenticity and personal happiness.

Unwritten Chapters: A Mosaic of Me

In the library of life, a book remains unbound,
Pages fluttering loose—a story profound.
A draft of dreams and heartbreaks stored,
A narrative deep, yet never scored.

Kyles's Chapter: The First Flame
Kyle stormed in with wit and fire,
A love that sparked my heart's desire.
Drama swirled, lessons learned,
In Gemini's glow, passion burned.

First Love's Echo, Early Bloom
Jace's shadow, love's first room,
Friendship dressed in tender care,
Hearts entwined in youthful snare.

Crossroads Kissed by Passion's Flame
Mark came and went, a fleeting name,
A spark that burned too bright, too fast,
In love's great book, not meant to last.

Vows Weaved with Worry's Thread
Darren's chapter, lines of dread,
A marriage marred by bottles drained,
Love's architecture, joy refrained.

Renaissance of a Solitary Soul
Divorce, the tolling of a bell,
In solitude's embrace, I found my swell.
A virus raged, the world stood still,
Yet in my silence, grew my will.

Brandon's Tale of Shadows Deep
Mental mazes, steep and steep,
A dance with demons in the mind,
Lessons harsh, but truths defined.

Farewell's Freedom, Heart's Release
Goodbye to Brandon, a heart's peace,
From tangled ties, I took my leave,
Towards Mexico, my soul to cleave.

Mexican Sun, Love's New Tongue
Nico's eyes, a song unsung,
A dance of words, a test of heart,
Two worlds collide, a brand new start.

Nico's Dark Unveiled
First the break, then still we stayed,
Living together as trust decayed.
Drama ensued, a line was crossed,
In shadows, a side of him I lost.

Authentic Threads in Life's Great Loom
Rafa's steady hand, respect so true,
A love that grows in shades of blue.
Through life's embrace, we've learned to see,
Our path entwined, in maturity.

A Future Painted in Present Tense
Aspirations high, no pretense,
Rafa and I, with hearts aligned,
Together, through all, we're intertwine.

In Playful Prose, The Story Bends
No book to bind, no settled gloom,
Just chapters lived, then set apart,
For a poem's pulse beats in my heart.

A Future Etched in Love's Own Dance
My future husband, our love's expanse.
Through every challenge, hand in hand,
We plan our bond, forever stand.

Perspectives of a Shared World
The world spins on, elections rise,
Truth and lies beneath our skies.
With loved ones near, we brace, we fight,

For a shared world, we seek the light.

Inspiration behind "Unwritten Chapters: A Mosaic of Me"

Emotion: Introspection

This poem serves as the final piece of my introduction chapter, setting the tone for the chronological journey of love that will unfold throughout this book. It provides a template for you to understand the path I'm taking you on, from the early moments of love to the deeper connections that have shaped my life.

Through this poem, I aim to guide you through pivotal moments—relationships that have marked my path, love's complexities, and the introspection that has emerged along the way. The poem starts with youthful infatuations and progresses to the mature love I share today, followed by reflections on the shared world we all navigate. This poem encapsulates the essence of my story and is your guide to understanding the emotional, chronological progression of love and life that follows.

More than just recounting events, this poem offers a mosaic of memories and lessons, bridging the personal and the universal. It invites you not only into my story but into your own experiences as you explore love, loss, and growth. The poem, and the book as a whole, I hope to create a connection that resonates beyond the words, encouraging reflection and a shared sense of humanity.

This poem is not just a prologue—it's the key to understanding the narrative ahead, guiding you through my life that is still evolving, with the hope that it inspires introspection and connection along the way.

Childhood
Emotion: Nostalgia

In this "Childhood" chapter, I take you through the formative years of my life, reflecting on experiences from birth until the summer of 2006, with a strong focus on my high school years. These poems capture the moments that shaped me, from the challenges and triumphs of entering Cass Tech to the deep connections and lessons learned within my family. Through anticipation, fear, love, and revelation, this chapter explores my journey of self-discovery, resilience, and the profound impact of those early years. It sets the foundation for understanding who I am, the person I've become, and how I've come to embrace and love with depth and authenticity.

Rooted in Detroit

In Detroit's heart, where the streets run cold,
a story begins, in resilience bold.
Malcolm Alexander-Neal, my name you'll hear,
raised by love that conquered fear.

My roots are deep, in the city's embrace.
Born to Brianna and Eli, but in a different place.
My grandparents, Mitchell and Sonia Neal,
stepped in with love, a bond so real.

At five years old, I found a new start.
In their home, they nurtured my heart.
From an abusive world, they pulled me away.
In their care, I learned to sway.

On Jefferson Avenue, in a high-rise grand,
with wide spiraled stairs, where life was planned.
Rooms filled with laughter, stories, and play,
a fortress of love, where I'd lay.

East Side Vicariate, a school of grace,
taught me more than just the race.
But as high school loomed, I felt the dread.
Would I keep up? Where would this path lead?

Yet in that home, high above the ground,
with cousins close, and love all around,
I grew, a worry-free child in a world so vast,
mature beyond years, in a life unsurpassed.

But there was more to this love I'd learn
from my grandfather, whose heart did yearn
for my grandmother's smile, her every quirk,
loving her deeply, even her "dirty socks" at work.

His love wasn't just in words but deeds,
helping others, fulfilling their needs.
A pillar of strength, my guide, my light,

he showed me how to love, to fight the good fight.

In their embrace, I found my creed,
to love unconditionally, with every deed.
But this love, so pure, sometimes was a test,
opening my heart, leaving me no rest.

Yet, it's the only way I know to be,
loving fully, unconditionally, just like he.
Though it made life harder, it's a love I hold dear,
for it's the foundation that brought me here.

This poem sets the tone, the beginning you see,
of a life shaped by love, and what's to be.
Rooted in Detroit, with lessons so bright,
a journey of love, of strength, of might.

So as you read on, through stories untold,
remember the love, the wisdom of old.
For it's in these roots, where my story begins,
in Detroit's embrace, where love always wins.

Inspiration Behind "Rooted "in Detroit"

Emotion: nostalgia

This poem is deeply personal, weaving together the foundational experiences that shaped who I am today. This poem is an introduction to my childhood and the early influences that guided my journey.

I was born and raised in Detroit, Michigan, a city known for its resilience and rich cultural history. My story begins with the love and care of my grandparents, Mitchel and Sonia Nash, who took me in at the age of five, rescuing me from a troubled and abusive household. Their strength and determination became the bedrock upon which I built my identity.

Growing up in their home, I learned independence early on. My grandparents instilled resilience, self-reliance, and resourcefulness in me, traits that I have carried into adulthood. Yet, this independence also cultivated a low-key hustler mindset, navigating life's challenges with determination.

My childhood in Detroit was sheltered and secure. We lived in a large apartment just off Jefferson, in what I considered downtown Detroit, though most would call it the east side. My cousins, Mara and Tavian, were my closest friends, and I spent much of my time with family, having conversations with grown-ups, playing cards, and soaking in their stories. This environment made me more mature than other kids my age, but it also kept me insulated from the social dynamics I would later encounter.

One constant, unwavering influence shaped my understanding of love: my grandfather. He is my first and most significant example of unconditional love. He adored my grandmother, even down to the smallest details, like loving her "dirty socks"—a simple expression of his affection. His love reached everyone he encountered, creating an atmosphere of warmth and kindness that taught me what it means to truly care for others.

Their relationship set the standard for what I believe love should be, and I have tried to emulate that love in my own life. Whether with family, friends, or anyone I meet, I pour that same unconditional love into my relationships. This is the only way I know how to love, and it has sometimes made life more challenging, allowing me to be taken advantage of—intentionally or unintentionally. Yet, I wouldn't trade it for anything because it's rooted in the love of my grandfather, the purest example I had.

My grandfather is more than just a role model; he is my pillar, my support system, and the person who shaped me into the man I am today. He is my honor system, guiding me with his actions and commitment to those he loved. Through him, I learned that love is not just a feeling but an action—a constant, unconditional giving of oneself for the well-being of others.

The first poem in the childhood chapter of my book, "Rooted in Detroit" sets the tone for everything that follows. It introduces the context of my upbringing and the foundational values that have influenced every relationship in my life. It's a way of grounding the reader in my story, showing how the lessons of love and selflessness I learned from my grandparents have permeated every aspect of my life.

In this poem, I aim to convey that love, as I understand it, is all-encompassing and unconditional. My hope is that you will see this love reflected in the stories and relationships that unfold in the poems that follow, understanding that it all began with the love and example set by my grandfather. Through this reflection, I aim to inspire others to think about the examples of love in their own lives and how those examples have shaped the way they love today.

New Beginnings in a Family Mosaic

In the weave of family, a new thread appeared.
Kara stepped in, as the summer neared.
Her bond with Uncle Arlen, a gentle tie,
introduced new kin under Detroit's sky.

Uncle Arlen, the elder twin, his heart robust,
Evan his shadow, in whom we trust.
Uncle Mitch, a soldier's stance, fleeting scenes,
Father Eli, a rolling stone, in and out of dreams.

But it was Kara' tribe that brought fresh air,
three young souls with stories to share.
Tanner Kearn, just two, her words a curious flow,
Tyrell, a tactician at three, a show of woe.

Trent, the peacemaker, at four, his calm a balm,
Their early wisdom, like a soothing psalm.
Middle school summers, their laughter my guide,
A camping first, with Kara's kin by my side.

Bernadette's talks, profound, drew me in,
My novice camping praised, a newfound kin.
Rain or shine, a tent I'd secure,
Skills honed without a manual, pure.

Kara's home became my weekend retreat,
Where game nights and fish fries were a treat.
Family reunions, a festive embrace,
Halloween parties, a spirited chase.

Tessa Jensen, of sandy hair,
Golden eyes that shift, a fiery flare.
Her spirit fierce, a friendship's test,
In debates, a fervent zest.

This "New Family," my adolescence's frame,
Their presence a comfort, life never the same.
From Kara's kitchen, the aroma of BBQ,

To the unity felt, in everything we'd do.

In this family mosaic, I found my place,
A gallery of moments, time cannot erase.
In Detroit's arms, these bonds were cast,
A foundation of memories, built to last.

Inspiration Behind "New Beginnings in a Family Mosaic"

Emotion: Belonging

This poem was inspired by a new family dynamic that entered my world during middle school. My Uncle Arlen started dating Kara, who brought three vibrant children—Tanner, Tyrell, and Trent, affectionately known as the "Three Ts." Their entrance marked a turning point in my social and family life, expanding my universe beyond the confines of my earlier, more sheltered experiences.

I had an instant connection with Kara and her family. They introduced me to new experiences, like camping, which became a cherished memory. Bernadette, Kara's mother, praised my natural aptitude for outdoor living. These new, exhilarating experiences contrasted sharply with my previous interactions, mostly confined to family.

This time in my life was filled with weekend visits to Kara's home, where I was enveloped in a lively atmosphere of game nights, family reunions, and seasonal celebrations. It provided a sense of community and familial warmth that I had not known in my own childhood. Kara's exceptional cooking and the general vibrancy of her home life left a lasting impression on me.

Kara's niece Tessa became one of my closest friends. Our friendship blended admiration and challenge, given her strong personality and readiness to engage in spirited debates. Her unique characteristics, from her sandy hair and color-shifting eyes to her fiery spirit, helped shape my adolescent experiences.

This poem reflects how Kara's family quickly became intertwined with my own, creating relationships that defined my middle school years and beyond. It celebrates the joy, learning, and growth of being part of a larger, lively, and loving family environment.

Echoes of East Side Vicariate

Four years within East Side Vicariate's walls,
a beacon where youthful ambition calls.
Through shifting classrooms, friendships took form,
in corridors, quiet, away from life's storm.

Tobias Winslow, the gentle giant in our midst,
his laughter a balm, too heartfelt to resist.
Taller each year, he soared above,
in jest and in spirit, he taught me of love.

Amos Taylor, with his jokes so light,
a touch of corn, yet a friendship bright.
Hours on the phone, silly dreams we'd share,
superpowers wished, floating through the air.

Rafiq, with her tough veneer,
a tomboy's grace, drawing me near.
Usher tickets and teddy bears, gifts I gave,
silent hopes of love, quiet and brave.

Alma's sketches, strokes of thought.
Daphne's fervor, battles fought.
Each a character in my unfolding play,
guiding me through each challenging day.

Middle school, a whirlwind fast,
memories fleeting, shadows cast.
Bradley Tanner, with his golden hair,

a class clown's exit, teacher's despair.

Lessons of self, of laughter and fight.
The word 'gay' whispered, a new kind of light.
Otis's taunt, a curiosity stoked,
in shadows of youth, my identity cloaked.

Harry Potter's pages turned in haste,
a wizard's world, my first true taste.
From reluctant reader to avid fan,
J.K. Rowling's magic, part of my plan.

Ms. Saunders's' math, her voice would ring,
lessons in numbers and life she'd bring.
Voicemails festive, a holiday treat,
her nurturing soul, none could defeat.

Cass Tech's challenge, an appeal to fate.
Rejection first, then acceptance great.
A portfolio thick, my dreams compiled,
business over architecture, a path restyled.

East Side Vicariate, where roots took hold,
in its classrooms bold, my story told.
From sheltered youth to a world embraced,
each lesson a step, in time well placed.

Inspiration Behind "Echoes of East Side Vicariate"

Emotion: Nostalgia

I spent four years at East Side Vicariate School, which inspired this poem. These formative years were the longest period I ever stayed at one school due to frequently. This school was the backdrop for many firsts in my life: my first real friendships, my first brushes with school dynamics and cliques, and my first steps toward understanding my identity.

Tobias Winslow and Amos Taylor were my pillars during these transformative years. Tobias, with his incredible sense of humor and towering presence, and Amos, with his light-hearted, corny jokes, made school life enjoyable and memorable. Our countless hours on the phone, discussing everything from the mundane to the fantastical, such as what superpowers we would choose, played a significant role in my adolescence.

Rafiq, with her tomboy coolness and indirect role in my early romantic stirrings, and other classmates like Alma and Daphne, each added unique hues to my middle school palette. These years also included challenging moments, like standing up for myself against bullies, which was a significant turning point in how I viewed myself and dealt with adversity.

The poem also captures how literature, specifically J.K. Rowling's "Harry Potter," unexpectedly captivated and transformed me from a reluctant reader into an avid one. This discovery opened up new worlds of imagination and learning.

Ms. Saunders was a teacher who took a tough-love approach that made learning engaging. I have cherished memories of her festive voicemails and holiday greetings, showing the warmth and care she extended beyond the classroom.

This poem reflects my middle school journey—a time of growth and learning that laid the groundwork for my future challenges and achievements. It celebrates the environment and the people who contributed to my development during a pivotal phase of my life.

Journey to Cass: A Prelude

Part I: The Fear and Transition

In the waning days of East Side Vicariate,
a cloud of trepidation shadowed my gate.
Cass Tech loomed, a giant so vast,
a leap toward adulthood, coming fast.

Afraid of the rigor, of paths unknown,
standing on thresholds, far from home.
From eighth grade's comfort into the storm,
where futures are forged, new selves born.

Graduation spoke of endings and starts,
among cheering family and hopeful hearts.
Spoke of gratitude, our Ms. Saunders praised,
her tough love, the beacon through our phase.

Part II: The Summer of Transformation

Summer at Cass, a prelude to more.
Math was a delight, English a chore.
But in those classrooms, life unfurled,
friendships blossomed, a new world swirled.

Daphne Emery, laughter and light.
Jada and Julian, through long summer nights.
Truths and dares in hidden school spaces.
Adolescent games, testing our paces.

Fumbling with feelings, learning the ropes,
navigating desires, harboring hopes.
The puzzle of texts, of meanings obscure,
finding my voice, becoming sure.

Part III: Independence Unleashed

A phone to my name, selling beads at the mart.
Crafting my way, practicing the art.
From East Side to Cass, a journey profound.
In every new challenge, my spirit unbound.

I sold my creations, stones rich and rare,
learning to hustle, always aware.
Riding the buses, the city my stage,
from one side to another, turning the page.

The fears I had harbored slowly receded,
as Cass and its lessons were fully heeded.
By summer's end, Cass was no longer dire,
but a promise of growth, of rising higher.

Part IV: Realization and Readiness

I learned to embrace each daunting new task,
realizing that growth is but courage unmasked.
No longer fearful of the high school fray,
ready to tackle whatever comes my way.

Daphne, Jada, Julian—the friends I'd keep,
part of my journey, etched in memories deep.
And as I prepared for the high school dawn,
I knew I was ready, my fears all but gone.

Inspiration Behind "Journey to Cass: A Prelude"
Emotion: Growth

These poems were inspired by the transition from my middle school days at East Side Vicariate to the more demanding environment of Cass Technical High School. This series captures the blend of apprehension, excitement, and growth that defined this period of my adolescence.

"The Fear and Transition," reflects the mix of fear and anticipation I felt as I graduated from middle school.

Despite being excited about moving forward, I was also scared about stepping into a more challenging and adult phase. The graduation ceremony, which all of my loved ones attended, marked both an ending and a beginning, encapsulating my mixed feelings about moving on.

In "The Summer of Transformation," I delve into the experiences of my preparatory summer classes at Cass. This was a time of academic challenge and social exploration, where I met new friends and started to find my place in this larger school community. The interactions with peers like Daphne, Jada, and Julian during these classes played a significant role in easing my initial fears about high school.

"The Independence Unleashed" part of the series highlights my entrepreneurial spirit through the bead jewelry business I ran during the summer. It was not just about making money; it was about asserting my independence and applying my creativity in a practical way. This experience was instrumental in building my confidence and helping me understand the value of self-reliance.

Finally, "Realization and Readiness" encapsulates the growth and readiness I felt by the end of that summer. It reflects the realization that I was capable of handling the challenges ahead, thanks to the foundations laid during those transformative months. This poem celebrates the personal evolution that occurred as I prepared to step into high school, no longer as a fearful incoming freshman but as a young man ready to take on the world.

Together, these poems chart the journey of my young self as a student, stepping out of the comfort zone of middle school, navigating through the challenges and opportunities of a preparatory summer, and emerging ready and eager to tackle high school and beyond. They celebrate the universal themes of growth, resilience, and the journey towards self-discovery.

First Steps at Cass Tech

I. Orientation and Beginnings

Cass Tech's halls, a labyrinth vast.
Echoes of footsteps from students past.
A square of old, and new wings spread,
rooms where countless dreams are bred.

An auditorium grand, a stage set wide,
where Mr. Corbin's words abide.
Talk of fisticuffs and edifice tall,
matriculation tales that enthrall.

The freshman crowd in wonder gaze
through the maze of Cass's intricate ways.
Lockers on high floors, a strategic art,
navigating these halls takes more than heart.

II. Freshman Strategies

Assigned a locker on the distant fifth.
My schedule a puzzle, classes adrift.
From seventh to first, with no time to spare,
cleverly claiming lockers here and there.

Veteran moves in a freshman's guise,
quickly learning, swift to rise.
In corridors filled with upperclassmen's calls,
finding my footing within these walls.

III. Academic Challenges

Mrs. Davison's English, a beacon bright,
from hated subject to a favored light.
Poetry recitations, a daunting task,
each stanza conquered, no need to ask.

From Jaberwocky's fanciful flights,

to Jack Frost's wintry nights.
A standing ovation for a performance keen,
finding joy in what once made me keen.

IV. New Friendships and Trials

In the bustling life of Cass's realm,
new faces and friendships overwhelm.
Daphne, Estelle, and Jillian by my side.
In their company, I take pride.

Forging signatures, a risky play.
Hall passes that let us stray.
Academic Decathlon, a club reborn.
Under Mrs. Davison's care, we're sworn.

V. Growing Pains and Achievements

From homecoming dances to everyday class,
each step at Cass, a significant pass.
Navigating social labyrinths with care,
learning that high school's more than just fair.

A GPA that marks a strong start.
Math honors beckon, a path apart.
Each challenge met with newfound might,
Cass Tech's lessons, my guiding light.

Inspiration Behind "First Steps at Cass Tech"

Emotion: Exhilaration

This poem stems from my transformative experiences at
Cass Technical High School. Through these poems, I aim
to capture this time filled with anticipation, challenges,
and personal growth. Starting high school was like

stepping into a vast new world. Cass Tech, with its complex layout and bustling corridors, was intimidating yet exhilarating. I remember the awe of navigating this enormous space—its old and new wings, each with distinctive features, and the unique architecture that made it feel like stepping into a storybook. Mr. Corbin's welcoming speech, filled with unusual words like 'edifice' and 'matriculation,' reminded me of a character out of a J.K. Rowling novel, setting the stage for our high school journey.

These poems also reflect my strategic adjustments as a freshman, like securing lockers on different floors to manage the daunting transitions between classes. These small victories helped me feel more seasoned and less like an overwhelmed newcomer.

English class with Mrs. Davison significantly shifted my relationship with the subject. Her engaging teaching style and the poetry recitation challenges transformed English from my least favorite to a favored subject. This change was pivotal, helping me find my voice and confidence in public speaking.

The poems explore the new friendships that became central to my high school life. Friends like Daphne and Jillian became integral parts of my journey, contributing to fun, mischief, and the everyday drama of high school life. Our adventures, from forging signatures to navigating social dynamics, added dimension to my school days.

These poems are a tribute to Cass Tech's impact on me from the start. They celebrate the academic and extracurricular activities and the personal growth and self-discovery that defined such an important phase of my life. The poem captures the challenges, triumphs, and social tapestry of my freshman year, highlighting how each experience contributed to shaping the person I have become.

Winter Reflections at Cass Tech

I. Contrasts of Learning

Winter semester, a haze in my mind,
with health class lessons, and vodka finds.
In the back of the room, a deal discreet,
Smirnoff Ices, a secret treat.

Health class irony, the irony deep.
Learning of alcohol, while secrets I keep.
Hiding bottles in walls of built-in drawers.
Nightly cocktails, breaking all laws.

II. Academic Struggles and Social Drinks

A 'B' in Health disrupts my stride,
chasing perfection, with nowhere to hide.
School days long, nights even longer,
in Aunt Kara's kitchen, her cooking made stronger.

Late-night feasts, laughter ringing clear,
her drunken joy, a moment so dear.
Yet, in the classroom, my focus held sway,
determined to excel, come what may.

III. Awkward Discoveries

A first awkward encounter in the dead of night.
Truth or dare, a curious plight.
Explorations of youth, too bold, too raw.
Learning of limits, and the flaw in awe.

Painful lessons, a secret shared.
A friendship fleeting, nothing spared.
Youth's clumsy steps into the dance of desire,
each memory a spark, each touch a fire.

IV. Celebrity Beginnings

Bio class memories, a face across the way.
Sean Anderson, before his celebrity day.
Silent exchanges, a future untold,
in the heart of winter, a story bold.

V. Pathways to the Future

A drive for the future, a college dream.
Accounting courses, a flowing stream.
Mrs. Stratton's class, a revelation,
finding joy in financial calculation.

From a hundred schools to just twenty.
Harvard at the helm, opportunities plenty.
Pre-SATs conquered, a Harvard letter.
Winter's end, nothing felt better.

Inspiration Behind "Winter Reflections at Cass Tech"

Emotion: Contemplation

This poem comes from the experiences of my 2002 winter semester, freshman year of high school.. This period included a mix of academic challenges, personal growth, and unexpected adventures, each contributing to a complex tapestry of memories that shaped my teenage years.

In health class, the stark irony of learning about the dangers of alcohol while secretly buying Smirnoff Ices highlights the rebellious undercurrents of my youth. This juxtaposition inspired the first poem, capturing the clandestine thrill and the hidden contradictions of my actions against the backdrop of classroom lessons.

The academic frustrations and social life at my aunt
Kara's house, where the nights were filled with the
warmth of her cooking and the joyous noise of family
gatherings, provided a rich contrast to the daytime
demands of school. These moments of familial comfort
among academic rigor inspired reflections on how
personal environments influence and shape our
educational experiences.

My first awkward encounter with sexuality was both
eye-opening and disconcerting. This inspired a poem
reflecting on the complexities of growing up, exploring
identity, and the often-painful lessons of early sexual
experiences.

Sitting across from Sean Anderson, who would later
become a successful celebrity, added a layer to my high
school memories. This proximity inspired a poem
contemplating the unexpected paths and future fame of
schoolmates, reminding me of the hidden potentials within
every classroom.

Lastly, the rigorous pursuit of academic excellence and
the strategic planning for college shaped another major
theme. The transition from a broad interest in architecture
to a focused passion for accounting, spurred by an
influential teacher, reflects my evolving academic interests
and the decisive steps toward future goals. The excitement
of receiving an acceptance letter from Harvard was
pivotal, symbolizing the culmination of my efforts and
aspirations, which naturally found expression in the final
poem of the series.

Sophomore Year Shifts

I. Finding Myself in Transition

Sophomore year, a canvas blank,
a time of change, in rank and flank.
Clothes, voice, and interests align,
identity's quest, subtly divine.

Amid the search, a truth unveiled,
desires of heart, in whispers, exhaled.
A yearning for love, not fully confessed,
from Harvard's summer, to heart's quiet quest.

II. Classroom Leadership

In Principles of Accounting's steady beat,
Mrs. Stratton's trust, a feat so sweet.
Left in charge, a classroom lead,
guiding peers, planting the seed.

Jace Bryant, the back-row sage,
questioning, talking, setting the stage.
From annoying to intriguing, a shift in sight,
a crush unfurling, hidden in plain light.

III. The Chase Begins

An unrequited dance, steps misaligned.
Jace, unknowing, the target of mind.
Strategy in motion, friends drawn near,
MSN chats, closing the fear.

Danica Blackwood, a conduit, found,
through digital words, a battleground.
Predator mode, a friendship's guise,
learning of him, a prize in disguise.

IV. An Unlikely Bond

Daria "Sweetie" Hinton, a friend by fate.
Sweets and calls, sealing the date.
Persistence in pursuit, a friendship's birth.
Laughter and cupcakes, increasing their worth.

A bond cemented over baked delights,
from forced beginnings to cherished rights.
Sophomore year, a mix of sweet and sour,
friendships and crushes, gaining their power.

Inspiration Behind "Sophomore Year Shifts"

Emotion: Self-Discovery

The poems were inspired by my experiences and personal growth during sophomore year. During this time of exploration and change, I began to more seriously consider my future and identity.

The first poem, "Finding Myself in Transition," reflects on my internal shifts. During this time,I actively tried to define my identity through my clothing choices, interests, and even my voice. After my experience at Harvard over the summer, I also started to acknowledge my sexuality more openly and began longing for a romantic relationship..

In "Classroom Leadership," I explore the responsibility and pride I felt when Mrs. Stratton, my accounting teacher, entrusted me to lead the class in her absence. This was a significant moment for me, highlighting my academic strengths and leadership capabilities. It also marks the beginning of my complicated feelings for Jace, a classmate who initially annoyed me but gradually became the object of my affection.

"The Chase Begins" is about the strategies I employed to get closer to Jace. This poem captures the intensity of my first crush, where I navigated friendships and social media to learn more about him and find ways to connect, despite the challenges of his existing relationships and my uncertainty about his orientation.

Finally, "An Unlikely Bond" celebrates the unexpected friendship that developed with Daria "Sweetie" Hinton. Our connection started over her cupcakes, which I initially bought and resold, but quickly grew into a genuine friendship filled with laughter and support.

Summer School Silhouettes at Harvard

Prelude to Harvard: Tesa's Friend

Before the Ivy halls beckoned,
I tied a knot, not with love, but friendship—
Tessa Jensen, a name I wore
like a badge to a battle I scarcely understood.
I asked her to be mine, not out of passion,
but perhaps as a shield, a guise
worn at the edge of self-discovery.
We never kissed, our love, a platonic dance,
a melody of companionship without the crescendo of
romance.

Harvard: A Theatre of Dreams and Revelation

Harvard unfolded like a map of the world I yearned to
conquer,
surrounded by minds like stars in a vast, unexplored
galaxy,
their brilliance sculpted from lineages of gold,
echoes of success I wished to echo.
I walked through this whirlwind of potential,
each day, a lecture from the future I envisioned.

Faces of Ambition

Amongst them, Danica Ainsley, her life a canvas
of metropolitan dreams, legal prowess, and political
tapestries.
Her home, a museum of affluence I walked through,
each corner whispering possibilities of what could be.
And there was Milan Singh, with his genome maps and
future scrubs,
words like 'bio-genetics' coloring his ambition,
his path as clear as the prestige of Exeter hallways.

Solitude in Diversity

In my sphere, few faces mirrored my own,
Omari, with roots reaching deep into African soils—
Black like me, yet worlds apart.
Cambridge's charm was inviting, yet isolating,
a reminder of the spaces we occupy,
both physical and metaphorical.

Boston and the Charles River

Boston's architecture, a new fascination.
Buildings speaking in stony tongues of history and design.
I embraced the city's skeleton in my courses
while the Charles River held my secrets,
its waters flipping my kayak in a moment of careless
zeal—
a plunge into the cold clarity of who I was becoming.

Reflections and Resolutions

Now, the memory of Harvard is a mosaic,
pieces of who I was, shadows of who I wanted to be.
Though paths changed and facades fell,
the lessons linger like the aftertaste of a potent brew.
As I chart the course of my true desires,
Harvard remains a chapter of exploration—

a summer of silhouettes, shaping the contours of my identity.

Inspiration Behind "Summer School Silhouettes at Harvard"

Emotion: Inspiration

These poems were inspired by my attendance at Harvard's summer school. Receiving my acceptance letter was a moment of pure elation; it marked the beginning of a journey that challenged my perceptions and significantly shaped my aspirations and personal growth.

At Harvard, I was thrust into an environment brimming with intellectual vigor and success that seemed worlds apart from my own experiences. Surrounded by peers whose lives were narratives of privilege and achievement, I grappled with feelings of impostor syndrome, yet I embraced these feelings as motivation instead of barriers. This environment was a vivid tableau of what life could offer—an eye-opener to the myriad possibilities that lay ahead.

Living on my own at such a young age in such a stimulating environment accelerated my maturity and broadened my perspective. Every lecture, every interaction was a stepping stone in defining the life I envisioned for myself. It reaffirmed my desires to travel, to engage deeply with diverse disciplines, and to carve out a path that was uniquely my own.

Reflecting on this time through my writing brings back a sense of nostalgia and reinvigorates the drive and passion I felt then. It reminds me that the experiences at Harvard shaped my life trajectory, propelling me toward creating a personal and professional life filled with purpose and exploration. Even today, as I reflect and write about these experiences, they continue to inspire and

excite me, fueling my ambitions and reminding me of the
vast horizons I yearn to explore.

11th Grade Confessions

11th grade… what happened there?
Let me clarify, let me lay it bare.
In 10th grade, Jace was just a thought,
a spark that hadn't fully caught.

It started with a few late interactions,
but by 11th grade, I had deep attractions.
I went full stalker mode, it's true.
Not quite out, but starting to break through.

The first I told was 1.   Samanika Halsey,
a friend who'd left, it felt safe to say.
She became my confidant, my secret keeper,
listening to tales of love growing deeper.

I befriended Danica, Jace's best friend,
hoping through her, my love I'd send.
We chatted on AIM, AOL, MSN, too.
I'd use any means just to talk to you.

From messengers to texts, from texts to phone,
Jace became the best friend I'd known.
But in my heart, he was so much more,
the secret lover I quietly adored.

Every day, he made me smile,
a love that stretched for miles and miles.
In my soul, I knew he felt it, too,
but he'd pull back, claiming he wasn't true.

He'd give me glimpses, then shut it down,
leaving me spinning, joy turned to frown.
My love was silent, my heart was loud,
but I kept it hidden under a shroud.

In the closet still, my love had to wait
til the 12th grade, when I'd open the gate.
But in that 11th grade year, so intense,
I learned of love, of hope, of suspense.

A love unspoken, shown through deeds.
A friendship deep, but my heart still bleeds.
For in the silence of that secret year,
I loved so hard, yet lived in fear.

Jace, my secret love, my true best friend,
a love that drove me near the end.
But I held it in, kept it tight,
waiting for the day, I'd bring it to light.

11th grade, a year of dreams,
of love that's hidden, bursting at the seams.
But I'd hold on, just a little while,
til I could show the world my love, my style.

Inspiration behind "11th Grade Confessions"
Emotion: Yearning

This poem is rooted in the intense, formative
experiences of 11th grade, when my feelings for Jace began
to take shape and grow into something deep, yet
complicated. This poem reflects the confusion, excitement,
and emotional turmoil that defined that period of my life.

In the 10th grade, Jace was just a fleeting thought, a
spark that hadn't yet ignited into the fire it would become.
But by 11th grade, that spark grew into something I
couldn't ignore. I found myself drawn to him in ways that
were new and overwhelming. It was the beginning of my
journey of self-discovery, of realizing and coming to terms
with my identity, even if I wasn't fully ready to share it
with the world.

The first person I confided in about being gay was
Samanika Halsey. It felt safe to tell her because she had left
Cass, so there were no immediate consequences or fears of
exposure. She became my confidant, the one who knew
about my growing feelings for Jace. Through her support
and understanding, I began to navigate this confusing
time.

As my feelings for Jace deepened, I strategically
befriended his best friend to get closer to him. We chatted
on AIM, AOL, MSN—whatever platform allowed me to
connect with him. Our communication evolved from
online chats to text messages to phone calls. Jace quickly
became someone I spoke to every day, someone who made
me smile, feel seen and believe there could be a future for
us.

But this love was complicated. I was still mostly in the
closet, so my feelings had to be kept hidden. Jace would
give me glimpses of affection, making me believe he felt
the same, only to pull back and claim to be straight. This
back-and-forth and push and pull caused me immense
emotional turmoil. I was falling in love with someone who
seemed to love me back, yet denied it, leaving me in a state
of constant uncertainty and longing.

The poem captures the silent love I carried, the intense
friendship that served as the foundation for my feelings,
and the emotional rollercoaster that Jace unknowingly put
me through. It reflects the struggles of unrequited love, the
pain of hiding your true self, and the hope that those
feelings will be fully reciprocated and acknowledged one
day.

Writing this poem was a way to process those emotions
and acknowledge how that time in my life shaped who I
am today. It's about the complexities of love, identity, and
the journey toward self-acceptance. The poem is also a
reminder of the lessons learned during that time—the
importance of being true to oneself, the pain of unspoken
love, and the growth that comes from those experiences.

The Summer of Revelation

The summer sun beamed, casting light on shadows deep.
In the space between 11th and 12th grade, I began to leap.
E-commerce program—a stage to test the waters clear,
s summer of truth, a time to conquer fear.

First day jitters, but a girl's question caught me off guard,
"Do you know Sam? Do you know Tyrone?"—her inquiry,
hard.
She fished for the truth I hadn't yet fully claimed,
assuming all gays knew each other as if it were a game.

But that summer, I chose to let my truth unfold,
told everyone in the program, before the season grew cold.
Each word felt like freedom, a piece of myself unveiled.
I moved with confidence, my true self never derailed.

I went further, decided my family needed to know.
Jaya, my high school friend, stayed with me, her support a
steady glow.
She stayed on the phone as I wrestled with my words,
cheerleading, encouraging, her presence never blurred.

My grandfather, hesitant, withdrew into his space,
but my grandmother asked questions, trying to find a
trace.
"Did you wreck the car? Get a girl pregnant?" she
inquired,
Each question a blow to the courage I had acquired.

"What would you think of me if you didn't know me?"
"Gay?" she answered, and I felt no shame.
Relieved, she said she'd tell him what I couldn't express,
and he, concerned only with legacy, asked, "Will you still
have kids?"—no less.

My mother, a quicker conversation in the car we took,
"How do you know?" she asked, with a puzzled look.

"Have you been with a girl?" she questioned, somewhat annoyed,
I asked her the same, and the conversation, we both enjoyed.

The rest of my family found out in stages, slow but sure,
a revelation that began that summer, a truth so pure.
From a summer of e-commerce to a lifetime of being free,
that summer of revelation was the summer I became fully me.

Inspiration behind "The Summer of Revelation"
Emotion: Liberation

This poem comes from the moment in my life when I began to embrace my authentic self and openly share my truth with those around me. This marked the transition from hiding who I was to stepping into the light and claiming my identity as a gay man. For many LGBTQ+ individuals, the journey to self-acceptance and coming out is often fraught with emotional and psychological challenges. The process of coming out is not just about revealing a secret; it's about affirming one's true self, shedding the weight of societal expectations, and finding freedom in authenticity.

For a gay person, being their authentic self means living openly and honestly without fear of judgment or rejection. It involves acknowledging and embracing one's identity in a world that often demands conformity. The act of coming out is a significant milestone in this journey. It is a declaration of self-worth and a refusal to be confined by the closet's oppressive walls. Psychologically, coming out can be both liberating and terrifying. It involves confronting internalized shame, overcoming fear, and challenging the narratives that society imposes on those who deviate from the norm.

The experience of coming out is often accompanied by a profound sense of relief and liberation. It's like releasing a pressure valve that has been building up for years, allowing the individual to breathe freely for the first time. This release is emotional and psychological as the person begins to integrate all aspects of their identity into a cohesive whole. The freeing emotion that follows is akin to shedding a heavy burden, allowing one to step into their truth with confidence and pride.

My journey can be understood through the stages of gay identity development in the book, "The Velvet Rage" by Alan Downs. According to the Downs, gay men often go through phases of shame, compensation, and eventually, authenticity. At this point in my life, I was transitioning from shame, where I had hidden my identity and conformed to societal expectations, to compensation, where I began to assert my identity and seek validation through coming out and embracing my true self.

During the summer between 11th and 12th grade, I began to move away from shame and closer to authenticity. By testing the waters in the e-commerce program and eventually coming out to my family and friends, I took significant steps toward living authentically. This crucial period in my journey to self-acceptance allowed me to explore who I was outside of the closet's confines and begin to build a life that reflected my true identity.

The poem captures the emotions, struggles, and ultimate triumph of embracing who I am. It is a reminder that the journey to authenticity is not always easy, but it is essential for personal growth and fulfillment. Through this poem and the reflection on my experience, I hope to inspire others to embrace their truth, to find the courage to come out, and to live authentically, knowing that the freedom and joy that follow are worth every challenge faced along the way.

First Day of Senior Year

Stepping into senior year, bold and bright,
lip gloss pink, shining in the morning light.
Diamond studs clipped, a glimmering sheen,
a belt that spelled "Mac," a statement unseen.

Cream Rockport shoes, laceless and sleek,
ripped jeans and a shirt that made me feel unique.
Extra, yes, but that was the plan,
to show up as myself, to take a stand.

I wanted the world to see me, no more hiding away.
I'm Malcolm, I'm gay, and this is my day.
A year of being out, a year of being free,
living life as I am, just unapologetically me.

No more questions, no need to explain,
I'd learned to love myself through the struggle and pain.
From that day forward, I knew I'd be true,
to show up in spaces as me, as new.

This was the template, the path I would take,
to live in my truth, for my own sake.
No longer bound by the closet's tight seams,
I'd step into the world, chasing my dreams.

Inspiration behind "First Day of Senior Year"

Emotion: Empowerment

This poem comes from a pivotal moment in my life
when I decided to fully embrace my identity as an out gay
male. After years of internal struggle, hiding who I was,
and grappling with societal expectations, I chose to make a

bold statement on the first day of school. My outfit that day wasn't just about fashion; it was about declaring to the world that I was no longer hiding. The lip gloss, diamond-studded earrings, and sparkly belt spelled out more than just my name—they symbolized my courage to be authentically myself.

This moment set the tone for how I would live my life moving forward. I wanted to show everyone that I was stepping into my truth and embracing it fully. This day was a template for how I would continue to show up in the world: unapologetically me, unafraid to be seen, and determined to live on my own terms.

The Orbit of Unrequited Love

In the halls of youth where echoes dance,
I found myself caught in your inadvertent glance.
Not just a classmate, not just a friend,
you were the dream, beginning to end.

Your laughter a melody, so light and free,
in every crowd, it was you I'd see.
Your touch, though fleeting, burned so sweet.
In those moments, my heart skipped its beat.

Your skin, a canvas of night's own hue,
held stories untold, of depths I never knew.
Your eyes, a fortress, gateways kept,
held dreams within where secrets slept.

I confessed my soul, laid bare my heart,
hoping, praying, for a start.
But "just friends," you said, with gentle decline,
your path lay elsewhere, diverging from mine.

So I ran from the pain, from your side,
from the torrent of feelings I failed to hide.
The door of rejection, heavy, swung wide,

under its shadow, a part of me died.

Yet the yearning lived on, a river so deep,
from moon to Pluto, it haunted my sleep.
Your essence, a phantom, in my every night's dream,
from the sky to earth's core, a relentless stream.

Love, overwhelming, a force untamed,
in your presence, my spirit aflamed.
Yet, in your absence, I learned to thrive,
for even in parting, our memories survive.

From adolescent halls to the whispers of fate,
you were my lesson in love, in hope, and in wait.
I would eventually have my chance, unaware of the ride,
the rollercoaster we'd embark on, with you by my side.

But in that moment, the truth I had to face,
perhaps the first sign that I'm a runner in this emotional
race.
I regret the time lost in that silent semester.
I missed you so dearly, my heart's quiet confessor.

Yet, we would orbit each other once again.
In hindsight, not much love was lost, but found as I began.
to understand the rhythms of heartache and bliss
in the gravitational pull of your eventual kiss.

Inspiration behind "The Orbit of Unrequited Love"

Emotion: Yearning

This poem comes from my intense, unbridled feelings
for Jace during our high school years. It captures the
overwhelming emotions I felt from unrequited love—a
mix of joy, desire, and pain. Jace was more than just a
crush; he was the epitome of beauty and allure to me, his

presence electric, stirring feelings deep within that I could barely comprehend or control.

This poem also explores what I learned about myself through this experience. It was a pivotal moment that revealed my tendencies in relationships, particularly how I handle rejection and emotional pain. The intensity of my feelings for Jace taught me about my capacity for love and the necessity of managing my emotions responsibly. It was a period of significant emotional growth, where I learned to cope with the heartache of unreturned affection and the importance of resilience in the face of emotional challenges.

This poem is an homage to the formative experiences of young love, the pain of letting go, and the personal growth that comes from navigating the complexities of heartfelt emotions. It's about the power of first loves and the indelible marks they leave on our lives, shaping our approach to future relationships and personal understanding.

Unspoken Acceptance

Senior year brought a truth I didn't intend to share,
an email sent in anger, raw and bare.
To parents who hadn't raised me as their own,
I lashed out with words, seeds of anger sown.

In that moment, I didn't realize the weight,
of outing myself, of sealing my fate.
My father found out in a scathing line,
but we never spoke of it, he never asked why.

Instead, he focused on mending the rift
between me and my mother, offering a lift.
Since that day, our bond has grown,
a silent understanding, a love fully shown.

No need to discuss, no need to explain.
He accepted me as I am, without any pain.
We speak openly now, with nothing to hide,
a relationship built on respect and pride.

In that year, I learned to stand tall,
to love myself first, above it all.
The journey was hard, but the reward was sweet,
finding acceptance in places I feared defeat.

Inspiration for "Unspoken Acceptance"

Emotion: Gratitude

This poem is drawn from an unexpected moment during my senior year of high school. In the heat of an emotional exchange, I inadvertently came out to my father in an email meant to express my frustration with my parents. The email was raw, filled with anger and hurt, and it included revelations about my sexuality that I hadn't planned to share.

What followed was a silent moment of acceptance from my father. We never discussed what I had revealed, and he never questioned me about it. Instead, he focused on repairing the relationship between my mother and me, showing his love and support in a way that required no words. This unspoken acceptance became a cornerstone of our relationship, allowing us to move forward with mutual respect and understanding.

This poem reflects the complexities of coming out, the unexpected ways acceptance can manifest, and the deep emotional connections that can form when we allow ourselves to be vulnerable. It's about finding love and support in places we didn't expect and realizing that sometimes, silence speaks volumes.

Kyle
Emotion: Introspection and Personal Growth

The "Kyle" chapter is about the complexities of my first significant romantic relationship and captures the intense emotions, challenges, and growth that defined our time together. These poems reflect on our journey from the early sparks of connection to the deeper struggles that tested our bond. Spanning from the beginning of our relationship through its various phases, this chapter highlights the lessons I learned about love, trust, and self-discovery. While it focuses on my time with Kyle, it also touches on the influence of other relationships, like the one with Jace, and how they shaped my understanding of love. This chapter reflects on my growth and the enduring impact of this relationship, offering insights into how it has contributed to the person I am today.

How We Met

In the days before Grindr's quick connections,
there was Adam4Adam, the digital intersection.
Kyle and I met in that virtual space,
two souls in proximity, finding a place.

We started chatting, just passing the time,
but soon, our bond began to climb.
From pixels on screens to friends in real life,
we met up quickly, with no hint of strife.

Then, fate played its hand in ISS 225,
a class on power, making us barely survive.
Professor Molloy, the bane of our days,
together, we grumbled through his tedious maze.

We formed a trauma bond over this shared despair,
studying together, a duo without a care.
Kyle, my first gay best friend, a trusted guide,
listening to my stories, standing by my side.

I told him of Jace, my high school woe,
how I loved him deeply, but he said no.
How he claimed friendship, denying the rest,
yet, I felt our connection was something blessed.

Kyle heard it all, my heart's deepest ache,
and in him, I found comfort, no need to fake.
We hung out often, just two friends in stride,
no romance, just trust, with nothing to hide.

In those early days, our bond was pure,
a friendship built on trust, one that would endure.
Kyle, the first to see my heart's true form
as I navigated love's unexpected storm.

Inspiration behind "How We Met"

Emotion: Camaraderie

Meeting Kyle on Adam4Adam.com—a dating website that was essential for LGBTQ+ people before apps like Grindr—felt like a gateway into something larger than just surface connections. Adam4Adam was one of the main platforms where people could connect, and at that time, for someone like me, it provided a safe space to explore who I was and to meet others who might understand the complexities of being young and gay.

Kyle and I didn't meet under romantic pretenses, at least not initially. We started talking online simply because we were nearby, which is how these platforms often worked. Proximity brought people together, and soon we met in person. There wasn't this immediate spark of romance—rather, we became instant "grill" friends. I remember hanging out and realizing that we were both in the same ISS class—Power, Authority & Exchange—at Michigan State University. We had Professor Folloy, and let me tell you, that class was a nightmare. The professor was impossible, and the coursework felt like a slog. Through that shared hatred, our trauma bond began.

A trauma bond is a deep emotional connection that forms between two people who experience a shared, often distressing, event or environment. The shared suffering glues you together in ways you don't even realize at the time. For us, that "trauma" was the class. We studied together, complained together, and vented about how difficult it was. It became the foundation of our friendship. But, I later learned that a trauma bond can be more than just a shared annoyance over a class. It can tap into deeper insecurities and emotional experiences, and in our case, it's what made our friendship so strong early on.

Kyle was my first gay best friend; huge for me because, up until then, I didn't have anyone I could truly talk to about my experiences, my feelings for Jace, or my anxieties around being gay. He was the first person I could talk to about all the details—the sleepless nights thinking about Jace, how Jace would tell me he wasn't gay, how much that hurt, and how much I was still in love with him despite it all.

This bond with Kyle wasn't just about the class or our shared frustrations—it was also about the emotional labor we were doing for each other. I was leaning on Kyle in ways I hadn't leaned on anyone else. He became a safe space for me to vent, explore what it meant to be gay and to process my feelings, and that created a deeper bond than I was initially aware of.

At the time, I didn't really understand the term "trauma bond." Our struggles were emotional and deeply rooted in our personal growth as young gay men trying to figure out who we were and what we wanted. These bonds can create security but also an emotional dependence that can complicate things later on. I think that's what happened with Kyle. We bonded over our shared experiences, but we also leaned on each other for emotional support in ways that perhaps we didn't understand or weren't ready for.

That friendship, born out of both online spaces and real-life struggles, shaped the way I approached relationships and love going forward. Kyle was there for me in ways I didn't even know I needed at the time. He helped me navigate my feelings for Jace, even as he harbored feelings for me, which I was too emotionally distracted to see.

This poem also taps into the broader experience of being a gay man in the mid-2000s, using platforms like Adam4Adam to find community, to connect, and to feel less alone. The digital world offered a sense of safety and anonymity, but once we crossed that threshold into real life, the emotions became very real, very fast. There was something beautiful and raw about those early connections because they weren't just about finding love or hookups—

they were about finding people who understood you on a deep, fundamental level.

This poem is, in many ways, about the beauty of connection, the complexity of trauma bonds, and the importance of having someone to lean on when you're discovering yourself. Kyle was that person for me in that chapter of my life, and this poem reflects that unique, formative experience.

Journal Entry: A Love Beyond the Reefs

In the Virgin Islands, where the coral reefs thrive,
I journeyed with Kyle, our friendship alive.
Exploring the reefs, the mangroves, the land,
hand-in-hand, learning nature's grandstand.

Journal by journal, I captured each day,
from coral's beauty to mountains of clay.
But beneath the waves and hikes so tall,
there was a feeling I couldn't recall.

Kyle, my first gay friend, so near,
started showing signs that weren't so clear.
In the reefs, he revealed his heart,
and slowly, unknowingly, we began to part.

From friendship's shore to a love untold,
in the Virgin Islands, our story unfolds.
I asked him to be mine, thinking it was right,
but Jace's shadow loomed in the night.

I wanted Jace, my heart knew so,
but Kyle was there, and the feelings did grow.
A mistake, perhaps, as I now reflect,
but we both learned, our paths intersect.

Through the mangroves, over Sage Mountain's peak,

our friendship endured, though love was weak.
Now, we remain friends, the love set aside,
but the memories linger, like the ocean's tide.

This journey taught me of nature's grace
and the fragile balance of love's embrace.
In the coral's beauty, in the mountain's climb,
I found the lessons of love and time.

So here's to the reefs and to friendships true,
to mistakes we make, and the growth we pursue.
For in the Virgin Islands, I learned to see
that love, like nature, must be wild and free.

Inspiration behind "Journal Entry: A Love Beyond the Reefs"

Emotion: Reflection

In 2006, I had my first study-abroad trip to the Virgin Islands. Through this journey into the natural wonders of the coral reefs and the islands' ecosystems, my relationships with Kyle and Jace became intertwined.

Kyle was my first gay best friend, and we had already established a close bond before the trip. However, during our time in the Virgin Islands, Kyle started showing signs that his feelings for me went beyond friendship. While captivated by the beauty of the coral reefs and the knowledge I was gaining, I also grappled with the emotions stirred by Kyle's growing affection. I knew deep down that I was in love with Jace, but Jace's feelings for me seemed uncertain, and I found myself at a crossroads.

In that vulnerable state, I made a decision that would shape the next chapter of my life: I asked Kyle to be my boyfriend. I realize this decision was likely a mistake—not because Kyle wasn't a good person, but because my heart wasn't fully in it. I was trying to move on from my unrequited love for Jace by embracing the love that was right in front of me, without fully considering the implications for our friendship or the long-term consequences.

This poem captures the internal conflict I felt between what I wanted and what was available to me. It's a therapeutic exploration of how we often make decisions based on immediate emotions or the need for comfort, rather than taking the time to truly understand our desires and what will fulfill us in the long run.

Don't do something just because it wants you; do it because you truly want it. It's important to think about what you want, understand your needs and desires, and not rush into decisions that might compromise your true feelings.

As I reflect on that winter, I see how much I've grown and learned. We do grow, we do learn, and it's essential to reflect on the past, taking what's best from it to better our present. Kyle and I had good moments in our relationship, but it wasn't meant to be more than a learning experience. The beauty of that time in the Virgin Islands wasn't just in the natural world I explored but also in the personal growth I experienced.

Kyle and I remain friends, having moved beyond that romantic entanglement, and I can appreciate the lessons taken from our relationship. This poem, inspired by my journal entries from that trip, is about the complexity of emotions, the importance of self-awareness, and the value of reflecting on our past to create a better present. It reminds me, and perhaps others, to think deeply about what we truly want and to let that guide our decisions in life and love.

A Trust Unraveled

Kyle, my confidant, my bff, my friend,
you knew of Jace, the love that wouldn't end.
You heard every secret, every whispered plea,
yet still, I leaned into you, perhaps foolishly.

When I asked you to be mine, you hesitated, unsure.
But eventually, you said yes, despite the love I bore
for another—Jace, whose name you knew well,
the one who held my heart in a silent, secret spell.

Just a month before, I visited him at U of M.
Our connection grew deeper, closer than it had ever been.
A massage on his back, my desire hard to hide,
but I waited, I hesitated, I didn't take the stride.

I came back from that visit on a euphoric high,
but you, Kyle, were distant, something amiss in your eye.
I should've seen it then, the seeds of mistrust sown,
but I was too wrapped up in love, afraid to be alone.

You were sick, bedridden, with a sadness so deep,
Your breath smelled of Doritos, your pain hard to keep.
You knew I had left to be with the one I loved true,
and that knowledge, Kyle, it broke something in you.

Our friendship was strong, but the foundation was flawed,
built on secrets, on feelings, on love that was raw.
You knew my heart belonged to someone else's name,
and that truth, Kyle, would set our bond aflame.

I learned a hard lesson, one that I carry still.
You don't have to say yes just to fill the void, to feel the
thrill.
Love isn't about grabbing at straws in the dark.
It's about trust, about truth, about a solid spark.

Our love was rooted in friendship, but trust was never
there,

Mistrust, jealousy, and secrets filled the air.
You don't have to love everyone who loves you in return,
That's a lesson, Kyle, that took me years to learn.

So here's to the love that wasn't meant to be,
To the lessons learned, the truths that set me free.
You were my friend, my first gay best,
But our love, Kyle, was a test I couldn't pass.

Now I know better, now I see clear,
Love is about timing, about trust, about steering clear
Of the entanglements that bind us in doubt,
And learning that true love doesn't have to shout.

Inspiration Behind "A Trust Unraveled"

Emotion: Betrayal

    This poem is about confronting the choices I made in my past, especially when it came to love and relationships, and understanding how those choices shaped who I am today.

    Kyle knew everything about me, especially my deep, unwavering love for Jace. He knew I had just visited Jace at the University of Michigan, where we had one of our closest moments yet—me giving Jace a massage, feeling every ounce of my desire and love for him. But as close as we were, I never closed the loop or pushed for more, because I was waiting for him to make the first move.

    When I came back from that visit, I was on cloud nine, filled with hope that things with Jace were finally moving in the direction I'd always wanted. But when I saw Kyle, something was off. He was distant and withdrawn. I didn't realize it at the time, but Kyle was deeply hurt. He had feelings for me that I didn't fully acknowledge, and seeing me so happy after being with someone else that he knew I loved must have been devastating for him.

I now see how flawed our relationship was from the start. I asked Kyle to be my boyfriend because I was desperate to feel loved and to move on from Jace, who wasn't giving me the love I craved. I leaned into the signals I thought Kyle was giving me, but I didn't consider how unfair it was to start a relationship with someone who knew how deeply I loved someone else. Kyle's hesitation when I asked him to be my boyfriend should have been a red flag, but I ignored it because I wanted so badly to feel wanted and to fill the void that Jace's rejection had left in me.

Through therapy, I've learned that you don't have to love everyone who loves you in return. Love isn't about grabbing at the first opportunity just to avoid feeling lonely or to fill a void. It's about mutual understanding, timing, and fulfillment. It's about what two people truly want, not just one person trying to fill the gaps in their heart with someone who happens to be there.

Kyle and I started with a strong friendship, but it was built on shaky ground—secrets, unspoken feelings, and a lack of trust. The foundation was already cracked before we even began, and that mistrust only grew as our relationship progressed. I've learned that love requires boundaries, respect, and clarity about what each person wants. It's not about settling for the thrill of being wanted or about trying to escape the pain of unrequited love. It's about finding someone who is truly right for you and ready to give and receive love in a way that is fulfilling for both parties.

This poem is about recognizing the mistakes I made, the people I hurt, and the truths I've come to understand about love and relationships. It's a reminder that love is not just about filling a void or seeking happiness at any cost. It's about connection, timing, and a mutual desire to build something real and lasting.

Reflections on Kyle

In the quiet of the night, my pen speaks true,
expressions of feelings I rarely construe.
Kyle, you've ignited a spark within,
a dance of joy that's seldom seen.

When first we met, thoughts skeptical and shy,
a "little black boy" who caught my eye.
Yet, through stories of cars and mutual distaste,
a friendship formed, not a moment to waste.

Cerynna and Daria, their teasing light,
whispered of more in the library's quiet night.
My first true friend who shared my way,
a golden coin I hoped would stay.

But fears of tarnish, of love lost in rust,
haunted the corners of newly formed trust.
The Virgin Islands trip, whispers grew loud.
Everyone saw a cloud where I saw no crowd.

Three weeks before my trip to UofM,
your care, your fear, began to stem.
Actions and words, not boldly said,
revealed a love that quietly spread.

You fought for us before I knew,
broke past bonds to start anew.
Yet, I wrestled with the fears inside,
scared to jump with no place to hide.

Afraid of attachment, of pain too deep,
of losing more than I could keep.
Yet there, in your smile, your dimpled grace,
I found a peace in the love we'd chase.

Jace's shadow, a friendship still,
but with you, Kyle, my heart does fill.
A partnership beyond mere friends,

a bond I hope never ends.

For in your laughter, in every call,
in every challenge, through every fall,
it's you, Kyle, who holds my heart,
A perfect puzzle, a work of art.

So here I write, my fears aside,
ready to walk this path, wide-eyed.
With you, my love, my chosen one,
underneath the same bright sun.

Inspiration Behind "Reflections on Kyle"
Emotion: Affection

On January 22, 2007, I sent a letter to Kyle, marking a turning point in our relationship.

In writing to Kyle, I tried to explain my complex emotions—my initial hesitations, the growing realization of my affection, and my fears about entering into a relationship that might change the dynamic of our friendship. It was a candid letter about my inner conflicts and desires, expressing how Kyle's presence transformed my usual reservations into a hopeful anticipation for something deeper.

Our relationship evolved from skepticism to a deep, meaningful connection. This poem explores the transition from seeing Kyle as just a friend to recognizing him as someone incredibly important to my life, whose companionship and affection could lead to lasting happiness.

In this poem, I revisited the feelings of vulnerability and courage it took to write that letter, channeling the mixture of fear and excitement that accompanied my decision to open up about my feelings. It was an attempt to capture

the emotions and thoughts I shared with Kyle on that day,
marking an important step in our journey together.

Endless Love: A Valentine's Memory

Valentine's Day, a first for my heart,
Kyle, my first real love, where romance would start.
With roses in hand and balloons in the air,
I decorated the room with tender care.

Endless Love played soft, in the background, it swayed.
Boyce Avenue and Connie, our anthem, our serenade.
"For you, I'd give a lifetime of stability," they sang,
and, in that moment, my heart truly rang.

I learned that night how deep my love could flow,
a river of warmth, where tender feelings grow.
How I pour myself into love's embrace,
making others feel they're in a sacred space.

But with love that pure comes a hidden plight,
a tendency to hold others too tight.
Not in the chains of possession or fear,
but in the comfort I give, so crystal clear.

Kyle and I, we didn't last long, it's true,
yet the seeds of my heart found fertile ground to renew.
A glimpse of the romantic I'd grow to be,
in the way I love, in the way I see.

For that night, we were wrapped in magic's spell.
Our hearts, like candles, burned bright and well.
"Two hearts that beat as one," they crooned,
and in that melody, our souls attuned.

Kyle was my Valentine, the first of a few,
a reminder of how I love in all that I do.
Endless love, a concept I'd come to know,
in the way I give, in the way I grow.

A night of roses, songs, and a room adorned,
where my romantic spirit was truly born.
Valentine's Day, a lesson in love so grand,
a memory that still holds my hand.

For every Valentine since has been a reflection
of that night's deep love and affection.
In endless love, I've found my way,
guided by the memories of that first Valentine's Day.

Inspiration behind "Endless Love: A Valentine's Memory"
Emotion: Romantic Nostalgia

Kyle wasn't my first love, but he was my first real, significant relationship. It was the first time I truly leaned into the idea of being in love and sharing my life with someone in a way that felt mutual. Our love was strong, our connection was real, and our relationship, in many ways, had the potential to grow into something even more beautiful.

Valentine's Day with Kyle was the first time I expressed my romantic side fully, and it was when I realized just how much love I have to give. I decorated the room, bought roses and balloons, and played "Endless Love" by Boyce Avenue and Connie Talbot—songs that still transport me back to that night. We shared a magical evening, and I discovered just how much I enjoy making someone feel special and loved.

In therapy, I've come to understand how my tendency to pour so much love, care, and support into a relationship can sometimes lead to an imbalance. This can create a dynamic where people lean too heavily on me, becoming dependent in ways that might not be healthy for either of us. While Kyle and I didn't date long enough for this to

fully manifest, my therapist and I have discussed how he
began to experience this.

Our relationship, though brief, was true and beautiful.
We eventually succumbed to our insecurities, trust issues,
and drama—things that could have been avoided, but we
were young, and we were still learning. Despite
everything, I have no regrets about our time together. Kyle
and I still share a deep bond, and he remains a life-long
friend, someone who knows me in a way that few others
do.

This poem is a reflection of that Valentine's Day, of the
love we shared, and of the lessons I've learned about love,
care, and boundaries. It's about the beauty of our
relationship, even in its imperfection, and a reminder that
love, in all its forms, is a journey of growth and discovery.
Kyle may not have been my first love, but he was the first
to show me what it means to truly be in a relationship, and
to give and receive love in a way that leaves a lasting
impact.

NYC Ambulance

We set out on a journey, Kyle and I,
Grand Rapids had been our escape, a sigh.
A weekend of love, of laughter, of rest,
proved we could travel together, passed the test.

So, New York City became our spring break dream,
driving through states, the road our gleam.
Upstate New York, we dropped off a friend,
then onto the city where the streets never end.

Memories blurred, the details faded,
but one moment in time has forever stayed.
Driving through the city, the lights, the rush,
an ambulance siren, the world's harsh hush.

I pulled to the right, but the road was too tight.
The ambulance couldn't pass, no room in sight.
They pushed forward, side-swiping my car,
got out and yelled, their voices like tar.

"You're making us late, someone might die."
Their words hit hard beneath the city sky.
A ticket in hand, my heart sank low,
had to return to court, a future blow.

But there was Kyle, my Gemini fire,
who stepped out, fueled by a fierce desire.
He let them have it, defending me true,
protecting us both, his temper flew.

That moment, so vivid, etched in our minds,
a glimpse of the strength in love's binds.
Kyle, my protector, fierce and bold,
a memory that lingers, a story retold.

In the chaos of NYC's relentless pace,
we found in each other a steadying grace.
Through sirens and shouts, we stood our ground
in each other's arms, love profound.

Though the photos are lost, the memories remain,
of a city, a siren, and love's sweet refrain.
And though we've moved on, and life's paths have split,
that day in the city, our hearts were lit.

For, in the end, it's the journey we take,
the roads we travel, the love we make.
And I've learned that when travel's a test,
it's a sign that love may truly be blessed.

Inspiration behind "NYC Ambulance"

Emotion: Resilience

I've come to understand that if you can travel well with someone, they might just be a real candidate for a lasting romantic partnership. When I was with Kyle, I hadn't fully grasped this , but looking back, I realize I was laying the groundwork for what I now see as vital in a relationship.

Kyle and I had already shared a memorable weekend getaway to Grand Rapids–a glimpse into how we navigated the world together. From staying at a bed and breakfast, enjoying good food, making love, and simply reveling in each other's company, that trip showed me that we could travel well together. It set the stage for our next big adventure: a road trip to New York City for spring break.

Our trip to NYC was a blend of excitement and unexpected chaos. We drove all the way from Michigan, stopping to drop off one of Kyle's friends in upstate New York before heading into the city. While many details of the trip have faded from memory, one event remains vivid: the ambulance incident.

We were driving through the busy streets of New York City when an ambulance came up behind us, sirens blaring. I pulled to the right as far as I could, but the street was too narrow for them to pass. Instead of waiting, the ambulance forced its way through, side-swiping my car in the process. The paramedics jumped out, furious, blaming me for potentially delaying a life-or-death emergency. I remember feeling a mix of shock, guilt, and frustration. I ended up with a ticket and had to return to NYC for court, though the case was dismissed when the ambulance drivers didn't show up.

But what stands out even more is Kyle's reaction. I'd seen hints of his protective nature before, but in that moment, I saw something more intense—something almost crazy. Kyle didn't just stand up for me; he was ready to nut up and shut shit down. He unleashed that fierce Gemini personality, showing a side of him that was both alarming and awe-inspiring. He was someone you didn't want to cross, and this moment was a clear preview of the wild, unpredictable side that would surface in our relationship later on. Looking back, I should have recognized this as a sign of the craziness yet to come— Kyle was not someone to be taken lightly or underestimated.

Now, I half-joke that a third date should involve a trip. Why? Because traveling together reveals so much about a person's true character—how they handle stress, support you in difficult moments, and navigate the unexpected, like an ambulance side-swiping your car in the middle of Manhattan.

Traveling with someone can show you who they really are beneath the surface. It's not just about enjoying the destination; it's about how you deal with the journey, with all its twists, turns, and surprises. That's why I now see it as essential in building a relationship. If you can survive a trip together, especially one that involves chaotic moments, then you might just have something worth holding onto.

"NYC Ambulance" is more than just a recounting of an event; it's a reflection on how that moment—and others like it—shaped my understanding of love, partnership, and the importance of truly knowing who you're with. It's about recognizing the signs of someone's true nature, understanding that love isn't just about the highs, but also about navigating the lows together. And it's about realizing that the journey you take with someone— whether across the country or through life—truly defines the strength and future of your connection.

Betrayal's Edge

I walked that night, phone to my ear.
Jaya's voice, a comfort, so sincere.
We talked of school, of life, of him—
Kyle, the man who made my heart brim.

Yet beneath the joy, a shadow crept,
a worry so deep, it quietly wept.
Was I enough? Could he be true?
These doubts I carried, they slowly grew.

Jaya listened, as friends do well.
Her words, a balm, a gentle spell.
She warned of doors I might reopen,
of Jace's name, a word unspoken.

I reached his dorm, the night was late,
expecting warmth, but met with fate.
Kyle's room, a scene that shattered trust,
another man, where love once was.

Heart heavy, confusion reigned,
a storm of feelings, all uncontained.
Anger, hurt, they mingled there,
But heartbreak? No, it was despair.

Why did he cheat? Was it my flaw?
Or was it his fear of what he saw?
A love that trembled, built on sand,
crumbling fast, slipping from my hand.

Beyoncé's words became my cry,
a song for all the tears I'd dry.
A spiral started, down I fell,
Kyle and I, we broke the spell.

Irony thick, as the story goes.
Kyle's fear of Jace, the one he chose
to cheat, to push me far away,

yet closer to Jace, I'd stray.

And so, the cycle came to end
with lessons learned and hearts to mend.
Insecurities, they tore us apart,
but they couldn't break my healing heart.

Inspiration behind "Betrayal's Edge"
Emotion: Betrayal and Despair

During my freshman year of college, things with Kyle
began to spiral out of control, leading to a painful and
enlightening unraveling. One night, I was on the phone
with Jaya, my confidante and friend who knew everything
about my life—my struggles, loves, and fears. As we
talked about school, life, and Kyle, I felt a mix of emotions.
I was happy, but I also had an underlying worry and a
sense that something wasn't right. Jaya, always perceptive,
voiced her concerns that Kyle's insecurities might push me
back toward Jace, the very thing Kyle feared the most.

As I walked across campus, lost in conversation, I
arrived at Kyle's dorm. What I found there shattered me—
Kyle, scrambling with another man in his bed. In that
instant, everything changed. I was confused, hurt, and
angry, but more than anything, I felt betrayed. The trust
we had built, fragile as it was, came crashing down.

This moment with Kyle was just the beginning of a wild
ride that would continue throughout the spring semester
of college.

"Betrayal's Edge" speaks to the complexities of love, the
pain of betrayal, and the lessons learned along the way.
This moment set the stage for much of what was to come
and ultimately helped me grow and better understand
myself. The ride with Kyle was tumultuous, but it was also
a necessary part of my story—a story that I continue to
unravel, one poem at a time.

Through with Love

Verse 1

As a Pisces, I'm tethered to the currents of emotion,
each note, each lyric, a wave of pure devotion.
Destiny's Child played the soundtrack of my pain.
"Through with Love" became the echo in my brain.
Freshman year, college days, Kyle was my muse,
but his insecurities made our love a bruise.
Fear of Jace, the love I couldn't hide,
Kyle's jealousy pushed me to the other side.

Chorus

"I'm through with it, love, I'm through with it, love,"
the words a release, a cry to the skies above.
"I'm giving it up, I'm giving it up,"
in those lyrics, I found the strength to rise up.

Verse 2

Driving fast down Grand River, tears in my eyes,
Destiny's Child blaring, my heart full of sighs.
Kyle's cheating, his words laced with doubt,
I was done trying to figure him out.
Jaya said it clear, friends saw it true,
Kyle's sabotage led me back to you-know-who.
Through with the lies, the fear, the fight,
Destiny's Child sang my soul's truth that night.

Chorus

"I'm through with it, love, I'm through with it, love,"
a mantra, a prayer, a push and a shove.
"I'm giving it up, I'm giving it up,"
letting go of the past, rising above.

Bridge

Through with the tears, through with the pain,
through with the cycle of love's endless strain.
I sang with passion, I sang with fire,
Destiny's Child fueled my heart's desire.

Chorus

"I'm through with it, love, I'm through with it, love,"
driving away, soaring like a dove.
"I'm giving it up, I'm giving it up."
No more trying, I've had enough.

Outro

Now, when I hear that melody play,
I'm transported back to that fateful day.
Destiny's Child, you carried me through,
I'm through with that love, and I found someone new.

Inspiration behind "Through with Love"
Emotion: Empowerment

During my freshman year of college, I was in a
relationship with Kyle, and our love was passionate, yet
fraught with insecurity and doubt. Music has always been
more than just sound for me—it's a portal to specific
moments and a way to relive emotions and experiences.
Destiny's Child's "Through with Love" became the anthem
of my pain and frustration during that period.

Music has this incredible psychological connection to
our memories. Certain songs can instantly transport us
back to a particular place, time, or feeling. For me,
"Through with Love" is one of those songs. I can still
remember driving fast down Grand River, the song
blaring, my heart heavy with the weight of a relationship

that felt like it was falling apart. Kyle's jealousy, fear of my feelings for Jace, and actions that seemed to sabotage what we had become too much. As I sang those lyrics, "I'm through with it, love, I'm through with it, love," I felt a sense of release, like I was finally letting go of something that wasn't right for me.

But as much as I felt done with love in that moment, I wasn't truly through with it. I was through with that particular love, or at least I thought I was. However, I would love again. I would love Jace, even though that love brought its own challenges. And beyond Jace, I would find love again with others. I didn't realize that love isn't something that just happens—it evolves, sometimes fails, and takes work.

I was hurt and tired, feeling like love was slipping away. But I've learned since then that love is out there, and we have to work at it if we want it. It has to be with someone who is willing to make it work with you, and you have to be in a place where you're ready to receive that love. Love is also about timing—being in the right place, at the right time, with the right person.

"Through with Love" reflects where I was at that moment—a young man caught up in the emotions of a difficult relationship, unsure of what love really meant or how to nurture it. But it was also a stepping stone, a part of my journey in understanding that love isn't just about the highs and lows—it's about the commitment to making it work, the readiness to embrace it, and the realization that love, when it's right, is worth all the effort.

Jace and Kyle Night

Jace, my best friend, my constant through it all,
we shared secrets, stories, and the rise and fall
of my love with Kyle, the highs and lows,
the happiness on Valentine's Day and the hurt that
followed close.

I told you of the joy Kyle brought, of being out,
of someone proud to stand by me, without a doubt.
But I never meant to twist the knife in the truth
that you, Jace, hid from your feelings, uncouth.

Three years deep in friendship, so much for just nineteen,
but I couldn't hide from you the pain I'd seen.
Kyle's betrayal, the cheating, the lies,
left me shattered, tears welling in my eyes.

You insisted on a visit, a reunion at MSU,
but I knew Kyle wouldn't handle it—knew what he'd do.
I begged you to stay away, to keep the peace,
but you came anyway, and the chaos didn't cease.

Lies spun to cover our tracks.
Jace, just a friend, but the truth cracks.
Kyle found out, his jealousy ignites,
a storm brews, and we brace for the night.

He burst into Shaw Hall, fury in his stride.
Jace ran while I tried to calm the tide.
Daria and Cerynna, caught in the fray,
and I held Kyle back, trying to keep the rage at bay.

No fists flew, but the whispers spread,
the "big black scary guy" they misread.
I pleaded with the cops, "Check the tape, it's all there,
but go stop him from tearing my life apart, I swear."

They found Kyle tossing my clothes in a heap,
threatening with bleach, a promise to keep.

But Latoya, my guardian, saved what she could,
while the police took Kyle, as they understood.

In Michigan, the law takes its toll.
Even without charges, it controls.
Kyle faced the consequences, served his time,
and in the end, found peace in the climb.

We talked later, as grown men do.
He thanked the charge, the classes he knew,
Helped him heal, work through the pain,
turning a moment of rage into long-term gain.

And I'm grateful for the growth we've both found,
for the loops we've closed, for the peace unbound.
What started in chaos, in heartbreak and fear,
led us to a place where the future's clear.

Jace and Kyle, a night to remember,
a story of fire, but also of ember
that burns down to reveal the truth
of growth, of healing, and of youth.

Inspiration behind "Jace and Kyle Night"
Emotion: Turmoil

   This poem comes from one of the most chaotic and
emotionally charged nights of my life—a night that, at the
time, felt like everything was crumbling, but with time,
perspective, and growth, I've come to see differently.

   I was in the thick of my relationship with Kyle while
navigating the complicated emotions I had for Jace. Jace
and I had this undeniable bond, yet complicated by the
fact that he wasn't out and couldn't fully embrace the
feelings I knew we shared. Kyle knew about my history
with Jace, which seeded an insecurity in our relationship
from the very start. Despite that, Kyle and I became a

couple, and for a while, we were good—really good. But the cracks were always there, just beneath the surface.

When Jace decided to visit MSU, I knew it would be a problem. Kyle was already feeling insecure, and Jace's presence was like gasoline on a smoldering fire. I tried to keep the peace and convince Jace not to come but he came anyway. That weekend was a mess of lies and half-truths as I tried to juggle my friendship with Jace and my relationship with Kyle. But the truth has a way of coming out, and it all exploded when Kyle found out Jace was on campus.

I'll never forget the way Kyle stormed into Shaw Hall, his anger palpable, his jealousy out of control. I was scared—not just for myself, but for Jace, who had to run to avoid the confrontation. I tried to calm Kyle down and contain the situation, but it was too late. The damage was done. Kyle's rage spilled over, and I was caught in the middle, trying to keep everything from falling apart.

When the police were called, and the accusations were thrown around, it felt like the world was against me. But even with the pain and chaos of that night, I can look back and see the growth that came from it. Kyle's actions led to consequences that ultimately helped him confront his own issues and grow as a person. He later told me that those anger management classes and the legal wake-up call were exactly what he needed to avoid a darker path.

What could have been a purely negative, traumatic experience has, with time, become something else. It's a reminder that not all dark situations are entirely dark. Sometimes, they hold the seeds of change, growth, and something better. I've learned that it's all about perspective and how you choose to see the events in your life. I could focus on the betrayal, the hurt, and the anger, but instead, I choose to see the progress, the healing, and the loops we've been able to close.

    This poem is about that shift in perspective. It's about acknowledging the pain and chaos, but also recognizing the healing and the positive change that can come from it and that sometimes, the most challenging experiences can lead to the most significant growth.

Reflections on a Broken Mirror

This is the type of storm I weathered in our time,
when anger spilled from his heart like unfiltered wine.
Kyle, in his rage, threw words like stones,
but what I saw were fears, deeply honed.

He claimed to be strong, to stand his ground,
yet his words echoed with a hollow sound.
"I am me," he said, "and I won't change,"
but it felt like a mask, a desperate exchange.

He pushed away love, friends, and light,
wrapped himself in shadows, ready to fight.
His reactiveness, a shield so tight,
running from the mirror I tried to hold upright.

I didn't know then how to speak with care,
to show him that change isn't something to fear.
He felt attacked, exposed, laid bare,
but I was only trying to show him what was there.

I disagreed with the venom he hurled,
felt his pain but couldn't heal his world.
He saw enemies where I saw love,
a struggle within, a push and a shove.

Now I see what I couldn't then,
the wounds he hid, the walls so thin.
But back then, I lacked the words,
to soothe his fears, to calm the surge.

Kyle, if only I could have shown

that change is growth, a seed that's sown.
But instead, we clashed, we tore apart,
leaving scars on both our hearts.

So here's the truth, as I reflect,
we all have demons we must inspect.
But running from the mirror's gaze
only keeps us trapped in a darkened maze.

I wish I knew then what I know now,
to guide us both, to help somehow.
But life has taught me, through love and pain,
that growth is worth the price of strain.

And so I leave this here to say
that in our struggle, I learned my way.
I hope you've found your peace and light
and faced the mirror in your own fight.

Inspiration behind "Reflections on a Broken Mirror"
Emotion: Regret

Kyle's anger and defensiveness led to him sending a harsh email to my friends, including Daria, Jace, Cerynna, Jaya, and Shayna. In this email, Kyle lashed out, declaring his commitment to being his unfiltered self and rejecting any efforts to change, even if it meant pushing people away.

Kyle's email was a response to a growing tension between us, where he felt misunderstood, unappreciated, and isolated. He expressed a deep-seated need to protect himself by becoming more private, locking away his thoughts and feelings, and distancing himself from my friends, whom he blamed for many of our problems. His words, though harsh, reflected the pain he was experiencing, which he projected onto others rather than confronting within himself.

In his email, he insisted that he didn't have low self-esteem despite admitting that he didn't like himself but loved himself for being "Kyle." He was grappling with internal conflict—wanting to be true to himself but struggling with the reality of who he was and how others perceived him.

Kyle also made it clear that he would no longer try to change for anyone, including me, because he felt that trying to change had only led to self-destruction. This statement showed me his resistance to growth and his fear of vulnerability. Instead of embracing the possibility of change as a positive force, he saw it as something that would destroy him, leading him to retreat further into himself.

In the poem, I tried to capture this moment—the tension between us, the hurtful words, and the underlying fears that drove Kyle's behavior. I didn't agree with his accusations or the way he lashed out at my friends, but I also recognized that his reactiveness was a way of running from the mirror I was trying to hold up to him. I didn't know how to communicate this to him in a way that he could understand or accept.

Seeing someone you care about struggle with their own demons while not being able to reach them is frustrating. We all have our battles; sometimes, those battles manifest in ways that push others away. Looking back, I realize that I, too, had my own learning to do—how to communicate better, how to support without pushing, and how to recognize when someone isn't ready to face the truth.

Kyle's email was a turning point in our relationship, making me understand the importance of self-awareness, communication, and the courage to confront our reflections. It's a lesson that has stayed with me and one that I continue to apply in my relationships today.

Missing You, Finding Me

You're so far away, yet close in my heart.
Cerynna, it's strange to be so far apart.
You say you're growing, day by day,
becoming a woman, finding your way.

I miss you more than words can say.
It's weird not having you here every day.
So much has happened since you've been gone.
I've been lost in my thoughts, feeling withdrawn.

I wrote you a letter, pages long,
but I held it back, trying to be strong.
Honoring what others tell me to do,
I sent it to the one it was meant for, too.

We talked it out, but it wasn't quite right,
I didn't get the outcome I hoped for that night.
But closure came, a door slightly closed,
and with it, a lesson, I suppose.

Then Kyle and I had our turn to speak.
He gave me an ultimatum, left me weak.
But when choosing between years and a single year,
the answer was clear, though it brought some fear.

So here I am, navigating my way
in a world that feels different every day.
I'm growing too, just like you,
learning to love myself in all I do.

It's beautiful where you are, I know,
and I'm finding my own beauty in the ebb and flow.
Miss you, love you, more than I can say,
But we're both on journeys, come what may.

Love you so much more.

Inspiration behind "Missing You, Finding Me"

Emotion: Longing

The first part of this poem is inspired by Cerynna, my best friend who studied abroad during our college years. I can't remember where she went, but , the feelings of missing her and the bond we shared are still vivid. This poem captures the longing I felt while she was away, as well as the complexities of maintaining friendships during pivotal moments in our lives.

The second layer of inspiration comes from a challenging situation with Kyle, who had given me an ultimatum: either stay at MSU or agree to an open relationship if I chose to go home for the summer. This hurt deeply because it felt like he was unable or unwilling to be faithful to me. Now I realize the importance of honest and mature conversations about needs, desires, and boundaries in a relationship. It's important to speak openly about what is or isn't acceptable and to make decisions with clarity and confidence.

That summer, Kyle broke up with me, and just a month later, I found myself with Jace. Kyle later accused me of cheating, but in my mind, I was single, hurt, and ready to pursue what I had wanted for so long. My connection with Jace felt undeniable. Deep down, I believed that his claims that he wasn't gay and didn't share my feelings were lies he was telling himself, and I moved forward with the conviction that our bond was real.

This poem is a nod to the emotional turmoil and growth I experienced during that time. It's about missing what once was, questioning what could be, and recognizing the importance of honesty and self-awareness in relationships. As I look back, I see the need to address unresolved issues, both in therapy and in life, and the importance of giving energy to what truly matters. The poem captures the bittersweet nature of change, the pain of letting go, and the hope that comes with understanding and growth.

A Summer of Transition

When I went home, the final thread snapped—
Kyle broke up with me, his ultimatum lapsed.
A month later, the dust settled and cleared,
and there I was, with the one I had always revered.

Jace, the one I had desired for so long,
a longing that echoed in every love song.
Kyle would later say I cheated, but truth be told,
he gave me the out, and I grabbed hold.

I was single, hurt, but ready to pursue
the feelings I had for Jace, deep and true.
I had wanted him since high school days,
and now, in that summer's golden haze,
I moved in closer, heart on my sleeve,
feeling the signals that I wanted to believe.

Jace, who once claimed he wasn't gay,
and that his feelings didn't sway that way,
but I felt it in my soul, my body, my bones,
in every whispered word, in every undertone.

That summer, he grew more vulnerable, more near,
signaling truths that erased every fear.
Though he told me otherwise, I knew inside,
that it was a lie he told to keep his pride.

Years of longing, now converging in time,
when I started with Kyle, Jace's jealousy chimed.
Supportive but torn as I navigated my fate
through emotions with Kyle and Jace's quiet wait.

The moment I was free, Jace saw his chance.
He became more comfortable, a subtle dance.
I felt the build-up, the tension so sweet,
that summer marked a transition where two hearts would
meet.

An ultimatum led me to this new beginning.
The next five years of a love story spinning.
From longing to reality, from doubt to trust,
that summer was the start of a love I'd always discussed.

A summer of transition, decisions so clear,
Led to a journey with Jace, year after year.
The past and the present collided that day,
and love, at long last, found its way.

Inspiration behind "A Summer of Transition"

Emotion: Anticipation

This poem, like the one before it, draws on the deep emotional experiences I went through during that transformative summer. I had just returned home, and Kyle broke up with me, ending our relationship with an ultimatum that left me hurt but also free. Kyle accused me of cheating, but in reality, he had given me the out, and I took it. I had been single, vulnerable, and searching for something more meaningful, which led me directly to Jace, the person I had desired for years.

That summer, after Kyle and I ended things, I found myself with Jace, whom I had longed for since high school. Jace started to act differently—more comfortable, more open, and subtly signaling that our connection was something more. Despite his insistence that he wasn't gay and didn't have mutual feelings, I felt in my soul, my body, and my bones that this wasn't true. Our conversations, our time together, and the deep bond we shared all pointed to a truth that he was perhaps not ready to fully acknowledge.

The poem reflects the move from a relationship with Kyle, marked by ultimatums and unresolved emotions, to a new chapter with Jace, where long-held desires finally began to surface. The build-up of emotions and subtle shifts in behavior came together, leading to the next five years of my life being intertwined with Jace.

This period was marked by both pain and joy and by the end of one relationship and the beginning of another that I had longed for. This poem is about the complexity of human relationships, the choices we make, and the ways in which our past and present collide to shape our future. It's a story of longing, transition, and the inevitable pull of love that finally found its way after years of waiting.

Jace
Emotion: Passion and Heartache

In the "Jace" chapter, I reflect on a love that spanned years, a relationship that was both deeply passionate and profoundly challenging. These poems chronicle the highs and lows of being in love with someone who kept us hidden in the shadows, from the intensity of our first kiss to the struggles of long distance and the pain of being kept out of the light.

This chapter explores the emotional turmoil of loving someone who couldn't fully embrace our relationship, the heartache of being unseen, and the lessons learned from a love that was both beautiful and flawed. From high school through college and beyond, this chapter captures a love that shaped me, revealing the complexities of my journey toward self-worth and the realization that true love must be seen, valued, and shared openly. The reflections span from the beginning of our relationship to its final test, highlighting the emotional growth and understanding that came from this significant chapter in my life.

The Love That Spanned Years

In that high school accounting class,
where numbers danced, and I caught your glance—
an annoying thorn, or so I thought.
But beneath that blue jean jacket,
those JROTC robes, those nerdy specs,
I saw a beauty, not yet fully grown,
a man you'd become, a seed yet sown.

Our story started with irritation's spark,
but soon, it blossomed into something stark—
A friendship deep, so close, so true,
it felt like dating, though it wasn't, yet knew,
the late-night calls that lulled to sleep,
library footsies, secrets we'd keep.
Each time I'd drop you last or pick you first,
I craved those moments, a love unversed.

I was sure, so sure, you felt it too,
even if you said, "I'm not gay."
But I saw through those words you spoke,
you were confused, drawn, beneath that cloak.
You were the object of my every affection,
the dream I held, my heart's projection,
from the first glance in that class of numbers,
to the silent dreams that filled my slumbers.

Through 10th grade, 11th, and our senior year,
our bond grew stronger, despite the fear.
Every movie, every stolen glance,
blurred lines between friendship and romance.
I told the world, I sang your name,
declared you the love that lit my flame.
Even as Kyle stood in our way,
I knew you'd be mine, come what may.

But this was more than a fleeting crush,
a love that soared, yet didn't rush,
from high school halls to college dreams,
we danced on the edge of fate's bright beams.

Yet, despite that love, despite my plea,
time would prove we weren't meant to be.

You were my object, my cherished affection,
the future I dreamed, my heart's connection.
Though we didn't last, our love held fast.
It shaped my soul, through every blast.
A love that spanned the fleeting years
taught me the depths of joy and tears.
And though forever wasn't ours to claim,
you'll always be the fire, the spark, the flame.

Inspiration behind "The Love That Spanned Years"
Emotion: Nostalgia

This poem comes from the deep and complex feelings I had for Jace, starting from our high school days. I first noticed him in our accounting class—he was that annoying guy who seemed to always be in my way, but there was something about him that caught my attention. He wore that blue jean jacket, those JROTC robes, and those nerdy glasses, and somehow, I saw the man he would become, the beauty he would grow into. Even back then, I knew there was something special between us. I couldn't quite put my finger on it, but I felt it deeply.

As our friendship grew, I realized how much I cared for him. We were best friends through high school—talking on the phone late into the night, studying together, sharing those quiet, intimate moments that seemed to blur the lines between friendship and something more. I was sure he felt the same way, even though he wasn't ready to admit it. He'd say things like, "I'm not gay" but I could see through that. I knew there was more beneath the surface, a mutual attraction that was just waiting to be acknowledged.

When I got to college, I couldn't stop talking about him. Everyone knew his name because I couldn't keep my feelings to myself. I was so in love with him and so sure

that he was the one for me that I would tell anyone who
would listen about our story, our secret moments, and my
dreams of a future with him. Jace became the object of my
affection and the center of my world. I was so
overwhelmed by my love for him that I even wrote and
recorded a song called "Object of My Affection."

This poem reflects that love that started in high school
and grew stronger over time, even as life threw obstacles
in our way. It's about the romantic and poetic journey I
experienced with Jace, from those first sparks in
accounting class to the intense longing that carried me
through college. Though our love didn't last forever, it
shaped me in profound ways, teaching me about the
depths of affection, the power of connection, and the
bittersweet reality of loving someone who might not be
yours in the end.

Our First Kiss

Our first kiss, a moment carved in time,
the summer began with an ultimatum's chime.
Kyle and I, our tumultuous affair,
ended with hurt, but left me bare.

I walked into the summer, single yet free,
hurt but hopeful, a door closed on thee.
But another remained, never truly sealed,
a love I longed for, a love revealed.

Love that filled my dreams, love I sought,
a love that consumed every waking thought.
Jace, the one I believed was mine,
the love that would complete me, so divine.

We had our moments, the tension grew.
In whispered words, our feelings flew.
He visited MSU, our hearts spoke plain,
yet he dodged my love, causing silent pain.

But one evening, at 8905 E Jefferson's light,
where we spent our nights, alone in the quiet,
Jace came over, our internships done.
We sat close together, our bodies as one.

Cuddled on the couch, hearts pounding loud,
he looked at me, his eyes shrouded in doubt.
But I leaned in, hesitant yet bold,
hopeful that this moment would unfold.

As our lips met, the world disappeared.
Passion poured out, everything I feared.
Tongue entwined, in a dance so deep,
our kiss was hot, heavy, and sweet.

In that embrace, time seemed to freeze,
a kiss that brought me to my knees.
Left me wanting more, yet feeling complete,
as if life could end, and I'd taste the sweet.

Jaya knew without a word from me.
She saw the glow, the joy set free.
Our first kiss, a memory so pure.
In that moment, I was sure.

A kiss that marked the start of dreams
of love so deep, bursting at the seams.
But also, the start of a journey unknown,
With twists and turns, yet to be shown.

Inspiration behind "Our First Kiss"
Emotion: Euphoria

After years of longing, dreaming, and hoping, I finally
shared a kiss with Jace—a kiss that I had imagined
countless times. This was the love I had been waiting for,
the love that filled my thoughts day and night, and the
love that I believed would complete me.

Our relationship had always been a dance of unspoken emotions and of feelings that were felt but never fully expressed. When Jace visited MSU that last time before the summer, we had a heartfelt conversation, one that I hoped would finally break down the walls between us. But even then, he dodged my love, leaving me to wrestle with my emotions alone. Still, I clung to the hope that we were moving in the right direction and that the door I had kept open for him would finally lead to something more.

That night, at 8905 E Jefferson, the place where we often spent our evenings alone, something shifted. We were on the couch, our bodies close, the air thick with unspoken tension. I could see the hesitation in his eyes, the fear that was holding him back. But when our lips finally met, all of that melted away. The kiss was everything I had ever dreamed of—passionate, deep, and so full of the love I had been waiting to express. In that moment, I felt complete, as if all the pieces of my life had finally come together.

But then, as quickly as the moment had come, it was tempered by his request. He asked me not to tell anyone, to keep our kiss a secret. It was a request that stung, a confirmation of the hesitation I had seen in his eyes. But I was so overwhelmed by the joy of finally having kissed him, by the momentum in the direction I had longed for, that I didn't fully process the hurt. I agreed to keep it a secret, burying the red flag deep within me because I was too happy to let it overshadow what had just happened.

I kept that secret as best as I could, but when I saw Jaya, I didn't have to say a word. She took one look at me, saw the glow, the happiness that I couldn't contain, and she knew. "Shut the fuck up! Y'all kissed!" she exclaimed, and all I could do was smile. The happiness I felt was undeniable, and in that moment, it didn't matter that it was meant to be a secret. My dreams were coming true, and for the first time, I felt like I was on the path to the love I had always wanted.

Lust in the Concrete Jungle

After that first kiss, we couldn't stop
lusting all over Detroit, from block to block.
Like teenagers, new to the thrill,
addicted to each other, couldn't get our fill.

Jace was my first in ways that mattered.
Not my first lover, but the one who shattered
every notion of love, of passion, of fire.
Together, we reached higher and higher.

At red lights, in garages, in the dead of night,
we gave in to the urge, to the burning light.
Work was no exception, desire knew no bounds,
from the corner of his block to the office grounds.

We explored each other, body and soul,
learning every inch, every way to make us whole.
It was exhilarating, steamy, pure ecstasy,
a stretch of lust and love, wild and free.

I'd drive hours just to be by his side,
to feel his warmth, to take that ride.
We were crazy in love, blinded by the heat,
but sex, I'd learn, isn't the only treat.

Yet, it was great, it was intense,
it kept me holding on, in past tense.
We even got fired for the love we made,
in the showers at work, where we often played.

His father was the president, and we got caught,
but all I cared about was if Jace was distraught.
Was he out now? Would this end us for good?
But all I wanted was him, in every way I could.

I left that day, fired for the thrill,
but I smiled, remembering every time, every spill.
My grandparents asked, "How was your day?"
"It was okay, I got fired for having sex," I'd say.

We moved past it, our love remained strong,
but looking back, maybe it was wrong.
Yet, for five years, he was mine
and I was his, our hearts intertwined.

I wanted him in my life, in my bed,
every thought of him running through my head.
His lips, his body, his warmth, his love,
he was the one I couldn't get enough of.

Lust in Detroit, that summer of heat,
our love story, wild, reckless, sweet.
But as time would tell, it wasn't enough.
Sex isn't everything, love's road can be tough.

But for those moments, those days, those years,
we were lost in each other, drowning in tears.
Of joy, of pain, of passion untamed,
our love was wild, never ashamed.

And though it ended, though we moved on,
those days in Detroit, our love was strong.
A memory now, but a lesson learned,
that love and lust, when mixed, can burn.
But still, I'd do it all again,
just to feel that fire that once was then.

Inspiration behind "Lust in the Concrete Jungle"
Emotion: Intensity

This poem comes from a time in my life fueled by
intense passion, lust, and the kind of love that blinds you
to everything else. This poem reflects on those summer
days with Jace, where our connection was so powerful that
it overtook everything—logic, reason, even common sense.
After our first kiss, it was like a dam had burst, and all the
emotions, the desire, the longing I had been holding onto
for years came rushing out in an unstoppable wave.

Jace was the first person I truly felt that kind of deep, physical connection with. He wasn't my first lover, but he was the first one who made everything feel complete, who made sex feel like more than just an act—it was an experience, an exchange of energy that left me both satisfied and craving more. We couldn't keep our hands off each other. We were like two teenagers discovering sex for the first time, completely addicted to the thrill, the excitement, the secrecy of it all.

I wanted him in every possible way, and we found ourselves giving in to that desire in every corner of Detroit—from red lights to parking garages, even at work. We didn't care; we were so consumed by our need for each other that we crossed lines, both physical and moral. I still remember the day we got caught at work, having sex in the showers. His father was the president of the company, and that only added to the complexity of the situation. When we were caught, it wasn't just embarrassing—it was terrifying. Would this end us? Would this expose him? Would we be okay?

I remember driving hours just to be with him, to feel his warmth, to escape the reality of everything else. It was wild, it was reckless, and at the time, it felt like everything. But now, looking back, I realize that while the sex was great, it wasn't enough. Lust can only carry you so far, and eventually, you start to see the cracks, the parts that aren't as fulfilling as you'd like them to be.

When I was fired from that job, I walked away with a strange sense of satisfaction. I had been fired for something that felt so important to me at the time—our love, our passion. But it also marked the beginning of understanding that love and sex aren't everything. They're powerful, yes, but they aren't the whole story. There's so much more to a relationship, and while Jace and I had an incredible connection, it wasn't enough to sustain us in the long run.

    This poem is a raw and honest reflection of that time of
intense passion, crossing boundaries, and learning hard
lessons. It's about the power of lust and love, but also
about the realization that there's more to a lasting
relationship than just those things. And even though it
didn't last, and we eventually moved on, I don't regret a
single moment. Those were some of the most intense,
exciting, and passionate days of my life, and they taught
me a lot about what I want, what I need, and what love
truly means.

Unspoken Truths

It's 5:19 a.m., and sleep escapes me,
thoughts tangled in the silence, too loud to be free.
I asked you once, why I wasn't there
at your Circle of Unity, where memories share.

You brushed it off like it was nothing at all,
but I saw the texts, the invites, the call.
You invited others but left me behind.
Was it because of Micah, buried in your mind?

I can't live with secrets, with truths untold.
Loving you is scary, as our story unfolds.
You say you love me, but actions speak loud.
Show me, Jace, beneath that cloud.

I've watched shows just to talk with you,
but our conversations feel like a déjà vu.
A quick hello, a goodbye too soon,
like a married couple, under the same moon.

You're like a father who loves, but stays far.
I know you care, but it's like chasing a star.
I needed to see you, to feel you near,
but your joke about being a drug wasn't clear.

It hurt me, made me feel obsessed,

like loving you is something I must suppress.
But you make me smile, even when I'm mad.
You drive me crazy, but it's not all bad.

I love your soft lips, your eyes, your grin,
but I'm tired of being the one who begins.
I need you to meet me halfway, to show
that love isn't something I chase, but something we grow.

I'm scared, Jace, of where we stand,
but I'm willing to work, to hold your hand.
I think about the first time we kissed,
how happy I was, how much I missed.

I want us to be that way again,
to talk, to laugh, to be more than friends.
So tell me how you feel, don't hold it inside,
even if it's hard, even if you've tried.

I've been up too long, with too much time,
but I need you to hear, to feel this rhyme.
I didn't know I could love this much,
but I do, Jace, and I need your touch.

Let's talk, let's work, let's try once more,
because I love you, and you're the one I adore.
Don't let silence be the end of our song.
Let's make it right, where we both belong.

Inspiration behind "Unspoken Truths"
Emotion: Vulnerability

This poem comes from an emotional email I wrote to on January 23, 2010, at 5:19 a.m. I was wide awake, grappling with the frustration, confusion, and hurt that had built up in our relationship. The poem reflects the intense emotions I felt as I tried to understand why Jace was distancing himself from me, why he wasn't being as open and communicative as I needed him to be, and why he seemed to be keeping me at arm's length.

The email was a raw and honest outpouring of my feelings—questions about why I wasn't invited to his Circle of Unity event, suspicions that Micah might have been the reason, and how our relationship was changing. I was frustrated that Jace wasn't showing his love in the way I needed, that our conversations had become shallow and routine, and that I often felt like I was the one putting in all the effort.

The poem captures these sentiments, turning the questions and concerns from the email into verses that express the pain of feeling overlooked, the desire for more connection, and the fear of losing someone you deeply love. It also touches on the vulnerability of loving someone who seems distant, the longing for deeper communication, and the need for mutual effort in a relationship.

At the heart of the poem is the tension between love and frustration—the deep affection I had for Jace, mixed with the pain of feeling like I wasn't getting the same level of commitment in return. The poem reflects my plea for him to meet me halfway, to show his love not just in words, but in actions, and to help rebuild the connection that seemed to be slipping away.

This poem reflects a critical moment in our relationship, where I was questioning whether we could work through our issues and find our way back to each other. It's a plea for honesty, for openness, and for the kind of love that isn't just spoken but lived.

2009's Missing Memory

"Why am I not in your 2009 favorite memories?" I cried
in an email sent with fire, with all the hurt inside.
"You better remake that damn thing, take out that kiss,
remove that bitch, and put me in where I should exist."

How bold it was, how clear it became.

Micah, in and out of your memories, like a claim.
Yet here I was, your boyfriend, your love, your truth,
not a single mention, no nod to our youth.

This wasn't just about a list or a year.
It was about being unseen, feeling my fear.
Throughout our time, five long years in tow,
I often felt hidden, your love didn't show.

You kept me in the shadows, out of sight.
Though your friends and family knew, it didn't feel right.
They knew who I was, more than just a friend,
but your closet kept me, and it wouldn't bend.

I stayed, hoping, yearning for more,
for the world to see what we had in store.
But time and again, I found myself here,
sending emails, fighting back tears.

Unfulfilled, undervalued, in love's hidden den,
questioning where I stood, again and again.
Your closet, our barrier, kept me apart,
from the world, from your life, from your heart.

So 2009 came and went, without a trace of me
in your favorite memories, where I thought I'd be.
A painful reminder of what we lacked,
Of the love we shared but couldn't act.

And though I loved you and tried to stay,
the feeling of being hidden never went away.
It wasn't just one year, one list, one fight.
It was the pattern, the hurt, the endless night.

So here's to the memory that should have been,
a love not in hiding, but out in the wind.
To being seen, valued, and loved in the light,
not just in secret, but in everyone's sight.

Inspiration behind "2009's Missing Memory"
Emotion: Hurt

This poem comes from a painful chapter in my life, where I felt undervalued, unseen, and hidden in my relationship with Jace. In early 2010, Jace shared his favorite memories of the previous year, and I wasn't included. Instead, Micah, someone else who clearly didn't hold the same place in his life as I did, was featured several times. This omission cut deep. It wasn't just about being left out of a list; it was a reflection of the larger issues in our relationship.

Throughout our time together, I struggled with Jace's reluctance to openly acknowledge our relationship. Although his friends and family were aware that he was gay and that I was more than just a friend, he kept me in the shadows, never fully embracing or showing the world that I was his boyfriend. This lack of public acknowledgment led to many moments, like the one in here, where I found myself questioning my worth and my place in his life.

The Velvet Rage delves into the phases of shame that many gay men experience. Jace was deeply entrenched in shame, unable to fully accept and live his truth. His internalized shame about his sexuality bled into our relationship, casting a shadow over what could have been a beautiful and open love. The shame he carried became a barrier between us, affecting both how he saw himself but also how he treated me.

The Velvet Rage describes this phase of shame as a time when gay men often hide parts of themselves, fearing rejection and judgment. Jace's inability to step out of the closet fully, to show the world who he really was and who I was to him, placed a strain on our relationship. His shame became my burden, as I was forced into a role that didn't reflect the depth of our connection or my importance in his life.

This poem reflects the pain and frustration I felt during those years. It's about the struggle to be seen and valued, not just in private but in the public eye. It's a reminder of the importance of living authentically and the damage that shame can do to the person carrying it and to those they love.

For those reading this, the lesson is clear: shame is a powerful force, but it doesn't have to define your life or your relationships. Confront it, work through it, and emerge on the other side with pride and self-acceptance. The closet may feel safe, but it's also a prison, and the love that's hidden there can never fully thrive. If you find yourself in a relationship where shame is holding you or your partner back, address it openly and honestly, seek help if needed, and remember that true love deserves to be seen in the light.

A Plea for Us

In Ann Arbor, where we laughed and played,
where friendship felt real, where memories stayed,
But apart, something always seemed to shift.
The bond we had began to drift.

Back in ninth grade, when I was just a boy,
uncertain of love, of joy, of ploy,
I didn't know what "gay" even meant,
but by eleventh grade, the truth was sent.

I lied to friends, to family, to you,
hid behind shadows, unsure of the view.
But in time, I let the truth unfold,
to Daria, to Jaya, to those who held.

I felt a weight lift, a burden eased.
Friendship grew, I felt more pleased.
But there was still you, the one I feared,
to tell my truth, to speak sincere.

Yet when I did, our bond did grow,
or so I thought, in the moments slow.
Told my grandparents, my mom, and more.
Found comfort in truth, in love, in core.

But you, my friend, my best, my love,
I fear we've lost what once was above.
Kappa, Twitter, the lies you've spun,
where's the friend with whom I'd run?

You twit your thoughts, your jokes, your fears,
but do you share them with me, dear?
You've become a ghost, a shadow, a blur,
and I'm left wondering who you are, for sure.

Think back to when we first kissed,
to nights of talk, of what we'd missed.
You shared your secrets, your bottled dreams,
but now, it's like you've ripped the seams.

I want to know you, to see you, to trust,
but it's hard when lies turn friendship to dust.
I know I breached, I crossed the line,
but do you truly not trust me, love mine?

I want to be happy with you by my side,
but I need to know, what do you hide?
Who are you, Jace? What do you seek?
Are you lost in a lie, afraid to speak?

I miss the jokes, the laughs, the fun,
the friendship that felt like it had just begun.
Please respond, please start to care.
I miss the friend I thought was there.

So, in closing, I ask with all my heart,
Can we find a way to make a new start?
Think about us, about life, about truth,
and please, be my friend again, as in our youth.

Inspiration behind "A Please for Us"
Emotion: Desperation

This poem captures my emotions, frustrations, and longing as my friendship and romantic relationship with Jace began to unravel. It's from a time when I noticed the distance growing between us, both emotionally and physically, despite our shared history and deep connection.

I wrote a long email to Jace on March 26, 2010, where I poured out my heart, addressing our relationship's painful and confusing shifts. I reflected on the bond we shared when we were together in Ann Arbor, where everything felt more real, where we laughed, played, fought, and watched TV together. But when we were apart, something always seemed to change. The connection that felt strong in-person weakened, and I was left feeling like I didn't know who Jace was anymore.

This moment was particularly challenging because it brought old wounds and insecurities to the surface. I recalled how, in high school, I struggled to come to terms with my identity, lying to friends, family, and even myself. I was relieved when I finally came out, and I found that my relationships grew stronger with the truth. But with Jace, the same pattern of hiding and distance hurt our friendship and our love.

The poem captures my plea for honesty, communication, and a return to the closeness we once had. I missed our deep conversations, late-night talks, and being truly seen and understood. But as Jace became more involved in Kappa and other activities, and as social media became a bigger part of his life, I felt like I was losing him to these external forces. He shared his thoughts and feelings with Twitter and Facebook instead of me, leaving me excluded and unsure of my place in his life.

This poem reflects my complex emotions of love, frustration, and a deep desire to reconnect. It's about the pain of watching someone you care about drift away and the fear that you might not be able to bring them back. I was trying to understand who Jace was becoming, and I was pleading with him to be honest with himself and with me.

The underlying message is about the importance of communication and trust in any relationship, especially when it feels like things are falling apart. It's a reminder that without open, honest dialogue, even the strongest bonds can weaken. This moment in time represents a turning point where I asked Jace—and myself—to confront the truth and to work toward a better, more authentic connection.

The Structure of Trust

In the halls of learning, where knowledge resides,
integrity stands tall, a pillar that guides.
Like the steel above, holding the roof high,
we trust in the builders, as time passes by.

But trust isn't just for buildings alone.
It's the foundation upon which friendships are grown.
In the bonds we form, both honest and true,
lies the essence of life in all that we do.

Gary Pavela spoke of this truth in his speech,
to students eager, with futures to reach.
He told of trust, the honor code's might,
how fidelity to truth brings friendships to light.

It's not just about grades or the tasks we complete.
It's about the people we meet and the trust that we keep.
For in every exchange, in every deal made,
integrity shapes us in the choices we trade.

But the lesson extends beyond the academic sphere
to the friendships we cherish and those we hold dear.

For in a world that's dog-eat-dog and tough,
it's fidelity to truth that makes love enough.

Think of the friendships that never grow old,
where honesty and loyalty are worth more than gold.
They're built on trust, on a foundation so strong,
a partnership in truth, where we all belong.

But there's a warning in Pavela's wise words
of friendships that falter, of truths that are blurred.
When ambition and deceit take the place of the heart,
The structure of self begins to fall apart.

He spoke of "Gamesmen," who play to win,
but lose themselves in the game, trapped within.
For when the thrill of the contest fades away,
what's left is a hollow, with no truth to say.

So let's build our lives like that ceiling above,
with integrity, trust, and friendships of love.
For in the end, as the years pass by,
it's the truth we live that keeps us high.

In every bond, in every hand we take,
let fidelity to truth guide the choices we make.
For the structure of self, like a building so grand,
stands firm when we trust in the truth we demand.

Inspiration behind "The Structure of Trust"
Emotion: Reflective

    While in college in 2010, I had to take an integrity class
as a consequence of doing something I wasn't supposed to
do in another course. As part of that class, I read Gary
Pavela's speech on academic integrity, social trust, and the
connection between truth and friendship. Jace helped me
with the citations for the paper I had to write, but this
particular speech stood out to me. Pavela's words
resonated deeply, especially the line, "With integrity, trust,

and friendships of love. For in the end, as the years pass by, it's the truth we live that keeps us high." This line made me think about what I wanted in my relationship with Jace and my friendships.

At that point in our relationship, I questioned whether I was getting what I needed and whether I was fulfilled. I hadn't started therapy, so I didn't fully understand the concepts of fulfillment or the boundaries I should have been setting. But I certainly felt the lack of those things, and Pavela's speech pushed me to consider what was missing.

The inspiration for "The Structure of Trust" comes from the impact of Pavela's powerful speech. Delivered at Trinity University in 2004, his speech was a call to uphold an honor code—and a reflection on the role of honesty and fidelity in shaping our academic lives and ourselves and relationships.

Gary Pavela eloquently explains how social trust is the cornerstone of any functioning society, using the metaphor of a building's structure to illustrate the importance of integrity. Just as we trust that the steel and concrete above our heads will hold firm, we rely on the honesty and integrity of those around us in countless aspects of our lives. This trust is a social necessity and it's essential in forming our identities.

Pavela also suggests that integrity isn't limited to academic or professional settings—it's a fundamental part of building who we are as individuals. He draws a connection between the values we uphold and the friendships we form, suggesting that true friendship is grounded in a mutual commitment to truth. This idea speaks to the importance of choosing friends who support us and challenge us to be our best, most honest selves.

In writing this poem, I wanted to capture Pavela's message and emphasize this aspect of human interaction. Trust and integrity are not just abstract concepts; they are the foundation of our relationships and the structure upon which we build our lives. By staying true to ourselves and to others, we create bonds that are strong, resilient, and enduring.

A special shout-out to Gary Pavela for his insightful work, which continues to inspire discussions on the importance of integrity and the role it plays in our personal and academic lives. His speech is a reminder that the choices we make, the truth we live by, and the trust we cultivate are all integral to who we are and who we become.

Sasha's Swipe: A Christmas Surprise

One chilly December, at the ATM,
my Comerica card slid in smooth,
I punched in a few digits, confident,
but then, a beep—and the news wasn't so cool.

"Insufficient funds," blinked on the screen.
Twice, thrice—I thought, What do they mean?
Lowered the amount, still no success,
Now I'm thinking—I must be in some sort of mess.

Back to basics, I pull up the app,
scan my transactions, look at the map.
What's this charge?—$1,500 flat?
I don't remember buying gold bricks or a platinum hat.

A call later, the truth came clear.
Jace, my then-love, with holiday cheer,
had swiped my card for a surprise, no doubt—
but this wasn't the gift I would've picked out.

You see, I'm not made of money; I'm not Rockefeller.
Grad school had me in a financial cellar.
A $1,500 Pomeranian? Was he out of his mind?
I couldn't even afford peace of mind!

Enter Sasha, tiny, malnourished, and frail—
a black puff of fluff, with a wagging tail.
Too small to be healthy, but already attached—
I couldn't just return her; our bond was unmatched.

Her eyes, like twin galaxies, dark as the night,
she'd follow me everywhere, my shadow in flight.
She didn't ask for this life, neither did I,
but there we were, just Sasha and I.

Jace's "gift," wrapped up in my funds,
left me less cash but plenty of puns.
And though I shot him a look of death—
it taught him to think before stealing my breath.

Sasha, though, became my ride-or-die,
born too small, but now strong enough to fly.
A Christmas present, with a twist of fate—
my money, his card swipe—but she's worth the wait.

So here's the moral, let's get it straight:
Check your bank balance, before it's too late.
And if your boyfriend buys you a gift on your dime—
make sure it's something you'd actually like, next time.

Inspiration Behind "Sasha's Swipe: A Christmas Surprise"

Emotion: Amused Frustration

This poem comes from a situation that blended humor, frustration, and lessons in boundaries. It's crazy to think that my ex-boyfriend purchased my dog, Sasha, with my own money—without my knowledge—only to reveal her as a "gift" for me later. As funny as it might seem now, this moment reflected so much more than just an overdraft in my bank account. It spoke to how I've allowed the lines between love and responsibility to blur in my relationships, often at the expense of my own needs.

This situation was a teaching moment about boundaries, communication, and taking control of my own narrative. I wasn't rich at the time—far from it. I was in grad school, scraping together funds to help out my uncle, and trying to stay afloat financially. So when I found myself staring at an insufficient funds message at the ATM, only to later realize that it was the result of a decision made without my consent, it was like a punch to the gut.

Sasha, a malnourished and tiny black Pomeranian, became a symbol of resilience. I nursed her back to health, even though I hadn't been the one to choose her. I felt responsible, and even though I hadn't planned for her, she was now mine. Bonding with Sasha showed me the depth of my ability to care for others, even when things don't go according to plan. But it also made me realize that I needed to be more assertive about my wants and not let others impose their choices on me.

Setting boundaries and having honest conversations is important, even when it feels difficult. Instead of saying more about how I felt at that moment, I let the situation slide, silently accepting behaviors that I didn't approve of. Therapy has taught me to speak up for myself, to honor my own desires, and to recognize when I'm being taken advantage of—even in small, seemingly insignificant ways.

There's also a lesson here about self-care and being clear about what we want in relationships. Sometimes, it's easy to let things go, to keep the peace or avoid confrontation, but that doesn't serve anyone in the long run. Relationships thrive on communication and mutual respect, and resentment builds when those things are lacking.

I learned that love isn't about sacrificing to the point of neglecting your own needs. It's about finding balance, advocating for yourself, and ensuring that you aren't left footing the bill for someone else's choices—literally or metaphorically. Sasha was a gift I didn't ask for, but she became part of my life. And while I wouldn't trade that, I now know that moving forward, I'll make sure that I'm actively choosing what comes into my life.

The key takeaway? Speak up, set boundaries, and don't let love blind you to your own needs. I've worked through these issues in therapy and I now understand the importance of making sure that my voice is heard in my relationships, that my choices are mine, and that I'm not just a passive participant in someone else's plans.

Sasha may have been bought with my card, but she ended up being my heart. I learned the hard way, but the lesson is clear: my life, my choices, my boundaries.

In the Shadows of Love

Five years in the closet, five years in the dark,
with Jace by my side, yet always apart.
A love that spanned college, grad school, and beyond,
but hidden from the world, where did we truly belong?

My family knew, my friends all could see,
he was my boyfriend, but what about me?
Who was he fooling, keeping us concealed?
While my heart ached with wounds that never healed.

I was hurt, disrespected, left feeling small,
crying out loud, but did he hear my call?
The weight of his silence, the burden of his fear,
left me drowning in sorrow, year after year.

I remember the nights, leaving Ann Arbor's glow,
sitting in my car, tears a flow.
I couldn't speak, couldn't find the words to say,
how much it hurt to be hidden away.

Ilana answered the phone, listened to my cries,

but even her comfort couldn't dry my eyes.
Those moments of darkness, so heavy and cold,
should have been the end, but I couldn't be bold.

I chose the idea, the dream of what could be,
blind to the reality that he didn't choose me.
I poured in my love, my time, my care,
but the imbalance was more than I could bear.

He went all out for others while I stood in the shade.
A birthday passed by, no grand gesture made.
I realized then, in the pain of that slight,
he knew how to love, but not in my light.

I cried then, and I cry now as I write
for the love that was lost in the shadows of night.
I let love blind me, let it steal my worth,
but now I know, I should have come first.

When he wouldn't come out, wouldn't stand by my side,
I knew it was time to let go of the ride.
I chose myself and ended those years,
but the pain of that love still lingers in tears.

Being in the closet, loving in the shade,
it's a hurt that doesn't fade.
But I've learned now, I am my priority,
and that's the love that will set me free.

Inspiration behind "In the Shadows of Love"
Emotion: Heartache and Self-realization

This poem is drawn from some of the deepest and most painful memories of my relationship with Jace, which spanned nearly five years, most of it spent in the shadows, hidden from the world. I look back on that time overwhelmed by a mix of emotions—love, hurt, confusion, and, eventually, a profound sense of loss. This poem captures those years, the intense highs, and the crushing lows of loving someone who wasn't willing to fully embrace me or our relationship in the light.

Jace and I shared so much—years of memories, moments of passion, and dreams that I believed we both wanted. But the reality was different. While my family and friends knew who he was to me, he kept us hidden, confined to the shadows of his fears and insecurities. It was a constant battle between the love I felt so deeply and the pain of being kept a secret, of being loved only in the dark.

I remember how often I cried and how many times I felt disrespected, unimportant, and overlooked. The pain was emotional and physical, manifesting in the tears that seemed to never stop and in the heaviness that settled in my chest every time I was reminded that I was not a priority. I poured so much of myself into that relationship—emotionally, financially, physically—because I believed that's what love required. I thought that if I gave enough and showed him how much I cared, he would eventually choose me, and he would step out of the closet with me into the light.

Knowing that Jace knew how to love, show grand gestures, put someone in the light and celebrate them when he truly cared was even more painful. I saw him do it for one of his best friends for two years in a row. He went all out for her birthday, making it clear to everyone how much he valued her and how much he cared. The elevated celebrations were impossible to ignore, and I couldn't help but observe them with a sharp sting of pain. I wasn't given that same treatment. I wasn't celebrated or placed in the spotlight in that way. It was a glaring reminder that while he was capable of these beautiful, thoughtful gestures, I wasn't the one receiving them. It hurt then, and it still hurts now writing this, remembering how much I longed for that kind of love and attention from him that never came.

I ignored the red flags, the hurtful moments, the times when he went all out for others but never for me. I kept choosing the idea of our future, the dream of what we could become, over the reality that was right in front of me. Love blinded me to my own needs and my own worth.

It took me years to realize that I was losing myself in that relationship and that I was sacrificing my own happiness and mental health for someone who wasn't willing to do the same for me. Loving myself, which I've come to understand through therapy, was something I had neglected. Loving yourself means recognizing your own worth, setting boundaries, and not settling for less than what you deserve. It means putting yourself first, even when it's hard; even when it means walking away from someone you love.

This poem was born out of that realization. It reflects on those dark years, on the love that I gave so freely and the pain that came with it. It's about understanding that I should have chosen myself sooner and that I deserved to be loved fully and openly. It's about the importance of loving yourself enough to walk away from a love that hurts more than it heals and from a relationship that doesn't bring you the happiness and fulfillment you deserve.

In the end, I had to learn that my love for myself needed to be stronger than my love for someone else. It was a painful lesson, but it was necessary. Now, as I look back, I can see that those years, though difficult, were an important part of my journey. They taught me the value of self-love, the importance of prioritizing my own well-being, and the strength it takes to let go of a love that isn't right.

The Grad School Realization

In cap and gown, I walked the stage,
a future ahead, but trapped in a cage.
Beside me, Jace, my love, my fight,
yet shadows loomed, dimming the light.

Grad school was our tethered bond,
but whispers of doubt were growing strong.
How do we build a life, a plan,
when he clings to Detroit, a grounded man?

He wouldn't tell his mother our truth,
our love confined, hidden from youth.
Every day together, yet nights alone,
a grown man fearing the truth at home.

I helped him get his car, his start,
but in the closet, we lived apart.
Our conversations turned to what could be,
but he chose safety, not you and me.

He spoke of grad school, a hopeful delay,
but I knew deep down, he wouldn't stay.
The clock was ticking, the end was near,
yet I fought on, despite the fear.

He couldn't see a life away,
From the streets of Detroit, where he'd stay.
He couldn't see himself free,
or living a life openly with me.

I wanted more, I needed more,
but he couldn't give what I was asking for.
In the shadows, I realized at last,
our future together was fading fast.

I deserved to be loved out loud,
to be his choice, to make him proud.

But he chose the closet, his own path,
and in that choice, I felt the wrath.

So I stood on that grad school stage,
ready to turn another page.
Leaving behind the shadows and doubt,
to find a love that would shout, not shut out.

Our time was ending, I felt it in my soul,
but I kept fighting, losing control.
Now I know, I deserved so much more,
than a love hidden behind a closed door.

Inspiration behind "The Grad School Realization"
Emotion: Disappointment and Awakening

This poem stems from deep introspection when I began
to see the cracks in my relationship with Jace during grad
school. It wasn't that I had made the decision to end
things—I hadn't. But I was beginning to see the reality of
our situation, the growing divide between us, and the
incompatibility of our paths.

I was grappling with understanding that while we
loved each other, our relationship wasn't as strong as I
needed it to be. I was ready to step into a new chapter of
life, but Jace was still hesitant, choosing the safety of the
closet and unwilling to move forward in the way I hoped
we could together. These realizations were painful because
I knew deep down that I might need to choose myself, my
mental health, and my future over a love that wasn't
fulfilling.

I valued communication deeply and tried to have those
necessary conversations about our future—where we were
heading, how we would navigate life together, and
whether we had the tools and adaptability to grow as a
couple. But every time I tried, Jace's responses were
hesitant, non-committal, and rooted in fear. He didn't see

himself leaving Detroit, coming out to his mom, or fully committing to me.

I was starting to see these signs, but I kept fighting for us, hoping we could make it work. I was so focused on the future I wanted that I didn't fully respect or acknowledge the direction of Jace's growth. I didn't see that his growth was different from mine and that his fears and hesitations were part of his journey, just as my drive to move forward was part of mine.

This poem reflects my understanding that I was on a path where I would eventually need to choose myself. It's about the therapeutic work that I couldn't fully grasp at the time but would later learn was essential in any relationship. Communication, self-awareness, respect for each other's growth, and the importance of mental health were lessons I couldn't see then but have since become clear.

In this poem, I express the conflict of knowing what I needed, even if I wasn't ready to act on it yet. It's about the growing awareness that while love is important, it's not enough on its own. It needs to be nurtured, communicated, and aligned with mutual goals and respect for each other's growth. This poem is about how, at the time, I wasn't ready to choose myself over the relationship, but I was beginning to see the necessity of it.

Betrayal Unveiled

In whispered tones of casual jest,
the heart's deep wounds are left undressed.
Your words, once sweet, now shards of glass,
reflect the shadows of all that's passed.

We planned a gift with laughter light,
yet drifted to desires of the night.
In text, you flirted with other skins,

unaware of the ache that grew within.

Your laughter hid the brewing storm,
your casual banter, a hurtful form.
How quickly joy turned to betrayal's dance,
leaving me lost in a painful trance.

I asked for simple camaraderie,
But your words hinted at a treachery.
Not just with others did your interests lie,
but in the spaces where my trust did die.

So here I stand amidst the debris,
of broken trust and a love not free.
Your actions speaking louder than any vow,
leaving me to wonder what, where, and how.

The veil has lifted, the truth now clear,
your distractions a signal of my deepest fear.
Was it ever us, or just your play?
A game of hearts, you chose to sway.

Now I pen this verse, a solemn ode,
to love once bright, now an empty road.
From gifts to betrayal, a path so worn,
in the cold light of truth, my heart is torn.

So I'll gather pieces, mend the breaks,
learn from love and all its aches.
For even in this pain, I shall not dwell
in the ruins of a love, a lessoned shell.

Inspiration Behind "Betrayal Unveiled"
Emotion: Betrayal

This poem unfolded through a seemingly innocent
conversation about a birthday gift. This poem was born
from the realization that my trust was being compromised,

not through direct confrontation but through the subtle,
yet hurtful, exchanges hidden within casual banter.

Our conversation started light-heartedly as we
discussed birthday plans for a friend. However, it quickly
shifted to a more flirtatious tone that involved others,
revealing a layer of interaction that deeply hurt me. It
wasn't just the flirtation that stung, but the ease with
which it seemed to happen, and the realization that such
exchanges had possibly become a norm rather than an
exception.

As I reflected on these messages, the sense of betrayal
grew. What was meant to be a simple coordination for a
gift became a window into a deeper disloyalty. This breach
of trust was particularly painful because it was not just
about the acts themselves but about the casualness with
which my feelings were sidelined.

"Betrayal Unveiled" is my way of processing these
emotions and giving voice to the hurt and confusion that
such revelations bring. It is about acknowledging the pain,
confronting the betrayal, and ultimately, finding a path to
heal. The poem captures the betrayal and the journey from
shock to the resolution of moving forward, learning from
the experience, and slowly rebuilding the trust in myself
and my relationship judgment.

The Last Test

Long distance is a bitch,
spoils the sex life, makes you itch
for the warmth of skin close by,
leaves you desperate, asking why.

They say it makes the heart grow fond,
but I say it's the final bond,
the last test love must endure
to see if it's steadfast, pure.

I wanted to weather every storm,
wanted Jace's love to be the norm.
But in Chicago, feeling so alone,
I saw the cracks, the seeds we'd sown.

We tried to bridge the miles apart,
but I was left with a heavy heart.
The effort felt one-sided, unfair,
no plans to move, no future to share.

Long distance didn't fail us, no—
it simply made the truth show.
The great sex, just a week before,
left me yearning, aching for more.

It was so good, it made me mad,
for everything we never had.
The hurt, the pain, the endless wait,
the broken promises, the sealed fate.

Long distance didn't break our ties.
It opened my heart, opened my eyes.
The space I needed to see it clear,
that what we had wasn't near.

We failed the test, couldn't hold on,
and in that truth, I found the dawn.
Long distance showed me what was real,
that love needs more than just appeal.

We failed it, yes, but now I know
that sometimes, letting go helps you grow.
Long distance didn't break our love.
It set me free like a flighted dove.

Inspiration behind "The Last Test"
Emotion: Resignation

This poem is about trying to navigate a long-distance relationship with Jace while living in Chicago. This poem captures the emotional turbulence and the harsh realities that long-distance relationships often bring.

Therapists often say that long-distance relationships can work, but they require an extraordinary amount of communication, trust, and a shared vision for the future. They emphasize that both partners need to be on the same page, making plans to eventually close the distance. Without that, the relationship can feel like a perpetual state of limbo, eroding the bond over time.

When I moved to Chicago, I was determined to make things work with Jace. I wanted us to weather every storm, to prove that our love could endure anything, even the miles between us. But as the days turned into weeks and the weeks into months, the distance began to take its toll. I found myself feeling increasingly alone, despite our attempts to stay connected.

The physical separation amplified my feelings of loneliness and made me desperate for the intimacy and closeness that were so easy when we were in the same city. It was a constant reminder of what I was missing. The more I lay in bed at night, staring at the empty space beside me, the more I realized that our relationship wasn't fulfilling me. The late-night phone calls and occasional visits weren't enough to bridge the emotional gap that was growing between us.

I was putting in more effort, making more sacrifices, and increasingly frustrated with the lack of progress in our relationship. We had conversations about the future, but they didn't result in concrete plans to be together. I wanted him to choose us and to prioritize our relationship, but it felt like we were on different paths.

One of the most confusing aspects of this time was that, just a week before we broke up, we had one of the best sexual experiences of our relationship. It was intense, passionate, and everything I wanted—yet, it also made me angry. I was angry that I couldn't have that experience every night and angry at the hurt and disappointment that had built up over time. The high of that moment was overshadowed by the lows of our reality.

Looking back, I realize that long distance didn't fail us—we failed it. The distance was the clarity I needed to see that our relationship wasn't what I thought it was. It highlighted the gaps, the unfulfilled promises, and the lack of a shared future. In a way, the distance was a gift, forcing me to confront the truth that I had been avoiding.

"The Last Test" is about that painful realization and how long distance, rather than being the enemy, became the mirror that reflected the cracks in our relationship. It was the time I needed to see clearly what I truly wanted and deserved. It was a test we couldn't pass, but it was also a wake-up call to start prioritizing myself and my own happiness.

To My Soulmate, Departed

Do you think, my love, we're meant to be?
The word "soulmate" dances 'round me.
Yet anger whispers doubts into the night,
claiming if true, you'd still hold me tight.

I've read that soulmates love the flawed just so,
in them, a perfect love they know.
And thinking back to laughter shared,
the way you loved the quirks I bared.

I miss you, yes, the tears do fall.
Without you, life's a hollow call.

No anger now, just aching blues,
believing still, my soulmate's you.

Our moments sweet, when life felt right,
your smile could chase away the night.
But life, it shifted, paths diverged.
In Chicago's winds, our futures surged.

You seemed to stall as I pressed on.
Our sync lost, the closeness gone.
Communication faded into thin air.
Your passion for others seemed unfair.

Yet here I am, still holding fast
to love that's gone, to dreams now past.
I wish for you to find your way,
to love me as I do, come what may.

The pain's still sharp, will it ever mend?
With every "A," it's you I want to commend.
Sasha's eyes, the neighborhood's embrace,
every corner shows me your trace.

When the night is quiet, and I'm alone,
I think of all the love we've known.
Can time heal this gaping wound?
With every beat, to you I'm tuned.

Please know this, though we're apart,
you hold a sacred place in my heart.
Forever my soulmate, this remains true,
I'm sending a virtual hug to you.

Smelling the scent that's only yours,
my soulmate, across distant shores.
Take care, my love, find peace, find light,
for you'll be in my dreams tonight.

Jace's Response

I. On Soulmates and Separation

Do I believe in soulmates? Yes, perhaps I do.
But perfect matches in this vast world? I'm unsure, too.
Last night's emotions, deep and raw,
reveal your pain, your final straw.

You say my absence tears you apart,
yet staying might poison the heart.
Love so fierce, it draws tears for a month,
isn't love that can sustain, it's too much.

II. On Needing Space

I need moments to myself like Carrie needs her hour.
Not indifference, but space to regain power.
Your inquiries, though caring, feel like chains,
restricting, confining like endless rains.

Tumblr's quiet, Twitter's buzz,
offer me solace, just because.
A quiet time to find my peace,
from daily toils to find release.

III. On Independence and Growth

When you cut ties, a part of me woke,
sobbing, yes, but independence spoke.
It's time to stand on my own two feet,
manage my bills, face life's heat.

This break, perhaps, is what we need
to grow, to heal, to plant new seed.
If joy is what you seek in me,
then let me find what I can truly be.

IV. On Our Bond and Future

If friendship is the path we take,
let's tread carefully, for both our sake.
I cherish you, your laugh, your mind,
but need to ensure our ties are kind.

If back together, our paths do wind,
let's ensure it's not just to bind,
but because it's right for both our hearts,
not just picking up broken parts.

V. On Forever and Always

No matter where our journeys lead,
in your happiness, I'll find my creed.
Sunshine, rainbows, laughter light,
I wish for you every day and night.

Always in my life, I hope you'll stay,
in whatever form, come what may.
Our love, deep and complex, a woven art,
forever, you'll hold a piece of my heart.

Inspiration Behind "To My Soulmate, Departed" and "Jace's Response"
Emotion: Introspection and Emotional growth

"To My Soulmate, Departed" and "Jace's Response"
came from an email exchange between Jace and me, where
I asked him about his beliefs in soulmates and expressed
my complex feelings about our relationship.

In my email, I poured out my frustrations, my longing,
and my confusion over what it meant to be soulmates. I
was deeply entangled in my emotions, feeling unfulfilled
and voicing loudly what I needed from him, almost
drowning out his own needs and perspectives.

Reading Jace's response now, I see clearly how it wasn't just about his need for independence but also about my own co-dependence. He was trying to communicate his need for space to be himself—a concept I struggled to accept. His words were a mirror, reflecting his feelings and my intense demands and how they impacted our relationship.

Creating these poems allowed me to transform our real-life dialogue into art, giving voice to both our perspectives. "To My Soulmate, Departed" encapsulates my side of the story, filled with longing and a plea for understanding. "Jace's Response," on the other hand, articulates his need for individuality and space, his love for me, but also his struggle with the pressures of our relationship.

This artistic process was cathartic, helping me to appreciate the balance needed between love and individuality, and highlighting the lessons I needed to learn about respecting both our needs. It was a powerful reminder of the growth that sometimes comes from painful realizations and the enduring impact of heartfelt communication.

The Love I Closed Down

After Jace, I think I secretly vowed,
To never love again with a heart so loud.
I felt a love so deep, so profound,
That when it ended, I buried it underground.

With Mark, it was lust that led the way,
A love built on nights that turned into day.
But nothing deeper, nothing to last,
Just fleeting moments, lost in the past.

With Darren, I loved, but it wasn't the same,
It lacked the fire, it lacked the flame.
A love more quiet, steady, and calm,
But not the kind that heals or soothes the balm.

Bax came next, with logic at the helm,
A love more reasoned, a different realm.
There was care, yes, but passion was thin,
A love more measured, not from within.

Nico felt like family, a comforting hand,
A love built on support, a steady stand.
But even there, it was love out of need,
Not the kind that lets your heart bleed.

I didn't realize until I met Rafaa,
That all these loves were logic's trick.
Manufactured, safe, controlled by thought,
So I wouldn't be hurt, or so I thought.

I closed my heart, locked it tight,
Turned down the love that felt too bright.
I let logic guide, let reason reign,
But in doing so, I avoided the pain.

Yet with Rafa, and many therapy sessions too,
I learned that love isn't always new.
It's a space, a safe one to grow,
A place where true love can overflow.

I let my heart open, just a crack,
And realized the love I'd held back.
The love that could endure, stand the test,
The kind of love that feels like a rest.

Now I see, looking back,
How I let fear control the track.
But with Rafa, I've found a place,
Where love is safe, and I'm free to embrace.

So here's to the love I almost lost,
To the lessons learned, to the cost.
I closed down, but now I'm free,
To love again, to just be me.

Inspiration behind "The Love I Closed Down"

Emotion: Self-awareness

This poem stems from the aftermath of my breakup with Jace, a relationship that, in hindsight, I never truly mourned or processed in a healthy way. The breakup left me closed off to the possibility of true love. I didn't do the necessary work or go through the therapeutic steps to properly grieve the end of that relationship, nor did I take the time to learn from it in a way that would allow me to grow and open myself up to love again.

After Jace, I moved aimlessly from one relationship to another, trying to avoid the hurt and disappointment I had experienced. With Darren, I was careful not to repeat the mistakes I made with Jace, but in doing so, I kept my heart guarded. With Bax, I tried to avoid the emotional disconnect I felt with Darren, but again, I approached the relationship with more logic than emotion. Nico was different, but I still wasn't fully present—my heart wasn't completely in it. I was avoiding something in each of them, trying to protect myself from the pain I had never fully dealt with after Jace.

It wasn't until I met Rafa that I began to see things differently. He's someone who has also done the work in therapy, who understands the importance of communication and emotional intelligence. With Rafa, I've found a partner who meets me where I am, and sometimes even exceeds me in maturity and understanding. He's the person with whom I can be completely vulnerable, knowing that he'll stand strong with me, just as I will with him.

In therapy, I've learned that my journey has been about learning to love myself first, to heal from past hurts, and to understand the patterns that have shaped my relationships. I've come to understand that true love requires both partners to be willing to grow together, to communicate openly, and to support each other's individual journeys. What I've learned is that Rafa is that partner for me. He's the person I've been waiting for, and through our relationship, I've found a love that is not only deep and passionate but also healthy and enduring.

My therapist has helped me recognize that the way I approached love after Jace was a form of self-protection. I wasn't fully allowing myself to be vulnerable again, fearing the hurt that I had experienced before. But with Rafa, I've learned that love isn't just about logic or intention; it's about opening your heart completely, even at the risk of being hurt. It's about building a safe space where both partners can grow and thrive together.

Mark
Emotion: Passion and Nostalgia.

In the "Mark" chapter, I reflect on the whirlwind romance and complex emotions that spanned over eight years between Milo "Mark" Parker and me. These poems capture the magnetic pull of our love affair, from steamy nights in Miami to the blurred lines between loyalty and desire. Our connection was more than physical—it was a deep, passionate bond that lingered despite other relationships and life changes. This chapter explores the highs and lows of our love, the thrill of our secret rendezvous, and the lessons learned from a connection that couldn't last but forever left its mark.

The Night at the Conrad: Meeting Mark

In the heart of Miami, on Brickell's high rise,
alone in a room where the city lights lie,
I felt the pull of the night, both empty and deep,
yearning for something my heart couldn't keep.

The Conrad Hilton, with its elegance and view,
a work audit's guise hid the loneliness I knew.
A screen's soft glow, a message sent—
and soon, our paths crossed by digital intent.

You arrived, Milo Park, with your slim silhouette,
a smile that held secrets, a meeting well set.
But then, the door closed, and you were gone
to the car, you said, as I thought you'd withdrawn.

Minutes ticked by, doubt's shadow did creep,
but back you came with a bottle to keep.
Dark liquor that warmed as conversation flowed,
A moment stretched out where time gently slowed.

We made love that night in a dance so profound
it stitched us together, where hearts were unbound.
Your touch was a fire, your kiss, a sweet tease,
and in that moment, we found our own ease.

For eight years and more, our paths intertwined,
not bound by a label, but by moments aligned.
You, my Miami lover, my secret embrace,
in the shadows of Darren, you found your own place.

With a waist so slender, a body so fine,
an accent that lingered, like aged, sweet wine.
Your lips, oh those lips, so full and so right,
could kiss for hours, losing track of the night.

You are the definition of my deepest desire,
the spark in the dark, the flame in the fire.
That night at the Conrad, where it all began,
a love affair etched in the lines of a man.

Inspiration behind "The Night at the Conrad: Meeting Mark"
Emotion: Passion and Longing

This poem stems from a night in Miami, where an unexpected connection blossomed into a long-lasting affair. The setting—a luxurious room at the Conrad Hilton off Brickell Boulevard—served as a backdrop to a moment of vulnerability and desire, where loneliness and the allure of the city intertwined.

The poem captures the anticipation, uncertainty, and eventual connection that unfolded with Mark, a man who became a significant figure in my life. Our encounter, which began with a simple chat on Adam4Adam, quickly evolved into a profound experience, marked by the physical and emotional chemistry that we shared. The act of Mark leaving and returning with dark liquor symbolizes the delicate balance between doubt and commitment, a momentary lapse that ultimately deepened our bond.

Mark, who became my Miami lover, occupied a unique space in my life—one that was both transient and enduring. The physical attributes that attracted me to him, from his slender build to his full lips, are woven into the poem, highlighting the intense physical connection that defined our affair.

The poem is as a tribute to the love we shared, even as it eventually faded into the background with the arrival of Darren, my future husband. The poem is not just about a single night but also about the lasting impact of that connection and how it shaped my understanding of love, desire, and companionship.

From Digital Sparks to Miami Nights

It began with a digital spark,
a chance meeting at the Conrad,
where the city's pulse synced with my own,
and soon, Miami became more than just a place.

I found myself drawn to its embrace,
not just by the sun and sand,
but by the warmth of Mark,
whose presence turned every trip into a dream.

Miami, with its beaches that kissed the sky,
its warmth that melted away the northern cold,
The vibrant streets, the art deco hues,
each visit, a canvas painted with new colors.

But it wasn't just the city,
though its beauty called to me—
the rhythm of the waves,
the allure of its nights,
the dance of its architecture against the sunset.

It was Mark, my island lover,
with his accent like a breeze from Saint Martin.
His touch, a compass guiding me through unknown
streets.
His laughter, the soundtrack to our Miami nights.

We made love as the ocean whispered beneath us,
our bodies wrapped in the warmth of the city's glow.
We'd eat well, nap deep, and lose ourselves in the rhythm,
dancing through the night, our hearts in sync.

Each weekend stretched into magic,
a series of moments where time stood still.
We'd cry when it ended, our hearts heavy with the parting,
but the anticipation of the next rendezvous was sweet.

The thrill of the trip, the rush of the night,
the taste of the city on our lips.

I loved Mark—or so I thought—
but maybe it was the love of it all,
the city, the man, the dream we built.

Miami became my favorite place,
not just for the sun or the sand,
but for the memories we carved
in those magical weekends,
where love seemed as endless as the horizon.

This digital meeting turned into a love affair,
full of excitement, passion, and the unknown.
And though it may have faded,
the echoes of those nights still linger
in every corner of Miami,
where our love was both born and left behind.

Inspiration behind "From Digital Sparks to Miami Nights"
Emotion: Nostalgia

With its vibrant energy and captivating allure, Miami became more than just a favorite destination—it was a backdrop to an equally thrilling and transient relationship. The poem explores how the city's beauty and excitement intertwined with my growing affection for Mark, creating a potent mix of desire, connection, and adventure.

However, the poem is also a cautionary tale about the importance of grounding love in more than just the thrill of the moment. The excitement of travel and the allure of Miami's nights were intoxicating, but they also masked the deeper work that was necessary to sustain and nurture a lasting connection. Mark and I shared many magical weekends, but we failed to engage in the difficult conversations to solidify our bond beyond the immediate gratification of our encounters.

While it's easy to be swept away by feelings and the excitement of new experiences, true love requires more. It demands vulnerability, honesty, and the willingness to dive into deeper conversations that address fears, expectations, and long-term intentions. The allure of a place, the thrill of a trip, and the excitement of a new relationship can be powerful, but they are not substitutes for the foundational work that builds lasting love.

While I loved Miami and the excitement it brought, I also recognize that both Mark and I missed the opportunity to "true up" our connection. We allowed ourselves to be carried by the wave of the moment, rather than anchoring ourselves in the deeper waters of understanding and commitment. This realization is a reminder of the importance of balancing the joy of the present with the necessary work of creating a future that is rooted in more than just the allure of the now.

A Birthday in Miami

When I start to love, my heart is all in.
My love is strong, my love is giving.
It's a love that shines, so obvious, so bright,
and when I fell for Mark, it felt just right.

I was already in love with Miami's charm.
The city's embrace, so warm, no alarm.
So, for his birthday, I made a plan
to spend it with Mark, with friends, hand-in-hand.

We flew to Miami, my best friends and me.
Rented an Airbnb, where laughter flowed free.
Mark, the guide, took us through the night,
showing us the spots where our memories took flight.

He showed my friends the magic we knew,
the places where we danced, where our love grew.
But now, looking back, I see a red flag,
a moment at a club where his temper did snag.

He tried to control how things should unfold,
but I was too young, too blind to be bold.
I brushed it aside, too deep in the thrill,
unaware of the boundary I should have set still.

But my love was strong, my love was pure.
I shopped at Barneys, an experience so sure.
With my AMEX in hand, I searched for his gift,
aging cream he wanted, my spirits did lift.

We dined in the sky, a five-star delight,
eating and laughing, the Miami night.
A moment so funny, my best friend's slip,
talking uncut, the car quieted quick.

And then at the beach, a mix-up so neat,
misheard "nude beach" as "new beach," a treat.
Charmaine laughed, we all joined in,
these memories in Miami, where our love did begin.

Each trip ended with hours so sweet,
passionate kisses, our love complete.
I could just eat him up, my heart on fire.
My friends saw it too, our love's desire.

That trip was memorable, a time so true,
where laughter and love painted skies so blue.
A chapter in Miami, a story of us,
a love that was young, so full of trust.

Inspiration behind "A Birthday in Miami"
Emotion: Affectionate Nostalgia

This poem stems from a vivid memory of a birthday
trip I planned for Mark, a man I was falling deeply in love
with, in Miami, a city I had already grown to adore. The
poem captures the excitement and passion of that time,
when my love for Mark and the allure of Miami
intertwined to create unforgettable moments. I wanted to

share how my love was so strong and giving that I may have overlooked important signs. I planned an elaborate trip, inviting my closest friends to celebrate Mark's birthday, and went out of my way to find him a special gift—aging cream from Barneys in Chicago, an extravagant purchase for someone I cared deeply about.

Looking back, I realize that there were red flags in our relationship that I was too young and inexperienced to recognize. For example, Mark displayed controlling behavior at a club during that trip. I was blinded by love and didn't have the tools or experience to set boundaries or recognize that this behavior needed to be addressed. I brushed it aside, too caught up in the thrill of our connection and the fun of the moment.

When we start to love someone, it's natural to be excited and giving, but it's also important to remain grounded and aware of the dynamics at play. Overlooking red flags or failing to set boundaries can lead to unhealthy patterns in a relationship, where one partner's needs or expectations overshadow the other's. The excitement of new love should not cloud our judgment or prevent us from addressing issues that may arise.

In therapy, I've learned that love isn't just about the thrill and passion—it's also about communication, setting boundaries, and being aware of behaviors that might be problematic. I now understand that it's crucial to recognize red flags early on and to have those necessary conversations that true up the relationship. For anyone reading this, I would encourage you to enjoy the excitement of new love, but also to be mindful of the importance of addressing concerns and setting boundaries. Don't be afraid to have those difficult conversations, as they are essential in building a healthy, lasting connection. The allure of the moment should not come at the expense of long-term emotional well-being.

The Night I Let Go

My Caribbean lover, ten months in,
trips to Miami, where our love would begin.
A long-distance dance, not terrible, not bad,
but leaving you, Mark, always left me so sad.

Tears on the tarmac, on flights back home,
leaving the warmth where our love had grown.
But this time was different, you were coming to me,
a visit to Chicago, where our love could be free.

Excitement built as the days drew near.
Cerynna and Bridgette also planned to appear.
A magical night, under the city's lights,
a limousine, a film crew, reality TV's heights.

An elegant dinner, a boat on the lake,
fireworks above, a night we'd make.
But looking back now, it's clear to see,
without drama or gossip, it wasn't meant to be.

Still, I cherished the night, a spark in the dark,
but another moment was where we'd leave our mark.
I cooked us a meal, candles softly aglow.
The food was divine, but my heart felt the blow.

In the privacy of night, I whispered to you,
three little words, so simple, so true.
But you didn't say them back, and in that silence,
I felt the shift, the fading of our reliance.

"What are we doing?" I questioned in my mind.
In that moment, our love began to unwind.
That was the night I let go of the dream.
We weren't official, just lost in the stream.

Later, we talked, and you confirmed my fear.
That night was the turning point, the change so clear.
It's funny how decisions, each one so small,
can alter life's course, affect it all.

Yes, it led me to Darren, but I'm not glad
that love is now a memory, one that turned sad.
We never know what could've been, what might unfold,
so speak your heart, be brave, be bold.

Leave nothing unsaid, no feelings untold,
for regrets can weigh heavy, and time can be cold.
In the end, we learn, through joy and through pain,
to live with no regrets and, in truth, remain.

Inspiration behind "The Night I Let Go"
Emotion: Heartbreak and Realization

I was in a long-distance relationship with Mark, my
Caribbean lover. Our connection was strong, filled with
passionate visits and emotional goodbyes. I remember the
excitement of his visit to Chicago and the magical night we
spent with friends, surrounded by elegance, laughter, and
the dream of something more.

But amidst the joy, a moment changed everything—
when I told Mark I loved him, and he didn't say it back.
That silence spoke volumes and made me question where
we stood, what we were doing, and what our future held.
It was then that I began to let go of the relationship,
recognizing that we weren't communicating on the same
level, that we hadn't had the important conversations that
could have solidified our bond.

Looking back, I realize that we were both enjoying life
and each other, but we failed to truly connect on a deeper
level. We didn't take the time to learn each other's
communication styles, to understand how to express our
feelings, and to ensure that we were both heard. In
therapy, I've learned the importance of speaking your
mind and your heart, of leaving nothing unsaid.
Communication is the foundation of any relationship, and

it's crucial to make sure that you're not only expressing yourself but also that the other person is truly hearing you.

In this relationship with Mark, we missed that opportunity. It's not that I would have wanted anything to change—I've since been married, divorced, and had various other relationships that have all led me to where I am today. I wouldn't change a thing because life is about living, learning, growing, and pivoting. Every mistake, every trial has brought me to this point, and I'm grateful for the lessons they've taught me.

"The Night I Let Go" is a reminder that while we may look back with a sense of what could have been, it's important to recognize the value of those experiences. They shape who we are, and they teach us the importance of communication, of being present in our relationships, and of making sure that nothing is left on the table. Because in the end, it's through these moments that we learn to live without regrets and continue to grow into the people we are meant to be.

When Darren Called

After I let Mark go,
I started to entertain Darren, slow.
And if I'm being real honest—
no filters, no gloss—
Darren was like Jace,
a ghost from my past
wrapped in everything I wished for,
but couldn't grasp.

He looked like him
until he didn't,
packaged in all I wanted,
a partner that fit.
He was out, independent,
introducing me to his crowd,

a man who wasn't afraid
to love me out loud.

In time, I'd learn in therapy's chair,
what a true partner means,
how to truly care.
But back then, my pattern was clear:
The next had to be what the last one wasn't near.

Darren wasn't Mark—
no fear in his voice,
He wasn't Jace—
no hesitation in his choice.
He was neither and both
in his own unique blend.
My equal in life,
not just a trend.

When Darren called, I picked up the line,
our first date at Bar Louie,
sparked by a cousin's shoe design.
A Louis Vuitton quest led me to a drink,
and soon, Darren was more than a passing link.
We dated heavy, fast and deep,
and in my mind, I knew
Mark and I couldn't keep.

I had to tell him,
but when? How?
A trip to Miami,
work was my cover
to see Mark one last time
before it was over.

Two weeks in the fall,
our final dance,
Using business as a tool
for a last romance.
The first week was easy,
though I felt the weight,
We made love, we laughed,

but something didn't feel straight.

The weekend came,
And I flew away
to New York City,
For Darren's friend's birthday.
Under the skyline's glow,
I asked him to be mine,
and with that, I knew
I had crossed a line.

Back to Miami,
to finish the game,
but on a moonlit beach,
I had to stake my claim.
With tears in my eyes,
I told Mark the truth,
that distance had grown,
and Chicago held my youth.

He looked at me,
with a question so soft,
"I should've said it back,
shouldn't I? Lost in thought."

We didn't dissect it then,
years later, we might.
But I whispered, "Yes,"
and walked into the night.

So that was the end—
or so I thought—
But life, like a moon,
is full of naught.
You never know what could've been,
what paths might have crossed,
so speak your heart,
don't let love be lost.

Leave nothing unsaid,
no feelings on hold,

For, in the end, it's courage
That turns stories to gold.

Inspiration behind "When Darren Called"
Emotion: Transition and Reflection

After I let go of Mark, a relationship that filled my life with passion and excitement, I began entertaining Darren. If I'm being honest, and I mean real honest, Darren reminded me so much of my first true love, Jace. He had the same kind of presence and outward confidence and independence that I had always wished for in Jace. But Darren was different too—he was everything I wanted Jace to be, but wasn't. He was out and independent, introduced me to his family and friends, and wasn't afraid to show the world who we were together.

In those days, I was still figuring out what I needed in a relationship. Therapy and experience had not yet taught me the importance of communication, of knowing what fulfills me beyond the surface level. I was stuck in a pattern: the next person had to be what the last one wasn't. Darren wasn't Mark—he voiced how he felt without hesitation. He wasn't Jace—he showed me the world without fear. He was his own man, my equal, or maybe even more. And when he called, I answered. We began dating, and it felt like a fresh start and a step forward.

But I was still tethered to Mark, emotionally if not physically. I had planned a trip to Miami under the guise of work, using it as an excuse to see Mark one last time before fully committing to Darren. It was easy to fall back into old habits with Mark—making love, laughing, enjoying each other's company—but I knew in my heart that something had changed. That weekend, I flew to New York to be with Darren, and I asked him to be my boyfriend.

Returning to Miami, I realized I had to end things with Mark. During a late-night walk on the beach, under the light of a full moon, I told him we couldn't see each other anymore. I told him I was dating someone in Chicago and that I wanted to go in a different direction. Mark looked at me and asked one simple question: "I should've said it back, shouldn't I?" We didn't talk about it in detail that night, but I whispered, "Yes." I thought that was the end of Mark, but life had other plans.

Looking back, I realize I never fully closed the door on that relationship, and that would later become a problem in my relationship with Darren. Mark never truly left; he lingered in the background, a ghost of what could have been. This experience taught me the importance of closing doors completely—locking them, even—when you're ready to move on. If you don't, those unresolved emotions and connections can come back to haunt you, affecting your new relationships in ways you might not expect.

I didn't know what I really wanted. I was moving through life, making decisions based on what felt good in the moment, what was more fun, what was convenient. I wanted love to be close, to be sure, but I didn't have the words or the experience to articulate what truly fulfilled me. I didn't know how to communicate my needs, and as a result, I found myself in situations that were complicated and unresolved.

Even now, with more communication skills and a better understanding of myself, it's easy to fall into the trap of making decisions based on what feels good at the moment. We all want to avoid pain, to seek out comfort and joy, but the challenge is to balance those immediate desires with long-term fulfillment.

Take the time to really understand what you want and need in a relationship. Don't be afraid to speak your heart and communicate openly with your partner. And when it's time to move on, make sure you close that door fully—lock it, even—so that you can give your new relationship the attention and energy it deserves. It's not just about what feels good right now; it's about building something lasting, something real, and that requires clear intentions, honest communication, and the courage to let go of what no longer serves you.

A Love Affair That Lingered

For my birthday, the tension in my chest,
Darren and I, already facing our tests.
Marriage problems brewing, infidelity's sting,
his hands on the apps, the lies he would bring.

Permission granted, to Miami I'd fly.
Called up Charmaine, my partner in crime.
She said, "Sure, let's do this right."
We stayed at the Marriott, under the city's light.

"Baking soda, I got baking soda,"
the lyrics that set the weekend's quota.
Coco on repeat, Mark's jam.
The anthem of our weekend, and damn—

He came right away when I called.
Our connection, magnetic, always enthralled.
He took us out, showed us the town,
made my birthday a night to drown.

In fun, in laughter, in old flames rekindled,
the love affair that never dwindled.
Charmaine asleep, Mark and I,
on the balcony beneath the Miami sky.

There was something about us, animalistic and raw,
a pull so strong it broke every law.
Of loyalty, of faith, of vows made in vain,
but in that moment, I felt no shame.

It wasn't the first time, wouldn't be the last,
sneaking away, leaving the past.

On a family trip with Darren and his mom,
I slipped away, to Mark's calm.

We met up, did what we always did,
shared a secret that neither could rid.
Another time, with my mom in tow,
I found myself in Mark's glow.

Couldn't get him out of my system,
blamed the cracks in my marriage's prism.
Darren's betrayals, the sex that was lacking,
justified my affair, no guilt in backing.

He wasn't just anyone, Mark was more,
a love that existed long before.
Before the apps, before Darren's games,
in my mind, it was different, not the same.

I told myself it was necessary, a need,
a flame that Darren's actions would feed.
I slept fine at night, with that excuse in hand,
and reveled in the moments we had planned.

That birthday, that weekend, I enjoyed every bit,
the laughter, the love, the fire we lit.
Eight years of a lingering affair,
in Mark's arms, I found what was fair.

So here's to the love that never quite ended,
a connection too strong, too deep to be mended.
A story of lust, of love, of sin,
a tale of what was, and what could have been.

Inspiration behind "A Love Affair That Lingered"
Emotion: Conflicted

This poem comes from a chapter in my life where the
lines between right and wrong, love and desire, blurred.
My marriage to Darren was already facing significant
challenges. Infidelity had crept in almost immediately—

Darren's inability to stay off gay dating apps, his inappropriate conversations with others, and the way he gaslighted me, calling it his form of "porn." On top of that, our intimacy was strained. I wanted more than what I was getting—more connection, more frequency, more satisfaction. It was 60/40 at best, and that imbalance left me feeling unfulfilled.

When the opportunity to go to Miami for my birthday came up, I took it, not knowing what I would do, but feeling the pull of the city and the memories of Mark. I called Charmaine, my best friend, and we planned a fun, carefree weekend. We stayed at a nice Marriott, and the weekend's theme became "I'm in love with the COCO!"— a song that Mark introduced to us. Mark had already met Charmaine, and when I told him I was coming, he immediately joined us. He showed us a great time, taking us out, celebrating my birthday in the way only he could.

But it wasn't just about the fun. There was something primal, something irresistible about my connection with Mark. We were drawn to each other like magnets, and that weekend, while Charmaine slept, Mark and I made love on the balcony. It was a moment that reignited our lingering love affair—one that would stretch over eight years. Even during later trips with Darren or my family, I found ways to sneak off and meet Mark. The lack of fulfillment in my marriage, Darren's infidelity, and the issues with our sexual connection all became excuses for me to continue the affair. I told myself it was necessary, that it wasn't the same as Darren's betrayals because Mark had been there before. I convinced myself that I wasn't really cheating, that it was different, and I slept fine at night with that lie.

One quote that encapsulates the theme of this story is: **"The most dangerous lies are the ones we tell ourselves to justify the things we know are wrong."** In therapy, I've learned that we often create narratives to avoid feeling bad, to sidestep guilt, and to continue doing what feels good in the moment. But those narratives can keep us stuck in patterns that ultimately harm us and our relationships. We can lie to ourselves to make the present more bearable, but those lies can catch up with us.

What I want readers to learn from my experience is the importance of honesty—first with yourself, and then with others. In relationships, communication is key, and if something is lacking, it needs to be addressed head-on, not avoided or replaced with something else. Therapy has taught me that true fulfillment comes from within, and it's essential to confront the issues in your relationship directly rather than seeking comfort elsewhere. If you find yourself justifying actions that don't align with your values, it's a sign to pause, reflect, and consider what you really want and need.

I've come to understand the importance of being raw and honest with yourself. Opening up—whether through writing, speaking with a therapist, or simply acknowledging your own feelings—can help you realign with your values and learn from your mistakes. Understand why you do what you do so you can grow and improve upon yourself. We all make mistakes, but those mistakes don't have to define who we are. If you have the capacity to change and grow, then you are not the same person in the future as you were in that moment of error. You were simply in the wrong situation, perhaps with the wrong partner, and it's from those moments that you can learn and evolve.

One of the biggest lessons I've taken from this experience is the importance of closing doors on the past completely. It's easy to be drawn back into old patterns, especially when they offer comfort or familiarity. But to truly move forward, you have to make a clean break—lock that door and focus on what lies ahead. Don't let the past linger and affect your future relationships. Learn from your mistakes, understand what you need and want, and don't repeat the same behaviors with a new partner. Growth is about making those changes, evolving beyond who you were, and becoming a better version of yourself.

Two Lovers

In New Orleans, under a Southern sky,
Mark and I, no questions of why.
Creole flavors on our tongues,
jazz in the air, where the city's song is sung.
The Marriott's sheets, our playground once more,
animalistic pull, a love to explore.

But the timeline blurs, affairs and life,
juggling Mark and Darren, a husband and a wife.
The year blends into another,
when Christmas came, we headed south
to Miami's warmth, where the truth would slither out.

Mark invited us to his Christmas cheer.
I hesitated, but we went, no fear.
By then, our marriage was open, a tangled thread,
Darren knew, though nothing was said.

At Mark's party, the room hummed with light,
and everyone saw how our eyes ignited the night.
Even Darren couldn't ignore what was clear,
the love that lingered, the pull so near.
I wasn't trying to show it, but there it was,
that magnetic force, like the buzz of a bee's cause.

No sex this time, though temptation ran deep.
Mark looked so good, I could barely keep
myself from taking him right there in the crowd,
but I played it cool, didn't want to be too loud.

Then Darren, with a drink in hand,
Showed the red flags of a crumbling man.
He got so drunk, broke a glass in a rage,
offended Mark's house, turned the page
on a night that started off fine,
but ended with me dragging him, drunk, back to mine.

It was good seeing Mark, though strange to mix
two lovers, one past, one current, in the same fix.

We even snapped a selfie, the three of us there,
posted it online, reactions to spare.
Followers who knew both, their comments so sly,
but I just leaned into it, not asking why.

These are the situations I've found through the years.
Lovers entwined between laughter and tears.
I wouldn't change it, not the good, not the bad.
The night was fun, until it wasn't, until it got sad.

But you never know how things will unfold,
So, I leaned into it, let the story be told.
Two lovers in the same space,
a tangled web, a complicated embrace.

Inspiration behind "Two Lovers"
Emotion: Entangled

Mark and Darren, two significant figures in my life, found themselves in the same space, leading to surreal and revealing situations.

It all started with a trip to New Orleans, where Mark and I continued our long-standing love affair. Our connection was undeniable—eating Creole food, vibing to jazz, and making love in the comfort of hotel sheets. It was another chapter in our ongoing, almost magnetic relationship. But life with Darren, my husband, was complicated. By this time, we were already facing problems in our marriage, including Darren's infidelity, his struggles with staying off gay dating apps, and our intimacy issues. When Mark invited us to his Christmas gathering in Miami, I hesitated, but we went anyway. At that point, Darren and I had transitioned into an open marriage, another layer of complexity in our relationship.

The party was a strange experience—having two lovers in the same room, feeling the tension and the undeniable pull between Mark and me. Everyone noticed it, even Darren. It was an odd mix of emotions, trying to balance the past with the present. But then, Darren's alcoholism reared its head. He got so drunk that night, offending Mark's friends, breaking a glass, and ultimately turning what started as a good time into a mess that I had to manage.

I realize how naïve I was—and maybe, how I can still be. It was a mistake to bring my two lovers into the same space and to think that I could navigate that situation without consequences. It seems obvious in hindsight, but I was too caught up in the moment to see it clearly. This experience is something I've added to my therapy self-growth list, a reminder to be more mindful of the choices I make and the situations I put myself in.

It's probably best not to mix your past and present lovers. The complexities and emotions can lead to unexpected outcomes, ones that are difficult to manage and can hurt everyone involved. In therapy, I've been working on understanding my patterns, recognizing when I'm being naïve, and making better decisions moving forward. We all have moments where we don't see the full picture, but the key is to learn from those moments, grow, and become better versions of ourselves.

The Fork in the Road: A Poem on Decisions and Destiny

In the eye of a storm, Mark flew north,
from Miami's wrath to Detroit's embrace.
A hurricane's fury, a twist of fate,
a moment where life's paths diverged.

He turned me off with his brash demeanor,
a weekend of friction, emotions frayed.
Crying over Darren, my heart in shreds,
his insensitivity like salt on wounds.

At Toya's house, the games were soured.
Friends met with annoyance, not camaraderie.
It wasn't all bad, but mostly it was,

and when he left, I let him go.

Chicago called, with Brandon's smile,
not yet deep, but something more.
Two weeks later, Cancun's sun,
a new beginning, love unfurled.

That choice, to lean into Brandon,
led me to Mexico's vibrant lands.
A house in San Diego, an Airbnb,
security in retirement, a home once more.

What if I'd stayed with Mr. Miami
through pandemic's isolation, who knows?
A different story, a different life,
but I don't dwell on might-have-beens.

I'm happy with the lessons learned,
the road I've walked, the things I've gained.
The growth, the therapy, no regrets,
that fork in the road was mine to take.

Small decisions, a pivot, a turn,
can change your story, shape who you become.
In that moment, I chose my path,
and it led me here, where I belong.

Explanation behind "The Fork in the Road: A Poem on Decisions and Destiny"
Emotion: Reflective

This poem reflects on a significant moment when a seemingly small decision drastically altered my life's course. It begins with Mark coming to Detroit from Miami due to a hurricane. His visit was marred by his insensitivity and our lack of connection during a time when I was emotionally vulnerable due to my ongoing divorce and feelings for Darren. His behavior during our weekend together, particularly at a game night with friends, was disappointing and led to our drifting apart.

After Mark returned to Miami, I spent time with Brandon in Chicago. Although our relationship was not yet deep, our trip to Cancun two weeks later marked the true beginning of our bond. Focusing on my relationship with Brandon shaped my future. It led to frequent travels to Mexico City, the purchase of a home in San Diego, and the creation of an Airbnb that provided both financial security and a sense of home.

The poem contemplates the alternate path I might have taken had I continued with Mark, especially during the pandemic lockdown. However, I don't dwell on these potential outcomes because I am content with the lessons I've learned, the experiences I've had, and the personal growth I've achieved. Seemingly small decisions can profoundly impact one's life trajectory, ultimately leading to fulfillment and happiness without regrets.

Darren

Emotion: Heartache and Personal Growth

In the "Darren" chapter, I reflect on the final chapter of our relationship, capturing both the beauty and the pain that defined our journey together. From our marriage in the heart of Chicago to our dissolution in Cook County, these poems navigate the highs and lows of our love story. This chapter delves into the emotional complexities of separation, the weight of shared dreams, and the bittersweet memories of our time together. From grand trips through Europe to intimate evenings over cocktails, each poem reflects the evolution of our relationship, marked by moments of joy, sacrifice, and, eventually, loss. Through the dissolution of our marriage and the therapeutic journey that accompanied it, I examine how love transforms, unravels, and ultimately teaches us about ourselves. This chapter not only closes the book on our relationship but also serves as a reflection on the lessons learned, the love shared, and the person I've become as I move forward, guided by the peace I've found in choosing myself.

Cocktails and Beginnings

We met in the shadows of the digital age,
where connections flicker and fade.
An exchange of numbers, forgotten names,
but fate had plans beyond the screen's frame.

A year later, a text from the past,
a Chicago number, a connection cast.
"What's up?" it read, simple, unplanned,
yet the voice behind it felt close at hand.

I didn't save your number, didn't recall your face,
but something familiar hung in the space.
You echoed, "Let's get a cocktail," not once, but more,
until one weary evening, I opened that door.

I had driven to Michigan, miles on my soul,
to gift my cousin, but it took its toll.
Tired and stressed, I needed a break,
and there was your offer, for a cocktail's sake.

We met at Bar Louie, where the city hums.
Lemon drop martinis, the night begun.
We talked, we laughed, it all felt right.
Our shared Detroit roots lit up the night.

Similar schools, similar streets,
our lives intertwined in unexpected beats.
Your friends were mine, the ties ran deep,
but in hindsight, there was something I'd keep.

The talk of cocktails, frequent, unmissed.
A red flag waved, but I'd never been kissed
by the knowledge of what addiction could be.
I was blind to the clues right in front of me.

What started with a drink, so easy, so light,
would later reveal shadows in the night.
But for now, it was just the beginning
of a story unfolding, of losses and winning.

In that moment, we were two souls
finding comfort in shared goals.
But the cocktails we toasted, carefree and wild,
held secrets that would later be reconciled.

Looking back, I see it clear,
the signs I missed, the hidden fear.
But for now, it was a night of firsts,
a cocktail, a meeting, and the start of thirsts.

Inspiration behind "Cocktails and Beginnings"
Emotion: Nostalgic

The connection and relationship between Darren and I began with a simple text and an invitation for a cocktail. Reflecting on that time, it's clear to me now that there were subtle signs—red flags—that I wasn't equipped to recognize back then.

We initially met online, a fleeting connection that I didn't pay much attention to. I wasn't fully comfortable with the gay online forums, as they often seemed geared more toward hookups than genuine connections. I closed my account, and with it, I thought, closed the door on that chapter. But somehow, Darren still had my number, and almost a year later, he reached out to me again. It was just a simple "What's up?" from a Chicago number, but I didn't realize then that Darren was actually in Detroit, reaching out because of my Detroit number.

His message was persistent, almost insistent: "Let's get a cocktail." It seemed like an easy and casual way to reconnect. I didn't think much of it—after all, who doesn't enjoy a drink after a long day? But in hindsight, I see that this repeated suggestion and focus on meeting over drinks, could have been a red flag. I was naive to the signs of alcohol dependency then, but now I understand that for some, alcohol can be more than just a social lubricant; it can be a crutch, a way to cope, or even a mask for deeper issues.

That night, after a long, exhausting day of driving to Michigan and back, I found myself in need of a break. Darren's offer of a cocktail came to mind, and I finally took him up on it. We met at Bar Louie in downtown Chicago, shared lemon drop martinis, and instantly connected. Everything felt familiar and easy, like we were on the same wavelength. We had so much in common—our Detroit roots, similar schools, and overlapping friend circles. It felt like a natural beginning, but I now realize that the foundation of our meeting was built on something I didn't fully understand.

In relationships, red flags like a constant focus on alcohol can often be overlooked, especially when everything else seems to align so well. Common phrases like "Let's grab a drink" or "We should meet for cocktails" can be harmless, but when repeated consistently, they can also be signs of someone who is alcohol-dependent. I didn't see it then, but now I know to pay attention to those patterns.

This poem was born out of the understanding that what seems like an innocent beginning can sometimes be tinged with signs we're not yet ready to see. We shared good moments, but there were also underlying issues from the very first toast.

Law School Planning

We sat at the table with dreams in hand,
you with a heart full of justice, a mind so grand.
Kent Law whispered your name, a beacon so bright.
I saw the fire in your eyes, the future in your sight.

Through the lists and courses, each step mapped with care.
From Criminal Law to Torts, you were ready to dare.
Every class, every credit, a brick in the road,
as you built a path where your passion flowed.

I watched you navigate the twists and turns.
Supported you in decisions, in the lessons you'd learn.
With every form you filled, every school you declined,
I stood by your side, knowing you'd find
the place where your purpose would finally align.

Tulane tempted, but Kent was the one
where your journey in law had truly begun.
You poured over contracts wrote with precision.
I saw you grow, with each new decision.

The excitement in your voice, the light in your stride.
I was there through it all, beaming with pride.
From Legal Writing to Civil Procedure,
every late-night study, I was your believer.

Financial support was my gift, no strings to bind.
Just the joy of seeing you excel, your future defined.
You tackled Employment Law, crossed hurdles with grace,
determined to win, to claim your rightful place.

Now, as you stand with that Kent Law degree,
know my support was the foundation, the key.
For every moment spent, every dollar invested
was in faith, love, and the dreams you manifested.

Your name on the roster, your goals set so high,
I knew you'd reach them, with a determined sigh.
And now, as you step into the world, so vast,
know my pride in you is something that will forever last.

For in your success, I see our shared dream,
a journey we took, hand in hand, like a well-woven seam.
So go, my love, let your legal path shine,
knowing that forever, your victories are mine.

Dear Darren,

With joy, I pen these words to you.
Accepted now, your dreams break through.
Chicago-Kent, the path you'll tread.
A scholar's journey lies ahead.

Your merits, bright, like stars they shine.
A scholarship—proof of the climb.
Fifteen thousand each year to hold.
No strings attached, no GPA to mold.

Four years, they say, this gift is yours,
to walk through law's demanding doors.
No burden placed upon your name,
just promise of your future fame.

And as you ponder what's to come,
know that your strength won't be undone.
For in these halls of justice, tall,
you'll rise above, you'll stand, you'll call.

The road is clear, the way is set.
In this new life, no room for regret.
We hope to see you in the fall,
to watch you conquer, give your all.

So take this letter as a sign
of all the greatness yet to find.

With every step, a world awaits
in the Windy City beyond the gates.

Best Regards,
From those who see
the lawyer, the leader
that you will be.

Support Through Law School

In those early years, I wore many hats,
a career chameleon, shifting through paths,
From one role to another, seeking the light,
chasing the dawn, for dreams felt so right.
US Foods to FINRA, the journey was long,
but each step I took, I made you strong.

When law school began, you took up the fight,
and I became your anchor, your guiding light.
Built businesses with hands that wouldn't tire,
Mac Neal LLC, a venture of fire.
Taxes, travel, and deals in real estate,
all woven together, securing our fate.

Hustling through chaos, I carved out the way,
so you could focus on your long school day.
We built a house, not just with stone,
but with dreams and ambitions, deeply sown.
Every corner furnished, each room a dream,
a fortress of love, or so it did seem.

The debts we cleared, the plans we made,
A future written, where success played.
I gave you space to learn, to grow,
and in that time, my love did flow.
You passed the bar, you took your stand.
With top-paying work, our future was grand.

But shadows lingered in the gleam,
for what I gave was more than a dream.

Undervalued, unseen, my efforts stood
as love's tender pulse turned to wood.
Jealousy brewed like a hidden storm,
and alcohol's grip began to deform.

The logic was sound, the numbers aligned,
But in the math of love, something declined.
Communication, broken, failed the test,
and love, once pure, laid to rest.
We rode on reason, on paper's grace,
but love lost its tender place.

The truth I now accept, though bittersweet,
that support alone couldn't make us complete.
For in the waves of life, logic can't mend
what love and vulnerability blend.
The house we built, the dreams we sought
were symbols of strength, but love was fought.

In the end, I found the truth inside
that even the strongest dreams can divide.
But from this journey, I've learned and grown,
and in that, a deeper love has shown.
For now, I know love must be free,
not bound by logic, but by vulnerability.

Inspiration behind "Support Through Law School Series"

Emotion: Bittersweet Reflection

The "Support Through Law School Series" is a deeply personal reflection on the journey Darren and I undertook together, beginning even before he was accepted into law school. This series of poems, including "Dear Darren," "Law School Planning," and "Support Through Law School," chronicles the unwavering commitment, love, and partnership that guided us through this challenging but rewarding chapter of our lives.

When Darren first expressed his desire to attend law school, I didn't just see it as his dream—I saw it as ours. From the moment we sat down to plan his path, I was all in. We meticulously reviewed every potential school, considered every course, and weighed every decision together. It wasn't just about finding the right school; it was about laying the groundwork for a future that we would build together. Kent Law ultimately stood out as the perfect fit, and the moment he received that acceptance letter, it felt like the culmination of all our hard work and planning.

"Law School Planning" captures the essence of those early days—the excitement, the anticipation, and the deep sense of purpose that drove us. Every decision, from choosing schools to mapping out his coursework, was made with careful consideration and love. I wanted Darren to have the best possible start, and I was determined to support him every step of the way. This poem is a tribute to that planning phase, where we envisioned the life we were about to embark on together.

"Dear Darren" marks the beginning of his formal journey into law, capturing the moment when his hard work and our shared efforts were recognized and rewarded. The scholarship he received was a testament to his academic potential, and it solidified our belief that we were on the right path. This acceptance wasn't just an achievement for Darren—it was a validation of everything we had worked toward together.

"Support Through Law School" reflects the years that followed, where I took on the role of provider and cheerleader. I supported us financially so that Darren could focus on his studies, clerkships, and gaining the experience he needed to succeed. It wasn't always easy, but it was a labor of love. I juggled multiple jobs, started businesses, and planned our future, all while ensuring that Darren had the space and resources to thrive in law school. This poem is about the sacrifices and the joy that came

from seeing him grow, excel, and eventually achieve his
goal of becoming a lawyer.

But beyond the practical support, this series is about the
emotional journey we shared. It's about the strength of our
partnership, the way we navigated challenges together,
and the deep love that underpinned everything we did.
Even as our relationship evolved and eventually ended,
the foundation of love, commitment, and shared dreams
remained a central part of our story.

As I reflect on this journey, I realize that the "Support
Through Law School Series" is not just a recounting of
events but a celebration of the power of partnership. It's
about what we can achieve when we believe in each other,
when we support each other unconditionally, and when
we work together to make our dreams a reality. Although
our love didn't last forever, the legacy of what we built
together—both in our relationship and in Darren's law
career—continues to resonate.

This series is a testament to the importance of
communication, shared goals, and the willingness to invest
in each other's success. It's a reminder that love is not just
about the good times but also about the work, sacrifice,
and dedication that goes into building a life together. Even
though our paths have diverged, I'm proud of the journey
we took and the dreams we realized along the way.

The Proposal

I spun it all from whispers of light,
each detail a thread in the loom of the night.
Weeks of labor, crafting our tale,
stitching moments where love would prevail.

A scrapbook thick with the gravity of time,
our story pressed in ink and rhyme.
I sifted through memories, text-by-text,

binding our laughter, our love, perplexed.
Pages breathing with our past's embrace,
pictures and words, woven in grace.

A CD tucked in, not just a song,
but the pulse of us, carrying along.
Earth, Wind & Fire as our witness to fate.
The universe listened, aligning the date.
A soundtrack synced to the rhythm we set,
each beat falling where the sun hadn't yet.

Dinner shimmered, soft under flame.
Flowers like whispers, calling his name.
The air stood still, waiting for the mark.
Everything quiet, love sparked in the dark.

He followed the pages, tracing our thread.
Each moment stitched tight, every word we'd said.
And when the music swelled to its peak,
I knelt with my heart, my soul left to speak.

"Will you be mine?" I asked with the sky.
The ring, a constellation, caught in his eye.
White diamonds laced with violet's hue,
a galaxy bound to the story of two.

He said yes, and the stars seemed to bloom.
The room stretched open, wider than the room.
Our vows floated, tethered by grace.
Two hearts entwined in sacred space.

The night was a sonnet, the air turned sweet.
Time bent gently beneath our feet.
Though the ring's meaning may blur in the years,
our love stays sharp, undimmed by fears.

The perfect evening, the stars in tune.
Two souls swayed to the rhythm of the moon

Inspiration behind "The Proposal"
Emotion: Anticipation with Fulfillment

I wanted to create a detailed and personal proposal that reflected the depth of my love for Darren, the journey we had taken, and the future I hoped we would build together. The process of putting the proposal together was laborious, but it was also incredibly fulfilling. Every part of it was designed to remind Darren of the special moments we shared, from our first date to the life we had created together.

The scrapbook was a monumental task, but one that I threw myself into wholeheartedly. I bought an app that let me extract every single text message we had exchanged. I spent hours poring over those messages, selecting the ones that held the most meaning, and placing them next to photos that captured that exact moment in time. I was creating a tangible manifestation of our love story that would remind him of every step we had taken together. Each page was carefully crafted, leading us chronologically through our shared journey, and it took weeks of effort to get it just right.

The music also brought the proposal to life. I created a CD of songs that represented different moments in our relationship, synchronizing them with the pages of the scrapbook. Each song reflected the emotions and experiences tied to those memories. For example, The Earth, Wind & Fire concert we attended was marked by their music, and every page of that scrapbook had its own melody. I even designed the CD cover with a photo of us and the proposal ring.

On the day of the proposal, everything seemed to align perfectly. It was as if we were inside a 90s rom-com, with even the music syncing with the mood of each moment. The soundtrack that I had put together flowed effortlessly through the evening, timed so well that it felt like it was guiding us through the proposal, rather than the other way around. It was almost otherworldly how seamlessly everything fell into place.

I had already spoken with the women in Darren's life—his mom, aunt, and grandmother—to ask for their blessing. They had all seen the scrapbook and gave their support, which made the moment even more special. That night, I had prepared an exquisite dinner, and every detail, from the lighting to the flowers, was intentionally curated to create the perfect atmosphere. The proposal itself felt like a culmination of all our moments together—the beauty, the laughter, the struggles, and the love.

When Darren reached the last page of the scrapbook and the proposal song started to play, I got down on one knee and asked him to be my husband. I told him why I wanted to spend my life with him, why he was my person, and why this moment mattered so much. The ring I gave him was unique, featuring both white and purple diamonds. The purple held a significance I can't fully recall now, but at the time, it was deeply meaningful to both of us.

Everything about that evening went more smoothly than I could have hoped. It was beautiful, and Darren said yes. The proposal symbolized how much effort, thought, and emotion I put into our relationship. It was the embodiment of my meticulous nature, my desire to make everything perfect, and the love I had for him that transcended the everyday moments.

The love, the partnership, and the shared history we had built were all wrapped up in that one perfect evening. It's a moment I will always treasure, not just for the outcome, but for the incredible care and love that went into planning it.

4435 S Indiana Series

4435 S Indiana: The House We Built

In the heart of our dreams, we laid down our plans,
two souls entwined, with blueprints in hand.
Darren and I, with visions so grand,
constructing a future, a love so well-planned.

From Hyde Park's embrace, we chased the skyline,
but downtown's allure wasn't truly divine.
We shifted our sights, found a new space,
a high-rise in the Loop, but it wasn't our place.

So we downsized to save, to build from the ground
a one-bedroom pause until our dream home was found.
A chance meeting with Jacob, our builder, our guide,
locked in a deal, and our hopes opened wide.

Day by day, I watched as our vision took flight,
brick-by-brick, rising in the fading light.
My heart leaped with each beam set in place.
This was our future, our dream to embrace.

4435 S Indiana, where our love took form,
a fortress we built to weather any storm.
Not just walls, but a testament of will,
a reflection of dreams, a space to fulfill.

We furnished it quickly, as if time stood still,
each room, a canvas, our passion to distill.
The housewarming echoed with laughter and cheer,
a celebration of us, of what we held dear.

But this wasn't just stone, or wood, or glass.
It was the life we envisioned, a love meant to last.
My name on the deed, yet our hearts intertwined.
In this space, we were both wholly defined.

Neighbors became friends, their dreams mirrored ours.

Together, we rose like twin shining stars.
4435 S Indiana wasn't just where we dwelled.
It was the dream we constructed, where our love excelled.

A testament to labor, to love, to ambition.
A symbol of a future, of shared vision and mission.
In those walls lived our hopes, our trials, our plans,
a home built with love by our own hands.

A Celebration of Dreams

In the heart of Chicago, where our dreams took root,
we built a home, brick-by-brick, truth-by-truth.
A place where love could flourish, and futures unfold,
4435 S Indiana, a story of bold.

The walls rose high, each beam a promise,
a future we shaped, no longer ominous.
From empty rooms to spaces filled with grace,
we turned this house into our sacred place.

And when the time came, with the keys in hand,
we decorated swiftly, as if by command.
Overnight, it became our sanctuary,
a home, a haven, a love legendary.

Then came the day, a convergence of pride,
a housewarming, a graduation, side by side.
Over 100 souls from near and far
gathered to celebrate under the same star.

Family drove in from Detroit's embrace.
Friends gathered, joy lighting every face.
The air was thick with love's sweet perfume,
as laughter echoed through every room.

Special invitations sent with care,
reflected the dual celebration we'd share.
Cupcakes adorned with little tributes, sweet,

a nod to milestones, a taste of dreams complete.

The day was beautiful, a perfect blend
of love, of support, of hearts to mend.
It wasn't just a house or a degree earned.
It was a life together, a page turned.

In every corner, the warmth was felt,
the life we constructed, the hand we were dealt.
It was a day where all things converged.
Our home, our love, our future emerged.

And as the sun set on that glorious day,
with hearts full, we looked ahead to the way.
A path we'd walk hand-in-hand,
building a life just as we'd planned.

4435 S Indiana, more than a place.
It's where we found our love, our grace.
A home, a dream, a future bright,
celebrated that day under soft evening light.

Inspiration behind "4435 S Indiana Series"
Emotion: Nostalgic Pride

Darren and I embarked on a journey that began with shared dreams and culminated in the construction of what I once believed would be our forever home. The poems in this series—"A Celebration of Dreams" and "4435 S Indiana: The House We Built"—reflect the love, hard work, and dedication that went into building our life together.

When Darren and I first met, we were two driven individuals with big dreams. We envisioned homeownership, businesses, and a life filled with success and comfort. We saw ourselves as a power couple in the making, and we set out to make those dreams a reality.

Our life together began in a beautiful condo in Hyde Park, but Darren had bigger aspirations. He wanted the vibrancy of downtown living, so we moved closer to the Sears Tower, trying to capture the energy of the city. When that didn't feel right, we relocated to a high-rise near Printers Row. But even then, something was missing—a sense of permanence and of truly building something together.

That's when we decided to cut our rent in half, save aggressively, and buy a home. This decision led me to Jacob, a builder who offered us the perfect opportunity. I met with him, negotiated the terms, and locked in a deal for a brand new 3,500-square-foot home at 4435 S Indiana. Building a home was exhilarating, but it was more than just excitement—it was pride. I was proud that I could make this dream a reality, with my name on the contract, my credit securing the loan, and my salary paying the mortgage.

As the house took shape, I became deeply invested in the process. Every day after work, I would drive to the construction site, taking pictures and imagining the life we would live in this space. It wasn't just a house; it was the physical manifestation of our commitment, our shared dreams, and the future we were building together.

The completion of the house aligned perfectly with Darren's last year of law school. We moved in and, in true fashion, had the entire place furnished almost overnight, transforming it into a warm and welcoming home. Our relentless pursuit of our goals was something I loved about us—we made things happen, often sacrificing sleep and comfort, but always with the belief that it was worth it.

To celebrate, we hosted a combined housewarming and graduation party, inviting over 100 friends and family members. It was a beautiful day, filled with love, support, and accomplishment. Family drove in from Detroit, friends gathered from all over, and the joy in the air that reflected

the significance of what we had built together. The special
invitations we made, the cupcakes commemorating the
occasion—everything was a tribute to the journey we had
undertaken.

The poems in the "4435 S Indiana Series" are not just
about a house or a celebration—they're about the journey
of realizing our dreams together. "A Celebration of
Dreams" reflects on the culmination of our hard work and
shared goals, while "4435 S Indiana: The House We Built"
delves into the emotions, challenges, and triumphs that
came with building our future.

While Darren and I are no longer together, this series
captures what we achieved during that time. 4435 S
Indiana was more than just an address; it was a testament
to our partnership, our ability to dream, and our
determination to make those dreams a reality. It is a
symbol of what love and dedication can accomplish, even
if the love itself did not last. The house represents the
strength and commitment we had in pursuing our shared
vision, a reminder that dreams do come true when you put
in the work and effort.

Though the love that helped build that home did not
endure, the lessons and the journey remain. This series
honors that journey, acknowledging the power of
partnership and the belief that with love and hard work,
we can achieve great things—even if the path eventually
leads us in different directions.

The Graduation Trip

We packed our dreams into a suitcase,
a journey through Europe, eighteen countries, thirty days.
A graduation gift, a gap between what was and what
would be,
I planned each moment, each stop on our spree.

From Chicago's hum to Brussels' cobblestone streets,
we wandered through cities where history meets.
Luxembourg's quiet charm, Copenhagen's sleek lines,
we sipped wine in Vienna beneath ancient designs.

This trip wasn't just a break, it was a bridge,
A passage between student life and the edge
of a world waiting for him, a world he'd soon claim,
but for now, it was ours, every street, every lane.

We mapped our way through castles and squares,
sipped on espresso without a care.
Each destination was a step closer to who he'd become,
but also a testament to what we had done.

The laughter in Warsaw, the quiet in Prague,
each moment was vivid, each night was long.
But it wasn't just the places that made it grand.
It was the freedom, the bond, hand-in-hand.

I took a leave, unpaid and unplanned,
but it was worth every penny, every grain of sand.
Because this was more than a trip, it was a dream,
a final hurrah before life's steady stream.

But beyond the itineraries and the detailed charts,
it was a gift from my heart to his heart.
A hope that we'd have many more days like these,
where the world was ours to explore with ease.

This journey was more than cities and sights,
it was a testament to love, to long nights.
To the sacrifice of time, of earnings set aside,
all for the memories, for the pride.

And though life has moved on, and things have changed,
that trip remains, in my heart, forever framed.
A moment of pure joy, of dreams unfurled,
in the corners of Europe, we discovered our world.

Inspiration behind "The Graduation Trip"
Emotion: Joyful Nostalgia

One of the most memorable and meaningful experiences I've ever had was planning and embarking on a 18-country, 30-day Euro trip as a graduation gift for Darren. This trip wasn't just a vacation; it was a bridge between the life we had known and the one we were about to step into. Darren had just finished law school, and while we couldn't afford the luxury of a year off, I wanted to give him something special, a moment to breathe before diving into the demands of his career.

I meticulously planned every detail of this trip, putting in weeks of research, mapping out each destination, booking flights, finding hotels, and creating itineraries that would allow us to experience the very best of Europe. Every day was planned down to the hour—where we'd eat, what sights we'd see, and how we'd get there. In addition to seeing as many countries as we could, I wanted to make Darren feel celebrated and appreciated for all the hard work he had put in to get to this point.

This trip also came at a personal cost to me. I didn't have the luxury of taking a paid vacation, so I had to take a leave of absence without pay. The financial sacrifice was significant, and there were moments when I wondered if it was the right decision. But deep down, I knew it was. This trip was a once-in-a-lifetime experience that would stay with us forever and I wanted to share it with Darren.

We started in Brussels, a city rich with history and charm, and from there, we explored the heart of Europe. Luxembourg, Denmark, Poland, Slovakia, Austria, Hungary, Romania, Bulgaria, Serbia, Switzerland, Germany, and Iceland. I still remember the laughter we shared, the awe we felt standing in front of centuries-old architecture, and the joy of simply being together in new, unfamiliar places.

What made this trip even more special was the fact that
it was just for us. It was a celebration of Darren's
accomplishments, a tribute to our relationship, and a
testament to the life we were building together. I poured
so much of myself into this trip—my time, my energy, my
love. It was an expression of everything I felt for him and a
way to show him how much I believed in him and in us.

As we traveled from city to city, I felt a deep sense of
fulfillment. I knew this was the right decision, despite the
cost and the sacrifices. This trip was the culmination of
years of hard work, not just for Darren but for both of us. It
was a moment of pure joy, where we could forget about
the stresses of life and just be present with each other.

This trip represents so much more than just the places
we visited. It's a reminder of what we were able to achieve
together, of the love and dedication that went into every
step of our journey. It's a chapter in our story that I'll
always cherish, a time when we were truly at our best,
exploring the world with nothing but excitement and hope
for the future.

When I Bought a Bike

It started with a bike.
An $800 decision
for my health, for my wallet,
for the peace of a ride to work,
pedaling freedom through the streets,
saving dollars on Uber fares.
A simple choice,
but it spiraled into something else.

April 2019,
the beginning of the end.
We'd gone from harmony to friction,
from quiet evenings to monthly arguments,
and by the spring,
the shouting was weekly—

fueled by alcohol,
fueled by words slurred and forgotten
by dawn.

I bought that bike,
not thinking it would be a battleground,
not thinking it would spark an inferno.
But there it was,
me trying to better myself,
to feel the wind on my face
and the ground under my feet,
and you, furious, calling it reckless.

Reckless?
I worked hard through tax season,
made my money, saved our bills,
paid down our debt.
This was mine—just mine.
My body, my health,
my ride through the city.
Why was this an argument?
Why were we even fighting?

It wasn't about the bike.
Was it ever about the bike?
It was the drinking,
the fog that crept in after every glass,
the slurred accusations,
the amnesia in the morning.
You'd forget what you said,
but I never could.
It all piled up,
one argument, then another,
until we were drowning in them.

Then came that day,
a Sunday like any other,
but nothing was the same after.
You were out with friends,
and I went shopping,
not thinking much of it,

not knowing the storm
waiting behind my door.

When I came home,
you were there—
not just you.
You and him,
on the couch,
our couch,
and you didn't stop.
You didn't stop when I walked in.

I stood there,
frozen,
the phone at my ear,
my aunt's voice,
her screaming panic
on the other side of the line.
I didn't even hear her at first,
just the sound of my breath,
the thudding in my chest.

Sasha,
my dog,
barked, pawing at my leg,
as if she knew
I wasn't in my body anymore.
I could feel the darkness,
the rage bubbling inside.
Unspeakable thoughts.
Terrible, dark thoughts
of what I could do,
how I could flip that couch,
make them regret every moment.

But my aunt's voice,
Sasha's paw,
pulled me back,
pulled me out.
I left the house,
went next door,

to my neighbors,
spent the night there,
and surprisingly,
I slept well.

The next day,
a hotel,
and soon after,
a plane to the Middle East.
And that's when I knew,
when I truly knew,
this was the beginning of the end.

It wasn't the bike.
It wasn't even the couch.
It was the unraveling
of everything we once were,
all the things we didn't say,
all the ways we lost ourselves
before we even knew it.

That bike,
that ride,
wasn't just about work,
it was the moment I chose myself.
And now,
I pedal forward,
leaving the wreckage behind.

Inspiration behind "When I Bought a Bike"
Emotion: Betrayal and Self-realization

This poem came from one of the darkest moments of
my life—a moment that shattered something inside me
and took me to a place I never thought I'd go. It all started
with the purchase of a bike. I didn't realize at the time that
a simple decision—an $800 bike for my health, for saving
money on Uber rides, for a bit of peace—would become
the symbol of everything that was going wrong between
Darren and me.

We were crumbling by early 2019 after years of feeling invincible together. Arguments crept in, starting as rare bursts in 2018, then picking up pace in 2019 until they became a weekly thing. By April, the tension was unbearable, and that bike, something that should've been a no-brainer, sparked an argument I never saw coming. I had worked hard all tax season and thought, "Why not? I deserve this. It's good for me." But Darren didn't see it that way. He called me reckless with money, accusing me of being irresponsible. But the real issue wasn't the bike. It was the drinking.

His drinking had become the elephant in the room, one I could no longer ignore. It showed up in every argument, every irrational blow-up, every forgetful apology the next morning. And I was tired. Tired of holding it in. Tired of tiptoeing around the obvious. His problem with alcohol was tearing us apart, and I wasn't afraid to call it out anymore.

Then came that Sunday in May, a regular day when I should've been able to relax. I went out with Lashonda to get away and focus on something simple like interior design shopping. When I got home, I expected to find an empty house. Darren was out, doing his thing with his friends, and I had no interest in joining. But when I opened that door, what I found instead was Darren, on the couch, with someone else. They didn't even stop when I walked in. They didn't even stop.

It was an out-of-body experience. I stood there, frozen, on the phone with my aunt. Her voice on the other end was frantic, but I couldn't hear her. All I could hear was the rush of blood in my ears, feel the thudding in my chest. My dog Sasha was barking, pushing her paws against me, sensing that I wasn't really there anymore. I felt myself slipping into a place I had never been before—a dark, twisted place where I understood, for the first time in my life, what it meant to go temporarily insane.

For the first time, I got it. I finally understood how someone could snap in an instant, how you could lose control of yourself and be overtaken by a rage so pure, so destructive, that it consumes you. I had always understood the phrase "temporary insanity," but I had never felt its potential so close, so dangerously near. I had dark thoughts in that moment—unspeakable thoughts—about what I could do, what I wanted to do. I could see myself flipping that couch, grabbing them both, taking them somewhere they'd regret. I was right there, teetering on the edge of something I could never come back from.

But I didn't. I didn't because of my aunt's voice screaming in my ear, and because of Sasha's frantic barking, grounding me back to reality. I walked out. I left the house, went next door to my neighbors, and spent the night there. And I'm glad I did, because in that moment, I saw just how easy it is for someone to lose everything. I saw how one moment of rage could cost you everything you love—your life, your freedom, your family, your future. I love life too much to throw it all away for a moment of fury. I love my family, my friends, and myself too much to go down that road.

That day taught me that sometimes, walking away isn't just the best option—it's the only option. Rage and betrayal can push you to a place you never thought you'd go, but you have to fight to stay grounded. I could have let the darkness swallow me whole, but instead, I chose to rise above it. And that's when I knew our story was over, that this chapter in my life had reached its painful, necessary end.

Thresholds Crossed

In our home, where love once dwelled,
lies betrayed, a story quelled.
Walking in, my world unmade,
on our couch, the trust betrayed.

"Open," we claimed, but boundaries blurred,
my heart screams, yet remains unheard.
Visions of infidelity, stark and keen,
shatter the facade of a tranquil scene.

Darren, with another, lost in embrace
on sacred space, our love's disgrace.
A chalice of affection, now broken, spilled,
on the fabric of commitment, unfulfilled.

This moment, this breach, so vivid, so vile,
strips the veneer of every false smile.
A week of torment, his scorn like a lash,
words that sear and actions that clash.

Alcohol, his shield, his constant crutch,
leaves me to grapple with the cold touch
of reality, where love morphs to disdain,
and companionship dissolves to pain.

I snapped, a mind teetered on madness' brink.
Into dark thoughts, I dared not sink.
Fleeing to refuge, where clarity's voice
urged a hard choice at a fateful cross.

Away I flew, to deserts afar,
seeking solace beneath a foreign star.
In solitude, the truth unmasked,
of open wounds and questions unasked.

The divorce, a gate to reclaim my breath,
from the ashes of love, from the specter of death.
For in the echoes of our fractured tale,
I choose to heal, to fight, to prevail.

Inspiration behind "Thresholds Crossed"
Emotion: Betrayal and Emotional Devastation

Over a year of couples therapy had failed to address the deep-seated issues between Darren and me, especially his worsening alcoholism and the increasingly toxic behavior that accompanied it. His constant disrespect, gaslighting, and lying eroded the foundations of our relationship. Finding Darren with someone else on our couch was the last straw. Supposedly justified by our "open relationship," this act shattered any remnants of trust and respect.

Fleeing to the Middle East was my refuge. Traveling alone through Cyprus, Lebanon, Israel, and Jordan, I found solace under foreign stars. The laughter, the sights, and the sheer distance from the source of my pain allowed me to heal and reflect. This journey was a pivotal period of introspection and empowerment. It was here, amidst the beauty and history of these lands, that I regained my strength and resolved to reclaim my life. The poem captures this transition from betrayal to self-reclamation and to surviving and transcending the trials of love.

The Therapy Series

A Couples Therapy Journey

In the quiet rooms where truths unfurl,
we sat, two hearts entwined in whirls
of hurt and hope, where love once bloomed,
but shadows loomed, and trust was doomed.
From fervent starts to painful ends,
our therapist, our guide, our friend,
saw through the cracks, the broken seams,
and led us through our darkest themes.

Unresolved Echoes

In the clamor of our heated talk,
I voiced my peace, yet felt the mock
of unresolved, a patchwork quilt,
where tears were shed, and guilt was spilt.
Our "Tuesday Talks," our structured truce,
an hour's peace, yet what's the use?
When every word and every plea
was just a bandage, not the key.

Jealous Words, Insecure Alarms

You spoke of jealousy and fears,
of how you drowned in unseen tears.
With every drink, a wall you built.
Behind your eyes, a sea of guilt.
I urged you see beyond your storm,
a therapist to help transform
your aching soul, your weary heart,
to heal the pieces, torn apart.

Promises on Shifting Sands

And yet, a cycle spinning wild,
from anger's lash to gestures mild.
Proposals made on fleeting smiles,
yet anchored not in steadfast miles.
Your words, they swing from high to low,
from "stay," "let's fix," to "let me go."
A pendulum that cuts the air,
in every tick, a wear and tear.

Boundaries Blurred, Lines Overstepped

You crossed the lines of me and mine.
In every call, a steep decline.
You turned my friends to pawns in games
and left me sorting through the blames.
Your actions, like a vise so tight,
left little room for me to fight.
For every boundary you'd ignore,
my heart would harden just a bit more.

Navigating Through the Fog

I spoke in therapy of peace,
of how I wished our strife would cease.
An avoider of the confront,
I sought a path less blunt.
Yet there you stood, with sharpened tongue,
unyielding words for old and young.
A wordsmith crafting cages fine,
to trap my thoughts and realign.

Therapeutic Reflections

In solo sessions, I learn to speak
of confrontation, of being meek.
Exploring self, where silence reigned,
In the language of therapy, my fears explained.
The art of avoiding, the dance around,
where my words are lost, and my hopes are found.
In the safety of counsel, I seek to learn,
how to speak my peace, how to discern.
As we navigate this therapeutic course,
seeking clarity, a lesser force.
The goal, not merely to coexist,
but to love, to cherish, and not to resist.

Therapist's Farewell

In closing doors, our paths diverge,
from therapy's supportive verge.
A journey through the mind's complex,
in search of growth, not just reflex.
The therapist's last note rings clear,
a benediction sincere and dear.
A wish for peace as we depart,
to find the calm, to heal the heart.

Inspiration behind "The Therapy Series"
Emotion: Self-reflection and Emotional Growth

The "Therapy Series" began as a deep dive into the turbulent waters of a relationship that increasingly felt misaligned, where communication broke down and personal boundaries were often overshadowed by overwhelming emotional demands. The initial inspiration stemmed from an assignment: a heartfelt letter crafted to articulate my feelings about our relationship to my therapist, which later extended to Darren, marking the starting point of this poetic journey.

These poems trace the contours of our couple's therapy sessions, reflecting on the struggles, the temporary patches on recurring issues, and the overwhelming discussions that often ended without resolution. They capture trying to navigate a relationship that felt more like a battlefield of words than a partnership, highlighting the emotional toll of constant questioning and the pressure to conform to expectations that didn't resonate with my true self.

As the series progresses, it delves into the individual therapy sessions that predated and paralleled our couple's therapy. "Therapeutic Reflections" is a window into the personal growth and insights gained from my own therapy journey. It reflects the challenges of facing one's vulnerabilities away from the storm of the relationship, focusing on internal battles and personal enlightenment about communication styles, emotional needs, and the quest for self-understanding.

Each poem is a stepping stone through the timeline of therapy—from hopeful beginnings, through the tumult of trying to mend irreparable cracks, to the eventual acceptance that some paths are meant to diverge. The "Therapist's Farewell" marks the end of an era of joint therapy sessions, acknowledging the effort and changes attempted but also recognizing the need to move forward separately for personal growth and peace.

This series is not just about the dissolution of a relationship but also about the journey of self-discovery and empowerment. It is about the importance of speaking one's truth, the courage in facing personal and joint demons, and the liberation found in recognizing when to let go.

Elegy for Peace

Dear Ryan,

I write in search of solace, seeking air,
from shadows cast in homes once filled with care.
I've left my hearth, a refugee of heart,
escaping storms that Darren's actions start.

Since last we spoke in session's bound embrace,
my home became a high-tense, haunted place.
A staycation to soothe the anxious tide,
yet even from afar, his woes collide.

His calls reach out like tendrils, thick and fast,
to family and friends both near and vast.
With words that twist the truths I've once confessed,
attempting to unsettle my hard-won rest.

His drinking peaks, as do his absent days,
a pattern set in such destructive ways.
He tries, perhaps, to draw me back to him,
but this, his method, makes returning grim.

Today, his mother calls, her words a plea,
intent on bridging gaps she cannot see.
A family meet she proposes, yet
we are grown men; our own paths are set.

My mother stands with me, her thoughts align,
that if I go, she'll join, our hands entwine.
For in the face of Darren's spiraled fall,
I seek to stand, though burdened, straight and tall.

Alcohol, the beast that clouds his sight,
dims every joy and turns day to night.
I hope she finds the key to mend his soul,
for on his wellness pivots my own whole.

Ryan, your guidance now would mean the most,
as I stand wistful, a near-distant ghost.
A week has passed, yet feels a lifetime's span.
Advise me, as you alone can.

Your counsel sought, in hopes to find a light
that leads us both from this perennial night.
To paths where peace might once again reside,
where healing waters flow, not ebb and tide.

Sincerely seeking, on a ledge of change.
Yearning for a life newly rearranged.

Therapist's Viewpoint

In rooms where silence spoke as loud as words,
you sat, we delved into the life's tough chords.
Each session spread like chapters in a book,
where pains were faced, and fears were bravely took.

I've seen you both through months of storm and stress,
grow tender roots amidst the harsh duress.
Your strides in seeking truth within your souls,
using learned tools to fill those aching holes.

Though unresolved, the conflicts may remain.
Your ways of coping never stayed the same.
Your growth, a journey, vividly expressed,
in every plea and need you've since addressed.

The time has come to part, our sessions end.
Respectfully, your choice I comprehend.
Our paths diverge, here's where our chapter closes.
Confirmed herein, no future poses.

Your privacy remains a guarded trust
in my hands safe, as fair and just.
Should future winds blow you back through my door,

My welcome warm, as it was before.

For now, I bid you strength to walk your lanes.
In separate worlds, to manage your own reigns.
May peace find you both, wherever you may go,
with heartfelt thanks, more than you'll ever know.

Inspiration behind "Therapeutic Gratitude Series"
Emotion: Closure and Self-acceptance

"Elegy for Peace" and "Therapist Farewell" emerged from the bittersweet conclusion to a relationship that was both emotionally enriching and challenging, and the therapeutic journey that helped navigate through it.

"Elegy for Peace" captures my internal struggle and the eventual serenity I found in solitude after my relationship that, while full of love, also brought significant turmoil. This poem reflects on the quiet aftermath of relational conflicts and the personal peace that comes from embracing solitude and self-reflection. It's about understanding the impermanence of certain relationships and the importance of finding inner calm amidst life's storms.

"Therapist Farewell" highlights the role of therapy in my journey. Ryan, our therapist, observed and facilitated our growth as we tapped into our feelings and needs. He witnessed how we used the tools developed in therapy to communicate more effectively and advocate for ourselves. This poem appreciates the therapeutic process that allowed me to understand and articulate my emotions and needs better, providing a structured environment where healing and self-discovery could occur.

Together, these poems encapsulate a journey of emotional maturation, from the tumult of unresolved conflicts to advocacy and communication fostered, and finally, to the peace found in acceptance and self-understanding. They reflect the impact of therapy in

navigating our challenges, marking an end to our sessions
but also celebrating the growth that they spurred. Through
these compositions, I aim to convey gratitude for the
therapeutic insights gained, the emotional resilience
developed, and the peaceful closure achieved as I moved
forward with a stronger sense of self.

Our Last Words Series

Darren's Farewell

I won't be there today, Ryan.
Forgive the chair that sits unclaimed.
I've turned it over in my mind,
discussed it with my own more private guides,
and still, the answer's clear:
I cannot face another pre-arranged defeat.

I feel ambushed, vulnerable to scorn,
wounded by setups, veiled in care but laced with harm.
And Malcolm, I'm certain,
won't shift his ground.

You've been great, truly,
a navigator in our stormy spree.
I thank you deeply, but must steer
on my own through these frosted tears.

Malcolm, to you—
I love you, perhaps more than I ever showed,
flawed and all, tethered to our shared dreams.
I've been your champion, quietly.
Not perfect, sometimes invisible in my own loud doubts,
but always, silently, irrevocably, on your side.

I've played roles ill-suited to us both,
the parent, the warden, the shadow in our shared light.
Too many questions, too much wine,
too quick to anger, too slow to soothe.

I regret the air I poisoned,
the paranoia over pennies,
the burdens, heavy, unfairly shared,
my part in your daily pill,
my failure to fill each outlined role
in the script we wrote together.

Our forever truncated to just a span of years.
Seven cycles around a sun that sets too soon.
I accept your leave, the exit you propose,
our paths diverging from the plan we supposed.

I'll not fight as we untwine.
I'll offer peace in every line.
Let's settle this with grace,
propose and negotiate face-to-face.
I promise fairness, devoid of spite,
for even in this ending, I seek to do right.

And a final note to clear the air:
I am wounded but not wanting of an end to all.
I am not plotting my final fall.
I drink, not to drown but simply to breathe,
missing days not due to bottle but the weight of grief.

I reached out in desperation, not deceit,
to family, not to wound you, but because I am weak.
And my mother, bless her, moved on her own accord,
a lioness protecting what remains of her pride's cord.

This is me, standing in the ruin of our shared dreams,
not a villain, just a man unraveling at the seams.
I am sorry for the storms I brewed,
for the quiet goodbyes and the solitude.

Sincerely,
Darren

Apology Not Taken

Darren, I've received your lines,
the weight of words, well-intentioned,
falling flat in the face of our fractured time.
I've pondered them, conferred with my own shadowed
guides,
and my heart's reply remains unchanged—
I cannot embrace an apology that stumbles,
fails to rise from the depths where our troubles lie.

Your absence today, a silence in the chair,
speaks volumes more than words could dare.
Yes, I feel ambushed, too,
not by you alone, but by the patterns we've sewn—
threads of care interlaced with harm,
a tapestry that leaves me cold,
Malcolm, the unmoved, standing firm in the storm.

Navigating these seas was never yours alone.
Your thanks, though kind, are notes left unplayed.
We chart our courses now through separate frosts,
your tears, your own, as are mine.

I hear your love echoing through time,
perhaps more than you ever showed,
flawed and tethered to dreams shared,
a champion in the quiet, unseen,
but love, unseen, unheard,
is a ghost in our shared light.

Roles miscast in our shared play,
the parent, the warden, the shadow—
questions too many, wine too much,
anger swift, solace slow.

The air you speak of, poisoned,
the paranoia over pennies,
burdens unbalanced, pills swallowed bitter—
our script, co-written,

failed in its lines,
forever truncated, just a span of years,
seven cycles, a sun set too soon.

Your proposal of peace,
a face-to-face grace,
is met with a heart that seeks more than words—
fairness, devoid of spite, a noble goal,
yet even in this ending,
right must be more than spoken.

Your final note,
to clear the air—
wounded but not wanting an end,
not plotting falls,
drinking to breathe, grief's weight heavy.
Reaching out in weakness, not deceit,
family, not wounds, a lioness moves alone.

Standing in our shared ruins,
not a villain, just a man,
unraveling seams.
Your storms brewed,
goodbyes quiet, solitude loud.

But Darren, some storms,
cannot be calmed by words,
some wounds, too deep for balm.
This apology, though given,
remains—unaccepted.

Sincerely, Malcolm

Malcolm Reads Darren's Farewell

Ryan,
Darren's bowed out of today's session.
Claims it's too much, too staged—
a feeling of being cornered, not heard.
He's stepping back, seeking closure on his own terms.

Malcolm,
He declares his love, unmatched and deep,
acknowledges his imperfections, his silent support.
Regrets his overbearing ways,
his storms of queries, his outbursts.
He's sorry for the shadows he cast,
for the everyday burdens that grew too heavy,
for the ends that didn't justify our means.
He accepts the close of our chapter,
Promises smooth negotiations, a fair divide.

And he clarifies—he's down but not out.
Lonely calls were just echoes of desperation,
not schemes or cries for attention.
He reassures us of his resilience,
despite the depths he's reached.

He's not asking for rescue,
just a nod of understanding as he finds his footing again.
As for us, he wishes well,
leaving with apologies,
not for the ending, but for the pains that led here.

Sincerely reading,
Malcolm

Inspiration behind "Our Last Words Series"
Emotion: Grief and Acceptance

"Our Last Words Series" emerged from the final
exchanges between my ex-husband and me at the
conclusion of our couples therapy sessions, each one
capturing our respective perspectives and the emotional
complexities of our parting.

"Apology Not Taken" reflects my feelings upon
receiving an apology that felt insufficient given the depth
of the issues that had surfaced in our relationship. This
poem is about the realization that not all apologies can

repair the damage, especially when the underlying issues are deep-seated and unresolved.

"Darren's Farewell" is written from Darren's perspective, voicing his acknowledgment of the relationship's end and his feelings surrounding our separation. It's an attempt to articulate his side of the story, expressing remorse and a recognition of the personal failings that contributed to our breakup.

"Malcolm Reads Darren's Farewell" is my reaction to Darren's farewell message. It's a blend of my reflection on his words and the tumult of emotions they stir up, from sorrow to a grudging acceptance of the reality that our paths were diverging.

These poems were birthed from a moment of closure, rooted in the final email exchanges that marked the end of our joint therapeutic journey. They give voice to the silent thoughts and unspoken feelings that often linger after such farewells. I titled this series "Our Last Words" to capture the finality and emotional weight of concluding a significant chapter in our lives against the therapeutic backdrop that had witnessed our final attempts at reconciliation and understanding. Through these compositions, I explore the intricate dance of coming to terms with the end of a relationship, marked by a poignant farewell that is both a lament and a cautious step toward future healing.

Ashes of Yesterday

The summer heat matched the fire in your eyes,
a blaze set to memories we couldn't revive.
I came home to silence, to closets bare,
and a backyard where smoke lingered in the air.
You burned more than fabric—you burned the past,
but I had already known this love wouldn't last.

A circle of ash where the old me lay,

yet I had no words left to say.
What's a wardrobe to peace of mind?
I packed my bags—two carry-ons, a book bag behind.
You kept the house, the couch, the sound,
but I kept the strength that I had found.

The papers, the terms, the debts we had,
I signed them away—what's left to be sad?
You took the furniture, the points, the stock,
but I took my soul, and that's worth a lot.

You can tally the numbers, divide the spoils,
but freedom was mine after all the toil.
Burn what you will, take what you may,
but my peace of mind won't go up in flames today.

And though the closet is empty, my heart is full—
starting over with little, but the price was null.
For in the ashes, I found my way—
what was left behind could never stay.

Inspiration behind "Ashes of Yesterday"
Emotion: Empowerment

On a scorching day, I went to the house and discovered my closet empty, every single piece of clothing gone. I knew something was off, but it wasn't until I saw the burn marks in the backyard that it hit me—he'd burned my entire wardrobe.

I stood there, defeated and heartbroken, staring at the circle of charred grass, realizing that everything I had bought were in ashes. But what could I do? The decision had already been made; I was leaving the relationship, and now I would be starting over with even less than I had imagined. All I had left were a book bag and two carry-on suitcases, but, at that moment, I knew that was all I needed.

After that summer, we reached a divorce settlement
agreement. The lawyers handled most of it, and though I
paid him more than I thought was fair, we split the house
and most things. He kept his condo, and I made no fuss or
mention of his other business ventures or houses. I came
out of pocket for more than half—an unspeakable amount,
really—but if I had to do it all over again, I wouldn't
hesitate. Because I would pay that price any day for peace
of mind.

I've learned through experience that protecting your
mental health is the foundation of living well. By
protecting your mind, you protect your whole being.
Mental health is like a garden—you need to nurture it,
tend to it, and remove the weeds before they choke the life
out of everything you've built. Darren did everything he
could that summer to destroy my mental garden. The
stress, the shock of seeing my clothes burned, the countless
small battles, all the chaos—it could have easily worn me
down, even broken me. But it didn't. And that's because I
had help, and I had the foresight to invest in my mental
well-being.

My therapist, Julie, was like a psychic, predicting
Darren's every move. She was always one step ahead,
guessing the manipulations and disruptions he would
throw my way, and together, we stayed proactive. Julie
kept me grounded and sane through the storm. No matter
how many clothes were burned, how many insane antics
Darren pulled that summer and into the fall and winter,
she helped me remain strong, unwavering, and, dare I say,
unbothered.

Thank you, Julie. Thank you to therapy. And thank you
to my healthy, sound mind. You saved me. You allowed
me to stand tall when it felt like everything around me was
burning down. Even though Darren tried to break me
mentally, I stayed whole. Peace of mind—there's nothing
more valuable.

The Planner in Me Series

2016: Inaugural Travel Email

Dear Friends,

In the heart of winter's chill,
when wanderlust begins to swell,
Darren and I, with dreams to chase,
lay plans for travels, time and place.

From Melbourne's sun to Cairo's sands,
we crafted trips mapped out with hands.
Punta Cana's beaches in February's grasp, Sydney's
skyline, in January's clasp.

March whispers of pyramids tall,
Egypt's history, a siren call.
Summer thoughts of Miami's heat,
End of season, Italy's streets.

London's Wimbledon, a 4th of July delight,
Las Vegas in fall with neon nights.
Seattle's drizzle or Dubai's gleam,
Each destination part of our dream.

But oh, the thrill of the unknown!
Botswana, perhaps, a place to roam.
For every plan we set in stone,
Adventure calls from lands unknown.

So here we are, an open invite,
To join us in these journeys bright.
The planner in me, with lists in hand,
Invites you to explore this wondrous land.

From emails sent to dreams we weave, Together, in travel,
we believe.
Let's share these moments, near or far,
For the world awaits beneath the stars.

260

Pack your bags, the time is near,
Let's venture forth with friends so dear.
For in every journey, every flight,
We find the world and our own light.

2017: Crafting Our Dream

There's a rhythm to my year, a dance with time,
mapping journeys, destinations, dreams to climb.
With Darren by my side, the world's our stage.
We chart the skies, turn over every page.

Italy in March, where history breathes, Montego Bay,
where the sun relieves.
Miami calls with its electric heat,
and London's charm, where past and future meet.

Singapore waits with its bustling streets as October
whispers of distant retreats.
Each plan, each flight, a thread we weave,
a tapestry of places, a map to conceive.

Other targets linger on the edge of thought,
Havana's rhythms, Peru's ancient plot.
From Vegas lights to Iceland's snow,
there's nowhere on earth we wouldn't go.

Each year, we plan, a tradition so dear,
we share our dreams, make it crystal clear.
A spreadsheet of hopes, a calendar of love,
each trip a testament to what we're made of.

Family and friends, join in when you can,
there's a place for you in every plan.
Europe in summer, a grand tour indeed,
from Denmark's shores to Bulgaria's creed.

Eighteen countries, ambitious, yes,
but that's how we roll, no settling for less.
We fly, we drive, we cross every border.

In the planner's world, there's always order.

I crave the thrill of what's to come,
the joy of planning, the journey begun.
It's more than travel, it's life's grand scheme.
It's the planner in me, crafting our dream.

So here's to the year, to the places we'll see,
to the memories made, where we'll always be free.
With Darren and I, the world's our domain,
in the planner's hands, there's nothing but gain.

We wander, we explore, we make our mark
in every city, every park.
With each new plan, my heart takes flight,
for in every journey, I find my light.

2018: Year of Wanderlust

Dear Friends,

Forgive the mass email,
but here I am, once more, to unveil
the travel plans for the year ahead,
dreams of destinations where we'll be led.

Darren and I, with our wandering souls,
map out the world, set our goals.
From Thailand's temples to Greece's shore,
each place a chapter, each trip a door.

January whispers of Thai delights
under tropical suns and starry nights.
March speaks of Amsterdam's charms,
With Greece's beauty nestled in our arms.

Tel Aviv in June, where Pride colors the sky,
London's Wimbledon, July's joyful cry.
Essence in New Orleans, with rhythm and beat,

Singapore in October, a journey complete.

West Africa calls, perhaps by year's end,
and Miami's warmth, where weekends blend.
Seattle's cool breeze may beckon, too,
with Portland's charm in our view.

These are the dreams we've laid in place,
a tapestry of memories time won't erase.
So, if any of this speaks to your heart,
Join us in this grand travel art.

We plan, we wander, we roam with glee,
the planner in me, ever so free.
For in these journeys, we find our light,
and in each adventure, our souls take flight.

Let's embrace the world, one trip at a time,
with friends by our side, in rhythm and rhyme.

Here's to a year of wanderlust's grace.
Let's explore together, find our place.

Best,
Darren & Malcolm

2019: A Year of Adventures

Hello All!

It's that time of year again,
when we share the dreams that we've carefully penned.
Our travel plans for the coming year,
a journey of wanderlust, far and near.

New Year's Eve 2018, in Stockholm we'll greet
the first of many adventures, where our hearts will meet.

January takes us to India's land,

Delhi, Agra, Mumbai, where history stands.
With Jaipur possibly in our sight,
we'll draft the itinerary, making it just right.

February's breeze will carry us south,
Alabama's history from Tuscaloosa's mouth.
A family trip to the DR's shores,
where laughter and love will echo once more.

March whispers of tennis under the sun,
Indian Wells and Miami, where games are won.
The courts will sing with each serve and volley
as we chase the thrill, so bright and jolly.

April brings us to Houston's embrace,
a Texan welcome with warmth and grace.
Then May unfolds in Croatia's view,
Split and Dubrovnik, where the waters are blue.

June calls us to Israel and Jordan's land,
where ancient tales in the desert sand.
Detroit in June to celebrate with glee,
Rowena Bentley turns 60, what a joy it will be!

July's fireworks will light the sky
in North Dakota and South Dakota, where the mountains
lie.
Mount Rushmore's grandeur, a sight to behold,
with family in Atlanta, where stories are told.

August's path leads to Boston's streets,
Providence whispers of history's feats.
September takes us to Argentina's grace,
Buenos Aires and Iguazu's pace.

October brings Hawaii's shores,
with grandparents dear, where aloha pours.
November's journey to Africa's heart,
Nigeria and beyond, where adventures start.

December returns us to Detroit's arms

for Christmas cheer and family charms.
And as the year closes, we'll find our place
in Edinburgh's beauty, where New Year's we'll embrace.

Other possibilities float in the air,
Cuba, Chile, Greece—who knows where?
South Korea's wonders, Alaska's wild,
each destination, a dream compiled.

So if these plans resonate with your soul,
join us on this journey, let the adventures roll.
Life is busy, but time we'll make
for the memories and bonds, we'll create.

Here's to 2019, a year of delight.
With family and friends, our travels ignite.
Let us know if you wish to come along,
in this dance of the world, where we all belong.

With love and excitement, Darren & Malcolm

2020: The Last Travel Email

August 2019,
I hit send without knowing
that this would be the last time
I'd share the joy of planning.
Mapping out a year of adventures,
each destination a beacon of light in a year filled with
shadows,
a year that would soon turn dark.

I was leaning on travel,
a crutch to bear the weight
of what began as a whisper of a divorce,
the start of a journey I hadn't planned.
May 2019, I stopped going home,
but by August, I had already wandered
through the Middle East's ancient sands,
Cyprus's shores, Panama's vibrant streets,

Myrtle Beach's quiet waves,
and Cancun was calling next.

The planner in me,
the love for the road,
sent out that email,
filled with hopes and dream of places to go
on weekends spent escaping,
of finding myself in foreign lands.
It was a ritual,
a tradition that Darren and I shared,
yet this time,
it was a lifeline for me.

January would begin with a divorce trip.
Three weeks of South American solace.
No attendees, just me and the path ahead.
Lebanon, Cabo, Acapulco, Puerto Rico,
Rome's clay courts, Alaska's icy embrace,
Sao Paulo's pride and joy.
Each trip a breath.
Each flight a step away
from the life I was leaving behind.

But then, the world paused.
COVID swept in, grounded planes, shuttered dreams.
And that email became a relic,
a memory of who I was,
of the plans I made
to keep moving,
to keep going
when everything else was falling apart.

I miss that part of me,
the one who could dream
in itineraries and flight numbers,
who could see the world
as a series of stops and starts,
each one an adventure waiting to unfold.
But life, divorce, and a pandemic put that part on pause,
left me grounded,

wondering if I'd ever fly again.

Yet, in reflecting,
I see a spark,
a hope that maybe,
in the near future,
I'll return to that email ritual,
start planning again,
send out another message
Filled with dreams of distant lands,
of journeys yet to be taken.

Because even now, after everything,
I still believe
in the power of travel,
in the magic of a map
and a plane ticket in hand.
And when the time is right,
when the world opens up again,
I'll be there,
ready to hit send,
To share the next chapter,
the next adventure,
with the ones I hold dear.

Inspiration Behind "The Planner in Me Series"
Emotion: Nostalgic Reflection

Darren and I cultivated a meticulous, shared passion
for travel throughout our relationship. It wasn't just about
the destinations; it was about the process of dreaming,
planning, and bringing those dreams to life. Each email
and itinerary was a manifestation of our love for
exploration, our desire to see the world together, and our
commitment to making those experiences as rich and
fulfilling as possible.

Planning our travels was an art form and a bonding
ritual that brought us closer with each discussion and
decision. I was the detailed planner who crafted itineraries

down to the hour, ensuring that every moment of our trips was accounted for, every meal was planned, and every reservation was made. On the other hand, Darren was the researcher who dug deep into each destination, identifying the must-see neighborhoods, historical sites and hidden gems that would make our travels truly special.

Together, we balanced each other perfectly. Darren's research and my attention to detail created a synergy that made our trips successful and memorable. Whether it was securing tickets to a tennis match in a far-off city or mapping out a journey through multiple countries in Europe, we approached every trip with the same level of excitement and dedication.

The series captures the joy of planning and the evolution of our relationship as seen through the lens of our travels. Our inaugural trip to Punta Cana in 2016 was the beginning of something beautiful—a tradition of yearly travel that brought our friends and family into the fold. By 2017, we had expanded our horizons to Jamaica, and although 2018 brought challenges and the beginning of the end for us, those travel plans were still a symbol of the life we built together.

As the years passed, our travels became a way to navigate our relationship. In 2019, as our marriage was unraveling, travel became both an escape and a way to cling to the memories of what we once had. The last travel email I sent in August 2019 was filled with hope and anticipation, unaware that the world would soon change and that COVID-19 would bring everything to a halt, including the life I had known.

This series is more than a chronicle of where we went and what we did. It's a story of love, partnership, and the shared pursuit of dreams. The emails and itineraries were the glue that held us together and the common ground we could always return to, even when other aspects of our relationship were falling apart.

Even though our marriage did not last, the memories of those travels, the experiences we shared, and the dreams we fulfilled together are forever a part of me. The "Planner in Me Series" reminds me of those moments and the power of dreams backed by love and hard work. It reflects a chapter of my life, where travel was a means of survival, a way to cope, and a way to keep moving forward.

While the format of my travels has changed since then—slowed down by life, the pandemic, and the realities of personal growth—the spirit of exploration and the joy of planning remain. One day, I hope to return to that ritual of sending out travel emails and inviting others to share in the adventures that lie ahead. But for now, I reflect on the journey, grateful for the memories, and look forward to the day when I can once again hit send on a new set of dreams.

The Final Verse of Us

In the hushed corridors of legal grace,
we sign the papers to unlace
the knot we tied with hopeful hands
in Cook County's solemn stands.

Malcolm and Darren, August's dream,
now just a whisper, a silent scream.
Married in the city's heart,
where skyscrapers rise and rivers part.

No children laughed within our walls.
No tiny footsteps echoed in our halls.
Yet, we built a life, a home, a plan,
two souls converging, man-to-man.

Irreconcilable, the differences grew,
like shadows at dusk, as darkness knew.
Attempts at mending, all in vain,
left us with nothing but this refrain.

Now, I stand in Cook County's sight,
asking release into the night
to dissolve the bonds that time has worn
from the love we pledged one summer morn.

Divide the world we built together,
amidst the storms we could not weather.
My non-marital goods in hand,
seeking solace in this unplanned land.

Darren, with skills to earn his keep,
no alms required, the slope's not steep.
May he prosper, may he thrive,
as separately, we strive to survive.

Judge, hear my plea, my final request,
to put our once-entwined hearts to rest.
Grant dissolution, clear and fair,
dividing what was ours to share.

Let us walk from court alone,
forging paths into the unknown.
Yet, in this formal parting's wake,
I wish you joy with every step you take.

For love once lived beneath these legal lines.
A story etched within Cook County's confines.
A chapter closes, letting go of strife.
Thankful for the dance, the music of our life.

Inspiration Behind "The Final Verse of Us"
Emotion: Somber Acceptance

In the Cook County Circuit Court, I went through the heart-wrenching process of legally ending a chapter of my life that began with hope and love but concluded in a courtroom.

As I navigated the legal intricacies and emotional turmoil of filing for divorce, I was struck by the stark contrast between the joyous beginnings of my marriage to Darren and the sobering end marked by court documents and legal procedures. What once felt like a union full of hope and promise had now dissolved into an unsettling mix of confusion, sorrow, and a quiet sense of grief. The notion of a marriage—a partnership built on dreams, shared lives, and intertwined destinies—being distilled into a series of legal points and requests felt gut-wrenching, as if the intimacy and love we once shared were reduced to mere formalities. It left me feeling vulnerable, exposed, and, at times, lost within a process that seemed so indifferent to the emotional weight it carried.

This poem was my way of articulating the complex emotions involved in this process. It reflects the bittersweet acknowledgment of the irretrievable breakdown of our relationship, while also expressing a wish for mutual respect and future happiness as we both move forward independently. I wanted to capture the dignity of this painful yet necessary conclusion, framing our separation as a respectful closure to a significant chapter of our lives.

Through "The Final Verse of Us," I sought to convey the legal and emotional journey from union to dissolution. It was important for me to express both the sadness of loss and the hopeful release into new beginnings, offering a voice to the silent emotions often overshadowed by the formalities of legal proceedings.

Dissolution of Marriage

Settled Accounts

In the quiet halls of judgment, papers whisper finality.
Two signatures, like soft echoes in a canyon.
A bond once formed in love, now disassembled by law.
Each clause, a chapter closed in the ledger of shared lives.

Equitable Distribution

Once shared dreams laid on the table,
now divided with precision—carefully measured fairness.
A house, a ring, accounts like autumn leaves,
scattered, each finding a new place to rest.

No Children to Speak Of

No tiny hands tug at the seams of their agreement.
Only memories populate the spaces between them.
Silent spectators to the division of years.
Invisible imprints on each signed page.

Uncontested Silence

Words unspoken hang heavy in the air
as the gavel's echo marks the end of shared paths.
Each walks away, laden with their portion,
from the love they once thought endless.

New Beginnings

Freed from the bond, but bound by history,
they step into separate futures,
their names still echoing in each other's past,
ready to rebuild from the fragments of yesterday.

Inspiration behind "Dissolution of Marriage"
Emotion: Resigned Reflection.

Inspired by the legal and personal documents that marked the end of a union, I explored the intertwining of love, loss, and legal finality. Each stanza reflects the stages of separation—the initial confrontation with the end, the negotiation of lives once entwined, and the eventual, inevitable acceptance. Through this creative process, I sought to capture the finality and division of assets, shared dreams, and intertwined lives. This poem navigates through the emotional and pragmatic aspects of ending a marriage, mirroring the legal intricacies of the Marital Settlement Agreement, but delving deeper into the personal shifts and realignments that the document signifies.

These legal documents marked not only the end of Darren and me but also the conclusion of a significant chapter in my life. It was the symbol, the legal direction, and ultimately the permission I needed to start anew. This dissolution was more than a court's decision—it was a pivotal moment of transition, freeing me from the past and allowing me to step into the next chapter of love in my life, with hope for future possibilities.

Brandon
Emotion: Resilience and Self-discovery

In the "Brandon" chapter, I explore everything from the turbulence of letting go to the complex dynamics of mental health, addiction, and love. I delve into the history of moving on from a broken relationship, traveling to new places, and finding my footing again in a different world. The reflections shared in this chapter are as much about transformation as they are about the moments that shape us. This collection isn't just a narrative about my past but an exploration of love, heartache, and resilience. Through these writings, I aim to illustrate how personal change can arise from the endings we sometimes least expect while showing how self-discovery, like the winds of Mexico, can carry us to new and unexpected places.

Meet Me in the Middle (East)

I was headed north, Alaska-bound,
but instead, I found myself turning 'round.
A Grindr chat, just a handsome face,
turned into something, but not at pace.
Bax was slow, communication thin,
but something about him pulled me in.

From schooling talk to travel tales,
not one conversation went off the rails.
No sexual hints, no dirty lines,
just light-hearted talk and witty signs.
I was escaping, needing light,
from couch disasters to hotel nights.
But when you're waiting on someone's "yes,"
you learn patience in this modern mess.

So, I skipped Alaska's icy air.
Instead, I flew to the Middle East fair.
Lebanon's streets, Cyprus's shores,
Jordan and Israel opened doors.
Wanderlust filled me, heart set free,
but I wondered, "What about Bax and me?"

Then, back home, we finally met.
A coffee date I won't forget.
A Middle Eastern restaurant's glow,
stories of my travels began to flow.
We talked, we laughed, we ordered drinks.
I started to feel the missing links.
Not just a date—this was the start
of something slow, thoughtful, heart-to-heart.

A peck goodnight, just lips so brief,
left room for mystery, sweet relief.
No rush to bed, no hurried thrill,
but something deeper, calm, and still.
I'm old school when love's in sight.
No need to rush what feels just right.

In therapy, you'll find a theme
of knowing your wants before you dream.
Don't skip Alaska for someone's text.
If they leave you waiting, you'll feel vexed.
The trick, my friends, is clear to see:
What do you want before "we"?

Set boundaries firm, make space for care.
Don't chase a love that's barely there.
If they're slow to speak, slow to act,
don't lose your journey, stay intact.
Romance is best when it's built with grace.
Not a sprint, but a steady-paced race.

Inspiration Behind "Meet Me in the Middle (East)"
Emotion: Hopeful Patience

This poem captures the unexpected beginnings of my
relationship with Bax when I was grappling with deep
emotional turmoil while seeking escape through travel and
new connections. When I met Bax on Grindr, I needed
something light to take me out of the darkness caused by
my relationship's collapse with Darren. I was in a hotel,
trying to avoid the mess at home. Darren had crossed a
line that I couldn't ignore, and I was done. My marriage
had already started its downward spiral, and I just wanted
to enjoy something—anything—without drama.

Grindr can often be explicit, but Bax and I connected
there in an easy, friendly exchange. I liked his demeanor
and how our conversation flowed about life, school, and
travel without ever turning sexual. It was refreshing and
promising, so much so that I delayed my Alaska trip
hoping we could meet before I took off. But Bax's slow
communication was a red flag I ignored early on, a theme
that would play out throughout our relationship.

Instead of heading to Alaska, I ended up traveling
across the Middle East—Lebanon, Cyprus, Jordan, and
Israel. That trip was a beautiful distraction. I rediscovered

pieces of myself in those countries, reconnecting with friends, making new ones, and soaking in the experiences. It was the mental and emotional break I desperately needed from everything that had been weighing me down. But even as I explored, I found myself thinking about Bax, hoping that we could meet when I returned.

When I came back, we finally had that first date. We shared coffee, dinner, drinks—all at a thoughtful, deliberate pace that I appreciated. Bax didn't rush things, and neither did I. The date was more than an escape; it felt like a start. And although it was slow and cautious, I was fine with that. I prefer to build something meaningful over time when I care about someone.

This story—and the relationship with Bax—taught me valuable lessons, some of which emerged later in therapy, as I worked to process my emotions and patterns.

- Know Your Own Needs First: Before trying to build something with someone else, you must be clear about what you want and need. I realized that I was seeking connection and healing with Bax, but I didn't ask myself enough early on if he was capable of providing that. Instead, I let his slow responses and uncertain behavior dictate things. Therapy reinforced the idea that you must center yourself in your own story before letting anyone else in.

- Set Boundaries Early: Bax's slow, non-committal communication should have been a signal for me to set boundaries earlier. If someone isn't clear about their intentions or can't commit to plans, that's a sign they may not be ready to meet you where you are. Learning to hold space for myself became critical in dating or friendships.

- Don't Ignore Red Flags: I learned that escapism and avoidance (like traveling or delaying trips) are temporary fixes for deeper problems. If someone isn't communicative or emotionally available at the start, it's likely a sign of what's to come. Therapy helped me realize that I was ignoring the signs, hoping for things to change, rather than accepting what was right in front of me.

- **Patience vs. Settling:** There's a balance between being patient and settling for less than you deserve. My date with Bax was sweet, but as time went on, his inconsistency became a pattern. Therapy taught me that there's a difference between giving someone time to show up and lowering your standards because they won't.

- **Escapism Doesn't Fix Core Issues:** Travel was my way of coping with the emotional trauma I was going through, but it wasn't a solution. Therapy helped me see that I needed to confront what was happening at home instead of always seeking an escape. Whether it's travel or a new relationship, you can't avoid dealing with what's hurting you.

- **Boundaries for Mental Health:** Finally, I learned the importance of boundaries in relationships. Bax had his struggles with communication and emotional availability, but I had to protect my mental health. Therapy helped me understand that keeping my peace is more important than holding onto someone who can't meet me halfway.

This poem serves as a reflection on these lessons, turning what started as escapism into a moment of clarity about what I truly need and want in relationships moving forward.

Taste of Chicago, Last Taste of Home

Chicago's skies, a taste of blues.
Restaurant Week, where dishes woo.
Bax by my side, my friends in tow.,
They said, **"He's so white,"** and if you know, you know.
Laughter bubbled like a glass of prosecco.
Their words weren't cruel, just cultural echo.

MDMA danced on the edge of lips.
A first flirtation, a risky trip.
"What the hell," I thought, "why not give in?"
One little pill and the high begins.
The Taste of Chicago turned to taste of bliss.
Every morsel, every texture, felt like a kiss.

And then—my house, the last weekend it'd see
My body, my soul, feeling truly free.
We rolled into the night, drunk on laughter and dreams,
and I found myself outside, under the moon's gleam.
The grass Baxeath me whispered in waves.
I was cradled by earth's rhythmic praise.
Touching the soil felt like touching the core
of nature's heartbeat, pulsing once more.

I was lying there, alive and alight,
connected to stars in a velvet night.
MDMA's magic swirled through my veins,
a cascade of beauty, a sweet release from pain.
For a moment, my worries melted away.
The divorce, the house, felt far from the fray.

But then, in the basement, a conversation stirred.
The air thick with tension, raw feelings slurred.
Bax's presence, a question not yet unspooled.
Is this my lover, or am I being fooled?
My mind started spiraling, doubts took hold.
Was this a friend or a love too cold?

MDMA made me raw, emotions so bright.
Every truth felt like fire in the night.
I saw Bax through a clearer lens.
Not all companions are meant to transcend
from friendship's warm, familiar flame
to lovers who share the same last name.

Circumstance and chemistry blurred the line.
I was houseless, restless, no place to call mine.
Bax's bed became my temporary stay.
His apartment, my refuge from the fray.

But looking back now, I can finally see
that some friendships were never meant to be
Anything more than a safe, quiet shore—
A place to rest, but nothing more.

Therapy taught me, intentions must lead.
Set boundaries first, don't follow the need
to rush into something undefined.
Let love and friendship take their time.

So, as I lay in my yard, grass brushing skin,
nature's pulse humming deep within,
I realized that love needs clarity,
not just passion or familiarity.
Chicago fed me, but not just with food.
It gave me a lesson, in friendship and truth.

Now when I taste those nights gone by,
I laugh, I learn, I don't even cry.
For every high, there's a grounded view,
and I know now what love can and can't do.

Inspiration Behind "Taste of Chicago, Last Taste of Home"

Emotion: Reflective Clarity

In early 2019, my marriage was crumbling. I had lived through a series of upheavals—emotionally, mentally, and practically. I wasn't even staying in my own home because the painful infidelity with Darren had left me feeling shattered. Seeing him with someone else on our couch was the beginning of me shutting the door on our relationship and opening a new chapter in my life. After that, I was living out of suitcases, couch-surfing, and looking for any escape from the chaos of my marriage ending.

I met Bax through Grindr during this turbulent time. Our first conversations weren't sexual–refreshing given the platform–and I was drawn to him. I was desperate for something lighthearted to take me out of my mental fog.

The escape he offered seemed like the right kind of distraction, and I latched onto it. I canceled my Alaska trip in hopes of meeting him before I left for the Middle East, but things didn't pan out as I hoped. In hindsight, that was just a reflection of how he operated—slow to commit, slow to show up, and slow to give clarity.

After I returned from an incredible solo journey to Lebanon, Cyprus, Israel, and Jordan, we finally went on our first date. It felt promising. Bax and I clicked in some ways, but there was always something just slightly off.

Then came Chicago Restaurant Week, a final weekend in what was once my home, now a painful reminder of the life I was leaving behind. That's when I tried MDMA for the first time. I was already in such a raw, emotional state, and the drug heightened my every sensation. I lay on the grass in my backyard, feeling like I was touching the very heart of the earth. I felt connected to the universe in a way I never had before. It was euphoric, but it also forced me to confront my deeper emotions about the house and the divorce, and my uncertainty about Bax.

A conversation in the basement that evening stuck with me and stirred up feelings of doubt about whether I could truly be with Bax. My mind, already spiraling from the MDMA, started to pick apart our dynamic, and it became clear to me that something was missing. Despite all the circumstantial reasons that had brought us together—my temporary homelessness and my need for connection—Bax and I were never really meant to be lovers. Our friendship was real, but in the absence of clear boundaries, I had mistaken it for something deeper.

Therapeutically, I've come to understand how essential it is to set intentions when entering any kind of relationship. When we let circumstance dictate the flow, without being clear about our needs and desires, we can easily end up in situations that don't serve us. I hadn't defined what I wanted from Bax, and as a result, I found myself slipping into a relationship that was never really meant to be romantic.

In addition to learning the power of boundaries in preserving my mental health and emotional wellbeing, I learned the difference between using relationships as an escape from pain and entering relationships with intention. My connection with Bax was largely circumstantial, born out of my need to fill the void left by my collapsing marriage. I've learned that entering into anything new without clarity—whether it's friendship or love—will often lead to confusion and hurt.

The MDMA heightened my emotions and allowed me to feel joy and a connection to nature, but it also gave me false clarity. The euphoria made everything seem clearer, but that clarity was temporary. It's important to understand that mind-altering substances don't provide solutions—they can offer perspective but often leave you more confused in the long run. My therapeutic journey has reinforced that I need to rely on sober, clear-headed thinking when making life decisions, especially in relationships.

My story with Bax is a cautionary tale about the importance of knowing what you want before embarking on something with someone else. Therapy taught me that the best relationships start with self-awareness— understanding your own needs, desires, and boundaries before you involve someone else. I went into things with Bax without clarity, and it left me feeling disoriented and unsure of how to proceed.

I now understand that not all friends are meant to be lovers. Through therapy, I've learned to separate the two and to not let circumstance blur those lines. It's a lesson I carry with me as I move forward in life, a reminder to always be intentional with my relationships.

In reflecting on this chapter of my life, I've gained so much insight into what I need from myself and others.

Boundaries, clarity, and intentionality are essential.
Therapy helped me navigate these lessons and avoid
repeating the same mistakes in future relationships. I'm
grateful for that growth, and I wish the same for Bax—
healing, clarity, and the ability to live with peace inside his
own head.

Cancún Confessions

Cancún, 9/5, the sun kissed our skin,
where the past and the present would blend and begin.
Mark, that fork in the road I'd ignore,
led me straight to Bax, knocking on my door.

Therapist said, "No, this one's a rebound,"
but I silenced her voice, didn't want to be bound.
Ignoring the red flags, waving like banners,
I packed up my doubts and my reckless manners.

"Let's Cancún!" I said, "Let's take a trip.
Let's see if we're solid or bound to slip."
Bax by my side, the beach at our feet,
it was magic and madness—a bittersweet feat.

MDMA under the moonlight's glow,
we drank and danced, feeling the show.
But Beneath the surface, the neediness grew.
We missed our tour, thanks to him, too.

So, I booked a private one, eager to see
Chichén Itzá's wonders, a treasure for me.
But the trip told tales in whispers and sighs.
Red flags flew high in Cancún's skies.

Serena lost the Open—my heart shattered loud.
I left the room, found solace in the crowd.
Blackout drunk, spilling stories of pain,
my divorce, my summer, my emotional rain.

Strangers listened, wide-eyed and confused.

Bax found me sobbing, my soul feeling bruised.
"I'm the new BF," he said with a grin.
They nodded, polite, not knowing where to begin.

Cancún, the start of a chapter so bold,
where the warning signs flashed, but I didn't hold.
The drinks, the tears, the laughter, the lies,
a love built on sand under Mexican skies.

So, what's the lesson from this sun-drenched affair?
Boundaries, grief—these burdens to bear.
Therapists are wise, don't dismiss their call,
or you'll find yourself crying, tequila and all.

For when the flags fly red, it's best to retreat
before your heart's tangled in a rhythm offbeat.
Cancún was fun, a weekend of bliss,
but looking back now, it's clear what I missed.

Inspiration Behind "Cancún Confessions"
Emotion: Regretful Realization

In September 2019, I was processing my separation
from Darren while also stepping into something new with
Bax. I can now see all the red flags that were present from
the start, yet, in the moment, I ignored them, eager for an
escape from the turmoil of my divorce and the
uncertainties of my future.

I had already spent a weekend with Mark before the
Cancun trip, and that weekend made me evaluate whether
I wanted to lean into my connection with Bax. My
therapist advised me against pursuing this relationship,
explaining that it was a rebound, but I didn't listen. I
wasn't in a state to listen. The thrill of escaping into
someone new overshadowed the red flags I was too tired
to address.

The trip was a whirlwind. We took MDMA, drank too much, and enjoyed the surface-level excitement of being in a beautiful place. But Beneath that surface, the cracks were already starting to show. Bax's neediness became apparent during the trip—shown through his inability to keep up with the plans, missing the tour we had been so excited about, and his dependence on me to lead the way. At the same time, I had my own red flags. I spiraled after Serena Williams lost the U.S. Open that year, not just because of the tennis match but because I hadn't processed my grief over the divorce. It all came flooding out as I sat at the bar, pouring my heart out to strangers. Bax found me crying, and I could see his discomfort when I had to face my emotional reality.

This experience revealed to me the importance of intentionality in relationships. The trip was a learning moment about the dangers of entering into a relationship without clearly processing the grief of a previous one. I had to learn that diving into something new, while attractive, wasn't going to heal the wounds that had been left from my past. Instead, it prolonged my healing process. By not taking the time to truly grieve the end of my marriage and understand what I wanted moving forward, I set myself up for more emotional turbulence.

Cancún was the start of my journey with Bax, but it also highlighted my struggle to heal and confront the difficult emotions I had been running from. The red flags were there from the beginning, but I ignored them, clinging to the hope that a new relationship would fix what was broken inside me. In reality, healing comes from within, and no relationship can do that work for you.

If I were to recommend anything from this experience, it's to honor your healing process. Don't rush into something new to escape pain. Listen to the advice of those you trust, set clear boundaries for yourself, and don't ignore the red flags, no matter how attractive the escape may seem. The more you work on yourself, the more prepared you are for healthy and fulfilling connections.

We Moved onto Ashland

We moved into Ashland—oh, what a thrill,
from Gold Coast high-rises to Andersonville.
Bax and I, hand-in-hand, took the leap.
Our very own place, a fresh start to keep.

Day by day, the key was mine.
Gold Coast's charm now left behind.
Valentines in magic, pure romance bliss.
San Diego sunsets, we sealed it with a kiss.

Then came Ashland, our sweet new domain.
A neighborhood where the gays reign.
Andersonville—oh, what a gem.
Every corner like walking on rainbow hem.

Cafés and bars, where love's on display.
A walkable haven where we'd spend the day.
Furnishing fast, with just a few clicks.
Our new home together, it felt like a fix.

But oh, COVID came knocking with its heavy, dark veil.
The world shut down, like a ship with no sail.
Stuck inside, two souls in one space,
trying to navigate this endless rat race.

Our Mexico City trip was my birthday delight.
Orlando followed with family in sight.
We did our thing before things froze.
Before life was locked behind apartment doors.

"Stay safe, stay home"—the motto of the day.
But we just wanted to live, laugh, and play.
Zoom calls with friends, and Netflix on repeat.
Ashland became the world Beneath our feet.

We watched the news—how many more gone?
When would we dance to life's old song?
Jailed to our homes, yet grateful, it's true,
that we had each other to muddle on through.

In that little spot on Ashland, love did grow.
Through panic and fear, it started to show.
But who could know what would come next?
Locked down together, unsure and perplexed.

Yet we laughed through the chaos, found joy in the pause.
Even in silence, we'd cheer with applause.
Ashland, our haven in that crazy storm,
where even in quarantine, love stayed warm.

Now, looking back, it's strange but so clear,
Ashland was more than just a pandemic year.
It was our trial, our dance in the dark,
proof that together, we'd made our mark.

Inspiration Behind "We Moved onto Ashland"
Emotion: Nostalgic Resilience

Moving into Ashland with Bax was a symbol of
commitment and a leap into shared living. We had just left
the safety and excitement of his Gold Coast apartment,
where our relationship had blossomed through romantic
evenings, trips, and adventures. We decided to take the
plunge into a new chapter—our own place in
Andersonville, a neighborhood that felt like it welcomed
us with open arms, was gay-friendly and full of life and
promise.

The excitement was real. We had come from magical
moments like celebrating Valentine's Day and trips to San
Diego , Mexico City and Orlando. This feeling of hope and
thrill was in the air, and we looked forward to what life
together would bring. Andersonville seemed perfect for
us—quaint yet lively, walkable, and vibrant. We imagined
summer nights exploring the neighborhood's cafes, bars,
and the community around us. We set up our home, fast
and determined, ordering furniture, decorating, and
dreaming of a bright future.

But then COVID hit, and everything changed.

Instead of the summer of exploration we had envisioned, we were locked down together, confined to this new home we had barely gotten to know. The world outside was full of fear and uncertainty. Every day brought more news of death, confusion, and worry. It felt surreal, like the universe had hit a pause button. All of our plans, like everyone else's, came to a sudden halt.

The lockdown tested us. Travel is where I feel the most alive and free, but here we were, unable to move, stuck in this tiny space. Our trips, our adventures, everything came to an abrupt stop. And yet, amidst the fear and chaos, we found moments of joy. We adapted, as humans do, finding small pleasures in the mundanity of life—Netflix marathons, Zoom calls with friends, and quiet nights where we clung to each other in an uncertain world.

In therapy, I've learned the importance of navigating the unexpected, especially in relationships. COVID taught us both that the "unknown" is a constant companion. It's something we can't predict or control, and sometimes, we just have to learn to coexist with it. The lockdown made me face aspects of our relationship I might not have otherwise noticed so soon. I had to reckon with my expectations—what I had hoped our life together would be versus what reality delivered.

Therapeutically, there's a lot to unpack from this situation. Moving into a shared space, especially during a time of global crisis, magnifies every emotion. You're forced to confront your partner in ways you never anticipated. The themes of patience, resilience, and adaptability come to the forefront. In therapy, I've often talked about boundaries and communication, and during that time, I realized how essential both are when you're confined together in such close quarters.

Life will throw the unexpected at you, and how you respond matters. COVID was one giant curveball, but it taught me that being adaptable—being able to go with the flow and make the best of the situation—is crucial in any relationship. Bax and I learned to find new ways to entertain ourselves and enjoy each other's company, even when the world outside felt like it was falling apart.

Through this process, I've realized that relationships are not just about the big moments or the grand plans. They are about how we weather the unexpected together, how we support each other in times of crisis, and how we remain grateful for the small moments that keep us going.

The move to Ashland and the experience of COVID lockdown taught me more about love, patience, and resilience than I could have imagined. It wasn't the journey I expected, but it was one that strengthened us, even as we faced so much uncertainty.

San Diego: The Sunny Move

We packed our past in boxes, taped shut with hope,
sent them west on Amtrak, San Diego's our scope.
Ashland sublet, Chicago house under the knife,
we flew out to sunshine, chasing a new life.

"Do the damn thing!"—Symone had said.
Her words in my head, a future to tread.
Thirty days later, no time to delay.
Off to California, no clouds, just sun rays.

The beach was our canvas, every day, a new hue.
Sand underfoot, the sky always blue.
Tennis by twilight, hikes under stars.
California living, no limits, no bars.

But Beneath the palm trees, a shadow grew tall.
Bax's mental health, the toughest of all.
I thought it was COVID that dimmed his bright spark.
Turns out, the struggles had long left their mark.

Weed masked the problems, gummies paved the way
for fun-filled nights and same-old days.
But soon, the haze couldn't hide what was clear.
The future we built couldn't just disappear.

I was funding the dream, building the base,
but in his panic, Bax couldn't keep pace.
San Diego shone, but inside, I was torn.
How do you thrive when love feels so worn?

Weed and worries, cycles on repeat.
Two to four weeks, then came the defeat.
Good days were fleeting, dark days too long.
I realized, through therapy, this wasn't where I belong.

A talk about drugs, addiction in tow.
Bax said he'd quit, but the progress was slow.
He wouldn't seek help, inpatient or not.
Said he'd fix it alone, but success was a shot.

Our move was a promise, a dream in the sun,
but life isn't perfect, no matter how fun.
San Diego gave me so much to achieve,
but love should be more than just learning to grieve.

So, lesson learned under that Californian sky.
No weed or worries can help you get by.
If love's what you seek, make sure it's aligned
with the life you want, not just what you find.

Inspiration Behind "San Diego: The Sunny Move"
Emotion: Disillusioned Hope

This poem reflects how the early stages of my
relationship with Bax were driven by a desire for a fresh
start, excitement about the future, and the charm of a new
environment. But as time went on, it became clear that
underlying problems, such as Bax's struggle with mental

health and dependency on substances like weed, were eroding the relationship from within.

Our move to San Diego symbolized a dream of living in sunshine and happiness, and in many ways, it provided that for a while. San Diego was a new beginning—full of sunshine, beaches, hikes, and the beauty of the West Coast. But no amount of sunny weather could change what was happening internally, both within Bax and in our relationship.

It is important to recognize early signs of struggle in a partner and to understand how unresolved personal issues can impact a relationship. In therapy, one of the themes I learned was that no matter how much I wanted to fix or help Bax, the work had to come from within him. You can't save someone from their own internal battles, no matter how much you love them or how many fresh starts you try to create together.

I learned that I couldn't carry both of our weights, especially when I was dealing with my own grief, change, and responsibilities. Therapy helped me see that I was taking on more than I could handle—financially, emotionally, and mentally. The relationship was draining me because I was trying to be everything for Bax when I needed to focus on my own needs.

The poem reflects the beauty of what we tried to build—a life together in San Diego, filled with travel, laughter, and the freedom of living in a new place. But it also reveals the cracks that form when one person isn't in a stable place mentally and the other is trying to overcompensate. Therapy taught me that love alone isn't enough to sustain a relationship when deeper issues are at play.

I also learned that masking grief and reality with substances or avoidance was not a healthy way to cope. Eventually, through therapy, I realized that while I could support Bax, I couldn't fix him, and staying in a relationship where I felt more like a caretaker than a partner was only harming me in the long run.

In reflecting on the move to San Diego and everything that came with it, I realize how important it is to be intentional about what you want in a relationship and to ensure that both partners are on stable ground mentally, emotionally, and physically. If one person is struggling with addiction or mental health, it can become impossible to build a healthy future together unless both individuals are willing to put in the work—individually and together.

Echoes of Reflection:

A Journey Through Shadows and Light Series

Between Lines of Color and Light

Beneath the stark glow of moon's introspective eye,
in the quiet aftermath of pulsing neon nights,
I sift through the remnants of a scattered mind—
words fleeting, thoughts incomplete, a frustrating bind.

A tapestry woven from black threads on white—
My life, a canvas where every stroke is a fight
for understanding, for space, within a sea of faces pale,
where my voice must shout against a gale.

Even the most 'woke' cannot fathom the depths
of a life painted with broader, darker strokes of breaths.
Privilege sits unbidden at their morning tables,
a menu of choices, while my narrative remains a fable.

But through this fog of chemical descent and rise,
I grasp a fragment of your strife as my prize.
It rings true, a bell in the night, clear and loud.
A connection, at last, breaking through the cloud.

Your journey, not unlike my own, yet worlds apart,
draws a map of empathy across the heart.
Together, perhaps, we can chart the unseen,
navigating channels where no light has been.

Echoes of Cass and Beyond

From the halls of a Detroit school, underlaid with historic
tones,
to the private classrooms where my future was sown.
Each word, each lesson, a stepping stone
in the city's heart, where Black excellence is grown.

I rose, a phoenix, from educational divides,
where rankings and statistics attempt to hide
the truth of disparity, the ongoing ride
from underfunded districts to achievement's tide.

The blackboard was my battleground, my theater of war.
Words, my soldiers, knowledge the core.
Struggling through textbooks, grades, and scores.
Emerging with a diploma, opening new doors.

Yet, it was not just about escaping or rising above,
but understanding my roots, and with push and shove,
making a space for myself, with love,
acknowledging the journey, the below and the above.

Now, as I pen down my life, my history,
I see how education shaped my mystery.
From Cass Tech's loyal halls to collegiate glory,
I write my own script, I tell my own story.

Vows of the Heart

In the silence that follows the storm's fierce cry,
as substances fade and the night draws nigh,
I see you clearer than ever before.
Your struggles, your strength, our core.

You, my first white love across cultural lines,
teaching me patience, reading the signs
of a world not made for us, but still we try.
Building bridges with words between you and I.

We talk, and I talk too much, maybe it's true.
But each word I spill is a bridge, my gift to you.
To explain, to express the world through my eyes.
To show you the colors beyond the skies.

Our love, a commitment, deeper than the sea.
You're more than a boyfriend, you're future to me.
We tackle life's challenges side by side,

in sickness and health, with nothing to hide.

I chose you, in a moment and forever more,
to walk this path with, to explore
every high and low, every joy and pain,
in love's sacred dance, in sunshine and rain.

Last Dance with Shadows

In the flicker of twilight's last defiance,
we danced with shadows, indulging silence.
Xtasy's whispers, G's quiet hum,
edibles lost in a night that succumbed
to a carnival of lights inside our minds,
where thoughts spun wild, untamed by binds.

Once, I stood firm—a stalwart against the tide,
scorning the very essence of the ride
that drugs provided, a vehement "no,"
marking boundaries where I'd never go.
But that night, as chemicals wove through my veins,
I found myself unchained, exploring new lanes.

Reflection came with the morning's sober breath.
A clarity born from the brink of death.
Though insights sparkled, sharp and profound,
they bore the weight of truth newly found—
That while the night offered a thought-provoking space,
it veiled true feelings—a momentary grace.

Love and commitment, entwined in that high,
seemed clearer, purer, under that starlit sky.
But as dawn broke, so too did the illusion,
leaving behind clarity and a quiet conclusion:
The essence of me was not in the haze,
not in the blur of those wandering days.

Now, standing in the aftermath, the choice rings true.
No more hard dances in the night's residue.
Occasional weed, a whisper of past calls.

Gummies and smokes in evening's soft falls—
But gone are the days of hard liquor's embrace,
Now, I walk a path clear in a steadier pace.

From ecstatic highs to reflective lows.
From the heart's quick beat to its composed repose.
This journey has taught me the strength of my will
to choose, to refuse, to be tranquil.
For every moment of weakness, there's a stronger day,
and in my heart, I know I've found my way.

Echoes of love, education, and identity's dance
all weave through my life, by chance and by stance.
And as I look back, with a heart firm and clear,
I cherish the growth from year to year.
For in the mirror of past with its shadows cast,
I see not just where I've been, but where I can last.

Inspiration for "Echoes of Reflection: A Journey Through Shadows and Light Series"
Emotion: Introspective Clarity

This is a collection that captures key moments in my life where growth, self-awareness, and hard decisions collided. It's a reflection on the powerful and sometimes destructive influence of relationships—how being with someone can introduce you to things that challenge your core, like drug use—and the realization that love alone can't save someone who isn't ready to save themselves. This series represents my third and final flirtation with drugs, and more importantly, it documents the moment I chose a different path, leaving behind both the substances and the relationship that pushed me toward them.

The poem "Between Lines of Color and Light" explores the complexities of trying to exist as a Black man in a relationship with someone who just couldn't understand that part of me. It's about the frustration of trying to explain my experience in a world that isn't built for people like me, and how love sometimes isn't enough to bridge that gap. This poem reflects on the deeper challenges of navigating racial identity in a relationship where privilege sits unexamined, and where my lived experience can't just be "explained" to someone who hasn't lived it.

The poem "Echoes of Cass and Beyond" I take a step back and reflect on my roots in Detroit, where my sense of self was first shaped. Growing up in underfunded schools and still pushing through to rise above—it's the story of a kid determined to make something of himself, despite all odds. My education wasn't just about survival; it was about learning how to thrive in a world that tried to limit me. Detroit taught me resilience, and this poem is my ode to that. It's about where I come from and how it made me who I am.

The poem "Vows of the Heart" digs into the love I once shared with Bax. It was the first time I crossed racial lines in a relationship. There was so much we shared, and in many ways, I thought this was it—that we could weather any storm. But love can't fix everything, and being there for someone, no matter how deep that love runs, doesn't mean you can pull them out of their own darkness. I wanted to be his rock, but I was only human. Sometimes you can't help someone if they're not ready to help themselves, and that realization hurt more than anything.

The poem "Last Dance with Shadows" is the heart of the collection. It captures my last experience with hard drugs—a night where I gave in, let go, and let the chemicals take over. That moment was everything I had once stood against, but it was also a turning point. I had always been strong enough to say no, but love can make you do things you never thought you would. That night was a blur of lights and hazy conversations, and by the time the sun came up, I knew I'd reached my limit. I haven't touched anything like that since. It was clear that while I could walk away, Bax couldn't—and that's when I knew our paths were diverging. I couldn't be the person to save him, and it broke us. This poem is about the moment I chose me, my health, and my future, leaving behind the lifestyle that didn't align with who I truly was.

This series reflects the duality of love and loss, of being pulled into someone else's orbit only to find your way back to your own center. It's about the realization that even when you love someone, there are things you cannot and should not fix for them. I had the strength to say no to the drugs, but I couldn't make Bax say no, and that was the beginning of the end for us. This journey—through love, identity, and reflection—has taught me the importance of choosing myself, and that's what this collection stands for.

Italy, a Verb

Italy became a verb,
a whispered joke,
a warning from friends:
"Don't Italy me," they'd say.
Charmaine was first to drop the line,
a lesson in love wrapped up in travel's disguise.

Italy, the stage where Darren's chapter closed,
where love crumbled like ancient ruins.
But this time, with Bax,
I walked in with hope,
not haunted by past shadows.

I planned Italy for his birthday,
crafted it like a masterpiece,
just like I did before.
From San Diego to Washington's misty peaks,
we reshuffled plans, dodged Canadian borders,
found ourselves in Italy's embrace,
where the air should have felt lighter,
where beauty should have blossomed between us.
But no, Bax brought his demons—
withdrawals from a pact he couldn't keep.

Cinque Terre's cliffs stood tall,
but Bax was a shell, a ghost,
detached from the vibrancy around us.
I was in Italy,
but Italy wasn't in me—
not with his moods twisting the joy
of the sun-soaked streets.

I tried to lift us up,
like I always do,
but the weight of it all,
his depression, his quiet battles,
dragged me into a place where I knew
there was no future.

We sat in Manarola,
the sky painted in Ligurian blue,
but the conversation was gray,
his tired eyes telling stories of medications untaken,
of struggles unspoken,
and I, always the hopeful,
thought maybe—just maybe—
we could fix it.

But the climb down from the hills
left me drained.
The whispers of hope faded,
replaced by the certainty
that we were over.
Italy did it again.

Florence, Rome—
we danced the awkward waltz of a relationship in ruins.
I played the tour guide.
He played the man fighting to get out of bed.
I tried to salvage what I could,
to show him the city he loved,
but we both knew the truth.
The end was near.

When the plane took off,

we parted ways,
him to New York,
me back to San Diego.
I was tired of the caretaker role,
tired of the weight of it all.
Italy broke us,
but it set me free.

I found my light again,
dropped 30 pounds of burden,
escaped the orbit of chaos.
That October marked the start
of my own rebirth,
and by the time COVID quarantined us,
the final straw was laid.
Italy, once a noun,
now a verb for endings,
but also,
for beginnings.

Inspiration behind "Italy, a Verb"
Emotion: Resigned Liberation

The period in my life transformed "Italy" from a place—
into a verb, a curse, a marker of the end of significant
relationships. Italy now holds a bittersweet place in my
life's story, tied directly to the unraveling of love with
Darren and later Bax. It became clear that if I couldn't find
joy in one of the most beautiful places on earth, then that
relationship wasn't meant to continue.

The first time I went to Italy with Darren, it was the
beginning of the end of our relationship. Our issues were
bubbling under the surface, but I realized on that trip that
something vital was missing. Fast forward to my trip with
Bax, and the same themes resurfaced, but this time with a
deeper understanding of my own needs. We were coming
off a months-long road trip from San Diego to
Washington, a trip that should have been full of adventure

and excitement, but the undercurrent of substance abuse had already started to shift the tone. The exhaustion of trying to maintain something with Bax while dealing with his mood swings, withdrawals, and overall disconnection became overwhelming. I planned this Italy trip as a birthday gift, hoping to share one of my favorite countries with someone I cared about. But the very thing I loved—travel—became a source of tension and frustration.

Italy, the country, didn't fail me. The experiences didn't let me down. But the relationship itself was no longer salvageable, and I couldn't force happiness into it. Italy, this time around, became a space for painful realizations. The trip was beautifully planned, with hopes that Bax would appreciate every aspect of it. I wanted him to experience Italy through my eyes, through the lens of travel being one of the happiest parts of my life. However, instead of bringing us closer, it tore us apart.

Bax had been struggling with substance abuse and mental health for a long time, but I didn't realize just how deeply it impacted his ability to be present in the moment. The withdrawal from drugs hit hard during our trip, and his depression cast a heavy shadow over every beautiful view, shared meal, and quiet walk. Even in Cinque Terre, one of the most stunning places on earth, I felt isolated and emotionally drained. I wanted to give Bax the gift of joy, but instead, I was met with his detachment. During the car ride back to our villa, I knew our relationship was over.

Breaking up with someone on their birthday trip isn't something I ever wanted to do. It felt cruel, but it was necessary. We tried to make the best of the rest of the trip, putting on brave faces, trying to salvage the remaining time. We toured Florence and Rome, and I did my best to show him the beauty of Italy and to honor his love for Roman history, but it was clear that we were just going through the motions. The dance of trying to be kind to each other while knowing we were no longer connected emotionally was exhausting.

The lessons I took from this experience are layered. One of the clearest is that if I'm not happy on a trip—something that usually brings me immense joy—then that relationship is not for me. Travel is a sacred part of who I am, and it's often where I feel most alive and connected to the world. If a relationship hinders that feeling, it's a sign that it's not right.

From a therapeutic perspective, it's important for anyone in a similar situation to recognize the signs of emotional depletion. Therapy teaches us to listen to our bodies and minds when they're telling us something is wrong. In this case, the emotional weight of being with someone who was battling addiction and mental health challenges became too much to bear. It's important to acknowledge when you've taken on a caretaker role in a relationship, and when that role starts to erode your own well-being.

Through therapy, I've learned ways to t heal and avoid future patterns:

1. **Boundaries:** Learn to set clear emotional and physical boundaries, especially when addiction or mental health is involved. Without boundaries, you risk losing yourself in someone else's chaos.

2. **Self-Care:** Prioritize your own well-being. If being with someone is detracting from your joy and your mental health, it's time to reassess the relationship. Self-care isn't selfish—it's survival.

3. **Emotional Honesty:** Don't delay difficult conversations. While breaking up on a birthday trip wasn't ideal, delaying the inevitable only prolongs pain. Honesty is difficult but necessary for both parties to move on.

4. **Recognizing Patterns:** Italy, for me, became a symbol of endings. It's important to recognize when

certain places, behaviors, or situations trigger the same emotional outcomes. Break the cycle, and don't repeat the same mistakes.

5. **Substance Abuse Awareness:** In future relationships, I'm clear about my stance on substance abuse. It's something I avoid because I've seen firsthand how damaging it can be. If addiction is part of the equation, it's important to set boundaries early and ensure your partner is in a healthy, stable place.

The Italy trip—and the painful breakup that came with it—was a necessary step in reclaiming my own happiness. It was a lesson in letting go and accepting that not all relationships are meant to last. Even the most beautifully planned trips can't fix something fundamentally broken. As I look ahead, I carry the lessons learned from Italy with me, hoping to break the curse of using travel as a way to mend what's beyond repair, and instead, using it as a tool for joy, discovery, and connection with the right person.

Beneath the Sun of San Diego

In the cool breath of March, my world unspun,
a tapestry frayed at the seams—
Divorce whispered its final decree,
as I wandered through life's in-between.

June's heat marked our parting of ways,
a retreat for the sake of my heart
from a home that no longer felt safe,
where love's light had dwindled to dark.

Then came Brandon, unexpected,
in the shadow of my solitude,
offering whispers of comfort,
a presence both calming and shrewd.

As the pandemic's grip tightened,
we clung to each other for ease.
His mind, a maze left unlighted,
succumbed to a silent disease.

Italy's skies bore our last dance,
on his birthday, under Tuscan sun,
where the threads of our romance
frayed further, coming undone.

His anger, a tempest at noonday.
My spirit, a vessel bereft
in the ruins of what we once called 'us.'
I left him heartbroken, yet deft.

Now home, in the arms of San Diego,
each corner whispers his name.
The life we had planned out together,
a memory, flickering flame.

He's moving on, steps growing firmer
on paths we were meant to explore—
Medicated, hopeful, and surging
towards a future away from our shore.

While I sit with our dog, dear Sasha,
Both hearts bruised by the echoes of loss.
In the quiet, I ponder the cost
of love's labor and time's albatross.

For in leaving, I've learned the hard lessons
of love that consumes and depletes,
Yet, in solitude's harsh confessions,
find strength in these bittersweet beats.

So here's to the healing, the hurting,
to the journey of finding one's peace
in the wake of a love's final curtain.
May my soul from this sorrow release.

Truth's Reckoning

In the silence of unspoken lies,
where comfort cradled us in deceit,
a harsh truth cuts through the quiet skies—
challenging the false retreat.

I yearn to be held, to be known,
cradled in arms that promise the morn,
yet stand as Superman, stark and alone—
Who guards my night until the dawn?

This moment, fleeting, is but a thread
woven through the fabric of our plight.
An echo of what the wise have said:
Truth's discomfort is the path to light.

It's a process, this painful unmasking,

of tearing down walls built by lies.
A daunting, solitary tasking,
under the ever-watchful skies.

Let me not fault the truth that stings
but the deceit in which comfort lies.
For only in truth's embrace, it brings
the strength to claim the awaited prize.

So here I stand, in the break of day,
Superman, with no hero in view—
Unmasking falsehoods along the way,
embracing the real, the brave, the true.

Lessons on the Edge of Love

I've learned the chase, a fleeting thrill,
where love and laughter filled the void.
Yet, in the hunt, I lost the will
to see what truly should be enjoyed.

Chasing dreams of family, of delight.
Lost in moments that felt so right.,
I overlooked the finer details in sight—
Who matches my journey, who fits just tight.

In giving care, I vanished into their days,
their needs, their chaos, their endless maze.
In seeking joy, I forgot my own ways
and strayed from the paths that deserved my gaze.

But now, I've grown in tastes and thought.
Podcasts charm and new tunes caught.
My eyes have opened to worlds untaught,
understanding depths previously fought.

I've learned the pain of love's disguise,
the sting of betrayal, the heavy sighs.
How can love be true amid the lies?

And why do these questions always rise?

He claimed my heart, yet spared his own.
A mirror held to truths unshown.
My voice, my pain, dismissed, unknown
in his story, where I'm merely a loan.

And yet, I stand, more whole, more keen,
to find the fit, not just the scene.
To be alone, to blend, to wean,
off love that's fleeting, not serene.

I dream now of a foreign touch.
A romance born from learning much.
In Spanish whispers, in gentle clutch,
finding love that feels just right, as such.

From Italy's lessons, harsh but true,
I saw the life that wouldn't do.
His path and mine, askew.
Relief in parting, as I pursue.

So here I learn, picky and wise,
to find a love that truly ties.
No more the traitor's sweet disguise,
but a bond that honors, satisfies.

In the Dance of Light and Shadow

In the ebb and flow of mind's tides,
where shadows stretch, and the bright side hides,
what's it like, you ask, to share a life
with one whose soul is a double-edged knife?

Bipolar whispers, a tempest's peace,
storms of silence, sudden release.
A partner's dance on a shifting floor,
where darkness looms when light is no more.

Education, our guiding star,

we learn the contours of each scar.
Both must navigate this delicate dance.
In understanding, we find our chance.

A healthy home, a shared endeavor,
holds us tight when we'd sever.
Accountability, a mutual creed,
forgiving the stumbles as we each proceed.

Sessions shared with a guiding voice,
in therapist's room, we make our choice
to see the person beyond the disease.
To love the depths, the soul's unease.

For though the illness casts a long shadow.
In its wake, misdeeds we must not allow.
Understanding, yes, but boundaries clear.
Love does not mean living in fear.

The ordinary becomes our case.
Within imperfection, we find our grace.
In this dance of shadow and light,
we hold each other through the night.

The Unseen Tides of the Mind

How many shades can a day wear
when the mind swings its pendulum unrestrained?
Awakening, no harbinger can declare
which hue from the spectrum will be gained.

On the crest of morning, I may find
a veil of gray draped across my thoughts,
heavy, obscuring the tasks aligned,
where vigor wanes and cheer distorts.

The world a canvas bleak and bare.
Nothing to sate the palate or will.
The inner hamster stumbles in its lair,

and the vibrant earth stands oddly still.

Yet, come another dawn, a vibrant surge.
Ideas teem like stars in night's embrace.
Energy boundless, on the verge
of spilling stars into the void of space.

Sleep flees from the electric pulse of my skin,
a restless ocean with no shore in sight.
Anger bubbles from within,
a tempest small provokes a storm to smite.

But with the grace of chemistry's quiet hand,
a middle path is carved from the stone of extremes.
Not to flatten, but to understand,
to dampen the peaks and elevate the dreams.

My mood, a solitary traveler through the day,
may shift the skies from clear to gray—
one transformation, sometimes two,
contained and cradled in medicinal dew.

In the ballet of highs and lows,
the swings are fewer than fears propose.
For those who shift with the sun's arc,
each day, a journey from dawn to dark.

Session Lines: Guidance Through the Maze

In the quiet office, words like threads weave
patterns of thought, CBT's tight cleave.
Julie speaks, her voice a calm, clear sieve,
filtering the chaos Bax's mind conceived.

"Dependent traits," she notes, "will strain the seams
of love and care till frayed are all your dreams.
Anxiety, depression, like dark streams,
flow deep, where rumination ever teems."

She speaks of cups that never brim with joy,
of pasts that haunt and futures that alloy.
"Not all had perfect starts, nor ploys
to skirt the shadows life might deploy."

"Trauma shapes," she says, "but doesn't dictate;
The past is set, yet now we navigate.
Hold not to griefs or slights that fate
might once have dealt, for new paths we can create."

Her counsel drifts to presence, being here,
"Live in the now," she urges, "hold this near.
Discard the 'what ifs,' drop the fear,
Embrace today, let tomorrow's skies clear."

On bipolar, undiagnosed, unseen,
she suggests a path where he might lean
towards stability, a keener sheen.
Of life where less is chaos, more serene.

"Speak with your therapist," a bridge to cross.
"Commit to treatments, count the real cost.
No more edibles, no more loss.
Prescriptions followed, no more chaos tossed."

The session's close, a plan somewhat defined.
Co-pays and calls, a checklist designed
to anchor Bax, to ease his mind
in hope that peace, they both might find.

Thus spoke Julie, in therapy's embrace,
a guide through mental health's intricate lace.
With every word, a step towards grace
in healing's journey, their shared chase.

Whispers in the Weight of Silence

In the quiet halls of our shared space,
echoes of my unspoken truths hang dense.
A tapestry of silence weaves its lace

around words unuttered, feelings intense.

I've become a friend, not a partner, in this dance.
Adored, perhaps, but never wholly heard.
Friendship's kisses, light as air, by chance,
miss the mark where deeper passions stirred.

I feel the ghost of touch, the faintest trace
of desire once declared in fervent embrace.
Now, the bed, cool and wide, leaves empty space
where warmth and want should interlace.

He sees my words as daggers, not keys,
unlocking doors to shared malaise.
When I voice my needs, it's as if a breeze
turns to hurricanes, my wants a maze.

He bears the look of one who's blamed,
when all I seek is to be known.
Not faulted, fixed, or even tamed—
just seen, just heard, not so alone.

The weight of worlds upon my back,
a solitary bearer of tomorrow's dreams.
In partnership, shouldn't there be slack?
A sharing of the load, a seam?

Italy looms, a test of trust.
Can I rely on him to thread
through COVID's needle as we must,
or will I navigate our path instead?

This dance of closeness breeds my doubt.
Compatibility's questioned tune.
My heart wants in, my head wants out.
Oh, how the silence fills the room.

Solitude in Companionship

In the quiet corners of our shared space,
lies a silence deep and opaque,
where understanding meets its boundary,
and love wrestles with isolation's quarry.

A partner's mind, a labyrinth unexplored,
where shadows play, and light is stored.
Mental tempests brew behind calm eyes,
a storm that love alone can't stabilize.

Significant misbehaviors, a turbulent wave,
born from a place dark and grave.
Understanding lends compassion's hand,
but doesn't excuse the acts that reprimand.

Not all misdeeds can wear this cloak.
Some are just echoes of pain evoked.
The illness is but one part of the soul.
Accountability—each partner's role.

Thus, in this partnership, I often find
a solitude that leaves one blind.
Together yet alone, in a silent plea,
longing for a harmony that's free from plea.

So we tread carefully on paths unseen,
navigating the space that lies between.
Loving deeply, yet from afar,
in the dance of the mind's bizarre bazaar.

Session Verses: Clarity in the Chaos

In the quiet refuge of our shared space,
I lay the terms of love and its embrace:
No tolerance for substance's chase,
a line drawn firmly, a necessary base.

I've been here before, the weary tread,
where promises dim and fears are fed.
I need my space when weariness spreads,
a moment alone, where no thread intrudes or weds.

Yesterday, my voice seemed lost in the gale.
My words, my needs, behind your narrative did pale.
You crafted letters, a recount of our tale,
but missed the heart, where true comforts prevail.

Therapeutic Verses: Navigating the Waves of Mental Health in Love

In the consulting rooms where silence speaks,
where echoes of 'us' blend with personal peaks,
we sat, Julie's words weaving through the weeks,
advice on balance when one's mental health seeks.

She spoke of dependence, a heavy chain that clings,
of anxiety and depressions with wide, sweeping wings.
"Rumination fills their cup but never truly brings
the solace or the closure that true understanding sings."

We all carry traumas stitched into our seams,
the patchwork of our past bursting at its beams.
Yet, ownership of actions must outweigh our dreams,
for healing lies in truth, not in escape's fleeting gleams.

Undiagnosed, yet shadows danced behind your eyes.
Bipolar whispers where manic highs disguise.
"Be present," she urged, a simple yet wise
directive to live now, where our true value lies.

This journey of 'us,' complex in its script,
requires that we're mindful, with our sails adeptly clipped.
Substance, a siren that has too many gripped,
must be navigated carefully, lest our bonds are ripped.

Julie outlined a path where together we could tread,

With strategies for coping and less fear of what's ahead.
Our commitment to each other, not bound by dread,
but a partnership in healing, where love is rightly fed.

Through cognitive reframes and sessions shared,
a future painted hopeful, less by fears impaired.
For in the therapy's embrace, we are both prepared
to face mental health with less being scared.

Our love, a vessel on this vast emotional sea,
requires that we navigate it most judiciously.
As partners and as lovers, where supportively,
we embark on this journey to set our burdens free.

Navigating the Noise: A Poetic Reflection

In a world so loud, I pause to ponder,
am I lost in waves of social wonder?
Texts like waves crash into days.
Do these digital whispers lead my ways?

Amidst the fray, thoughts drift to healers,
to rituals and faith, to spiritual dealers.
Can religion mend or just unfold
a path in the vast, to clutch or hold?

Now, a question lingers in the silence,
a whisper of need, a hint of defiance.
Am I tethered too tightly to desire's fire?
Is it loneliness or a primal mire?

My heart battles with the joy it seeks
in embraces found, in whispered peaks.
Is this fervor a flight from a deeper ache
or a genuine quest for connection's sake?

Anger, too, treads within this dance,
seeking its cue, waiting for a chance.
How do I tame this fervent beast?

Turn raging storms to a tranquil feast?

And as I stand at life's broad gate,
no home yet chosen, on destiny's slate.
Should I anchor or drift awhile?
Explore this phase, mile by mile.

Each thought, each fear, each wild delight
forms the mosaic of my inner fight.
In seeking balance, I find my role
to navigate the heart, to heal, to console.

Inspiration Behind "In Tandem: Poems of Love and the Mind's Maze Series"
Emotion: Reflective Compassion

In Tandem: Poems of Love and the Mind's Maze captures moments of discovery, understanding, and emotional negotiation with my partner, Brandon, whose struggles with bipolar disorder shaped our shared and individual paths.

Our story unfolds beneath the sunny skies of San Diego, where the warmth of the environment contrasted sharply with the cool undertows of mental health challenges. "Beneath the Sun of San Diego" and "Truth's Reckoning" reflect on the duality of our experiences—moments of connection overshadowed by the realities of mental illness.

"Lesson on the Edge of Love" and "In the Dance of Light and Shadow" are about the delicate dance of love and support alongside Brandon's unpredictable moods and behaviors. These poems explore the shifting dynamics of a relationship where love is both a binding force and a battlefield of emotions.

"The Unseen Tides of the Mind" and "Sessions Lines: Guidance Through the Maze" highlight our therapeutic journeys, both together and individually. These pieces show the importance of professional guidance in navigating the confusing and often overwhelming maze of mental health.

"Whispers in the Weight of Silence" and "Solitude in Companionship" contemplate the loneliness that can permeate even the closest relationships, particularly when one partner is battling an internal storm. The poems discuss the silence that can grow, filled with unspoken words and stifled emotions, despite physical proximity.

"Sessions Versus Clarity in the Chaos" and "Therapeutic Verse" reflect on the moments of clarity achieved through therapy—both the breakthroughs and the setbacks. They reveal how therapy served as a lifeline, offering tools and insights to manage the chaos that mental illness can bring into a relationship.

"Navigating the Waves of Mental Health in Love" combines all these themes, illustrating the journey of loving someone with a mental health condition. It speaks to the ebbs and flows of emotional wellness and the impact on a romantic partnership.

Finally, "Navigating the Noise: A Poetic Reflection" caps the series with a broader reflection on my internal dialogues and external expressions. It connects personal growth with the pursuit of understanding, acceptance, and peace within the tumult of a challenging but enlightening relationship.

Each poem, crafted from real-life experiences and heartfelt reflections, aims to articulate the often indescribable facets of love, mental health, and the pursuit of personal and relational harmony. Through this poetic series, I hope to offer insights and solidarity to others navigating similar turbulent waters, illuminating shared struggles and triumphs.

Winds of Mexico

March whispered in, cold as doubt.
Chicago wrapped me tight in its gray.
Six months past an October that should've severed us,
yet here I stood, tangled in the threads of yesterday,
a ghost in your studio, north side shadows clinging,
on the phone with my therapist, her words slicing clean.
"Why don't you go?" she asked, like a door flung open.
"Why not Mexico?"—a breeze sweeping away the weight
unseen.

And so I booked it, a flight to freedom.
Mexico City rising in my mind like an oasis.
But first, I had to break what had long been broken.
Rebreak a bond that no longer held its grace.
Midnight crept as I found you lost in the blur of bottles.
Bax, drowning in your own storm.
Your eyes, glazed like glass, too far to see me,
too lost to fight, too numb to warm.

Sasha at my side, like an anchor I had to drop.
I stood there, offering goodbyes that echoed hollow.
No fight left, just the quiet weight of things undone.
And I turned, the wind at my back,
ready to follow the pull of peace,
of a life not tethered to another's fall,
to caretaking a grown man's pain.
I drove through the night, Detroit-bound with Sasha,
a fleeting stop before the skies opened and I boarded my
plane.

In Detroit, I let go—left Sasha to wait for her new dawn.
And then it was me, just me, unburdened and bare.
Mexico on the horizon, a place to be reborn.
Leaving the ashes of Chicago's cold air.
Coyocan embraced me with warmth and stillness,
an Airbnb where I unpacked my heart.
In the streets, I shed the weight of forgiveness.
In the air, I breathed in the start.

The winds had changed, and I had followed.
A life of my own, untethered and free.
Chicago, a distant storm I no longer borrowed,
and in Mexico's sun, I found the key.
To break up again, with the ghost of us gone.
To walk away, and simply move on.

Inspiration behind "Winds of Mexico"
Emotion: Liberation

I found myself trapped in a cycle I thought I had broken free from, only to be pulled back into Bax's orbit again and again. We had already broken up, been apart, but somehow, I allowed his arms to reel me back in. It started with a simple ask: "Can you help me move?" A moment of weakness, perhaps, or a sense of obligation that I hadn't yet shaken. So, I went. Then came another ask: "Why don't you return to Chicago after your trip to Lebanon?" And I did, despite knowing in my gut that I shouldn't.

The Lebanon trip was a turning point, though. I remember the clarity that hit when Bax made that comment about my Instagram story: "It looks like you're single." He said it casually, but there was an edge, a sense of ownership that felt out of place. And in that moment, I realized—he wasn't wrong. I was single. But more importantly, I needed to start acting like it. That comment was a mirror, reflecting just how deep I had slid back into the role of someone else's caretaker, someone else's emotional anchor, when I had already decided to set myself free.

When I returned to the U.S., I immediately scheduled a therapy session. I knew it was time to rebuild boundaries and to get myself out of the gravitational pull that had kept me tethered to Bax for far too long. Julie, my therapist, was my guide through this process. She didn't just help me realize I needed to get out—she helped me see why. We talked about the importance of a clean break, the need to truly disentangle from someone, even if that person isn't physically holding you. Emotional bonds can be just as binding, and I had let those invisible ties linger long after the relationship should have ended.

Why was I even there? That was the question I had to ask myself in therapy. Why was I still showing up for him when I knew he wasn't showing up for me in the way I needed? It wasn't just about Bax—it was about my own boundaries, my own need to stop repeating old patterns, to stop letting guilt or nostalgia keep me stuck in a place that wasn't healthy. Therapy helped me see that, and it gave me the tools to do what needed to be done.

This poem is about that pivotal moment—standing in his studio, realizing that, although we weren't technically together, I was still trapped. Booking that flight to Mexico City wasn't just an escape—it was the first step in reclaiming my freedom. Breaking up isn't always one clean moment; sometimes, it's a process, and I was finally ready to complete it, charting a new course with every mile traveled.

Not Quite Friends

We're not quite friends,
but once I care, it's hard to unthread the tie—
unless harm cuts deep or peace slips away.
I'll always root for you quietly, from afar.
Even when the distance stretches long,
I still hold a space where you once stood.

With Bax, it was Sasha that bridged the gap—
the day I left Chicago for Mexico City,
he took a train to Detroit, picked her up,
brought her back to Chicago
like a traveler returning to the only light
that still flickered in the dark.

I saw then what I had always known—
Sasha wasn't just a dog,

she was his lifeline, the thread
pulling him through the fog of days.
I let her stay with him, with one simple test—
"Do it yourself," I said,
knowing if he made that journey alone,
it meant something real.
And he did,
through his deepest depressions,
Sasha walked him back to life,
her leash a tether to the world
he often tried to escape.

Years passed—
two and a half, to be exact—
since I watched him claim Sasha as his own.
Then came San Diego,
months later, Bax reached out—
an apology wrapped in reflection,
like a letter delayed by the weight of time.
He thought he was moving back into my life,
but I had to build walls,
told him I was dating,
that it was time for him to go,
that the past, though familiar,
could no longer take residence here.

But even still,
I found myself rooting for him in quiet corners,
like a distant fan in a stadium,
hoping he finds his footing on unsteady ground.
We exchanged words like bridges,
his guilt and shame seeping through,
and I, offering what I could—
reminders that he could still rise,
that redemption waits,
even for the weary.
I prayed for him,
not because I had to,
but because I knew
he needed someone who believed
he could stay afloat.

He apologized again
for the delusions of San Diego,
and I forgave him,
because I know him—
not the broken pieces,
but the man who still tries,
who still seeks the light.

And so, I stand at a distance,
not quite a friend,
but someone who once cared,
and still does,
in quiet moments, in passing thoughts.
Because once you've rooted for someone's survival,
it's hard to let go completely—
even when the roads diverge,
and the years press on.

Inspiration Behind "Not Quite Friends"
Emotion: Compassion

My experience with Bax has been colored by his struggles with mental health and substance abuse—a life-long battle that touches not just the person going through it, but everyone around them. It's a battle that often feels relentless, a cycle of highs and lows that can bring out the best and worst in someone.

Addiction is an insidious force. It can erode trust, chip away at bonds, and distort the person you once knew. With Bax, I saw firsthand the way his substance abuse strained his relationships, not only with me but with his friends and family. He went through periods of withdrawal, guilt, and moments of clarity where he recognized the destruction, but the road to recovery is long and full of setbacks. Despite everything, I've always wished him well because I know the pain that comes with addiction is more than just the substances—it's the mental health struggles that fuel it.

Because of this history, I've come to value sobriety and mental clarity in my romantic relationships. I want peace of mind and to live in a space where addiction doesn't hover like a storm cloud, waiting to ruin the day. My relationship with Rafa has been such a beautiful contrast. Rafa and I believe in avoiding substances and staying clear-headed, and that alignment brings a level of trust and stability that's incredibly important to me. It's a relief to be with someone who also values health and clarity and doesn't carry the weight of addiction into the relationship.

Bax will often have moments where he reaches out, apologizes, and reflects on the damage caused by his substance abuse. I maintain boundaries with him because I need to protect my own well-being, but that doesn't mean I stop caring. In fact, once I care about someone, it's hard to turn that off completely, as long as they haven't done irreparable harm. I've always hoped Bax could repair the relationships he's damaged, get his mental health in order, and regain control of his life.

Mental health is so important, and it's not lost on me how fortunate I am to live comfortably inside my own head. I can't imagine what it's like to constantly battle the inner chaos that Bax has endured for years. I hope he finds peace. Everyone deserves the chance to live without feeling like they're drowning in their own mind.

This poem is about the complex emotions that come with caring for someone who struggles with addiction. It's about wishing them well, but also knowing that there must be boundaries for your own sanity and protection. It's about the painful recognition that sometimes, despite your best intentions, you can't save someone from their demons—they have to save themselves.

Nico

Emotion: Growth and Resilience

The Nico chapter is a profound reflection on personal growth, a complex friendship, and the delicate balance between love and boundaries. It captures the luminous moments we shared—traveling, exploring Mexico, and discovering each other's worlds—while also addressing the shadows of miscommunication, emotional strain, and the weight of mental health struggles. Through these writings, I offer a lens into the evolving nature of our bond, where affection and tension intertwined, and where compassion, healing, and hard decisions ultimately reshaped our connection. This isn't just a story about two people navigating life together but a testament to the importance of mental health, self-awareness, and the power of boundaries in fostering growth. Like life itself, this chapter weaves together light and shadow, teaching me that love sometimes means letting go and, other times, learning to love differently—more mindfully, more intentionally, and, ultimately, more authentically.

Self-Discovery in Mexico City

On a brisk March day, resolve stark as night,
I booked my passage, my spirit alight.
A one-way ticket to new skies so vast,
to sever old ties, to break free at last.

Drove down to Bax's with my world in a car.
My dog Sasha beside me, we'd travel far.
But Bax was absent, not home to face fate,
so I found him out where new endings await.

A bar's dim glow, where I closed our last page,
then east to Detroit, through the cold's sharp cage.
Sasha safe with kin, I turned once more,
to Mexico City, its heart to explore.

A week into freedom, the city's embrace,
Nico appeared, a surprising grace.
His Spanish words, a melody new.
Kind, loving, a bond that grew.

But my heart still yearned for the roads untread,
for spontaneous jaunts, by no bounds led.
Torn between love and a soul unconfined,
in Nico's arms and in travels defined.

This dance of desires, of love and free will,
Mexico's charm, its power to thrill.
Here, in the pulse of a city so vast,
I seek myself in its mirrors cast.

Inspiration Behind "Self-Discovery in Mexico City"
Emotion: Liberation

I confronted the lingering influence of my past
relationship with Brandon during a pivotal conversation
with my therapist. After our breakup during his birthday
trip to Italy, my therapist challenged me to reflect on why I

was still allowing him to occupy such a significant space in my life and to consider what I truly wanted for myself.

Motivated by this conversation, I booked a short trip to Mexico City, intending to embrace a week of exploration and independence. The poem captures my aspirations for freedom and self-discovery, juxtaposed against the unexpected reality of meeting Nico during that very trip. Despite my intentions to remain single and explore on my own terms, I found myself drawn into a new and surprising connection.

This planned solitude and unexpected companionship form the core theme of the poem, highlighting the unpredictable nature of life and the complex interplay between personal intentions and the surprises life throws our way. It's a reflection on the continual balancing act between seeking personal independence and embracing the connections that come unexpectedly, shaping our journey and personal growth.

How We Met

I landed in CDMX, full of hope and drive,
eager to learn, eager to thrive.
Intentions clear: be single, have fun,
enjoy the city, date—under the Mexican sun.

Seven dates in, exhaustion hit.
But when Nico pinged, I wasn't feeling it.
Tired, distracted, watching Nadal play,
I almost said, "Nah, maybe another day."

But something in his pics, or maybe his vibe,
made me say, "Okay, come by, just chill—no tribe."
Ordered tacos, poured wine, "The Normal Heart" on.
Heavy movie, but hey, I was drawn.

Nico arrived, poco español.
My words were fumbly, but we found our stroll.

We didn't need perfect words to connect.
It was something more—we didn't expect.

"Chinga," I thought, "this guy's alright."
By day two, he stayed up all night
fixing my computer, like a techy dream.
Determined to help, like part of the team.

I wasn't looking for love, pero aquí está.
He gave me a reason to stay, no más andar.
We didn't plan it, it just felt right,
from tacos to Netflix to that first night.

Though I said I wouldn't—yeah, we did.
Morning, night, un mes sin lid.
He helped me stay so I could live.
And I gave what I had, all I could give.

No regrets in this wild journey we've run.
Though some things got heavy, it's been full of sun.
We met in Mexico under a crazy moon,
And even through the storms, I'll cherish the tune.

Nico and I, we had our ride,
from computer fixes to passion we couldn't hide.
No más dating, no más drift.
He secured my place, gave my life a lift.

And while the road's been rocky and true,
I wouldn't change it, ni tú.
Porque, in the end, what matters to me
is the love we built a little unexpectedly.

Inspiration Behind "How We Met
Emotion: Serendipity

Mexico City, I had a plan and a vision of what my life
would look like—exploring the city, meeting new people,
and immersing myself in the culture. But what I didn't

expect was meeting Nico and how that chance encounter would change my life in ways I couldn't have imagined.

When I arrived in Mexico City for a short visit, I was eager to dive into everything. I had every intention of keeping things casual, staying single, and just having fun. That week, I went on so many dates that it felt like a whirlwind—exhausting but also a thrilling way to experience the city. I let each person show me around, letting them pick the places we'd go because I wanted to see Mexico through the eyes of the locals. It was exciting, but by the end of the week, I was starting to feel worn out.

Then came the night Nico messaged me on Grindr. I was sitting in my Airbnb, drained from the whirlwind of dates, half-watching tennis and half-thinking about whether I had the energy for yet another new connection. Honestly, his pictures didn't grab me at first, and I wasn't even sure if I wanted to meet him that night. But something about his energy through the messages felt different. Maybe it was his persistence or the way he carried himself online, but I found myself telling him he could come over with the condition that we would keep things low-key. No pressure, no expectations.

We met, shared tacos, and watched "The Normal Heart," which, looking back, seems like such a heavy movie for a first meeting. But it didn't bother me. I've always been able to handle the weight of things that others might shy away from, and Nico seemed to meet me there, in that space of depth. Despite the language barrier—his Spanish and my near-zero ability to communicate in it at the time—we found a way to connect. The conversations weren't fluid, but the connection was.

There's something so profound in that—how two people who barely speak each other's language can still feel something that goes beyond words. And that's exactly what happened. By the end of the night, what I initially said I didn't want—sex—became inevitable. It was intense, passionate, and maybe unexpected, but it felt right. We found ourselves spending more time together, more nights, more mornings, until it became a rhythm.

But the true pivotal moment with Nico wasn't just the physical connection. It was his act of kindness and care. By day two, he had stayed up all night helping me resolve a personal computer issue related to my business. This wasn't just a quick fix; it was hours of him staying up, determined to help someone he'd just met. In that moment, I realized Nico wasn't just another date. He cared in a way that was beyond transactional. It was as if, even though we had just met, he already had a sense of protectiveness over me, a desire to make sure I could handle things and thrive during my trip.

That moment of him helping me solidified something between us. It wasn't just the sex or the fun of being with someone new in a vibrant city. It was the feeling of being supported in a way that was unexpected and deeply appreciated. He became someone important in my life, not because I was looking for it, but because of how naturally and generously he showed up.

The poem reflects this journey—the spontaneity, the fun, the unexpected connection that grew deeper than either of us likely anticipated. Even though our relationship had its highs and lows, I have no regrets. Every step and moment was part of a journey that taught me something about love, connection, and even myself. Yes, there were heavy moments, and not everything was easy, but the poem is reflective and celebratory. In the end, Nico helped me in a way that went beyond a typical romance—he supported me during a moment I needed it most, and for that, I'll always be grateful.

Our Journey in Two Worlds

I told him straight—"No quiero un compromiso,"
But my actions, claro, told another story.
We talked of past loves, goals for tomorrow,
of open doors and endless roads, no sorrow.

Nico listened, siempre quiet, siempre kind,
while I danced around, contradicting my mind.
He fixed my computer, made my life a breeze,
then asked softly, "Can I stay the week, por favor, please?"

I said, "Sure," thinking it's just time to share.
He came back with a duffle, ready to care.
We spent time in Coyoacán, streets full of life,
walking mercados, parks with no strife.

The talks kept coming, pushing the line
from just two friends to something divine.
The air was thick with love's slow creep.
In Coyoacán's rhythm, we let it steep.

Every visit brought new adventures to see,
from Condesa's charm to Ensenada by the sea.
A place I could breathe, take in the view,
play tennis, explore, and try something new.

Over the years, love bloomed and soared.
Through every trip, every memory stored.
Oaxaca, Chiapas, Puebla, Veracruz,
weekend escapes, no way to lose.

Tolantongo on my birthday, the caves and pools,
thermal rivers, we soaked in nature's jewels.
Traveling together, connecting the dots,
our love grew stronger in those warm spots.

But looking back, the lines were blurred.
He was my first Mexican friend, that's the word.
Best friends we could've been, claro, sí,
but we crossed a line, ya no podía resistir.

I traveled solo, came back to find
an ultimatum—"Decide, or leave behind."
So we made it official, chose the path.
No regrets, just love's aftermath.

Life's not for regrets, it's a journey we take,
learning from each twist, from each mistake.
We had fun, we laughed, we shared, we fought.
The friendship worked; the love? Maybe not.

But still, I cherish every day we spent,
from Coyoacán to Grutas, where our love was bent.
Nico and I, we danced through the flame,
and even when it ended, I'd do it again, just the same.

The Inspiration Behind "Our Journey in Two Worlds
Emotions: Bittersweet Reflection

When I first visited Mexico City, I had no plans for a serious relationship, and I was very upfront about that with everyone I met, including Nico. However, as life often goes, things didn't exactly follow my plan.

I began with the mindset that I would live freely, embrace my independence, and perhaps engage in casual connections, but nothing serious. Yet, from the moment I met Nico, something shifted, even though I couldn't quite admit it to myself.

After Nico stayed that first night, that night turned into more nights whenever I returned to Mexico City. We shared moments, deepened our connection, and started to build something that felt unexpected yet meaningful.

He leaned in, and slowly, without even realizing it, so did I.

During my visits, we spent time exploring Coyoacán, a vibrant part of Mexico City. Life during those visits became about more than just surviving—it became about thriving together in the moments we shared. We explored the streets, spent time in the parks and mercados, and enjoyed the vibrant atmosphere of the area. Our conversations started to change too. We began talking about more than just surface things. We talked about what we wanted, what we valued, and eventually, the lines between being just friends and something more began to blur.

I look back on our travels across Mexico as some of the best moments we shared. Traveling with someone—especially through the beautiful landscapes of Oaxaca, Chiapas, Puebla, and Veracruz—creates a bond. It deepens the connection. Our trip to Tolantongo for my birthday was a highlight. The thermal pools, caves, and rivers felt like a dream. That day stands out in my mind as a time when we were truly in sync, enjoying the moment, connected to each other and to the nature around us.

But, as the poem reflects, the story wasn't all about the good times. There were moments of tension and conflict. Nico wanted more; he wanted commitment, and I was still trying to live life on my terms—freely and independently. I traveled solo, and when I returned to Mexico City on one of my visits, I found myself facing an ultimatum: either we would commit and figure out what our relationship was, or we would part ways. He couldn't continue to deal with my freedom and with me seeing other people while he was emotionally invested in us. So, we made it official, even though deep down, I had my doubts about whether this was the right move.

Nico and I had an intense, whirlwind relationship that was filled with highs and lows. While a lot of things didn't work, especially the romantic aspect of our connection, I have zero regrets. I don't regret making it official because every experience and relationship teaches you something. I learned about myself, love, what I truly value in a relationship, and what works and what doesn't.

Our friendship was the foundation of everything. Even when the relationship part didn't work out, the friendship was strong. He was my first true Mexican friend, and that bond is something I'll always hold close. In hindsight, maybe we should've kept things at the friendship level, but life doesn't always allow for those clean lines. The sexual and emotional connections had already been made, and once you cross that line, it's hard to go back.

I wanted to capture that dynamic in the poem and the feeling of traveling together, growing closer, and the inevitable tension that comes when one person wants more than the other is willing to give. I also wanted to express the gratitude I have for the time we shared. Nico helped me navigate Mexico City during my visits. He made me feel at home in a place that was new to me, and I'll always appreciate that.

The poem reflects the bittersweet nature of our relationship—how we started as friends, grew closer through shared experiences, and eventually had to face the reality of what we were. But it's a happy reflection because there are no regrets. Life is a series of lessons, and Nico was part of an important chapter in mine. He taught me about love, patience, and the importance of friendship, even when things don't go the way you expect.

Our Language of Love

He spoke Spanish, I spoke English—
Neither fluent in the other's tongue.
But somehow, we communicated
before words ever found our lungs.

It began in silence, intentional and sure,
in gestures, in glances, in actions so pure.
Our language was movement, unspoken intent.
No need for words when our bodies were bent.

Making love became our first conversation,
a dialogue of touch, of pure sensation.
And when we needed more than the heat of the night,
we leaned on Google Translate to get it right.

I'd fumble through Spanish, my tongue unsure,
but he smiled, his patience made me endure.
And when anger flared, when my words hit fast,
I'd switch to English, emotions too vast.

If he wasn't too mad, he'd follow along,
but when his stubborn Capricorn kicked in strong
I'd translate each sentence, both angry and clear,
switch back to Spanish, hoping he'd hear.

Over time, we built a bridge of sound.
Our voices found a rhythm, a common ground.
His Spanish became mine, my English his own.
In this language of love, our words had grown.

He didn't master English the way I did his.
But after 2.5 years, he could speak, and I'd miss
not a word of his Spanish, not a turn of phrase—
We understood each other in so many ways.

Yet language wasn't the wall between us.
It was the minds, the desires, the fuss.
Two hearts wanting different things.
Trying to fly with mismatched wings.

Language, you see, wasn't the true barrier.
It wasn't about verbs or grammar errors.
It was communication beyond the sound.
The ability to listen, to stand our ground.

We grew, we learned, we tried our best,
but sometimes love isn't just the test.
It's not the words that fail to flow—
It's understanding when to let go.

In the end, we spoke a language of grace

but wanted different things, a different place.
No regrets, just lessons learned.
In this language of love, no bridges burned.

For even if words fell short in the end,
we once shared a language, my lover, my friend.

Inspiration Behind "Our Language of Love"
Emotion: Nostalgic Understanding

This poem captures one of the most interesting
dynamics of my relationship with Nico—our language
barrier and how we grew beyond it. When we first met,
neither of us spoke the other's language fluently. Nico
spoke Spanish, and I spoke English. That alone could have
been a barrier, but it wasn't. The language of
communication between us was always something deeper
than words.

In the early stages of our relationship, we
communicated through actions, non-verbal cues, and
physical connection. The love we built wasn't rooted in
conversations or deep philosophical debates—it was in the
way we moved around each other, the way we touched,
laughed, and just existed in the same space. We found
ways to communicate without needing perfect Spanish or
English. There was a simplicity that felt natural, even
though it wasn't easy.

One of the things I realized with Nico was how much of
our communication was silent, intentional, and action-
based. Our love language wasn't spoken—it was shown.
Whether through the intimacy we shared, the care he took
in helping me adjust to life in Mexico or the small gestures
of everyday life, we communicated in an effective way,
even if it wasn't through words. That's where the idea for
the opening lines came from: the notion that our love
started in silence, in touch, in understanding without the
need for verbal language.

As we moved forward in our relationship, we began to rely on more words. Google Translate became our best friend, especially when we needed to dive deeper into each other's pasts, feelings, or discuss more complicated topics. We used it as a tool to help us understand each other on a conceptual level. But over time, we also started to naturally pick up more of each other's language. I got better at Spanish, and he improved in understanding my English. Our conversations weren't perfect, but we had built a bridge where we could communicate effectively enough to understand each other's hearts, even when we lacked the right vocabulary.

One thing I found interesting was how emotions played a role in our communication. When I was upset, I'd switch back to English—because it was faster and more immediate. There was a comfort in expressing my emotions in my native tongue, and I hoped he would understand me even if he couldn't grasp every word. And for the most part, he did. But sometimes, when things got heated, I had to stop and translate everything I said. Those moments were frustrating, but they also showed how committed we were to making it work and to understanding each other despite the barriers.

The inspiration for the middle of the poem came from those experiences—the times when we had to navigate language with patience and effort, when we had to piece together meaning through context and tone, rather than relying solely on words. Over the years, Nico got to the point where he could speak to me entirely in Spanish, and I could understand almost everything he said. There was a beautiful evolution in how we communicated. But that wasn't enough to save the relationship, because the real barrier wasn't language—it was the difference in what we both wanted out of life and love.

This leads into the core theme of the poem, which is that language wasn't the true problem. We both grew to understand each other's words, but our minds were in different places. Nico and I wanted different things—he desired more stability, commitment, and perhaps a future that I wasn't sure I could offer him. Meanwhile, I was more focused on my independence, my freedom, and my ability to explore life on my terms. The clash wasn't about our ability to speak the same language; it was about being on different life paths.

That realization is what the poem reflects toward the end. It's not the lack of words that can break a relationship—it's the inability to understand each other's desires, to align your hopes and dreams. Communication isn't just about talking; it's about listening, comprehending, and being on the same page. Nico and I were great at communicating in so many ways, but when it came down to what we each wanted from the relationship, we were speaking two entirely different languages.

I don't look back with regret. I see it as a beautiful, complex relationship that taught me so much about love, communication, and the importance of truly understanding someone beyond just words. The poem reflects that—how we grew in our ability to speak to each other, but also how we learned that communication goes far deeper than language. Despite the fact that we weren't a perfect fit romantically, the bond we shared was meaningful, and I'm grateful for the time we spent navigating both language and life together.

This poem is my way of honoring that journey— acknowledging the complexities, the fun, the frustrations, and ultimately, the love we shared in our own unique language.

Seasons of Us

From day one, I knew you weren't my one,
but that didn't stop the laughter, the fun.
You weren't my soulmate, pero sí mi mejor amigo.
In you, I found a bond deeper than just ego.

You were my first Mexican best friend.
Through you, I learned how cultures blend.
You taught me life, aquí en la ciudad.
Navigating mercados, TelCel, ¡qué necesidad!

Learning the language, los pequeños detalles.
From panaderías to las calles,
you held my hand in this foreign space,
but deep down, I knew you'd never be my place.

Sexual lines we crossed, maybe too soon.
But even as desire waned under the moon,
we stayed together, por la amistad,
laughing for hours, no need to play hard.

We traveled well, side by side.
In you, I found a calm, a perfect ride.
And when the heat died down between us two,
it was our friendship that saw us through.

I am Malcolm, I need freedom to roam,
yet in you, I found a second home.
But even homes can have cracks in the wall
and by the end, we let it all fall.

You called me an angel, tu luz en la vida.
So why shoot me down, in tu propia caída?
We could've parted, still holding hands,
but instead, we broke under life's demands.

Now I mourn not the love, but the friend.
A brother lost, a bond that couldn't mend.
It wasn't the material things you let go,
but the guidance, the help, the love I'd show.

I'm sad for you, más que por mí,
because losing me, you lost the key.
Not just to things, but to a life we shared.
To the moments where you felt truly cared.

But life moves on, the cycle breaks,
We learn, we grow from the mistakes.
No regrets, only lessons to gain.
In the end, we both endured the pain.

You weren't my one, but you were my friend.
A chapter in life that had to end.
And though it's broken, I don't look back with sorrow,
Just gratitude for the love we borrowed.

Inspiration Behind "Seasons of Us
Emotion: Bittersweet Reflection

From the very beginning, I knew Nico wasn't "the one," yet that didn't take away from the fact that we built something meaningful together. Our connection wasn't born from a desire for romance or a fairytale ending but from a place of comfort, companionship, and shared journeys.

The poem reflects that truth. Nico was my best friend, the first person who helped me navigate Mexico during my visits—a completely foreign country to me when I first arrived. Traveling to a new place comes with countless small challenges that are easy to overlook from the outside, like navigating local supermarkets, figuring out cell phone providers like TelCel, or just understanding how daily life flows in an unfamiliar environment. Nico became my guide during those visits, helping me bridge the gap between what I knew and what I had yet to learn. In many ways, he was my lifeline.

But I always knew deep down that I didn't want a committed relationship with him. I talked about it openly—about my past, my future goals, about not wanting to tie myself down. I even toyed with the idea of open relationships and what that might look like. Yet, despite my words, my actions reflected something different. There was a circular codependency happening between us that I've only come to fully understand after talking to my therapist. I was relying on Nico to help me adjust to my time in a new culture, and in return, he was looking for a deeper emotional connection.

The sexual part of our relationship faded over time, probably sooner than it should have. But the reality is, while I'm a sexual being, I didn't feel that same desire for him as I had in the beginning. Still, we stayed together, not because of sex, but because of our friendship. We genuinely loved being in each other's company. We laughed for hours, shared countless experiences, and traveled so well together. I'm particular about how I travel, and Nico never once made it difficult. If anything, he enhanced those experiences, and in those moments, we were truly connected.

Looking back, it's clear to me that our friendship was always the foundation of what we had. And in that way, Nico became more than just a friend—he was like a brother. We admired each other's differences, and while that wasn't enough to sustain a romantic relationship, it was enough to keep us close for a long time.

Unfortunately, the relationship didn't end as it should have. It wasn't a clean break, and that's something I still feel sadness over. I had envisioned Nico being a lifelong friend, someone who I could always count on. But things fell apart. The bond we had was broken in ways that felt unrepairable by the end. I've accepted that now, but it doesn't make the loss any less significant. It makes me sad, not just because I lost a friend, but because I know he lost a lot too.

Nico once called me an angel in his life, and that's something that stayed with me. I was there for him in ways beyond material things. I helped him, supported him, and was a consistent source of care and guidance. So when the relationship ended, it felt like a harsh fall—why shoot down the very person who was there to help lift you up? It's a question I still think about, and one that forms the heart of this poem. It's about mourning not just the end of a relationship, but the potential of what our friendship could have been.

But even with that sadness, I don't have regrets. Life moves in cycles, and sometimes we have to break them to grow. We learn from our mistakes and our relationships, and in the end, I believe everything happens as it should. Nico wasn't my one, but he was my friend. We shared a season of life that was meaningful and important, and for that, I'm grateful.

The poem is a reflection of that bittersweet truth. It's about the fun, the laughter, the friendship, but also the lessons learned and the reality that not every relationship is meant to last forever. Some are meant to teach us, to help us grow, and to prepare us for what comes next. That's what Nico was for me—a season of learning, growth, and connection, with no regrets.

Unfolding Narratives

In the weave of our days, amor y comprensión,
your words, Nico, unfold in tender song.
I wanted to start with apologies so soft,
for the troubles we've faced, where our paths have often
crossed.

Tu lado especial, beside you I stand,
a newbie in love, trying to understand.
Te estoy dando todo, my all I pour,
yet fear in this dance, I might stumble once more.

Communication falters, language barriers tall.
Each of us learning, aiming to forestall.
Aprendiendo idiomas, crafting love's creed,
hoping our voices can meet every need.

Your past isn't mine to alter or claim.
Mis malas experiencias, not yours to blame.
Still, I offer my lifestyle, hope you embrace.
Finding our rhythm, in this vast loving space.

Espero que tú también, understand my plea.
In empathy's cloak, may we both truly see.
Not iPhones or diets that swiftly change pace,
but lasting and real, our hearts' tender trace.

Can we, two souls, rewrite rules that bind?
Finding new pathways, leaving old ways behind?
What if we fashioned a story so bold,
where love's not a cage, but a tale to be told?

My grandmother's note likened life to a ship.
Captain and crew on a familial trip.
Navigating waters where love writes the script.
Celebrating the journey, with every hardship eclipsed.

A toast to our future, to days not yet seen,
to love that survives, where others have been.
In stories of struggle, in the joy of our play,
In the quiet moments that end each day.

¿Será posible, amor, this new plot we draft?
In the sweep of our love, the wind in our craft.
With loyalty not shackled by fear or past pain.
In the love that we foster, again and again.

So here, in these lines, our story's new page.
Not fettered by norms, nor confined by an age.
A love that is living, constantly new.
Amorcito, let's discover, what love can truly do.

Lamentar y Amar

Nico, your words echo in a silent room,
"Me gustaría empezar diciendo que lamento..."
Your regrets paint the walls
where I hang my hopes and my heartbeats.
Quiero cuidarte, amarte—
Your promises whisper through our imperfections.
We're learners of love's language,
struggling with syntax
yet fluent in feelings.
In the crossfire of cultural confusions,
we write a bilingual bond,
Imperfect yet ours.

Reglas Rotas

"Why not just us?" you ponder,
Questioning the fences we're meant to uphold.
Quien escribió esas reglas?
Are they guardians or gatekeepers?
Together, podemos escribir something different,
Rewriting rules.

Redefining the road of loyalty,
not as a cage,
but as the sky—vast, open, ours.

Diferencias y Desafíos

Your lifestyle, un mapa of divergent paths,
opens my eyes to unseen streets.
It's not about blame,
"It's about understanding," you say.
And I try,
Porque te amo.
Yet love is not just feeling, it's facing,
facing you, me, and the truths we carry.

Nuevo Día, Nuevos Sueños

El pwróximo año, nuestro primer 14 de Febrero juntos
You dream aloud,
and your dreams dress my doubts in hope.
Valentine's Days envisioned in vibrant vistas,
celebrating the ordinary in extraordinary ways.
Let's not skip the beats of our hearts
but dance to them,
louder, closer, fearlessly.

No Perdernos

"Ahora hagamos lo más sencillo… No perdernos nunca."
Your plea pins itself to my priorities,
a simple request wrapped in the complex layers of
everyday living.
Through laughs, misunderstandings, through every tear
and touch,
let's hold on.,
For in holding, we acknowledge.
In the journey, we understand.

And in understanding, we love.

Amor en Equidad

This love, una mezcla de give and take,
where each glance, each gesture holds weight.
Equally distributed,
balanced on the scales of mutual respect,
where my strength fills your voids,
and your courage covers my cracks.
Together, forming a fortress,
Not impenetrable, but inviting.

A True Companion

Contigo, every day is a discovery,
each moment, a new map to explore.
From the simplicity of shared silences
to the complexities of shared smiles,
Cada día contigo es una promise,
to try, to trust, to continue
in the dance of our intertwined destinies.

Confessions Under the Quiet Sky

In the quiet that wraps our nights,
you confess—
A stream of Spanish whispers.
Lamentations of love lost in translation.
"Lamento lo que ha estado sucediendo…"

I listen,
straining to decode heartbeats
between each syllable.
Finding my own confessions lodged
between my limited verbs and your infinite emotions.

We are two souls charting stars in different skies.
Your words, a constellation I wish to understand.
Mine, a nebula forming slowly in the expanse of your
patience.

Nuevas Reglas para Viejos Juegos

Rewriting the Rules
Who wrote the rules we try to follow?
Those old scripts that bind and blind,
dictating how to love, who to be.

Together, we draft new laws in our digital diary—
Our notes, a rebellion against traditions that no longer
serve.
In our silent scriptorium, we question,
"¿Será posible que haya mejores alternativas?"

Our love, a crafted dialectic,
negotiating spaces between freedom and fidelity,
where loyalty isn't about chains but choices,
visible in the way we rewrite what it means to be us.

Desentrañando los Hilos

Unraveling Threads
Your fears unravel in text,
a tapestry of concerns and care.
"Yo no soy el culpable de esas malas experiencias…"

You speak of past pains, not as excuses,
but as chapters in the novel you let me read.
I respond not with ink but with empathy,
typing out my understanding, slow but sincere.

Together, we mend the frayed edges,
stitching a new story from old wounds,

believing in the fabric we weave.
Stronger in its repaired places.

Celebración de Contrastes

Valentine's Vows

You dream of our first February Fourteenth,
Each word, a petal laid down on the path to a future
together.
"Deseo que el próximo año..."

Your aspirations, bright as holiday lights,
illuminate my uncertainties.
Each hope you type casts a promise,
a vow to turn the ordinary into our own celebratory feast.

Our digital notes, the invitations sent out to the universe,
requesting the blessing of more shared tomorrows,
marked by laughter and the clink of glasses in cheers.

Encuentros y Entendimientos

Meet Me Halfway

Let's not lose each other in the crowded spaces
of missed cues and misunderstood phrases.
"Ahora hagamos lo más sencillo… No perdernos nunca."

In the garden of your sentences,
I find my footing.
Your affirmations guide me through thorny doubts,
each emoji a bloom in our ongoing conversation.

Our commitment, typed in twilight's glow,
promises to meet halfway.
In the middle of our mess, our magic,
where understanding grows wild and wonderful.

Inspiration Behind "Confesiones y Compresiones Series"
Emotion: Introspective Connection

"Conversations in Contrasts" and "Unfolding Narratives," along with the extended entries such as "Confesiones y Comprensiones," stems from the unique communication dynamic between Nico and myself, shaped by our linguistic differences and evolving bilingual interactions. Our relationship, like many, faced the challenge of expressing complex emotions in a language that wasn't our first. As Nico shared his thoughts in Spanish and I grappled with articulating my deeper feelings in an evolving Spanish proficiency, we turned to a method that bridged our communicative gaps—writing notes.

This digital notepad, our modern-day epistolary exchange, captured a stream of consciousness from both our perspectives, reflecting our thoughts, misunderstandings, aspirations, and the nuances of everyday interactions over our two-year journey together. The poems do not directly quote our written notes but are evocative interpretations that delve into the themes, emotions, and conversations that these notes encompass.

Each poem in this extended series continues to explore the depth of our digital dialogue. "Confesiones y Comprensiones," for example, delves further into the intimate confessions and mutual understandings that surface in our notes, highlighting the poignant moments of vulnerability and connection that define our relationship. This set of is a continuation of our digital notes, weaving in the passive and active voices that emerge in our ongoing communication, reflecting both the explicit and the unspoken elements of our exchange.

The authenticity of our exchanges and the genuine effort to connect beyond linguistic barriers, show the potential for intimacy and understanding despite the inherent challenges. This series celebrates the imperfect yet

beautiful ways we chose to communicate and connect as
our relationship evolved through shared words and
shared worlds. Our digital whispers transformed into a
poetic form, offering a richer, more textured
understanding of our relationship dynamics. Each poem is
a distilled from many moments—fragments of a larger
dialogue that encompasses love, cultural intersections, and
personal growth, revealing a landscape where love is both
a feeling and a practice, requiring patience, understanding,
and often, a reimagining of traditional narratives.

Growth Beyond the Garden

In the quiet corners of my soul,
I find a garden where my kindness grows.
Tangled vines of care and compassion,
tendrils reaching out to those in need.
Nico, like a wilting flower, drew my gaze,
and I, ever the gardener, offered my hands.
Nurturing his roots, feeding his fragile petals,
unaware that in doing so, I forgot to tend my own.

Each act of care a leaf, each gesture a bloom.
Yet, I see now, my garden became overgrown,
a lush entanglement where growth was stunted,
my own spirit, shadowed by the canopy of another's need.

My therapist's words, a pruning shears,
cut through the thicket of my understanding,
revealing the truth that my constant care,
though well-intentioned, binds rather than frees,
creates a dependency that chokes the light.

I see Nico's struggle, mirrored in my reflection,
realize my kindness can be a double-edged sword.
A blade that cuts through isolation
but also one that can weave a web of reliance.

To empower is to offer the soil, the water,

the sunlight needed for growth.
But to step back, to let the roots find their depth,
to allow the flower to seek the sun on its own.

In this realization, I find my own strength.
A resolve to foster interdependence, not dependency.
To be a gardener of resilience,
cultivating a garden where each plant stands tall,
fed by its own roots, reaching for the sky.

So, I turn the soil within my heart,
plant seeds of self-awareness and boundaries,
watered by the understanding that to truly care
is to let go, to trust in the inherent strength
of each soul to find its own way
to grow beyond the garden of my care.

Inspiration behind "Growth Beyond the Garden"
Emotion: Self-realization

This poem is my realization that continually helping Nico hindered my own growth, a behavior rooted in my innate tendency to take care of people. This caregiving nature, while well-intentioned, has often led to creating dependencies rather than fostering independence.

The poem is also influenced by the insights from my therapist, who helped me understand that my kindness, though genuine, can be misinterpreted and taken advantage of. Through therapy, I've learned the importance of empowering others to stand on their own, rather than allowing them to rely solely on my support. This shift in perspective was crucial for both my personal growth and for encouraging the growth of those around me.

Using the metaphor of a garden, the poem explores the balance between nurturing and enabling, illustrating how my constant care can create an overgrown environment where true growth is stunted. It emphasizes the need to cultivate resilience and interdependence, where each individual can flourish independently while still being part of a supportive community.

"Growth Beyond the Garden" acknowledges the complexity of caregiving and the necessity of setting boundaries. It celebrates the strength found in self-awareness and the courage to let go, allowing both myself and others to grow beyond the confines of dependency.

Beyond the Changes

No es que sea fácil, es que no estoy siendo nada,
In this journey together, no te voy a perder.
You're not leaving me, no hay puerta cerrada.
We live together in every dawn we share.

In any case, I'm gaining un hermano.
A better friend, to you I'm giving,
And to myself, space to be human,
to grow in this world so vast and living.

We're gaining more than what we're losing.
It's not like my love is thrown out the door.
We're just changing the way we're loving
and setting boundaries, so nothing's a chore.

But still, we're in each other's lives.
Nos apoyamos mutuamente, we're cheerleaders.
All that matters is to have you in my life
and to be good to each other without fears.

A relationship may or may not happen later,
but family and friends, siempre serán.
In this journey together, every step greater,
in love and life, always hand-in-hand.

Explanation behind "Beyond the Changes"
Emotion: Acceptance with hope

This poem was inspired by a conversation where Nico asked me if it hurt to end our romantic relationship. My response to him was honest: "No, it does not hurt. It doesn't hurt at all."

Despite the end of our romantic relationship, we are not losing each other. On the contrary, we are gaining so much more. The decision to shift our relationship from romantic partners to friends and brothers is rooted in love and respect for each other's growth and independence.

True love is not selfish. It does not seek to hold someone back or prevent them from growing. For both Nico and me, this transition allows us to explore new experiences, expand our minds, and pursue our own wishes, hopes, and desires. By giving each other space to be independent and whole, we are ensuring that if our paths cross again in the future, we will be bringing our complete selves into any potential relationship.

Our conversations revealed that even in the short time apart, Nico has experienced significant personal growth and happiness. Knowing that he is on a path that fulfills him brings me joy. Our bond remains strong, and our roles in each other's lives are still significant. We continue to support and cheer each other on, understanding that family and friends are constants.

This poem is about embracing change and recognizing the beauty of evolving relationships. Love can transform and adapt, and by prioritizing personal growth and mutual support, we are truly gaining more than we are losing.

Con Amor, Pero Solo Amigos

Te amo, my heart, pero no ahora,
Our journeys diverge, like noche y aurora.
Grow, learn, y vive tu vida,
Don't pause for me, no me esperes, querida.

You're my amigo, mi mejor compañía,
Discover new cosas, find tu alegría.
We may be juntos, who knows qué vendrá,
But for now, solo friends, por favor, entiende ya.

El tiempo dirá, no hay crystal ball,
Vive y aprende, answer your call.
Whether partners or amigos, forever near,
With love, siempre, let go of the fear.

Inspiration Behind "Con Amor, Pero Solo Amigos"
Emotion: Compassionate Detachment

I wrote a letter to Nico while he was struggling with his deep feelings for me. The letter conveys my love for him and my desire to maintain our friendship while emphasizing the importance of personal growth and independence for both of us:

Nico,

I love you dearly, and it pains me to see how much you are hurting because of how much you love me. You've asked me if there is hope for our future, and I've told you many times already: there is. I am not saying I have zero interest in a possible life with you, but I do not want to be with you right now. We both have our own journeys of growth, independence, and we need to give ourselves the opportunity to truly be friends.

I noticed from our conversation last night that you want to do things to try to win me over. I do not want that. I want you to be my friend. I want you to live your life, learn new things, discover new places, and focus on cohabitation and friendship with me. I do not want you to try to be my friend and my boyfriend at the same time. I do not want you to pause your life, pause dating, or put anything on hold because you are waiting for me.

I know you think I am the best, and maybe in many ways, I am, but that doesn't mean I am absolutely the best for you as a romantic partner. It also doesn't mean that we will definitely be together. I am not saying we will not and cannot be together, but it is not an absolute.

I am being true to my word and commitments, and I need your help. I need you to understand that we are just friends. Just because there is a possibility for the future, does not mean you need to act on that now. Now, you need to lean into being single, finding your way, discovering your likes and dislikes, and meeting new people.

The better our actual friendship is, the better the chances we have of either being together in the future as partners or staying in each other's lives as best friends for life. Do not look at the latter as a loss; you are gaining me either way.

Please think on this. I do not want to continue to see you hurt or limit yourself because you are waiting for me. I will always love you. I just want different things for myself, and I want more for you. We both have control over our actions and the direction things can go. Think about that.

With love,
Mac

Mt. Helix Series

Walking Around Mt. Helix

At Mt. Helix, steps light and free,
360 views stretch wide for me.
San Diego's sprawl, El Mar's blue sheen,
Mexico's charm, in vistas serene.

Flowers whisper, scents so rare.
Sage and California sagebrush flare.
A white bloom with yellow core,
pink like a caterpillar, leaves me in awe.

Purple thorns, yet beauty still.
Small white blooms like popcorn thrill.
Names unknown, yet love remains.
In scents and sights, my joy sustains.

Here they are, captured true.
Nature's palette, vivid hue.

Atop Mt. Helix

Atop this hill, where vistas spread,
my solace found, my heart is led.
In nature's calm, my spirit heals.
Among the flowers, life reveals.

With you, my ex, we shared this climb,
a moment paused, a bridge through time.
As friends, we grew, our hearts laid bare.
In whispered winds, we found repair.

Therapy's guide, a beacon bright,
grounded me through darkest night.
With words I found and courage gained,
atop Mt. Helix, peace maintained.

This mount, my refuge, steady, true,
witnessed our bond, refreshed, renewed.
Through valleys deep and peaks so high,
We walked as friends beneath the sky.

Our journey marked by blooming grace.
In every petal, a warm embrace.
With each new step, a path refined
by therapy's light and hearts aligned.

So here's to growth and moments shared,
to healing hearts and souls repaired.
Atop this hill, our spirits blend
in solace found and love, my friend.

Inspiration Behind the Mt. Helix Series
Emotion: Reflective Reconciliation

Mt. Helix, located in La Mesa, California, is a place of solitude and reflection for me. I love to share it with everyone who visits me in San Diego due to its stunning 360-degree views of the city and the ocean, and it even has glimpses of Mexico. Mt. Helix's beauty and tranquility make it a perfect retreat for those seeking peace and inspiration. I have many cherished memories there, including birthday mornings and enjoying breakfast while taking in the breathtaking scenery.

As Nico and I walked along the trail during a recent visit, I explained the various sights we could see from the top. Nico picked flowers for me during the hike, creating a lovely bouquet. "Walking Around Mt. Helix" was inspired by these flowers. Each bloom, with its unique color and fragrance, symbolized our journey and the beauty we encountered.

Before departing Mexico City for San Diego, Nico initially said he would not be able to go because he couldn't find dog care, leaving me to scramble for a solution. He eventually found care but didn't communicate his efforts, causing me stress. I needed to address these unresolved emotions, which led to a valuable discussion with Nico atop the mountain.

On top of the hill, Nico and I talked about our past relationship. We discussed why we are no longer together, what happened during our time together, and how we have both grown and experienced new things since the breakup. Nico expressed gratitude for the opportunities he has had in the United States, acknowledging that our relationship helped him see the need for growth and new experiences. He credited me for keeping my promise to bring him to the states, emphasizing my commitment to my word.

I addressed important action items from my therapy sessions, including my feelings of discomfort and frustration, expectations for the San Diego trip, and my need for closure. We also reevaluated the current arrangement where he stays in the place I use during my visits and discussed potential changes to that situation. We explored what this could mean for our relationship, whether it involved closure or finding a new dynamic that works for both of us.

Our conversation on the mountain allowed me to acknowledge my anger, hurt, and disappointment and work on addressing these feelings constructively. I apologized to Nico for my anger over the dog care miscommunication. By recognizing and discussing the root of my frustration, we were able to grow closer as friends.

Our visit and conversation inspired the poem "Atop Mt. Helix." The hill became a place of solace, where our hearts found common ground and grew closer as friends. It represented healing and understanding, guided by therapy and personal growth.

"Walking Around Mt. Helix" and "Atop Mt. Helix" capture the beauty of Mt. Helix and the significance of our

evolving relationship. This visit, the flowers, and our
heartfelt conversation symbolize the unknown future we
hold, and I am okay with that uncertainty. I look forward
to continuing our journey with an open heart, embracing
the beauty of our evolving relationship, and the solace
found atop Mt. Helix.

Boundaries and Bridges

Nico, last night we talked, our hearts laid bare,
about friendship's path and the past we shared.
Querías saber, should you fight for my love?
Or has my heart found a new home above?

Amigos primero, I said with a sigh,
Necesitamos espacio, and here's why:
Miscommunication, even if we cross the language divide,
frustration seizes us, leaves patience denied.

You're stubborn, secluding in your hide.
Don't communicate, making the environment feel weird
inside.
I am the rageful one, anger like a tide.
A harsh tone spoken, it's a promise I keep.

Remember the carnival, a fight so intense.
Words were weapons, in anger immense.
He pedido disculpas, but it lingers still.
I can't be with someone who ignites that will.

You sent me reglas, a guide to our path.
Para mejorar la comunicación, to avoid the wrath.
Escuchar para comprender, listen with care.
Expresar opiniones, en turns to share.

Evitar generalizaciones, nunca y siempre no more,
Hablar sobre errores, reparations at the core.
Valorar a tu pareja, with respect and love.

Practicar la comunicación no verbal, gentle as a dove.

Buscar el contexto adecuado, find the right time.
Evitar discutir en caliente, avoid the heat of the climb.
Realizar actividades juntos, together we'll grow.
Momentos tranquilos, for empathy to flow.

Trabajar en equipo, cede un poco, give and take.
Centrarse en el problema, stay focused for our sake.
No buscar culpables, no winners in this game.
Think before we speak, no blame, no shame.

Darnos espacio, to breathe and to heal.
Aceptar, not change, but understand what's real.
Identifiquemos las causas, conflicts to mend.
Recognize triggers, as we work to transcend.
Nico, I hope you see, this is our way
to build a friendship, where respect will stay.
May we find peace, en el camino we tread,
with boundaries set, and mutual respect ahead.

Infinite Possibilities

Nico, our talk was a breath of fresh air
A step toward a space where I can dare
to be my whole self, unguarded, free,
in this newfound peace, I hope you'll see.

I look forward to feeling safe, secure.
A place where our words are kind and pure.
Less repeating, more growing from here.
Let's cherish the now, cast aside the fear.

I know you love me, and that love won't die.
Our future's a mystery, but we'll get by.
Meeting you, I've gained a companion for life.
Whatever form that takes, we'll weather the strife.

Let's enjoy the present, no more drama or pain.

Respect my boundaries, and we'll both gain.
Focus on self, let our minds expand.
New experiences await, hand-in-hand.

The world is vast, with infinite ways.
But remember cause and effect in our days.
Things won't stay the same; we must evolve
in this ever-changing puzzle, we'll find ways to solve.

I see relationships as interdependent, you see.
Two individuals, whole and free.
We come together, our strengths to share.
Yet alone, we stand strong and care.

No co-dependence, no chains that bind,
but a dance of support, where we each find
our own friends, our priorities clear.
Together in love, yet without fear.

Become who you are, and I'll do the same.
We'll support each other through joy and through pain.
In time, we'll see how things unfold.
In this journey of life, let's be bold.

Infinite possibilities, the world's our stage.
Let's grow, let's pivot, let's turn the page.
Support one another, no doubt in mind,
and in time, we'll see what changes we find.

Inspiration Behind "Boundaries and Bridges" and "Infinite Possibilities"
Emotion: Acceptance with Affection

These poems come from my complex and evolving situation with Nico. We had been broken up for four months but continued sharing the same space during my visits, transitioning to a new normal within a friendship and shared arrangement. This period was marked by several spats and growing pains, highlighting the challenges of maintaining a respectful and supportive relationship while navigating this unique dynamic.

"Boundaries and Bridges" was inspired by a conversation with Nico about establishing clear boundaries and focusing on building a strong, respectful friendship. We addressed the miscommunication and frustration that often took place between us, partly due to language barriers and Nico's tendency to seclude himself, making the environment feel strange and uncommunicative. This poem captures my desire to avoid triggering negative emotions and emphasizes the importance of mutual respect and understanding.

"Infinite Possibilities" reflects the positive outcome of that conversation and my hope to create a safe space where we could both be our authentic selves. It expresses my optimistic outlook on having fewer repetitive and frustrating conversations and instead focusing on personal growth and respect for each other's boundaries. This poem is also about my understanding of interdependent relationships, where both individuals can thrive independently while supporting each other without falling into co-dependence.

I desired to balance my needs and wants while trying not to sacrifice too much more of my time or doing things I didn't want to do. It was a challenging situation when I cared deeply for someone, but I recognized the need to prioritize my own well-being and care more for myself.

Shadows and Light

¡Buenos Días! They say, as the sun rises high.
But beneath the glow, shadows whisper and sigh.
You never truly know someone until the mask slips away,
revealing the rawest colors, where light meets decay.

Sometimes, those colors shine, a beauty unexpected.
Other times, they unsettle, leaving us disconnected.
In Nico's eyes, I saw both shades—a spectrum of deceit,
A pathological dance where lies and truth would meet.

He took from me, not just things, but trust, piece by piece.
Denials so strong, they could silence my peace.
Yesterday, it came to a head—keys stolen, a heart torn.
His sister's presence needed in a day so forlorn.

We searched the room, uncovering more than just things.
Finding the remnants of his secretive stings.
He's gone now, out of my life, a chapter closed tight,
but the sadness lingers, even in this newfound light.

For in his vindictiveness, I see the depth of his pain.
A soul lost in shadows, trying to break free in vain.
I'd feel bad for him if not for the scars he left behind.
But even in this, compassion I still find.

I loved him once as a friend, a brother, a guide.
Gave all I could, with no regrets to hide.
But now it's his journey, his battle to face.
I'll pray for his healing, for him to find grace.

Mental health is a light in this world so complex.
A guide through the shadows when life's full of vex.
I care for my own, and for others, I do the same.
Embracing growth, compassion in this relentless game.

For we all have our shadows, and we all seek the sun.
In the dance of the light and dark, the battle is won.
So I'll move forward now, with love in my heart,
knowing I did my best, played my part.

Nico's chapter is over, and though the sadness remains,
I find solace in the knowledge that I broke the chains.
For in this life of complexity, compassion is key,
and mental health care is the light that sets us free.

Inspiration Behind "Shadows and Light"
Emotion: Compassion

Nico took Rafa's car keys and proceeded to engage in a series of manipulative behaviors. This situation unfolded over a harrowing 48 hours, revealing the darker aspects of Nico's character, including compulsive lying, disregard for others, and a deep-seated vindictiveness.

Despite claiming not to have the keys, Nico had hidden them on the roof and buried the AirTag in the dirt on the balcony. This behavior was not an isolated incident; it was part of a pattern of dishonesty and manipulation that had been building over several weeks, where Nico repeatedly took items and denied having them. His complete disregard for the truth and pathological lying culminated in him making a false police report and attempting to file a restraining order against me.

I found myself at the police station, grappling with the sheer audacity of Nico's actions. I knew that I had exercised restraint, but his behavior pushed me to a point where I questioned whether I should have acted more forcefully, given the unjust situation I was being dragged into. I had a moment of clarity when I realized that Nico's actions were not just impulsive but vengeful, and despite his later attempt to apologize and seek my help, it was clear that he had not taken responsibility for his actions or truly recognized the harm he had caused.

I realized then that I had enabled Nico's behavior over the past two years. By continuously forgiving, helping, and reaffirming his actions, I inadvertently reinforced his behavior—a psychological concept known as negative and positive reinforcement, where certain behaviors are encouraged or discouraged based on the responses they elicit. In Nico's case, my forgiveness and support acted as a positive reinforcement, allowing his negative behaviors to persist without consequence.

This experience taught me valuable lessons about boundaries, recognizing red flags early on, and establishing clear and healthy separations when ending a relationship. Physical and emotional distance are necessary to truly move on from a toxic relationship. Sharing the same space during visits after a breakup can prevent both parties from healing and moving forward, as the proximity keeps them locked in a cycle of unresolved emotions and conflicts.

This 48-hour nightmare led to significant changes in my life. I realized that you never truly know someone until they show you their true colors, and when those colors reveal possessiveness, deceit, and a lack of accountability, it's important to recognize these red flags and take immediate action to protect your well-being. I broke my lease, packed up the house, paid the penalty, and moved in with Rafa, closing this chapter with Nico for good.

The poem captures the complexity of human behavior, the shadows that people carry, and the importance of mental health care in navigating these challenges. It also reflects the deep sadness and disappointment that comes from realizing that someone you cared for deeply can act out of such a place of hurt and revenge. Despite this, I chose to move forward with compassion for myself and others, learning from this experience and prioritizing my mental health and well-being.

Rafa

Emotion: Love and Emotional Intimacy

In the "Rafa" chapter, I offer a poetic exploration of the deep and evolving relationship with Rafa. These poems capture the essence of our bond, from the first sparks of attraction to the layers of connection we've built together. Through reflections on love, growth, and the shared moments that define us, this chapter delves into the emotional intimacy and mutual understanding that characterize our journey. It's a portrait of love in its many forms—passionate, thoughtful, and enduring— illustrating how Rafa has become integral to who I am and how I've come to love deeply and authentically. Spanning from March 2024 to September 2024, this chapter marks a significant period in our story, though it's far from the end—just the point where I paused to bring this book to life.

First Date Series

Tinder Sparks and Tennis Courts

We met on Tinder, swiped right,
Started with "How are you?" and "How's your night?"
Quickly moved to deeper chats,
Work woes, laughs, and daily stats.

He's an accountant, sharp and neat,
Numbers talk—our shared feat.
Switched jobs, unsure, a bit of a fluke,
But his smile? A magnetic, Mexican look.

His beauty struck me, took me aback,
A bit nervous, wondering if we'd track.
His week was packed, Six Flags and friends,
A whirlwind schedule, no pretend.

We talked tennis, a sport I adore,
Set a date—our first score.
Tennis and tacos, a classic play,
He looked hotter in person, what can I say?

His energy was warm, a calming vibe,
Made me feel good, let worries slide.
Dinner was filled with first date chatter,
Family, work, dreams that matter.

Dates followed, a steady flow,
Tennis, dinners, a blooming glow.
Booked a room, a weekend retreat,
Polanco's Marriott, just to keep it discreet.

No talk of sex, just a chill day,
I couldn't host—ex in the way.
Dinner, a movie, set up on my screen,
Shared diet habits, healthy and lean.

Sugar-free ice cream, his sweet surprise,

My smile, wide, no need to disguise.
We napped, then woke, and in a tender touch,
We made love—oh, it was much.

His body, statuesque, a sight to see,
His back broad, lips soft, setting me free.
The look in his eyes, intense and real,
As we moved together, sealing the deal.

Our first date, a passionate start,
Tinder sparks, now love's art.
A connection deep, a bond so true,
With each glance, I wanted more of you.

The Turning Point

After Polanco's weekend bliss,
It was clear, this wasn't just a kiss.
Rafa and I, beyond the physical,
Something deeper, something lyrical.

Our connection, not just skin and bone,
He saw promise, a future unknown.
I felt it too, a mutual fire,
A budding love, a growing desire.

I left Mexico City, off to San Diego,
Travel blurs the details, but the feelings flow.
When I returned, he missed me true,
A surprise pickup, though I had a clue.

New and fresh, yet nerves ran high,
Realized I liked him, didn't want to lie.
Respect and care, I wanted to see,
If he'd want more with full clarity.

At Benito airport, back in the ride,
I confessed, with nowhere to hide.
"I have things to tell, do you want them now?"

And our destination—a Marriott vow.

He said, "Start talking," so I began,
Laid out the truth, as best as I can.
Told him about my ex and our shared space,
How we'd head to a hotel, a neutral place.

I needed to be honest, to let him see,
All the baggage that came along with me.
He didn't stay that night, but dinner we shared,
We talked more deeply, our feelings bared.

Nervous, yet hopeful, I felt a shift,
This was a test, a chance to uplift.
Rafa's maturity, his listening ear,
The beginning of a space safe and clear.

This was just the start, many talks to come,
A journey unfolding, not a race to run.
With each word, each honest confession,
The foundation of trust, our love's progression.

Inspiration behind "First Date Series"
Emotion: Nostalgia and Anticipation

These poems came from reflecting on the early stages of our blossoming romantic relationship. This series, comprising the poems "Tinder Sparks and Tennis Courts" and "The Turning Point," explores our journey from initial attraction to deeper emotional connections.

The first poem, "Tinder Sparks and Tennis Courts," captures the excitement and anticipation of meeting someone new through an app, discovering shared interests, and navigating our first few dates. It highlights the nervousness, attraction, and the unexpected connection that developed between us. The setting of our first date, playing tennis and sharing tacos, along with the subsequent intimate moments, showcases the natural progression from casual interest to deeper feelings. The vivid memories of our weekend at the Marriott Renaissance in Polanco, where we shared a heartfelt connection and physical intimacy, serve as a foundation for exploring the nuances of our new love.

The second poem, "The Turning Point," delves into the deeper emotional and psychological aspects of our relationship as it evolves. After the special weekend in Polanco, the realization of genuine feelings and the desire for a serious relationship set the stage for a crucial conversation. The poem reflects my awareness of the importance of honesty and transparency, especially when dealing with complexities like sharing space with an ex during visits. The experience of being picked up from the airport by Rafa, followed by the candid discussion about my past and current situation, becomes a pivotal moment in our relationship. It underscores the significance of open communication, the willingness to confront challenges, and the growth of trust and emotional safety between us.

These poems collectively explore our journey from initial attraction to a meaningful connection, emphasizing the importance of honesty, vulnerability, and the willingness to navigate the complexities of life together. They capture the excitement, challenges, and deepening bond as we build a foundation for a lasting relationship.

Distance in Love

We wandered through Chicago's vibrant streets,
A week that sped like seconds, not days;
Exploring corners where laughter meets,
With friends as guides in city's maze.

Now miles stretch, silence loud between us,
Heartbeats echo a longing new and deep.
Didn't foresee this yearn, this sudden fuss,
Missing you more, awake and in my sleep.

The heart, they say, grows fonder with some space,

Each day apart stitches longing tight.
And in that longing, a sweet embrace,
Of memories in morning and at night.

With each sunrise, I count down to your touch,
Recall your eyes, that soulful, deep blue hue.
When you whispered "Te Quiero," oh so much,
A simple phrase, yet it felt strikingly true.

My reply, a whistle, shy but sure,
In your gaze, a promise, soft and pure.
Safety and thrill in balance, so secure,
Our interdependence is the cure.

My therapist smiles, hearing of you,
Hope in her eyes, reflecting something true.
For once she hears joy, not the blues,
In tales of love that's budding, sweet, and new.

So here's to counting days till you're near,
To shared dreams and paths that we revere.
In this wait, there's beauty, crystal clear—
A love that's growing, cherished and dear.

Inspiration Behind "Distance in Love"
Emotion: Longing with Hope

This poem captures the bittersweet emotions of distance and the fresh excitement of a burgeoning relationship with Rafael Dominguez. Recently, we immersed ourselves in the urban allure of Chicago, where days felt mere moments and laughter was our shared language. This cityscape became a canvas for our growing connection, setting the scene for adventures with friends and intimate discoveries about each other.

As we parted ways, the sudden intensity of missing Rafael became palpable—a longing that seemed too vast for the few days we've been apart. This poem reflects not just the physical distance but the emotional closeness that's forming, illustrating how space can paradoxically deepen bonds.

Each line is a careful step in the dance of a new relationship—tender yet cautious. Rafael's first heartfelt "Te Quiero," gazing into me with his sunlight-amber eyes, marked a milestone in our journey, one that I celebrated with a mixture of shyness and confidence. It's a pivotal moment that resonates with the feeling of being seen and cherished.

The involvement of therapy in this phase of my life acts as a mirror and a guide, ensuring that as I navigate these new waters, I do so with intention and self-awareness. My therapist's positive outlook on my emotional narrative with Rafael serves as an affirmation that this time, things are moving in a hopeful direction.

This poem is not just an ode to the longing for Rafael's presence but an acknowledgment of the careful, deliberate pace we're setting for our relationship. It's about embracing the thrill of new love while securing a foundation built on mutual respect, understanding, and the kind of support that promises not just fleeting happiness but a lasting connection.

In the Beginning Days

In the nascent whispers of our beginning,
where every message flutters like a promise,
you bloom within the garden of my affections,
a bright dahlia in the sunlight of my days.

You make me very excited, a gentle thrill,
a quiet storm of anticipation in the calm.
Your kindness, a soft melody that hums
through the corridors of my busy life,
echoing gratitude, weaving joy
in the tapestry of ordinary moments.

"Babeeeeeeeeeeeeeeeee!!!!!" your text ignites,
a jubilant echo in the quiet of my anticipation,
your words in Spanish, a tender caress
across the miles that fail to diminish
the pulse of our growing closeness.

"Muchas gracias por tu mensaje, hermoso!"
Each word you send is a petal dropped
on the path of our unfolding story,
marking the trail with vibrant hues
of care, of passion, of an earnest tenderness.

You see me—not just the outlines but the shades within.
"Todo lo hago con mucho cariño porque tú lo vales,"
you say, as if love could be distilled into syllables,
each one a testament to the earnestness
of your affections, the depth of your regard.

And in return, I observe, I cherish:
your intelligence—a beacon when my thoughts grow dim,
your support—a pillar when my strength wanes,
your affection—a quilt in the chill of my doubts.

Together, we dance in the joy of discovery,
our conversations a bridge over any distance,
our plans a shared journey on a map yet drawn.
"Me encanta esto que estamos viviendo juntos,"
and in these words, our future takes shape,
painted in the hues of trust and mutual growth.

Here, in the heart of this beginning,
where every message, every call, is a seed planted,
we nurture the garden of what we could become,
eager for every blossom the new dawn will bring.

Inspiration behind "In the beginning Days"
Emotion: Joyful Anticipation and Tender Affection

This poem stems from the fresh, exhilarating beginnings of a new relationship with Rafa, a person who embodies the qualities I've longed to find in a partner. This poem is a reflection of the initial stages of our relationship, where each message and interaction is filled with the potential of deeper connection. It captures the essence of our mutual excitement and appreciation, translated through the heartfelt exchanges we share.

Interdependence in a relationship refers to a balanced dynamic where both partners support each other while maintaining their individuality. It's about being connected and supportive, yet each person is independent enough to stand alone. So far, my relationship with Rafa exemplifies this. His consistent communication, expressions of gratitude, and supportive actions reassure me that stepping into this relationship is a journey worth taking.

Despite the excitement, I remain cautiously optimistic. As we continue to explore this connection, the constant affirmations through our interactions serve as small lights along the path, illuminating our way forward. These moments of shared happiness and mutual respect reassure me that it's okay to venture deeper into this relationship, flashlight in hand, ready to discover what lies ahead in the unlit corners of our future together.

Portrait of Rafa: Lines and Light

In the gallery of life, walks a man,
Tall as the tales he lives, six-foot-one of grace,
A face that dances between jest and earnest,
A smile that holds both the sun and the moon.

His voice, a symphony of highs and lows,
Colors each word with a painter's precision—
Here lies laughter, there rests gentle whispers,

All wrapped in a voice that bends light into arcs.

Sculpted in the gymnasiums of discipline,
His arms, declarations of unwavering resolve,
And a silhouette that sings praises to effort,
His form, a testament to the labor of dreams.

Hair kissed by the fire of autumn's touch,
Carefully tousled, a crown of auburn and gold,
Eyes deep pools of a twilight mystery,
Hinting at stories only the stars can retell.

A blend of heritage, rich and diverse,
Skin that carries the light of far-off places,
Lips crafted for poetry and promises,
A nose sculpted by the hands of history.

But oh, his smile—wide, radiant, a beacon,
It's here his spirit dances free and bold,
In laughter, a fortress and an open gate,
In joy, a spark that sets the night alight.

Each gesture, each glance, each quiet moment,
He is a sonnet written by the dawn,
A melody played on the strings of the heart,
Rafa, a portrait of love's finest art.

Inspiration behind "Portrait of Rafa: Lines and Light"
Emotion: Admiration and Affectionate Reverence

This poem springs from my desire to capture the essence of someone who embodies an extraordinary blend of beauty and personality. Rafa, one of the most beautiful people I've ever met, is not just a feast for the eyes but a presence that enriches the soul. Observing him—whether he's moving through the routines of the day, sleeping peacefully, or simply being in the moment—is a source of deep joy for me.

This poem is an attempt to sketch the myriad details
that make Rafa uniquely captivating. From his expressive
face and the melodic cadence of his voice to the disciplined
strength of his physique and the thoughtful contours of his
personality, each line of the poem strives to mirror the
admiration and affection I feel. It's about more than just
physical appreciation; it's an ode to the qualities that make
him profoundly special to me.

Full Description of Rafael Dominguez:

Beneath the stretch of skies, there walks a man,
towering at six feet one, a canvas of expressions painted
vividly across his face. His smirk, a playful herald of his
wit, gives way to contortions so vivid and capricious they
could choreograph the comedy and drama of an entire
evening.

His voice, a melody that fluctuates with pitches of
humor and sincerity, echoes the nuances of his dynamic
persona—playful, teasing, an audible touch that colors his
every word with vitality. His arms, sculpted as if by an
artist's fervor for perfection, speak of disciplined mornings
and iron wills, while his rounded, impeccable derrière
declares the triumphs of countless squats and lunges.

Sprinkled with hints of red, his hair—a crowning glory
of meticulous cuts—flows just long enough to tempt
fingers to disrupt its perfection, though he guards it
jealousy against casual strokes. His eyes, deep brown
pools mistaken at times for the oceanic blue, hold secrets
and stories, beckoning one to peer closer into the depths
where laughter dances and sorrows are shielded. When
the sun is above, and you catch him smiling with his eyes,
you see a blend of sunlit amber and golden hues, swirling
like warm autumn leaves caught in a gentle breeze, full of
life and mystery.

His heritage, a vibrant tapestry of Mexican colors,
subtly blends with the lighter hues of his complexion,
presenting a visage not quite typical, marked distinctly by

the symmetrical grace of a well-defined nose and lips that
are neither too thin nor unduly full, but perfectly formed
for whispers and kisses.

Each smile, a gateway to his soul, reveals layers of
innocence entwined with mischief, as if he carries within
him a sprite-like spirit, playful and profound. His thick,
straight eyebrows frame his gaze, adding intensity to his
every look, while his laughter is an open invitation to joy,
resonating deep within the heart of the beholder.

In every aspect, from the playful tilt of his head to the
careful poise with which he navigates his world, he is a
portrait of the paradoxical blend of joy and depth, mischief
and intellect—a man who, like a cherished verse, becomes
etched deeply in the mind and heart of those fortunate
enough to encounter him.

Chasing the Contradictory Unicorn

I am a man riddled with contradictions,
A Pisces swimming in a sea of dual desires.
I crave what I reject,
Reject what I crave,
A walking paradox seeking clarity in the fog.

You, a towering presence, a unicorn rare,
Will you be the enigma that aligns with my dualities?
In moments I want you close—so close,
Yet in the same breath, I push for space,
A heart's tug-of-war between near and far.

I admire traits in you that also fray my nerves,
It's like we speak in tongues, languages of the heart
My contradictions—why can't they be understood?
Yet here you are, a unicorn, possibly my myth turned
truth,
Could you be the one who dances to the beat of my
shifting whims?

You embody all I've never known I wanted,
Tradition never tempted me until you,
They say insanity is doing the same but expecting change,
Perhaps I've been mad, ignoring the signs,
That I need a unicorn, your unique breed.

Someone who navigates my intricate tides,
Gives me passion until I retreat into solitude,
Listens intently, then knows when to leave,
Returns when the silence between us calls too loudly,
Your independence intertwining with my needs.

My therapist speaks of interdependence,
And in you, I see the potential of that dance,
A unicorn of a man, shifting my view from madness to
method,
A deliberate choice to indulge in my contradictions,
With you, the unicorn, redefining my every contradiction
into harmony.

Inspiration behind "Chasing the Contradictory Unicorn"
Emotion: Conflicted Yearning and Hopeful Introspection

This poem emerged during a heart-to-heart on May 24, 2024, with my closest friends in Nashville. As we delved into the nuances of my desires and contradictions, a light-hearted yet profound discussion unfolded about my nature: loving what I don't want and shunning what I crave. It's the delicate balance of these contradictions that often define our pursuits in life, particularly in love.

I've always had a penchant for Latin men, often finding that their emotional intensity both attracts and overwhelms me. However, in my current relationship with Rafael Dominguez, a notable shift has occurred. Rafael, uniquely taller than my usual type, represents a break from my past patterns. This divergence was playfully noted by my friends as a potential sign that he might be the 'unicorn' I've been seeking—a metaphor for that rare and perfect match who can navigate the complex landscape of my desires.

This revelation aligns with recent discussions in therapy, emphasizing the theme of interdependence rather than dependency. Historically, my relationships have started with fulfillment but tended to devolve into dissatisfaction due to a repeated pattern of agreeing without understanding. Rafael's approach is refreshingly different. Our communication is genuine; he shares his desires and listens to mine, creating a foundation built on mutual respect and understanding rather than one adapting to the other's wishes under false pretenses.

In this poem, I celebrate the idea of embracing my contradictions as strengths rather than flaws. It's about changing the narrative from one of insanity—repeating the same actions and expecting different results—to one of intentional action and self-acceptance. As I navigate this new relationship with both excitement and caution, I'm learning that being a contradiction isn't a downfall but a beautifully complex aspect of who I am.

So, as I sit here, surrounded by the warmth of friendship and armed with newfound insights from therapy, I'm hopeful. Maybe, just maybe, Rafael is the unicorn who can handle the beautiful chaos of my contradictions. This poem and our discussions is a reminder that it's okay to be a 'walking contradiction.' It's okay to be Malcolm, Mac—the complete, multifaceted person I am.

A Tale of Two Hearts

In My Voice:

In twilight's gentle hush, I write to you,
A note from my heart, both worn and true.
To navigate this path is fraught with pain,
Yet by your side, I find the strength to remain.

With baggage heavy, I know it's tough,
And at times, the road feels rough.
New to this dance of love and care,
I strive to be kind, honest, and fair.

Therapy's guide, my weekly confide,
In growth and change, I seek to abide.
Sorry for Eva, Nico's unjust wrath,
Yet I vow to follow this healing path.

Speak your truths, let feelings flow,
In this space, our love will grow.
I may stumble, not always right,
But in your heart, I anchor my light.

Rafa's Reply:

Remember, I'm here, steady and true,
Neither of us perfect, but we pursue
A love that supports, complements, and mends,
Together through all, our hearts transcend.

This journey may be shadowed and long,
But with you, my strength belongs.
My intent is never to wound or break,
Only to nurture the joy we make.

Concern for you, my heart's deepest care,
To see you happy, free from despair.
The past may cling, but let's release,
Together, we'll find our sweet peace.

I stand with you, in every tear,
Ready to listen, love, and cheer.
Towards a future bright and clear,
With love that conquers every fear.

Our Mutual Echo:

Te quiero, gracias—our hearts align,
In your words, I find the divine.
Understanding dawns, perspective bright,
Together, we face the night.

In this poetic dance, our souls connect,
Through honesty, love, and deep respect.
A tale of two hearts, one story told,
Of love that grows, and hands to hold.

In rhythm and rhyme, we write our song,
On the same page, where we belong.
Together we build, with every beat,
A symphony of love, complete.

Inspiration behind "A Tale of Two Hearts"
Emotion: Love

Navigating the waters of a new relationship while still entangled in the complexities of an old one is a delicate, often tumultuous journey. This poem emerges from my current life experience—trying to build a fresh, honest connection with Rafa while dealing with the unresolved remnants of my past relationship with Nico.

In the midst of this transition, I've faced moments of frustration and doubt, feeling the weight of my emotional baggage and the challenge of being truly open and vulnerable. My dedication to therapy has been a guiding light, helping me grow and address my issues head-on. Each week, my therapist gives me assignments to work on, encouraging me to confront my feelings and actions with honesty. This commitment to self-improvement and personal growth is a cornerstone of the poem.

The specific incident involving Eva and Nico became a pivotal point in my relationship with Rafa. Nico's behavior was unacceptable, and I felt a deep need to acknowledge this and apologize to Rafa, emphasizing my sincere commitment to change and growth. This moment of accountability is woven into the poem, illustrating my respect for Rafa's feelings and my desire to build a foundation of trust and understanding.

Rafa's response to my openness has been incredibly supportive and empathetic. His words reassured me that he is here for me, ready to listen and understand, despite the challenges we face. His commitment to our future together and his willingness to work through our pasts and present struggles inspired me to capture this dynamic in the poem.

Ultimately, this poem is a reflection of our journey— two people striving to be on the same page, communicating openly, and supporting each other through the ups and downs. It celebrates our mutual dedication to building a harmonious and loving relationship, highlighting the power of honesty, empathy, and growth. This poem is a testament to our shared hope for a future filled with love and understanding, where our hearts can find peace and joy together.

In the House of the Queen

One starry night, a dream almost real,
I met Rafa's mother, a jewel without equal.
The queen of the party, in a flowing black dress,
With fabric wings cascading from her arms, no less.

Eyes dark, filled with untold tales,
A curious gaze, deep as ancient wells.
Her smile, a light that could brighten the night,
Her elegance, a dance, an art form in sight.

Dressed for the occasion, with oyster pearls in her ears,
A long necklace, touching her dress, twinkling like stars, my dear.
Cream circles on her skirt, a dreamy contrast,

Enhancing her beauty, a vision to last.

Rafa's mother, with lips of dark red,
And hair in a bun, gleaming like the future ahead.
Every detail carefully chosen,
A touch of class that could never be frozen.

We sat to dine, her grace unmatched,
Eating with elegance, as if in a royal batch.
She worked the room like a politician on a mission,
Every smile, every gesture, a dance of precision.

I watched in awe and admiration,
As Rafa, her son, showed pure devotion.
He treated her like a queen, with care and respect,
A reflection of his soul, a love so perfect.

One night at the quinceañera, an enchanting encounter,
I felt welcome, wrapped in her warmth like no other.
Rafa's mother, a muse of tradition,
A beacon of beauty and high education.

I look forward to our future conversations,
For now, I'm held in the magic of these sensations.
The night I met the queen of the night,
A graphic dream, with a touch of delight.

Inspiration behind "In the House of the Queen"
Emotion: Awe and Admiration

As I sat down to reflect on my time at the quinceañera, I found myself filled with admiration and awe for Rafa's mother, and I wanted to capture those feelings in this poem. The night was enchanting, from the beautiful decor to the lively atmosphere, but what stood out most was my encounter with Rafa's mother. She embodied beauty, class, and grace, dressed in a stunning black dress with flowing fabric wings, her makeup and accessories carefully chosen to enhance her elegance.

Rafa's mother moved through the room with the poise of a seasoned politician, greeting everyone with a warm smile and a keen curiosity. Her presence was magnetic, and I was fascinated by her ability to make everyone feel welcome and appreciated. Observing Rafa interact with his mother, treating her with such respect and care, gave me a deeper insight into his character and values.

This poem is not just a recount of my observations but also a reflection on the potential future. As I enjoyed the festivities, my mind wandered to thoughts of what it would be like if our families were to merge. There are pending plans for family trips, and I wondered how these experiences would unfold, what dynamics would emerge, and how we would navigate the blending of our lives.

Meeting Rafa's mother was a small yet significant window into what might come. It made me think about the possibilities of our relationship, the merging of traditions, and the journey we might embark on together. This poem encapsulates my admiration for her, my experience at the quinceañera, and my contemplations about the future.

Echoes of Intimacy: Poems of Love and Self-Reflection

Embrace of the True Self

In the mirror's gaze, where shadows play,
True love finds its roots, deep in the clay,
Not in the illusion, not in the mask,
But in the embrace of the self, a sacred task.

To love another, you must first see,
The essence of self, raw and free.
Therapists say, and so do I,
Interdependence lets true love fly.

Dependence clings, a vine in the night,
Craving the sun, but losing its sight.

But interdependence, like trees side by side,
Stand tall together, in life's shifting tide.

In therapy's light, the truth is laid bare,
Loving yourself means showing you care.
A heart that beats with self-adoration,
Becomes a lover without reservation.

Boundaries set, not walls but gates,
In the dance of love, they orchestrate.
No enmeshment, no losing the core,
But growing together, being more.

To give your all, you must first be whole,
Heal the wounds, nourish the soul.
In this journey, you'll find your grace,
In your own reflection, your lover's face.

True love blooms when the self is known,
Roots deep in authenticity grown.
Embrace your essence, let it be,
For in true love, you must first be free.

Quiet Currents

In this hotel cocoon, where silence streams,
I drift through slumberous, reflective dreams.
Awake, the TV whispers like a distant shore,
As I, a Piscean, retreat to explore.

Silent tides guard my energy's spark,
Recharging my soul in this quiet, dark.
Thoughts flow freely, like rivers unseen,
Mapping my projects, life's vivid sheen.

The world outside spins, a distant hum,
In these tranquil depths, clarity comes.
Soon, I'll rise with the morning light,
Homeward bound, ambition in sight.

To my man, my projects, plans unfurled,
Ready to conquer the awaiting world.
Te quiero, mi amor, see you soon,
Under the sun and the rising moon.

Distance and Connection

Across the miles, our lives unfold,
With stories shared and moments told.
At weddings grand and quiet retreats,
Our hearts sync in digital beats.

You, amidst the laughter and cheer,
I, in the quiet, fighting tears.
Missed appointments and lazy days,
Yet love lingers in our gaze.

"Hola amor," your words so sweet,
Through messages, our hearts still meet.
Though busy schedules pull us apart,
In every text, I feel your heart.

A lazy day, distractions abound,
Yet in your words, solace is found.
"Miss you," you say, and I reply,
Our bond, unbroken, under the sky.

Through busy times and silent nights,
Our love persists, reaching heights.
For in the chaos, love still grows,
In every message, it clearly shows.

So, my love, though time seems brief,
In your absence, I find relief.
Knowing soon, we'll reunite,
Our love's embrace, a guiding light.

Inspiration behind "Echoes of Intimacy: Poems of Love and Self-Reflection"

Emotion: Introspection and Clarity

I was in a hotel room, experiencing a weird interaction with Rafa. It wasn't one of those good days, and the situation left me feeling uneasy. Rafa, who usually exemplifies interdependence in our relationship, was suddenly giving off a needy vibe, and I couldn't quite pinpoint the source of it. Instead of addressing it directly with him, I found myself reflecting on what I truly want and what I appreciate about our relationship. This moment of introspection and the therapy sessions I've been attending sparked the creation of the poem "Embrace of the True Self."

In the poem, I explore the idea that true love can only flourish when we embrace our authentic selves. It contrasts the concepts of interdependence and dependence, highlighting how healthy relationships grow from two individuals who are whole and self-aware. The poem emphasizes the importance of self-love and personal boundaries, suggesting that only by knowing and loving ourselves can we become better lovers.

During the same trip to Chicago, another poem, "Hotel Quiet Currents," was born from a similar feeling of reflection. In the quiet solitude of my hotel room, I found myself drifting through reflective dreams and recharging my energy. As a Pisces, I often retreat into myself to find clarity and recharge, and this trip was no exception. The interaction with Rafa made me question my identity and my need for personal space. Despite my efforts to communicate with Rafa about my need for space, there was a misunderstanding, and I felt a strange suspicion from him. This experience prompted me to write about the tranquility I found in the hotel room, mapping out my thoughts and projects for the future.

"Distance and Connection" was inspired by the physical distance often present in my relationship with Rafa and

the way we manage to maintain our bond through digital
communication. Despite the busy schedules and missed
appointments, our love persists. This poem captures the
essence of staying connected through messages and the
comfort found in each other's words. It reflects the balance
of our love, even when we are apart, and the reassurance
that soon we will reunite.

Layers of Us

Eres como una cebolla,
I told you, eyes meeting yours,
A metaphor, a mystery,
In words not quite your own.

Capas y más capas,
Layers and more layers,
Of who we are, of what we feel,
Unfolding, revealing,
In this dance of translation.

In your eyes, I see you open,
Yet still, I sense the depths,
Siento las profundidades,
Empathy as my guide,
I navigate the unseen.

American phrases, Mexican hearts,
We bridge the gap, we find the art,
Of saying what's meant, not just the words,
Conexión más allá de las palabras,
Connection beyond the phrases.

You say you're open,
And I believe you, truly,
But like an onion, you have layers,
Hidden, waiting,
For the right touch, the right time.

Therapy helps,
Guiding us to speak,
To share, to understand,
Comunicación es la clave,
Communication is the key.

Nervous moments come,
But we talk, we navigate,
Towards clarity, towards each other,
In this new, beautiful journey.

Estoy aprendiendo,
I am learning,
About myself, about you,
About language, and the spaces between.

Our differences, we marry,
Unimos nuestras diferencias,
Uniting in a common dance,
Exciting, daunting, beautiful,
All at once.

Layers of you, layers of me,
Peeling back, discovering,
In a shared language of love,
In the poetry of our hearts.

Eres como una cebolla,
With layers to reveal,
And I am here, peeling back,
With each word, each touch,
Embracing the beauty of us.

Inspiration Behind "Layers of Us"
Emotion: Vulnerability and Discovery

The poem draws from the rich, complex experience of navigating a relationship where language and cultural differences play a significant role. The inspiration stems from a conversation about the metaphor "you are like an onion," a phrase that encapsulates the idea of someone having multiple layers of personality and experiences that need to be gradually uncovered.

In explaining this metaphor to Rafa, my Mexican partner, I realized the challenge and beauty of translating not just words, but meanings and emotions. This process revealed how phrases that are uniquely American might not have direct translations in Spanish, yet they hold the same significance once explained. The effort to communicate these nuances highlights the depth of our connection and the learning journey we're on together.

Rafa's sense of openness with me, despite being in therapy and feeling more exposed than ever, shows how relationships can bring out new facets of ourselves. As an empath, I sense the layers beneath his surface openness, understanding that true depth takes time and patience to uncover. This dynamic adds an exciting, yet daunting, element to our relationship as we continuously discover more about each other and ourselves.

Our journey is a blend of learning about language, cultural differences, and finding common ground. It's a beautiful dance of bridging gaps, marrying our differences into a shared understanding. This poem celebrates that process, acknowledging the complexity, beauty, and excitement that comes with peeling back each other's layers. Through our good communication and the support of therapy, we've managed to navigate even the nervous moments, strengthening our bond.

This poem captures the essence of this ongoing journey, the joy of discovery, and the profound connection that grows as we embrace each other's multifaceted selves.

Baggage Claim

Yes, I'm dating just one guy,
Despite the whispers, don't ask why.
Nico's here, he's got a room,
But romance? Nah, that's not his bloom.

I see your doubts, those little jabs,
"Two-timing?" "Ex-love crabs?"
But listen close, let's set it straight,
I'm working through this hefty weight.

He's my past that's sticking 'round,
But our future? Solid ground.
It's messy, sure, this tangled mess,
But you and I, we're still the best.

We've made memories, trips to plan,
Despite this suitcase from my man.
No regrets, just looking ahead,
Sharing life, no more to dread.

So laugh a bit, and ease your mind,
Our love's the rare and wondrous kind.
Baggage claims? I've got a few,
But every step, I'm taking with you.

Inspiration behind "Baggage Claim"
Emotion: Reassurance and Humor

This poem emerged from a heartfelt and honest
conversation I had with Rafa about the complexities of my
situation with my ex, Nico. The inspiration stemmed from
my need to address Rafa's concerns and doubts, which
have surfaced through his witty yet pointed remarks like,
"So you are dating two people?" or "You are having sex
with your ex?" These comments, while playful, highlighted
his unease and the misunderstandings that can arise in our
unique circumstances.

Writing this poem allowed me to convey my feelings in a witty, snarky, and humorous manner, which aligns with our communication style. It was a way to clear the air and reaffirm my commitment to Rafa while acknowledging the realities of my past that still linger in the present. Despite the baggage, I wanted to emphasize the joy and excitement of our relationship, the memories we've made, and the adventures we have planned.

The process of creating "Baggage Claim" was cathartic, helping me to transform a potentially awkward situation into a lighthearted yet sincere expression of love and dedication. It serves as a reminder that while I may have some lingering complexities, my focus and affection are firmly directed towards our future together.

Pride in the City: A Colorful Symphony

Pride in the city, oh what a sight,
Mexico City's colors, bold and bright.
Reforma's parade, a vibrant stream,
A living, breathing, rainbow dream.

I wore my simplicity, white shorts, blue and white shirt,
Rafa with rainbow socks, suspenders, oh, the flirt.
He ditched his shirt, just suspenders remained,
Photogenic by a statue, his beauty unchained.

The streets were crowded, a colorful throng,
Characters, costumes, singing their song.
Mermaids, bears, cheerleaders, cats,
Men in period dresses, and sparkling hats.

We danced through the chaos, laughed with the crowd,
Every step with you, I felt so proud.
Sluts in their glory, queens on display,
The spirit of Pride in full array.

Through every costume, every cheer,

I felt our future, crystal clear.
With baggage in tow, yet here we stand,
Building dreams, hand in hand.

Inspiration behind "Pride in the City: A Colorful Symphony"
Emotion: Joyful Celebration and Pride

This poem was inspired by an unforgettable day spent celebrating Pride in Mexico City with Rafa. The day was a vibrant and joyous celebration, filled with the exuberance and diversity that epitomizes Pride. The parade on Reforma was a kaleidoscope of colors, costumes, and characters, each contributing to a lively and inclusive atmosphere.

Rafa and I approached the day with our own unique styles—me in simple white shorts and a blue and white button-up shirt, while Rafa embraced the spirit of Pride with rainbow socks, suspenders, and a tight black shirt. At one point, he even went shirtless with just the suspenders, capturing a stunning photo in front of a statue that showcased his photogenic charm.

The parade itself was a sensory overload of beauty and individuality, with people dressed as mermaids, bears, cheerleaders, and various flamboyant characters. The streets were packed, and the energy was palpable as everyone came together to celebrate love and identity in all its forms.

Our conversation after the event reflected the depth of our connection and the joy of sharing such experiences. Despite the complexities of my past and current living situation, this day reinforced the strength of our bond and our commitment to navigating our future together. The poem captures the essence of this vibrant celebration and the sense of clarity and hope it brought to our relationship, celebrating the beautiful journey we are on amidst the colorful chaos of life

You Have Me Intoxicated

Baby, can't you see I'm calling?
A guy like you should wear a warning
It's dangerous, I'm falling

As we drove, your eyes sparkling bright
Britney's voice, a playful delight
Our song, now forever tied to us
Cemented in love, without much fuss

Your family welcomed me with open arms
Brunch with mom and dad, your sister's charms
Aunt's laughter, cousins' smiles
Making every moment worthwhile

Your kiss, a sweet escape
Our cultures blending, taking shape
Like Rocío Dúrcal's graceful song
Passion and love, where we belong

With a taste of your lips, I'm on a ride
You're toxic, I'm slippin' under
A poison paradise
Don't you know that you're toxic?

Each note, a memory of love and glee
Of us together, wild and free
In this melody, we're entwined
Our hearts and cultures, forever combined.

Inspiration Behind "You Have Me Intoxicated"
Emotion: Playful Infatuation and Passion

This poem stems from a playful and deeply meaningful
moment shared between Rafa and me during a memorable
car ride. As we drove, Britney Spears' "Toxic" came on,
and in true Rafa fashion, he began singing the lyrics to me,
humorously declaring it as "our song." The lyrics resonated
with how he felt—intoxicated by our love, caught up in the

wild ride we were on together. He teased that I was "toxic" in the best way, making him feel overwhelmed in love, and even joked that we should both wear a warning because of how intense and passionate our connection is.

This moment occurred during a special family outing with Rafa, Zeus, and me. We had driven far out of the city to meet up with Rafa's mom, dad, sister, aunt, uncle, and cousin for breakfast. Though we missed the visit to the cemetery they had stopped at earlier, we arrived just in time for a warm and joyful meal. It was my first time meeting some of his extended family, and the interaction was filled with laughter and connection. What truly stood out to me was how Rafa's mom, who doesn't speak English, made the effort to narrate and translate the conversation for me in a Spanish I could understand, bridging the language gap and making me feel fully welcomed into their world.

After breakfast, Rafa, Zeus, and I wandered around a nearby carnival, enjoying the festive atmosphere and savoring the beauty of the moment. It felt like another layer of a rich cultural experience—one that deepened my sense of belonging in Rafa's life and in his family.

This poem captures the essence of that day—one filled with laughter, love, and the blending of our lives. Rafa's playful declaration that "Toxic" was our song, initially a lighthearted joke, became a meaningful memory forever tied to that experience. The poem intertwines the emotions of that moment with the cultural fusion we share, blending the pop world of Britney with the spirit of a Spanish diva like Rocío Dúrcal. It reflects the vibrant, playful, and richly layered love that defines our relationship. The banter, the love, and the joy we shared that day all come together in this poem, highlighting both the depth and lighthearted energy that make our bond so special.

Friendship's Voice

In the daylight, smiles paint my face,
Yet shadows of silence find their place.
I speak of politics, work, dreams spun,
But often, my voice feels like it's the only one.

His words tumble out, a river of tales,
I listen, I laugh, I sail his gales.
But when I speak, it's as if my breath,
Loses its power, fades to death.

He's vibrant with friends, a joyous sight,
While I feel alone in the quiet night.
Our moments of laughter, though bright they seem,
Are fleeting, like whispers in a distant dream.

Feeling bipolar, emotions swing high and low,
In his presence, happiness and loneliness flow.
I wonder why my heart feels this weight,
Am I lost in love or trapped by fate?

Today, the tears welled up, unbidden, unplanned,
Caught in the current of feelings so grand.
Reached out to Shayna, my anchor, my ground,
In her words, solace and strength I found.

"Do you ever feel like you could just cry,
Not wanting to, but emotions sky-high?"
"Yes," she said, her voice a balm,
Her empathy wrapped me in calming calm.

"I hate the loss of control," I confessed,
She understood, her words expressed,
Her own battles with waves of despair,
Together, we stood, a resilient pair.

The thug in me, holding back the tide,
Yet in public, emotions can't hide.
With her, I let go, felt free,
These unknown streets, they don't know me.

Her love, a beacon, through my stormy sea,
In her, I find the strength to be me.
Though love's path is fraught with doubt and pain,
In friendship, I find my voice again.

So here I stand, with heart laid bare,
Grateful for the love and care.
In this dance of joy and sorrow,
I hold on to hope for a brighter tomorrow.

Inspiration behind "Friendship's Voice"
Emotion: Vulnerability and Emotional Struggle with Isolation

This poem was born out of a day marked by a profound sense of emotional duality. Before Rafa and I had the heart-to-heart that helped ease the weight on my shoulders, I found myself bottling up my feelings. The sensation of being unheard and alone was like a storm cloud hovering over me, ready to burst into tears at any moment. I felt trapped in a cycle where my words seemed to evaporate, leaving behind an echo of silence.

One particular evening, this weight felt especially heavy. Rafa and I went to the grocery store to pick up a few items we had missed the first night. He stayed in the car while I ventured into the store, a mundane task that became my moment of escape. As I searched for marshmallows and other essentials, I retreated into the comforting voice of my best friend, Shayna, having just texted with her.

Talking with Shayna, even through text, brought a wave of relief. It was in those moments of laughter and shared confessions that I felt truly heard and seen. Despite knowing that I needed to communicate these feelings to Rafa, this escape provided the solace I needed to get through the night and the rest of the weekend.

The friendship I share with Shayna and Charmaine is a cornerstone of my identity. Their unwavering support, love, and the way they see me for who I am is interwoven into the very fabric of my being. This poem captures the essence of those feelings—of being weighed down by unspoken emotions, finding a moment of escape in a friend's understanding voice, and the immense gratitude I hold for the friendships that shape who I am.

Echoes of Understanding

Leaving San Miguel, driving to Ciudad de México,
A town where belleza whispers through each stone,
Rafa and I, hearts heavy with unspoken words,
As twilight painted the sky with oro and crimson.

I gathered courage like a precious gem,
To tell him of the silences that felt like sombras.
I spoke of feeling unheard, unseen,
Moments where his words reached others but passed
through me.

His gaze softened, truly listening,
Apologizing, a bridge forming with his words,
Explaining the language barriers that built walls,
How zoning out was a shield, not a slight.

We talked of presence, of being acknowledged,
Not just standing by but being a part of his mundo.
He admitted the habits of old amistades,
Routines that made me feel like a stranger.

In that car, under the San Miguel sky,
He promised change, out of amor y respeto,
Creating a space where I felt seen, heard,
A safe harbor in the growing storm of our relación.

He spoke of our open comunicación,
A drama-free sanctuary where we could both breathe,
Where emociones were bridges,

Building a future on trust and understanding.

And in that moment, our unofficial bond strengthened,
His love, my comfort, woven together like the colors of San Miguel,
Creating a tapestry of growth, potential, and mutual respeto.
Gracias, Rafa, for listening, for validating, for being open.

As the car moved forward, so did we,
Two souls learning the language of amor,
Building a sanctuary where both our hearts could belong,
In the ever-beautiful, ever-changing landscape of us.

Inspiration Behind "Echoes of Understanding"
Emotion: Vulnerability and Emotional Reconciliation

This poem stems from a pivotal moment during a car ride with Rafa, as we journeyed from the enchanting town of San Miguel to the bustling city of Mexico City. San Miguel, with its vibrant colors, cobbled streets, and soulful essence, served as a beautiful backdrop for a crucial conversation that deepened our relationship.

During this drive, I found the courage to express feelings of invisibility and being unheard, particularly when Rafa interacted with his friends. I felt like a shadow, present but unseen, and it weighed heavily on my heart. Rafa's response was nothing short of transformative. He listened with genuine empathy, apologized, and explained the language barriers that sometimes created misunderstandings. He reassured me that his actions were not intentional slights but habits formed over time and promised to be more inclusive and attentive.

This conversation was the turning point in our steady climb toward feeling absolutely connected and growing in love. After this day, everything clicked. Rafa's willingness to listen, validate, and work on our communication solidified my trust and love for him. I began to see Rafa as

my safe space, someone I could rely on and feel truly
connected with.

The trip to San Miguel played a significant role in this
transformation. It was not just about the beautiful places
we visited or the friends we spent time with, but also
about how we navigated challenges together. Even when I
felt a little lost and had things on my mind that needed
expression, Rafa's response was perfect. He made me feel
heard and understood, cementing our relationship.

This poem captures the essence of that car ride and the
profound impact it had on us. It reflects the growth,
understanding, and deepening love that emerged from
that moment, making it a cornerstone in our journey
together.

This Is Me: El Amor a Través de la Acción

I entered the weekend with a heart full of glee,
ending it with memories que nunca olvidaré.

Fuimos a San Miguel,
where the house was small but the compañía was grand.

Rafa and his besties,
a merry band, joking we're not in San Miguel,
though the supermercado is close at hand.

Rafa, con su energía vibrante y su risa contagiosa,
the leader, el capitán.

Mateo, his glasses like scholarly jewels,
an old soul, serene as un jardín en la madrugada.
Observador silencioso,
noticing la belleza in life's little cues,
cada flor blooms with quiet confidence.

Nuestro otro Rafael,
sus gafas catching la luz de la luna,

stands with una sonrisa suave yet exuberante.
Aura de calidez e intelecto,
ojos brillando con curiosidad,
un explorador finding joy en cada momento.

Cesar, con su sonrisa que es como una brisa de verano,
Bienvenidos con natural ease,
offering comfort and belonging,
un encanto desenfadado que hace a todos sentir a gusto.

Entré al fin de semana con nervios por la barrera del
idioma,
but left it feeling más conectado.

Una amistad floreciente vía Rafa,
cada uno revealing quién es en pequeñas ways.

A veces callado, siempre traduciendo,
catching la mayoría de las palabras,
lost in un par.

Es difícil pero disfruto las historias,
requiring silencio y enfoque.

Las veces que participé en la conversación,
creo que entendieron quién soy.

Me dicen que los mimo;
yo lo llamo mostrar mi amor,
actions louder than words.

Comparto mi amor through cooking,
asegurándome que los que amo están cuidados.

Gracias por invitarme a sus vidas, por su paciencia,
Conectando uno a uno,
conversando sobre threads comunes,

Pasando el fin de semana en las sombras de las montañas
verdes en la casita roja, Nourished by comida, charlas, y
risas.

Inspiration Behind "This Is Me: El Amor a Través de la Acción"

Emotion: Gratitude and Connection

This poem was inspired by a weekend retreat filled with joy, connection, and the beauty of new friendships. The setting is a picturesque small house near San Miguel, where the company of close friends creates a memorable experience.

The inspiration for this poem comes from a deeply personal experience of navigating a language barrier over the weekend. Despite my limited Spanish and often limited speech, even when my friends spoke English, I found meaningful connections through one-on-one moments with each of Rafa's friends. These interactions allowed me to lean into their personalities and get to know them better.

As a man who expresses love through actions—whether through cooking, caretaking, or making sure the people around me know how I feel about them—I wanted to use my words, in written form, to convey my gratitude and observations of their unique and beautiful individuality. Writing is where I feel most comfortable and expressive, and this poem serves as a heartfelt thank you to Rafa's friends for sharing the weekend with me.

I hope that through this poem, they can feel my love language conveyed through the food and actions over the weekend. Each stanza is crafted to reflect their distinct personalities and the warmth and joy they brought to our time together. The use of Spanish phrases adds depth and cultural nuance, enhancing the emotional resonance and authenticity of the experience.

The poem captures the essence of showing love through actions and expresses heartfelt gratitude for the shared moments, conversations, and laughter that defined the retreat. It is a celebration of new friendships and the beauty of connecting beyond words.

Between the Lines

You joke about the little things,
Like where we stand, what's next to bring.
A smirk, a laugh, a casual fling—
But never quite the whole darn thing.

You jest about the future, dear,
With words that twinkle, crystal clear.
But what's the punchline that I fear?
The truth, perhaps, is not so near.

We danced around the homeless chat,
You laid it bare, just like that.
But other times, you dodge, you bat—
The ball of truth, where's it at?

I'm not here just to play a part,
In your comedy or in your heart.
I seek a friend, a truest start,
Where jokes don't tear the truth apart.

I'm searching for a partner, yes,
But also one who'd gladly confess.
Their fears, their dreams, without the jest—
A best friend's bond, at its best.

So laugh with me, and let's be clear,
I'm here to love, to hold, to hear.
But joking's veil, it shouldn't steer,
Away from truths we both hold dear.

Let's build a bond that's truly free,
Where jokes and truths both equally,
Can share the stage, can simply be—
A love, a life, our comedy.

Inspiration behind "Between the Lines"
Emotion: Frustration and Longing for Authenticity

This poem was born out of a heartfelt and enlightening conversation with Rafa after our trip to San Miguel. Feeling safe, comfortable, and heard during our discussions about the trip, I had one more thing on my mind that I needed to express. This poem was my way of addressing a pattern I'd noticed—Rafa often jokes about certain topics, skirting around the core of what truly matters.

I wrote this poem to read to him, capturing my thoughts and feelings. The poem is intentionally vague and general, never touching directly on the topics that were joked about. At the time, I wasn't prepared or willing to delve into those specifics, but I felt it was important to address the pattern of joking itself. Rafa's mature and supportive response made me feel heard and validated, yet he also checked me, rightfully so. He reminded me that I can ask him directly about what he means or what I want to know in those moments.

Rafa's point was clear—we cannot change others; we can only change ourselves. We can communicate how we feel and hope others choose to respond, but I had to acknowledge that I hadn't asked the questions I needed answers to. There was a previous time when he joked too many times about the homeless—an inside joke a few would understand—and I did ask then. So if I truly wanted to know, I could ask.

This conversation revealed to me that I was avoiding an elusive topic we hadn't discussed before becoming official. It also highlighted that while Rafa is a direct person, he sometimes jokes when he's uncomfortable being straightforward. This is part of who he is, and those jokes are his way of signaling for me to ask the deeper questions.

Through this exchange, I realized the importance of addressing things directly and not relying solely on

indirect communication. I heard Rafa loud and clear—I
need to change because I want to, and I will. I hear you,
Rafa, and I love you.

A Partner I Must Have

In the quest for love, I seek a mate,
To fill the gaps, to co-create,
Grounded, mature, a steady hand,
Balanced, protective, strong to withstand.

I'm a soul so loving, I give too much,
Often losing in the eager clutch,
But my new partner, strong and wise,
Will guard my heart from hungry eyes.

He stands as a sword, sharp and true,
Defending against those who misconstrue,
With insight keen, he reads the room,
Knowing who's real and who's the gloom.

Opposites attract, a dance of two,
Yet in many ways, we align, it's true,
His strengths become my defense's shield,
In his embrace, my fears are healed.

A partner I must have, without a doubt,
In his presence, love's what it's all about,
Together, we form a perfect blend,
My lover, my protector, my true friend.

Inspiration behind "A Partner I Must Have"
Emotion: Yearning for Protection and Companionship

This poem is a heartfelt ode to my ideal partner,
someone who complements my weaknesses and brings
balance to my life. I tend to give excessively, often finding
myself vulnerable to being taken advantage of. Through
therapy, I have learned the importance of having a partner

who offers protection, discernment, and maturity. This partner not only understands my generous nature but also stands as a defender against those who might exploit it.

The inspiration for this poem came during a conversation with my friend Ilana. We talked about a range of topics, including my need to sometimes be seen as someone's villain and the complexities of truth-telling. This led me to reveal my deep and growing love for Rafa, sharing how great things have been going. Our communication has been on target, and I feel like we can tackle anything together. We discussed what qualities a partner must have, and as we talked, I realized that Rafa embodies what I need in a partner.

Ilana and I caught up on the last couple of months, and I expressed how Rafa makes me feel heard, protected, and truly valued. He is a true friend and someone with whom I can let down my defenses. This realization birthed this piece, capturing how Rafa's strengths bolster my defenses, creating a harmonious and supportive relationship.

The poem celebrates the union of opposites, where my partner's strengths reinforce my vulnerabilities, ensuring a balanced and fulfilling partnership. It underscores the therapeutic principle that healthy relationships are built on mutual respect, protection, and the ability to balance each other's strengths and weaknesses. Through my discussions with Ilana and my reflections in therapy, this poem was born, capturing the essence of what I need and have found in Rafa.

He Put It on My Calendar

He put it on my calendar, can you believe?
A simple act that made my heart heave,
I was at home, a notification came,
Our weekend plans, each time, each name.

Different things we're doing, at different times,

Ensuring I won't forget, making love's rhymes,
It's yet another thing, in the myriad of ways,
That strengthens my admiration, love ablaze.

He put it on my calendar, a thoughtful deed,
A man of my own kind, fulfilling my need,
Planning life together, step by step,
Being literally on the same page, where we're kept.

Our calendars in sync, a testament to us,
In the small things, our love finds its thrust,
A man who cares, who plans, who sees,
In these moments, I find my ease.

He put it on my calendar, a sign so clear,
That our love is strong, that he holds me dear,
In every detail, in every plan,
I see my future, with this thoughtful man.

Inspiration behind "He Put It on My Calendar"
Emotion: Gratitude and Affectionate Love

This poem was inspired by a simple yet profoundly meaningful gesture from my partner, Rafa, who added our weekend plans to my calendar. One day, I was at home and received a calendar notification. When I checked it, I saw that it was from Rafa. He had scheduled a birthday party we had committed to attend together and an invite for the Van Gogh museum experience with him and his mom. I cheesed very hard when I saw the calendar invite and shook my head, thinking, "This is going to work."

This act signifies thoughtfulness, organization, and a desire to be in sync with each other's lives. Not only does this type of action eliminate any confusion about our plans, but it also ensures I am reminded and can prepare. For some reason, it just made me really happy—everything Rafa does makes me love him more.

My therapy has emphasized the importance of small acts of consideration in building and maintaining strong relationships. This gesture is not just about planning but also about creating a shared future and ensuring both partners are literally and figuratively on the same page. The poem reflects the deep admiration and love that such thoughtful actions inspire, illustrating how these small, considerate acts contribute significantly to a relationship's foundation and growth.

Un Amor Como el Primer Beso

Rafa, you stir in me a love long lost,
A butterfly flutter, a nervous pit,
Excitement twined with memories glossed,
In my chest, a fire brightly lit.

This love, mi corazón, is not the usual game,
No logical steps, no calculated moves,
But a first love's fervor, all the same,
An energy that both thrills and soothes.

Life, it's worn its toll, its heavy tread,
Made love a practical, growing vine,
A deeper connection, logic-led,
But with you, it's a teenage love divine.

Terrifying, yes, this feeling reborn,
A fear that I'd forgotten how to feel,
Yet here I stand, both thrilled and torn,
Speechless before a love so real.

Making love, I lose my way,
In your eyes, I see my soul reflected,
A shared connection, a bright array,
In your gaze, my love perfected.

In awe, I'm speechless, lost for words,
Taken back to youthful days,
In love, where butterflies and nerves

Define our dance in fiery ways.

Rafa, you're my first love's thrilling beat,
A nervous, happy, endless bliss,
In your love, I find my heart's own heat,
In this teenage affair, our timeless kiss.

Inspiration Behind "Un Amor Como el Primer Beso"
Emotion: Youthful Passion

This poem was inspired by a profound realization and emotional experience I had with Rafa. After a night of intimacy, I saw something in his eyes that made me feel like our souls were connected. It brought back the fluttering butterflies I hadn't felt since my first love, Jace. This overwhelming sensation, almost akin to a good panic attack, made me realize I was falling in love again, and it was both exhilarating and terrifying.

My therapist encouraged me to embrace these feelings for Rafa. She told me to acknowledge the new affection and love, recognizing that my fear was rooted in past experiences. She emphasized that these feelings were natural and positive, and it was okay to trust and embrace the happiness I found in my relationship with Rafa.

Reflecting on this, I realized that my therapist's advice was instrumental in understanding what I was feeling. We discussed how love involves allowing oneself to be vulnerable and open, much like the innocence and intensity of a first love or "puppy love." This connection is built on mutual trust, exploration, and the sheer joy of being with each other. The butterflies and nervous excitement signify a deep emotional bond, one that transcends logic and reason, and dives into the realm of pure, unfiltered emotion.

Writing this poem was my way of capturing this whirlwind of emotions. It's about the rediscovery of that teenage love affair within my heart, a feeling I thought I'd never experience again. It's about the joy, the fear, and the exhilarating vulnerability of loving someone so deeply that it feels like your first love all over again.

In essence, this poem is a testament to the beauty of love that feels new and exciting, even after life's trials and tribulations. It's about allowing oneself to be swept away by the magic of a genuine connection, to feel the butterflies and embrace the nervous excitement, and to revel in the shared moments of vulnerability and joy.

In the Garden of Butterflies

In the garden of my heart, I tend to flowers,
Each petal a memory, each bloom a lesson learned.
But now, as summer dawns, I find new buds emerging,
A blush of love, a whisper of affection,
For Rafa, whose presence cultivates a meadow in my soul.

These feelings flutter, delicate as butterflies,
Their wings a pastel echo of my first love, Jace,
When the world was new and my heart, an open field,
Dancing with the innocence of untouched dreams.

Yet, shadows linger, woven from past heartbreaks,
A tapestry of fear that drapes over my joy.
I see the threads, the pattern of old wounds,
And I know these scars are maps of where I've been,
Not where I must go.

Rafa's eyes, a safe harbor, reflect the sun's promise,
A sanctuary where trust can take root and grow.
He is the gardener of my wild places,
Nurturing the soil, gentle with the thorns,
Understanding that beauty often hides in complexity.

My therapist's voice is a soothing rain,
Reminding me that trust is a seed, not a stone,
That to embrace this love is to embrace myself,
To allow these butterflies their flight,

To dance in the sunlight without fear of the fall.

And so, I breathe into the moment,
Acknowledge the tender ache of vulnerability,
Knowing that love is a garden always in bloom,
Ever-changing, ever-growing, ever-hopeful.

In Rafa's embrace, I find the courage
To let the butterflies of my heart take wing,
To revel in their delicate beauty,
And to trust that this garden, our garden,
Is a safe and happy place,
A sanctuary for our blooming love.

Inspiration behind "In the Garden of Butterflies"
Emotion: Hopeful Vulnerability and Evolving Love.

This poem stems from my evolving relationship with Rafa, viewed through my personal reflections and counseling sessions. The poem captures the fresh and exciting feelings I have for Rafa, reminiscent of the "butterflies" I felt with my first love, Jace. This metaphor of butterflies conveys the beauty and fragility of new love, encompassing the blend of excitement and nervousness that accompanies it. Jace was a love that made me take flight from these feelings, forcing me to calculate and love from the brain rather than the heart. With Rafa, the excitement and nervousness of actual love from the heart is both thrilling and terrifying, marking a very clear turning point in my growth. It signifies my evolution from the trauma I had been holding onto, as I learn to embrace love in its fullness—no longer guarded, but open and vulnerable.

After talking with Julie, I began to understand that the way I approached love since Jace has evolved during this courtship with Rafa. First loves, like the one I had with Jace, are often a safe space, where we enter with no context, full of blind trust. When that trust gets broken, it can leave scars that show up later in unexpected ways.

Julie reassured me that it's normal to carry that hurt, but it's important to recognize when a new love, like Rafa, is offering something different. While the connection between Jace and Rafa initially scared me—because they felt similar—Julie pointed out that Rafa had earned the space in my heart. His love isn't a naive, innocent first love; it's something cultivated and nurtured over time. This made me realize the butterflies I feel for him aren't signs of fear but of something deeper and safer.

Guided by Julie's insight, I now understand that my past heartbreaks are just part of my history. They don't define my future, and they don't cloud what Rafa and I are building together.

This revelation reminds me to embrace my feelings, trust the happiness Rafa brings, and let go of those shadows from the past. It's time to confidently nurture this new relationship, knowing that the pain of the past has taught me to be cautious but not closed. My heart is open, and I am choosing to trust it again.

Rafa's presence is depicted as a safe harbor where I can cultivate trust and vulnerability, symbolized through the metaphor of gardening. This imagery emphasizes the careful nurturing required in our relationship, with trust being a seed that needs time and care to grow. The poem ultimately celebrates the empowerment found in self-acceptance and the courage to embrace love despite past hurts. It reflects my journey towards interdependency, where both partners support each other's growth without creating unhealthy dependencies. Through these themes, "In the Garden of Butterflies" becomes a reflective and dynamic piece that honors new beginnings, personal growth, and the transformative power of love and self-awareness.

Love's Gentle Remedy

On days when clouds loom heavy, skies are gray,
When deadlines press and news brings disarray,
A restless night, with worries left to seep,
In love's embrace, my heart finds peaceful sleep.

For in your smile, my burdens softly fade,
Your voice, a melody that soothes the frayed,
Each glance, a beacon in the tempest's sway,
Your love, a dawn that brightens darkest day.

When stress and strife attempt to steal my cheer,
Your touch, a balm, makes every problem clear,
In you, I find a haven from the storm,
Your love, a fire that keeps my spirit warm.

With you, even the hardest day can mend,
In love's sweet refuge, all my troubles end.

Inspiration behind "Love's Gentle Remedy"
Emotion: Comfort and Solace in Love

This poem was born out of an incredibly demanding work week, one where I found myself pushing through over 80 hours of intense deadlines and relentless tasks. The pressure was almost overwhelming, and fatigue was my constant companion. Yet, amid the chaos and exhaustion, the immediate thought of Rafa brought an unexpected and profound comfort to my mind.

Just thinking of him made me smile, his presence in my thoughts a soothing balm to my weary spirit. Rafa's love provided a sanctuary, a gentle reminder that even in the toughest times, there's a light that can pierce through the darkest moments. It was this thought of him that gave me the strength to carry on, to push through the remaining hours of my day with renewed energy and hope. His love transformed a grueling week into a testament of how

deeply someone can impact your life, turning stress into
solace and weariness into warmth.

What a Difference Time Makes

In the realm where time and space entwine,
We find love's dance, so sweetly divine.
From moments swift, like lightning's blaze,
To gentle growth in love's warm embrace.

July 25th, a day to recall,
I penned a poem, my heart did sprawl.
"Will you be my boyfriend?"—words so true,
In a box of memories, crafted anew.

A pop-up explosion, love's story told,
With echoes of pride, stickers bold.
Pictures tucked in pockets, eight in all,
From Mexico City's pride to Malibu's call.

San Diego sunsets, Hollywood's sign,
Chicago's winds, San Miguel's wine.
Your mom, your sisters, moments so dear,
In the center, our first date so clear.

"Te amo," you whispered, a week had passed,
A fluttering feeling, my heart held fast.
I heard it, unsure, but couldn't deny,
The truth in your words, the sparkle in your eye.

Before, "Te quiero" was our gentle start,
A cautious phrase, a budding heart.
You asked, "Do you know the weight it bears?"
I smiled and listened, felt your cares.

In English, "I love you" comes slow,
One phrase for all, as you know.
But "Te amo," deep and strong,
Reserved for love that's lasted long.

You joked of houses, of life's grand plans,
But I knew the truth in your loving hands.
From "Me gustas" to "Te quiero," we grew,
Now "Te amo," my love, I'm complete with you.

What a difference time makes, indeed,
From early days to planting love's seed.
And in future chapters, we shall see,
What time will bring, for you and me.

Inspiration Behind "What a Difference Time Makes"
Emotion: Love's Deepening Progression

This poem is a heartfelt reflection on the journey of love and the significance of time in shaping relationships. On a special day—July 25th—marking our anniversary and the day I asked Rafa to be my novio. This moment was a culmination of our shared experiences and the deepening of our bond.

The day itself was a whirlwind of emotions and events. We had traveled to Puebla the night before, a spontaneous trip to pick up his car. Despite the exhaustion and the last-minute nature of the trip, I aimed to create a special and unique experience for us. As a perfectionist, I felt I didn't quite hit my own mark of flawless execution, but the sentiment and effort were there. What mattered most was that Rafa said yes, accepting my proposal with love and enthusiasm.

The day after, I had the honor of being introduced to Rafa's family as his boyfriend. His sisters, protective and caring, gently questioned my intentions, a gesture that showed their love and concern for him. It was a moment that I cherished, appreciating their care and the warmth of his family.

The following weekend, we continued our celebration by traveling to Cabo, where I introduced Rafa to my family as my boyfriend. This experience was filled with joy and new memories, further solidifying our relationship. Despite my initial hesitation and the thought of delaying the moment, it was clear that life would always be busy. I realized that I didn't want another day, trip, or interaction to pass without making our relationship official.

Rafa had playfully, yet earnestly, asked me several times when I would officially ask him to be his partner. I was ready, and there was no reason to wait any longer. The poem encapsulates the essence of our journey—from the early days of getting to know each other to the love we now share. It reflects on the significance of language, culture, and time in expressing love, and how these elements have shaped our relationship. Ultimately, it celebrates the joy and excitement of finding love and committing to a shared future.

Mi Amor, Mi Compañero

Hey Rick, mi amor, que tal?
From the start, it's been un sueño real.
Meeting family, amigos, travels, and pride,
In your love, I'm taking a joyful ride.

Plans we've made, and love we've shared,
In your embrace, I feel so cared.
Estoy enamorado, it's true,
And I want to tackle life with you.

So, will you be my boyfriend, por favor?
Together, let's open every door.
Tag team life, with laughter y más,
Making all our dreams last.

Inspiration behind "Mi Amor, Mi Compañero"
Emotion: Joyful Anticipation and Love

This poem is a heartfelt expression of my love for Rafa and my desire to ask him to be my boyfriend. To make this

moment even more special, I created a picture explosion
box filled with memories from our adventures since
March. Each photo captures the joy we've shared, from
meeting family and friends to traveling and celebrating
Pride in Mexico City. I decorated the box with stickers that
match our experiences, like Pride stickers for our Mexico
City Pride.

In the center of the box, I placed a picture from our first
date at Junior Club, where we played tennis and later
enjoyed tacos. On top of this cherished memory, I wrote
the poem on pretty sparkly paper, folded it into a small
box, and sealed it with a heart sticker.

For me, love inspires creativity and romance, which I
express through thoughtful gestures like this one. It's a
language of love that comes naturally when I'm deeply in
love, and it's a part of myself that I cherish. With Rafa, I
feel my full self, and for the first time in over five years, I
am ready for a committed relationship. I've deleted all my
apps and am fully devoted to him. I feel complete,
knowing we can communicate our needs and decide
together on any future pivots. This sense of puppy love
has reignited a spark in me, and I am thrilled to share my
life with him.

Our Love in Words

In whispered tones and midnight chats,
We weave a tapestry, where our hearts are at.
"I hate that you have to experience that," I say,
"But I love that we share this, in our own way."

Our families, silent, lost in their own strife,
Yet we choose to communicate, to breathe life.
"One of the many beautiful things I love about you,
Is how we resolve, how we see each other through."

You blush, you smile, with words so sweet,
"Can we get married now?" A love complete.

I wish I was there to see you, glowing with pride,
"In lieu of a big wedding, or one later," I confide.

"First a small one," you suggest, so wise,
"And then, a big one, when the house is our prize."
Priorities set, a future we build,
"Exacto," I reply, our dreams fulfilled.

"I love waking up to you," I confess, heart sincere,
"Tackling life together, I hold you dear."
"I love it too," you say, with a smile so bright,
"This is so sweet, it makes my heart light."

"Y por siempre," I promise, "es la verdad,"
Forever in love, in joy, and sometimes in sad.
"Te amo, bebé," you whisper as night falls,
"Te amo," I reply, as sleep calls.

In our dreams, we find solace, in our love so deep,
Together we face life, no promises we keep.
Our bond, our words, a testament so true,
In love and in life, we always make it through.

Inspiration Behind "Our Love in Words"
Emotion: deep love and intimacy

This poem was written after a heartfelt conversation between Rafa and me. My love for Rafa runs profoundly deep, rekindling feelings of butterflies and excitement that I once thought were lost forever. Through therapy, I have learned that it is not only okay to move forward with Rafa but that our connection is strong enough to tackle any challenge life throws our way. This realization has made my puppy love even more intense, and I am confident that Rafa is my husband; it is just a matter of finding the right time to make it official.

Our entrepreneurial spirits and shared passions drive us to move quickly on our dreams. We talked about the practicality of getting married sooner rather than later, not only because we love each other and want the world to know but also to safeguard our investments as we embark on buying a home and building a real estate empire. This will allow us to retire early and enjoy life and travel without constraints.

The poem captures our mutual understanding and unwavering belief that, together, we can achieve anything. Our communication, conflict resolution skills, and solution-oriented approach are the foundations of our relationship. These qualities make me confident that we can weather any storm and build a beautiful life together.

"Who is This? A Metaphorical Revelation"

People keep saying this love looks different on me,
Like a new outfit that fits just perfectly.
They notice I'm glowing, a brighter kind of hue,
Moving and grooving, like I'm brand new.

"Y'all dressing alike every day now?" they jest,
In love-love, they say, this phase is the best.
Cousin Alina smiles, "I like this new side,
You look good together, like a perfect tide."

Another chimes in, "He isn't your usual type,
But the chemistry, oh, it's so alive!"
Someone else adds, "Yes! Enjoy life with your boo.
I've never seen you THIS happy, it's true!"

Matching outfits, the comments abound,
We've heard it before, it's all around.
"They're like twins!" they joke, but we know the truth,
Our love shines through, in every little proof.

So, who is this in love, glowing so bright?
It's me, transformed, in pure delight.
A different side, a new chapter begun,
With him by my side, my forever one.

It's new for us both, this different kind of bliss,
We're happy, we click, and tackle life like this.
Fun, adventures, and love to share,
From here on out, we'll take on the world's dare.

Inspiration behind "Who is This? A Metaphorical Revelation"
Emotion: Joyful Transformation and Love

This poem was inspired by a recent trip to Cabo San Lucas, where I introduced Rafa to a few of my favorite family members. This trip was a significant moment for us as a couple, especially since it was Rafa's first time meeting my family. We were there to celebrate my cousin Brianna's 50th birthday, surrounded by a beautiful mix of loved ones including my cousin Alina, my auntie, cousin Tanner, Tanner's friend Jacinda, and my cousin Kendra.

Cabo, with its stunning landscape and vibrant atmosphere, was the perfect backdrop for this memorable weekend. We stayed at the Riu Palace, a luxurious resort that offered breathtaking views of the iconic rocks jutting out of the azure waters. The property itself was a paradise, with lush gardens, elegant architecture, and a lively atmosphere. The Riu parties were a highlight, filled with music, dancing, and a palpable sense of joy that made the celebration even more special.

The beauty of Cabo is undeniable, from its golden beaches to the dramatic rock formations known as "El Arco," which stand as a natural archway at the tip of the Baja Peninsula. This historic site has been a witness to countless sunrises and sunsets, and it added a sense of wonder and history to our experience. The vibe in Cabo is a perfect blend of relaxation and excitement, offering a serene escape from the everyday hustle and bustle.

This trip was not just about celebrating a milestone birthday; it was also a much-needed break for me. After three grueling 80-hour work weeks, fighting to win a telework case against my job, I finally secured a victory just before our departure. Knowing that I wouldn't have to relocate from San Diego to Chicago immediately allowed me to relax and enjoy this time away. It felt like a breath of fresh air to rest, recharge, and savor the sweetness of this new love that feels so mature and familiar.

During the weekend, I also had a therapy session with my therapist, who has been a guiding light in helping me navigate my love life. She expressed her happiness for me, recognizing the settled, secure, and healthy place I've reached. Her advice was to lean into this newfound happiness and embrace the journey ahead. She also provided valuable insights that helped me refine a part of my book, which I submitted to my editor this weekend.

I'm currently working on filling in the gaps of my story for Parts 1 and 2 of my book, and I'm motivated to meet my personal deadlines. This weekend was not just a time for celebration but also a balanced success in finding rest and clarity. It was a much-needed recharge, as the doctor ordered, allowing me to enjoy the company of loved ones, soak in the beauty of Cabo, and appreciate the deepening bond with Rafa. This trip encapsulated a moment of joy, growth, and the comfort of being surrounded by people who love and understand me, making it an unforgettable experience.

In addition to the beautiful backdrop and the special moments with my family, the inspiration for this poem also comes from the overwhelming response we've received from friends and family on social media. Our Instagram posts from the trip have garnered numerous comments and messages from people who see the love and joy radiating from us. They consistently remarked on how different I seem, noting a newfound happiness and confidence that shines through in every photo.

My cousin Alina and other family members echoed these sentiments during the trip, expressing their excitement and happiness for me. They noticed that I'm

moving and doing things I never did before, exuding a
new energy that they hadn't seen in me. The consistent
recognition from loved ones—both in person and online—
of this positive change in my life has been both
heartwarming and affirming. Their excitement for me,
coupled with their observations of this "new" me, has been
a delightful affirmation of the growth and joy I feel in this
relationship. This collective acknowledgment and support
have further solidified my belief in the unique and
beautiful connection I share with Rafa, making this love
feel all the more special and real.

All In, Forever Yours

Baby, te amo más que las palabras pueden decir,
I'm standing here, heart in hand, no games to play.
I've heard your pain, seen your tears,
and I'm here to make it clear, to wipe away those fears.

Yes, I've made mistakes, but mi amor, I'm learning.
Navigating this path with you, my heart is yearning.
I've listened, I've heard, and I want you to know,
in this dance of love, I'll never let you go.

You've seen my world, the chaos, the strain,
but through it all, mi corazón, I'm not causing you pain.
I see the insecurities, and I own my part,
but please know, I'm here, with an open heart.

I'm not perfect, but I'm perfectly yours.
I'm not asking you to fix me, nor to fight my wars.
I'm working through the mess, with therapy in tow,
but baby, you're my future, it's you I want to show.

That I'm all in, no hesitations, no doubt.
Our love, our bond, that's what it's all about.
I'll respect your process, your space, your time,
but know, in my soul, you're always mine.

Yes, I was wrong, those pictures, those trips,

but please don't let that cloud our love, or let it slip.
I was tired, overwhelmed, trying to make it through,
but baby, don't you see, all I want is you.

I'm here, I'm committed, I'm ready to fight,
to hold you close, through every day and night.
Te amo, con todo mi ser, with all my might,
and I promise you, I'll make it right.

Let's not let the past cast a shadow on today.
Let's build our future, in every possible way.
I'm not running, I'm standing here, arms wide open,
for you, for us, for the vows yet unspoken.

Yes, I'm pivoting, I'm learning, I'm trying to be true,
but all I want, mi amor, is a life with you.
You've given me hope, a reason to believe,
that together, there's nothing we can't achieve.

So, I'm asking you, from the depth of my soul,
let's move forward, let's make ourselves whole.
Te amo, mi vida, más de lo que puedes ver,
and I can't wait for the day when you're mine to wed.

I'm all in, no doubts, no fear.
With you by my side, everything is clear.
So let's take this journey, hand in hand,
together, forever, across this land.

Baby, focus on my heart, on my intention,
and know that with you, there's no hesitation.
We're a force, unstoppable, strong,
and with you, my love, I know where I belong.

Let's make this love last, let's make it shine,
because, mi amor, I'm yours, and you're mine.
I'm all in, I'm here to stay,
and I can't wait to start our forever, today.

Inspiration Behind "All In, Forever Yours"
Emotion: Devotion

This poem is about the real, raw emotions of navigating a pivotal moment in our relationship. It reflects my struggle of withholding the truth out of fear and uncertainty, even when my intention was never to cause harm.

Before I fully realized how deeply I loved Rafa and how safe I felt with him, I made the mistake of keeping something to myself, which ultimately surfaced and tested our bond.

My inspiration for the poem comes from the pain and growth that followed. When Rafa discovered the truth, it challenged the foundation of what felt like a perfect relationship. Yet, something even stronger emerged—our ability to communicate, ask the hard questions, express our hurt, and find a way forward together.

This poem captures the beauty of a love that isn't perfect but is resilient. It's about acknowledging mistakes, embracing vulnerability, and moving forward with even more honesty and commitment. It celebrates the fact that despite the flaws and the challenges, Rafa and I have built a relationship where we can talk through anything, and that is a love worth fighting for.

Our Equation of Forever

In the arithmetic of life, you and I are more than a sum,
an equation where balance isn't just a hope—it's done.
You, Rafa, my future husband, this I know with every breath,
not just for your looks, though, damn, they're beyond the best.

Born in Mexico, raised with roots deep and true,
yet you've wandered the world, learning,

speaking in tongues—two.
You bring me the kind of love that's both fierce and warm,
a shield and a sword in any brewing storm.

Two years in therapy, you've polished your mind,
now, we have conversations that are one of a kind.
We're careful with words, take steps back when we must,
building bridges with trust, not eroded by rust.

You solve problems with the skill of your trade,
balancing accounts of love in the ledger we've made.
Equally yoked, both dreamers, entrepreneurs at heart,
in every plan we draw, we each have a part.

I'm not just in love; I'm anchored in you,
a love that's mature, yet fresh as morning dew.
We're talking weddings, one small, one big—a Mexico affair,
but no matter the size, it's the love we'll wear.

And I've met your family, who love and support us, too.
They've welcomed me in, made our bond feel even more true.
I can't wait for our travels, our future, our schemes,
for all that we've dreamed and those yet to dream.

This life with you, where anything's possible, it seems,
feels like a journey where life is but a dream.

Inspiration Behind "Our Equation of Forever"
Emotion: Love and Commitment

    This poem came from me trying to put into words
through conversation my deep love for Rafa and my
certainty in the fact that I'm meant to spend my life with
him. I'm certain Rafa is my husband, and while he
definitely is attractive, this certainty isn't based on that. It's
about how our lives align in such a harmonious and
balanced way—how we are equally yoked in every aspect,

from our entrepreneurial spirits to our shared dreams and the speed at which we move to make things happen.

Born and raised in Mexico, Rafa spent time abroad where he honed his English, becoming nearly bilingual. This experience broadened his world; now, he brings that same open-mindedness to our relationship. He's loving but assertive and protective, making me feel safe and cherished. The past two years of therapy have been transformative for him, and I can see the results in how we communicate—I've never experienced such great communication in a relationship. We're incredibly sensitive to each other's words, careful in our conversations, and when necessary, we take a step back to ensure we're on the same page. This mutual respect and understanding reassures me that we can face anything life throws at us together.

We've talked about our future, even thinking about a small wedding and perhaps a larger one in Mexico later. But those plans are still up in the air, and I'm just focused on how good things are. Despite moving out after a recent bump with my ex, this overwhelming, beautiful love I have for Rafa has been the one constant in the chaos of resettling and finding my footing again. It's the kind of love that gives you butterflies, the kind that my past traumas once told me was foolish. But I see it differently through therapy, calling it "puppy love" instead of "stupid" and recognizing it as something mature and safe. For the first time, my therapist actually approves of me being in a relationship, which is a big deal considering her past concerns.

We plan to travel together through the fall, and I can't wait for everyone to meet him. Rafa is so full of life— social, energetic, and genuinely happy. I've met nearly his entire family, and they've welcomed me with open arms, supporting us wholeheartedly. Rafa has brought out a social side of me that I didn't even know I had, and somehow, I'm keeping up with it all—work, life, and everything in between.

   This poem is a reflection of all these feelings, of the
certainty I have in our future together, where anything is
possible and life feels like a dream.

Bésame, Mi Amor

In the stillness of night, I whisper to the stars,
our love, a secret written in celestial scars.
Kiss me, mi amor, as the moonlight bathes your face,
your golden red beard, a halo, a tender embrace.

Each day with you, I bask in the glow of our truth,
your love, a treasure, a fountain of youth.
I vow to never let you feel a shadow of doubt,
for in your arms, I've found what life's all about.

Bésame mucho, the words linger on my tongue,
a melody of love, forever young.
Our passion, a fire that never dies,
in your eyes, I see endless skies.

Together, we face the world, hand in hand,
building a life, a future so grand.
You are my anchor, my home, my safe space,
in your embrace, I've found my place.

Your lips, soft against mine, a sweet caress,
a moment of bliss, nothing less.
As I hold you close, our hearts beat as one,
tethered together, under the sun.

Te amo, Rafa, con todo mi corazón,
you are my muse, my endless song.
In this dance of life, we'll move with grace,
every kiss, a promise, every touch, a trace.

I'll remind you daily, in every breath I take,
that our love is real, no chance for heartbreak.
For in this rare, precious gift we've found,

our souls are bound, eternally wound.

So, kiss me, mi amor, let the world see,
our love, a beacon, vast as the sea.
In every word, in every gentle touch,
I love you, Rafa, so very much.

Inspiration behind "Bésame, Mi Amor"
Emotion: Deep Love and Devotion

This poem stems from the deep and passionate love I
feel for Rafa. It's a love that I cherish and want to celebrate
every single day. This poem captures the intensity of my
emotions, the desire to never take our love for granted,
and my excitement for our future together. It reflects my
commitment to ensuring that Rafa always feels secure and
loved, with no room for doubt in the strength and depth of
our connection.

The poem is also inspired by the timeless, beautiful
song "Bésame Mucho," a musical portrait of deep affection
and yearning. The song's lyrics weave through the poem,
serving as a metaphor for our eternal bond. Spanish adds a
layer of intimacy and rhythm, echoing how our love
feels—both familiar and endlessly new.

Through the imagery of tender touches, soft kisses, and
the warmth of our closeness, this poem conveys what it
means to be truly in love. It's about embracing every
moment, celebrating the joy of being together, and
recognizing that we have found something rare and
precious in each other. This poem is a testament to the love
we share– a love that is passionate, safe, and eternal.

Love, Green Cards, and Entrepreneurial Hearts

We're sketching out the blueprint of our days,
two entrepreneurs in love, finding our ways.
With hearts intertwined and dreams to share,

but oh, the whispers—let's tackle them with flair.

"Is it the love, or is it the card?" they say,
as if our plans were inked in some cliché.
But darling, they don't see the spark in our eyes,
or the late-night talks under Mexican skies.

We're plotting out futures, both work and play,
balancing spreadsheets, navigating each day.
"Is this about business or some grand design?"
Well, we're in love, but sure, the tax breaks are fine.

Let them giggle, let them guess.
We're in this together, no need to impress.
For us, it's more than papers or legal binds,
it's the way we laugh, our hearts and our minds.

Green card or no, our journey's our own,
with plans so grand and love well-known.
So let them talk, let them jest and debate.
We've got visas for life, and that's first-rate.

We're partners in crime, in love, and in plans,
building our empire with our own hands.
So here's to the love, the dreams we've sown,
together forever, in a life we've grown.

Inspiration behind "Love, Green Cards, and Entrepreneurial Hearts"
Emotion: Playful Resilience and Confident Love

This poem comes from a place of deep love and shared ambition. Rafa and I are entrepreneurs planning our life together. As we navigate the complexities of the green card process, we can't help but acknowledge the perceptions that arise from family and friends. Some might assume that our relationship is driven by the pursuit of a green card rather than the genuine connection and shared dreams we hold dear.

But our love is real, and so is our desire to build a future together—a future that involves both our hearts and our entrepreneurial spirits. This poem is a playful response to those assumptions, a way to laugh at the idea that paperwork could ever define the depth of our bond. It's a celebration of our journey, acknowledging the practicalities while embracing the love that underpins everything we do.

In this poem, I capture the balance between navigating legal processes and building a life together. It's about more than just immigration or business; it's about the joy we find in each other and the life we're crafting, hand in hand.

Quiet Love

I am quiet, my love,
not for lack of words,
but for the overwhelming joy
that swells within me.
It's not just butterflies,
it's something deeper,
something that fills my soul
and captures my heart entirely.

I search for the right words,
but everything feels small
compared to the love I hold for you.
You already know,
I want you as my husband.
You already know,
I love you more than words can say.

Yet, here I am,
pensive, lost in thought,
trying to describe this weight,
this beautiful weight of love
that presses on my chest,
making me quiet,
making me yours.

Inspiration behind "Quiet Love"
Emotion: Profound Affection and Introspective tenderness.

I often find myself lost for words when explaining my feelings to Rafa. One moment that stands out took place during trip to his house in Querétaro, Mexico. As we sat together on my last day there, I felt this overwhelming sense of love and happiness. It was stronger than anything I had ever felt, and I struggled to find the words to express it.

We had just come off two hellish weeks—key drama, Nico drama, police drama, me moving in with Rafa, and getting my place on Buenavista prepared for rental. This weekend getaway was the perfect escape and reset. And there he was–my boyfriend, my future husband–supporting me through it all.

As I sat there, pensive and quiet, I thought about everything—the happiness, the love, the relief of being with him after such chaos. I wanted to say something and tell him everything I felt, but the words wouldn't come out. It wasn't that I didn't have the words; it was that I couldn't utter them.

So, I stayed silent, reflecting on how deeply I love him. Writing has always been my outlet, so I wrote "Quiet Love." It was my way of explaining to Rafa that I was so quiet because I felt something far stronger than butterflies, something that butterflies could never describe. I didn't read the poem to him then, but later, I finally found the words to express my love to him out loud.

Navigating the Lows with You, Mi Cielo

Love isn't just about the highs,
it's weathering the stormy skies.
Rafa, with you, I sail each tide.
In calm or chaos, I'm by your side.

We've touched the heat, felt the strain,
but in your arms, I'll brave the rain.
When waters rise, we don't drift apart,
we row together, heart to heart.

Your intensity, a flame so bright,
it wasn't easy, but it felt right.
Through our deepest lows, we find the light,
we talk, we mend, until the night turns bright.

Mexicano de mi corazón, mi fiel compañero,
Your directness is my guiding faro.
"Nip it in the bud," you say with might,
forcing me to speak, to not take flight.

We create a rhythm, a dance so true,
healthy conversations, just me and you.
Cada palabra, cada sentimiento compartido,
Fortalece nuestro amor, nunca es perdido.

We learn, we grow, with every beat,
seeking what's different, never retreat.
You tell me what you need, and I the same.
In this game of love, we're both to blame.

With each passing day, my love ascends.
Through every trial, our bond extends.
Eres mi esposo, mi amor eterno,
In every struggle, our love turns vernal.

"Las parejas saludables discuten," they proclaim.
But we communicate, never play a game.
Diferentes perspectivas, frustraciones también,
yet we rise, creating harmony again.

Healthy's not perfect, but it's real.
It's how we dance, how we feel.
Respetando cada sentimiento, nuestro amor se expande,
You'll forever be my life, my light, mi Cielo grande.

Inspiration behind "Navigating the Lows with You, Mi Cielo"

Emotion: Resilient Love and Deep Commitment

This poem is drawn from the real-life dynamics Rafa and I navigate, especially as we work through our unique relationship challenges. The drama of the Nico chapter is just one part of our story. Spending a lot of time in Mexico, even with Rafa as my boyfriend and best friend, sometimes leaves me feeling isolated, particularly in all-Spanish-speaking spaces. The language barrier, combined with being gay, often makes me feel lost in conversations and jokes, which can be incredibly lonely.

There have been moments when my mood was written all over my face, and Rafa, ever attentive, would pull me aside to talk. These talks, deep and understanding, are filled with a genuine desire to support each other. I've never experienced the type of reasonableness Rafa shows and his attention to my needs in a relationship before. I feel truly heard, understood, and supported, which is rare and precious.

These moments of connection, where we communicate openly and experience the lows together, only reinforce what I already know in my heart: Rafa is my husband. I've already made up my mind, and these experiences just solidify that decision even more. I'm only waiting for the right moment to propose. I am even having a ring made and have a proposal place and day in mind. This poem is a reflection of that journey—of navigating the lows and highs, of feeling lost but finding solace in the love we share, and of knowing that this man is the one I want to spend the rest of my life with.

A Promise in Córdoba

Rafa, my love, this journey we're on
is more than just miles traveled, it's where I belong.
In your arms, through highs and lows, we stand,
navigating life together, hand in hand.

In Córdoba, beneath the Argentine sky,
where history whispers and the mountains lie,
I'll kneel with a ring, a 14-carat vow,
to ask you, my love, will you take this now?

Estancias Jesuíticas, where the sun sets low,
a place so serene, where our love can grow.
With "Tú de Qué Vas" softly played by a band,
I'll pour out my heart, and reach for your hand.

On November 24th, our anniversary date,
the moment will come, and I'll know it's fate.
From the first "yes" you gave on that July day,
to this moment, my love, I've been on my way.

I've told my family, prepared them with care.
They know what's coming, the love that we share.
My mom smiled and said, "You're such a lover, Mac,"
and my friends, they cheered, no doubts, no lack.

But first, I spoke to your family, you see,
seeking permission, so this love could be free.
Your mom, at first, took it slow with concern,
but then she smiled, her blessing we'd earn.
She said, "No need to rush, take your time,
welcome to the family, you're already mine."

Your dad, with a hug and a quick yes,
spoke of love and safety, wishing us the best.
"Look after mijo, stay smart, stay true,
and know we'll always support both of you."

Your mom saw the ring, nestled in a shell,
its blue-pearl beauty cast a silent spell.

In that moment, I knew it was right,
our families aligned, love shining bright.

We'll journey through South America's lands,
from beaches to mountains, with dreams in our hands.
But it's in Córdoba, where the rivers flow,
I'll ask you to stay, to never let go.

Your love, Rafa, has shown me what's true,
in every challenge, it's just me and you.
We talk, we grow, we learn every day.
You're my partner, my love, in every way.

So, as the Argentine winds gently blow,
in that sacred moment, you'll surely know,
That this love we share, it's meant to be.
Will you marry me, and set our spirits free?

With every conversation, my love deepens still.
You're my future, my forever, my heart's only thrill.
So in Córdoba's beauty, under that starry dome,
Rafa, say yes, and let's build our home.

Inspiration behind "A Promise in Córdoba"
Emotion: Anticipation and Deep Devotion.

The inspiration behind this poem is rooted in a momentous decision I'm planning to make, one that symbolizes the culmination of love, growth, and the future I see with Rafa. We've been through so much together, navigating challenges and building a deep connection that has only strengthened with time. It's this bond, this undeniable certainty in our relationship, that has led me to plan a proposal that reflects the depth of my feelings and the beauty of our journey.

The setting I've chosen for this life-changing moment is the Estancias Jesuíticas del Norte Cordobés in Córdoba, Argentina. Córdoba is a place rich in history and natural beauty, known for its colonial architecture, rolling hills, and the cultural significance that echoes through its landscapes. The Estancias Jesuíticas, a UNESCO World Heritage site, hold a special allure with their historical significance. These estancias were once the center of Jesuit missions, embodying a blend of religious, cultural, and agricultural heritage that played a crucial role in shaping the region.

The specific estancia where I plan to propose offers a serene, picturesque backdrop—a perfect blend of history and nature. The sprawling fields, the ancient buildings, and the tranquil atmosphere create an environment where time seems to stand still. It's a place where the past and present merge, making it an ideal setting to ask Rafa to build our future together.

However, the details are still being worked out. I'm hoping to secure the location at the Estancias Jesuíticas del Norte Cordobés, but I need to coordinate with the site to ensure that it's possible to have a photographer, a drone, and the privacy necessary for such an intimate moment. I envision the proposal happening on our anniversary date, November 24th, during our trip through South America. Everything is falling into place, but I need the final confirmation to make this dream a reality.

One of the most important parts of this journey was speaking to Rafa's parents and asking for their blessing. Since they don't speak English and I'm still studying Spanish daily, though not yet fluent, I prepared a script to guide me through the conversation. While I am strong in conversational Spanish, I understand more than I can communicate back, which made this moment both challenging and deeply meaningful.

As the conversation unfolded, I found myself listening intently, receiving their words and emotions, and reassuring them when necessary. There were moments where I could respond with the Spanish I had, and I spoke from the heart whenever I had the words. Rafa's father was immediately supportive, embracing me with love and offering his blessing without hesitation. He told me to look after his son and to be smart in the life we're building together. Rafa's mother, although initially concerned about how quickly we've moved, soon shared in our joy. When she saw the ring, housed in a diamond-studded, blue-pearl sea shell, her concerns faded. She welcomed me into the family and reassured me that there was no need to rush the wedding. With the blessing of both families, I now feel even more assured that this is the right moment to move forward.

As I work on these plans, I'm filled with excitement and anticipation. This proposal isn't just about asking Rafa to marry me; it's about creating a moment that encapsulates the journey we've been on and the life we're building together. The setting in Córdoba, with its rich history and stunning beauty, feels like the perfect place to take this next step in our relationship. It's a place that represents both the roots of our love and the wings that will carry us into the future.

I'm looking forward to the moment when everything comes together, and I can look into Rafa's eyes, in that beautiful, historic setting, and ask him to be my forever. The planning is in motion, and though there are still details to finalize, I know that whatever happens, the love we share will make it a moment we'll both cherish for the rest of our lives.

Perspectives of a Shared World
Emotion: Empathy and Reflection

"Perspectives of a Shared World" isn't solely about politics but rather a collection of diverse reflections and thoughts that represent my view of the world. These pieces explore everything from grief and loss to the history and significance of words that carry the weight of systemic racism, offering commentary on the resilience of marginalized communities.

Whether reflecting on personal gratitude or celebrating moments of triumph, each work provides a window into various perspectives. This chapter is about sharing my interpretations of the world around me through political landscapes, personal experiences, or cultural observations. My goal is to show how interconnected we are, bound by shared struggles, victories, and moments of growth.

Under Flushing Lights: Coco's Victory, A Poem

In the vibrant rush of New York's heartbeat,
Elle called with an echo of excitement—
"If Coco wins, are you in for the ride?"
Hell, yes, my bags were packed in spirit,
before the final serve of the semifinal set.

Ticketed dreams were booked as Coco swung,
a protest delay, a breath for us to find
our golden seats in history's lush script.
By the match's end, our plans were inked—
New York awaited, and adventure blinked with promise.

Flushing Meadows buzzed, a global village,
Elle's poster high: "Go Coco! NY Summer '23!"
We found our seats, first row above the elite,
close enough to hear the thrill, to feel
the pulse of thousands under Arthur Ashe's lights.

Celebrities dotted the stands, an assembly
of stardust cheering on the court's young queen.
The first set stumbled, but hope is a resilient friend.
Coco rallied in the second with fierce grace,
claiming the set as ours to celebrate.

With every volley, every precise backhand,
the stadium united in a crescendo of cheers.
Championship point—a pause in collective breaths—
then joy exploded as Coco conquered,
her victory a painting of pure, sweet triumph.

Tears were shed, ancestors felt,
as she climbed to her family's embrace.
We, so close, were wrapped in the moment's embrace,
our cheers a bridge to her joyful tears.

After the match, Elle and I retreated to the hotel,
a quiet sanctuary to reflect and feast.
The following day, vibrant with Jay Z's beats,
Sammie joined just for the museum's greet.

Each moment, a thread in the vibrant fabric of our
weekend.

That weekend, New York wasn't just a city;
it was a promise fulfilled, a dream lived.
Thankful for the call that brought me there,
for Coco's rise, for friendships that flare.
Under the lights of Flushing's courts,
we found a memory forever to hold dear.

**Inspiration behind "Under Flushing Lights: Coco's
Victory"**
Emotion: Exhilaration and Gratitude

This poem arose from an exhilarating and intensely
personal experience at the US Open, shared with my dear
friend Elle. The poem commemorates a historic event in
tennis and marks the 8th anniversary of my friendship
with Elle, which began at the very same tournament. This
connection adds a layer of sentimentality to the occasion,
blending personal milestones with public triumph.

Celebrating Coco Gauff's maiden Grand Slam victory
was about more than the sport; it was a moment of
significant cultural importance, particularly within the
African American community. Her victory as a Black
woman being celebrated on such a grand stage was a
powerful symbol of progress and representation. It
resonated deeply with me, witnessing the communal joy
and support for her, reflecting on the struggles and
triumphs of Black women throughout history. The
atmosphere was electric, charged with the collective pride
and hope of thousands, making it a tear-jerking,
heartwarming experience.

Sharing this moment with Elle, surrounded by fans who
embraced Coco's success as their own, displayed the
beauty of shared human experiences. It highlighted how
sports can transcend games to become platforms for larger
societal conversations and connections. The poem attempts

to capture the essence of this experience—how a single
game of tennis illustrated achievement and community,
and how it reinforced the bonds of a friendship forged in
the very same stands years ago.

To Latoya, on the Passing of Jerry

Latoya, my friend, on this longest night,
your father found peace, stepping into the light.
On the winter solstice, he always knew,
it was the darkest day, yet he'd guide us through.

He'd say with each sunrise, the light would grow,
a gentle reminder that healing comes slow.
Though yesterday brought us grief and tears,
today, we start healing, despite our fears.

Your dad's last words, "Don't worry, be happy,"
echo in my heart, uplifting and snappy.
He was always a beacon, our positive ray,
now, his sunlight guides us, day by day.

A massive THANK YOU to everyone near,
who supported your family, year after year.
Especially now, through this toughest fight,
to the hospice team that cared each night.

As life keeps "lifing," with its twists and bends,
may your family's strength shine, never to end.
And though life's woes might rise like a tide,
know I'm here for you, always by your side.

Jerry's spirit, like sunlight, remains,
a comforting presence through life's pains.
Rest easy, dear Jerry, in your celestial sweep,
your love surrounds us, vast and deep.

Inspiration behind "To Latoya, on the Passing of Jerry"
Emotion: Grief and Solace

The inspiration for the poem dedicated to my best friend Latoya and her father, Jerry, stems from a deep desire to offer support and solace during a profound time of grief. Watching Latoya and her family navigate the complexities of their loss moved me to craft words that memorialize a beloved father and illuminate the often under-discussed journey through grief.

The ultimate goal of this poem is to provide Latoya and her family—a family I hold dear—with a sense of enduring strength and community support. It is a reminder that they are not alone in their journey through grief. By sharing this poem with a wider audience, I hope to foster a broader understanding of grief, encouraging a more open dialogue about its impact and how we can support each other through the darkest of times.

Grief is a multifaceted response to loss, particularly the loss of someone to whom there is a deep bond of affection. It is more than emotional suffering; it involves a range of physical, cognitive, behavioral, social, cultural, spiritual, and philosophical responses. People often experience grief as a series of stages, though not everyone will go through all stages, and they may not occur in order. These stages, identified by Elisabeth Kübler-Ross, include denial, anger, bargaining, depression, and acceptance. These are not steps to be checked off but are more fluid experiences that ebb and flow over time.

Grief is not a process that ever truly ends; it evolves, changes, and becomes part of our narrative. It's important to acknowledge this ongoing nature because it allows us to understand that feeling grief long after the initial loss is normal—it is a testament to love and connection.

I aimed to create a piece that would not only serve as a tribute to Jerry's life and his impact on his family but also as a reflective piece for others dealing with their own grief.

By embedding the stages of grief within the verses, the poem invites readers to find pieces of their own sorrow and healing within its lines, offering a shared space for mourning and growth.

In creating this, I wanted to ensure that Jerry's legacy is celebrated and that the love and lessons he imparted continue to shine, guiding his family like the "sunlight" he was compared to in their lives. This poem is a testament to his life, a comfort to his family, and a beacon for all who navigate the turbulent seas of loss and remembrance.

New Year's Eve Resolution Series

Symphony of Aims

In the newborn year, I pen a pact,
a symphony of aims exact,
to fuse the personal with the chase
of career peaks in a balanced grace.

A union leader I resolve to be,
in service, strength, with diplomacy,
financial targets firmly set in stone,
$10k saved as seeds skillfully sown.

Language barriers I plan to breach,
with Spanish phrases, I'll fluently preach.
Duolingo's paths I shall stride,
advanced conversations as my guide.

A wanderer's heart, so wild and free,
aims to tread new lands, five or ten, maybe.
Each step a story, each mile a tale,
In foreign whispers, my spirit sails.

A book a month, to read and muse,
in literary seas, I'll gladly cruise.
Politics, a stage where I must play,
A voice in change, come what may.
A nonprofit dream to call my own,
where seeds of future good are sown.
From paperwork to mission clear,
a beacon of hope in the community near.
This year, a canvas broad and bright,
painted with goals in morning's light.
Each resolution a stroke of art,
crafted with wisdom from the heart.

As I march forth, let it be known,
these goals are seeds meticulously sown.
A blend of joy, work, and introspective flights,

in 2024's ambitious heights.

Echoes of Intent

I penned my goals, a blueprint bright,
but words alone won't win the fight.
It's not enough to wish and write;
accountability brings them to light.

Each day I wake, these goals in view,
a constant reminder of what to pursue.
Not hidden in drawers or lost in the fray,
but loud in my space where I work and play.

Hola! The word now rolls with ease,
Spanish lessons, climbing like the breeze.
With every teacher, each phrase takes flight,
A steady ascent toward my summit in sight.

Yet, as I traverse this year's ambitious track,
I'm reminded of the need to look back.
To check the compass, ensure I'm true
to the course I charted, the aims I pursue.

For what are goals if not to steer,
to tame the chaos we often fear?
They're not just dreams on paper cast,
but mandates for the future, from the past.

So, let each goal live, not just in thought,
but in action, in the battles fought.
Displayed on walls, in notebooks scribed,
in daily view, where they can't be bribed.

Still, there's time, the year's not done,
many a race is yet to be won.
The intentions I set, deep at my core,
call me to action, to strive for more.

With each review, each honest glance,
I give my dreams a fighting chance.
To grow from seeds to mighty trees,
in the garden of will, swayed by a breeze of tenacity.

Midnight Wishes in Puebla

In Santiago Atzitzihuacán, where echoes tell tales,
New Year's Eve unfolds under star-sketched veils.
In this corner of Puebla, where time gently scales,
we embraced a tradition, as old as the trails.

With twelve grapes in hand, as the church bell chimes,
each toll marks a hope in these festive times.
For each sweet burst, a wish entwines—
Luck and joy in these simple signs.

First, a grape for finances, may they find fertile ground.
Second, dreams of a home in Oaxaca, profound.
Third, a wish for a place in Mexico City's heart.
Fourth, to refinance debts, a fresh financial start.

Fifth, success in leading with wisdom and care.
Sixth, for Mac Neal's vision, a non-profit affair.
Seventh, travels and tennis, adventures to share.
Eighth, health and well-being, handled with flair.

Ninth, the courage to navigate ties of the heart.
Tenth, authenticity, whether together or apart.
Eleventh, a journey of purpose to smartly chart.
Twelfth, a year rich in reading, a literary art.

As each grape passed my lips, the future seemed bright,
with Nico and his family, in the festive night's light.
A tradition of wishes, in the new year's first sight,
Las doce uvas de la suerte, our hearts taking flight.

In this small town's embrace, where life's essence pours,
we welcomed the new, on Puebla's historic shores.
With laughter and hopes, in our festive outdoors,

we stepped into a year, where opportunity soars.

Inspiration behind "New Year's Eve Resolution Series"
Emotion: Reflection and Cultural Appreciation

These poems were inspired by a blend of cultural practices and personal reflections experienced during an unforgettable New Year's celebration in Santiago Atzitzihuacán, Puebla, Mexico. This small town, alive with rural charm and steeped in the rich history of the Mixteca Poblana region, offered a stark contrast with the typical American New Year's celebrations.

"Midnight Wishes in Puebla" was inspired by the Mexican tradition of "Las doce uvas de la suerte," where each grape, eaten at each stroke of midnight, carries a wish for the upcoming months. This tradition imbues the new year with hope and joy and symbolizes a deep connection to cultural roots and communal aspirations. The practice helped me appreciate the significance of ringing in the new year in a manner that emphasizes spiritual and communal growth over individual ambition.

"Echoes of Intent: A Poem on Keeping Promises to Oneself" and "Resolutions for 2024: A Symphony of Aims" are inspired by my own reflections and resolutions, set against his new cultural understanding. These poems explore the idea of resolutions as a symphony of earnest intentions toward personal and professional fulfillment instead of a list of goals. The contrast between American resolutions—often characterized by a focus on individual achievement and self-improvement—and the communal, hopeful spirit of the Mexican grape-eating tradition prompted me to rethink how resolutions can be both personal and inclusive, reflective and forward-looking.

With its outdoor kitchens and a lifestyle deeply connected to the land, Puebla exemplified a life of authenticity and simplicity. It provided a physical and metaphorical space that was almost "camping adjacent," where the lines between living off the land and festive celebration blurred. This environment, alongside the communal dining and shared hopes for the new year, deeply influenced my perspective on how we set intentions and follow through on them.

In "Echoes of Intent," I explore the personal commitment to keep the promises we make to ourselves, highlighting the need for consistency and reflection. This poem is a call to hold oneself accountable, emphasizing that while setting goals is crucial, revisiting and reassessing them is equally important for growth and fulfillment.

In "A Symphony of Aims," I articulate my goals across various facets of life—language learning, financial savings, personal development, and more. This poem is structured to reflect a holistic approach to resolutions, where personal ambitions harmonize with the desire to contribute meaningfully to society and maintain healthy relationships.

Together, these poems form a narrative that spans from cultural appreciation and personal reflection to actionable plans, each influenced by the vibrancy of rural Puebla and the enriching experiences of a new cultural celebration. They underscore a yearning to blend the best of multiple worlds: the communal warmth of Mexican traditions with the focused ambition of American resolutions.

Poems Inspired by an Australia and New Zealand Trip

Deposits to the Universe

In Melbourne's embrace, under the Australian sun,
with Elle Bellamy, tales of tennis spun.
From US Open's courts to breakfast shared,
connections formed and stories bared.

We met by chance, a delayed flight's gift,
at O'Hare, where weary travelers drift.
Sharon waited, a new friend in tow,
June Bentley's warmth began to glow.

Breakfast laughter with a lively crew,
Elle's smile caught the morning dew.
Social threads, woven tight and fast,
a friendship built to truly last.

Years unrolled like open courts,
from Wimbledon's greens to sporting sorts.
An 18-country journey across the Euro expanse,
Elle's insights gave my travels a chance.

She connected dots with tennis greats,
in towns and tales that fate creates.
And now, at last, the Aussie Open's call,
together, watching the tennis ball.

She spoke a truth, so simple and profound,
"Make deposits to the universe, let it abound.
So when you need to make a withdrawal,
it won't decline, no, not at all."

We laughed and vowed with heartfelt glee,
"Our withdrawals won't be declined," said we.
For life's about the give and take,
the moments shared, the chances we make.

In friendships forged on global stages,

we deposit laughs, loves, and sage pages.
So when we reach to claim our due,
the universe smiles, and sees us through.

A Tennis Love Affair

Beneath the Melbourne sky, so fair,
we stepped into the tennis square,
the Australian Open, vibrant, alive,
from Day One, the spirit did thrive.

We cheered for Sinner's fiery play,
admired Sakkari's brilliant sway,
Wozniacki's grace, Tiafoe's might,
each match a thrilling, joyful sight.

Day Two, the heat rose, not just in play,
Jessica Pegula's swings, oh, what a display!
Live tunes floated, lifting the crowd,
Margaret Court Arena, echoes loud.

A selfie with Hurkacz, our lucky charm,
amidst the tennis buzz, a delightful calm.
Then Day Three, courtside, we found our place,
Iga and Kenin's chase, a breathtaking race.

Zverev's night session, electric under lights,
snapped a pic with the Carrot Boys, heights
of fandom reached, our hearts swelled proud,
tennis tales woven in a jubilant crowd.

Rain on Day Four, yet spirits never waned,
with Coco Gauff, our excitement remained.
First Nations' flags waved in proud display,
Novak's prowess ended the day in the perfect way.

And though now we pause, Sydney's charm awaits,
New Zealand's adventures open new gates.
Eager for semifinals, where champions contend,
this tennis journey, may it never end.

Elle, with a smile, asked with each meal's spice,
"But is it hot?" her food's roll of the dice.
Tennis talks stretching into the night,
This trip with her, every moment a delight.

Anticipation for the final rounds grows,
back to Melbourne, where the tennis wind blows.
#AO24, you've been a splendid host,
ready for more, we cheer, and we toast.

Tournament Terminal

At the heart of the court, like a terminal gate,
where the world in miniature seems to congregate.
Not just a game played in fluorescent light,
but a vibrant junction of delight and sight.

Faces pass—a mosaic, vivid and vast,
each one a narrative, tethered to a past.
Stories unspoken but felt in the air,
each glance, each smile, a soliloquy rare.

Fashion parades in a riot of hues,
traditional threads merging with modern cues.
Silks and linens and jerseys entwine,
in a spectacle of textures, culturally divine.

Here, the art of people-watching excels,
each observer a story, their intrigue compels.
From the seasoned fans in their team's proud colors,
to the novices stunned by the game's fervent ardors.

The diversity here is the true game played,
not merely the matches that captivate and persuade.
It's a reminder of the beauty that diversity crafts,
as backgrounds blend and the audience laughs.

A tennis match—my terminal of joy,
where the world's diversity converges, coy.

As planes take flight, so too does the ball,
uniting us all, from the large to the small.

In this space, where the world softly collides,
amid cheers and claps and victorious strides,
both court and terminal in their transient grace,
remind us of joy in this communal space.

For here in the echoes of serves and flights,
lies the beauty of diversity—my heart's true delight.
Both my happy places, vivid and grand,
where the world meets and understands.

I.   Tall Poppies and Other Tales

In lands down under, where tall poppies grow,
I heard tales spun with a somber flow.
"Australians cut down their tallest blooms,"
a cultural scythe amidst their perfumes.
Success, they whisper, should not shine too bright,
lest it invite envy, cloaked by night.
Here, humility is more than just grace;
it's survival, in this competitive place.

II.   The Bogan's Way

In Aussie lands, 'bogan' dances on tongues,
not defined by poverty, but by songs unsung.
Urban yet outlandish, their culture spans,
beyond redneck labels that bind their hands.
A term so local, yet broad and wide,
where wealth and rough edges often collide.
Rich or poor, it's not the money they flaunt,
but a lifestyle, a culture, that they vaunt.

III.   Conversations in Contrast

Aussies, they say, gaze at stars and stripes,
admiring freedoms, ripe with types.
Yet, in their voices, a note so mild,
not as harsh as the Brits, but equally styled.
The tall poppy's roots, so deep in this ground,
where talk is cheap, yet smiles are found.
Contrast stark with the open American vibe,
their reserved nature, hard to describe.

IV.   Indifference and Insight

At first, their cool glances might just disguise,
indifference or a guise unwise.
But each interaction, deeper than seen,
reveals a warmth, a curiosity keen.
Yet a date turned sour, with words unkind,
a reminder that perspectives are often blind.
A struggle with indifference that masks as cold,
but beneath the surface, stories untold.

V.   The Racism Adjacent

Seeking a term for subtleties missed,
for those near hate, but never kissed.
By the depth of bigotry, their biases bare,
not full hatred, but an unaware stare.
'Racism adjacent,' a phrase to denote,
those who don't hate, but on prejudice dote.
Not active bigots, but still not quite clear,
Of the barriers they uphold, year after year.

VI.   Tennis Souls

In courts fluttering with national flags unfurled,
tennis becomes a language spoken round the world.
"Why support Coco?" they openly ask,
as if supporting one's own is an arduous task.
Yet in each rally, each serve, each play,
we find kinship in each sporting fray.
Celebrating all athletes, irrespective of race,
finding joy in each game, each match, each ace.

VII.   Food and Friendships

Though not a journey marked by culinary delights,
each meal told a story, lighting up the nights.
Grindr tales, where deeper connections were sought,
in cafes and courts, where companionship was brought.
Simon stood out, a beacon so rare,
who saw beyond the surface, showing true care.
A friend, a lover, who appreciated the soul,
in a world that often overlooks the whole.

VIII.   Waiheke's Wine and Waves

Waiheke Island, where vineyards meet the sea,
Onetangi Beach, where life feels free.
Races on sand, and wines that tell tales.
Here, among the vines, friendship prevails.
An island not just of scenic routes,
but of deep histories, and cultural roots.
A gem in the gulf, where life slows to a gaze,
celebrating sunsets in a vine-framed haze.

IX.   Māori Lands and Lore

Aotearoa, with its clouds stretched wide,
where Māori culture continues with pride.
From Hobbiton's hills to tales deeply told,
a culture rich, brave, and bold.
Yet shadows of past treaties linger still,
complex histories that time cannot fill.
Here, traditions thrive, not just survive,
in the land of the long white cloud, where cultures jive.

X.   A Global Heart

A dream to live, a year divided by four,
in Australia, the US, Europe, and more.
Each quarter a chapter, each season a tale,
of tennis matches and friendships that prevail.
From Aussie shores to European arts,
finding a home in the world's open hearts.
A global citizen with a suitcase in hand,
seeking new stories in every land.

Inspiration Behind "Poems Inspired by an Australia and New Zealand Trip"
Emotion: Wonder and Connection

This series was born from a vibrant and enlightening journey I embarked on with my dear friend Elle. This adventure took us through Melbourne, Sydney, and Auckland, weaving through the exhilarating atmosphere of the Australian Open and exploring the diverse cultures and landscapes of Australia and New Zealand.

The inspiration for these poems sprang from the profound experiences and observations made during this trip, particularly at the tennis matches in Melbourne. The dynamic environment of the tournament was reminiscent of the bustling scene at an international airport terminal, where every individual is a unique story embarking on a personal journey. This analogy deeply influenced my reflections on the trip—tennis, not just as a sport, but as a celebration of global diversity, culture, and connection.

In my notes, I captured this essence, likening the tennis crowd to a "rich tapestry of culture and diversity," where the art of people-watching reveals a "mosaic of faces" from all corners of the globe. This vivid array of spectators, with their varying fashions and backgrounds, created a parade of colors and textures that was both inspiring and visually captivating. Such observations were instrumental in crafting poems that delve into themes of cultural exploration, human connection, and the joy found in shared experiences.

Moreover, the concept of "Deposits to the Universe" emerged during a particularly reflective conversation with Elle. It encapsulated the idea that our interactions and experiences contribute to a larger cosmic account and that maintaining a positive balance ensures we can draw on it when needed. This metaphor became a central theme, representing the investments we make through travel, friendship, and learning, which enrich not only our lives but the broader human experience.

Each poem is thus a narrative thread, woven from the detailed tapestry of experiences, from the thrilling matches at the Australian Open to the quieter, introspective moments exploring the streets of Sydney and the cultural richness of Auckland. The joy of the trip, especially the time spent immersed in the world of tennis, was a reminder of my "happy places"—both at a lively international airport and amidst the cheering crowds of a tennis stadium. Each environment offers a unique window into the variety of human experiences, united by common passions and pursuits. This series of poems is a tribute to that unity and the personal fulfillment found in such diverse gatherings. These writings are a celebration of the journey and the profound impact of seeing the world through both a lens of wide-eyed wonder and thoughtful introspection.

Bali on Two Wheels

In Bali, a jewel embraced by sea,
I found my heart's untamed glee—
A motorbike, my steed for the week,
an adventurer's spirit, a freedom to seek.

With no prior dance with motorbike's thrum,
the roads beckoned, whispering, "Come!"
Through bustling streets and whispers of green,
where life unfurls serene and unseen.

Daunting at first, the island's wild roar,
each twist and turn, a new door
to landscapes painted with a vibrant brush,
where time slows down in a tranquil hush.

The wind wove tales in my flowing hair,
sun-kissed paths led to who knows where;
with every mile, my confidence soared,
Bali's rhythm, a tune adored.

I discovered, too, the nimblest dance,
Uber's bikes, weaving by chance
through snarls of cars and crowded ways,
in swiftest motion, my vibrant days.

The freedom found on those whirling wheels,
unveiled the heart of Bali, its deepest feels.
More than a journey from A to B,
a ride into the soul of the Bali sea.

Now, back at home, I dream of the ride,
of sunlit roads and the wide
open smiles of the island's embrace,
until once more, I visit that place.

Inspiration behind "Bali on Two Wheels"
Emotion: Adventure and Freedom

This poem was inspired by my unforgettable experience exploring Bali by motorbike. This trip was a deep dive into a new form of freedom, where I could discover the island's vibrant culture and breathtaking landscapes at my own pace. Having never ridden a motorbike, I found the challenge exhilarating, transforming from daunting to second nature. This adventure allowed me to weave through bustling streets and tranquil countryside's, feeling the wind and sun as constant companions. The mobility and agility of traveling by motorbike revealed Bali in a way that deeply connected me to its rhythm and beauty, inspiring reflections on freedom and exploration that I aimed to capture in the poem.

Bali, a renowned island in Indonesia, is as rich in history as it is in beauty. Known for its volcanic mountains, iconic rice paddies, beaches, and coral reefs, the island is a hub of spiritual and cultural magnetism. Bali's culture is deeply influenced by a unique form of Hinduism, evident in its daily rituals, numerous temples, and colorful ceremonies. The Balinese language, a form of Malay, is intricate, reflecting the island's historical layers of Javanese and Dutch influences.

Indonesian cuisine offers a palette of flavors characterized by a generous use of spices, coconut milk, fish, and pork. Dishes like "Babi Guling" (suckling pig) and "Bebek Betutu" (slow-cooked duck) are local favorites that provide a taste of the island's culinary diversity.

Beyond its shores, Bali's commitment to preserving its culture amidst tourism is evident in its arts—traditional dance, music, and painting. Each aspect of Balinese life is interwoven with a respect for both the spiritual and natural world, making it an enchanting place to visit and explore. This rich tapestry of experiences was transformative and educational, enriching my

understanding of a place where tradition and modernity
beautifully coexist.

Ode to a Shero on The View

On the stage of "The View," amidst a sea of lights,
Liz Cheney stood firm, advocating for political rights.
A Republican with a difference, her voice strong and clear,
discussing the future of the GOP, a topic so dear.

Her interview, a powerful moment of truth and grace,
unveiling the challenges her party must face.
With the post-2024 landscape stark and real,
she called for a shift, a new Republican ideal.

Her book, a deep dive into tumultuous days,
January Sixth's shadows and democracy's haze.
Through pages that echo with the weight of facts,
she maps the dangers of political acts.

Trump's presidency, under her critical eye,
revealed as a storm that darkened the sky.
Her words are a beacon for those who seek light,
in a realm where truth often loses the fight.

Liz Cheney, a shero, with courage unmasked,
her commitment to democracy fervently tasked.
On "The View," her insights a clarion call,
for truth and justice, desired by all.

Her book—a must-read, a journey to the core,
of a nation divided, its heart torn and sore.
#ReadToUnderstand, let the facts be your guide,
In Liz Cheney's words, let truth be your tide.

This ode celebrates not just a moment on air,
but a woman's resolve to challenge the snare,
of fiction and lies in political debate.
A shero's stand against a possible dire state.

Inspiration behind "Ode to a Shero on The View"
Emotion: Admiration and Resolve

This poem emerged from a moment of realization and respect as I watched Liz Cheney on "The View." Although I had always known of her, my understanding of her beliefs and actions had been superficial. It wasn't until I saw her articulate her concerns with such conviction about the future of her party and the country that I truly appreciated her depth. Listening to her on the show and subsequently devouring her book in just a few days, I was struck by her relentless dedication to assembling the January 6th committee, her unwavering commitment to democracy, and her tireless efforts to dispel lies.

Liz Cheney stands out as a true hero in an era where silence and sidestepping have become all too common among many political figures. When many chose to remain quiet, she spoke out; her voice did not waver, even when it cost her politically. Her courage to stand firm in her beliefs, regardless of the consequences, is not only commendable but also a rarity in today's political landscape. Her book provided an in-depth look at the crucial moments and decisions that defined the recent turmoil within American politics, especially those surrounding the events of January 6th.

As I turned the pages of her book, I was captivated by her dedication to truth and accountability. It's easy to align with those who share our views, but it requires a sincere integrity to stand against the tide within one's own ranks. Cheney's actions and her narrative in the book cement her as a pivotal figure striving to uphold the tenets of democracy against formidable challenges. This poem, therefore, is not just an ode to her appearance on a talk show, but a tribute to her role as a steadfast defender of democratic values and truth.

Cleansing Chants

On the first of March, as spring whispered near,
I took to my home with sage and cheer.
With each herb's smoke, twirling, light,
I cleansed each corner, banished the blight.

Sage whispered secrets of cleansing old,
its smoke like a story of wisdom told.
Canela's sweet spice in the air did twirl,
promising abundance in this new world.

Rosemary's fragrance, sharp and clear,
promised protection, brought comfort near.
Ruda's strong essence, with protective grace,
secured our haven, this new sacred space.

As the music played, "La Llorona" soft,
its haunting melody lifted aloft.
With every note, a prayer was spun,
binding the cleansing, till it was done.

"May peace dwell within these walls," I'd say,
as "Son de la Negra" lively did play.
A joyful close to a ritual so dear,
in our cleansed home, we welcome good cheer.

May this space be a sanctuary, true and bright,
filled with laughter, love, and light.
As herbs turned to ash, and music soared,
our home reborn, our spirits restored.

Inspiration behind "Cleansing Chants"
Emotion: Renewal and Serenity

This poem stemmed from my recent visit to Buenavista, a transition filled with excitement and a desire to embrace new experiences. During my stay, I carried out a cleansing ritual to purify the space I was using and infuse it with positive energy, a practice I hold dear for marking new beginnings. The use of sage and other herbs like canela, rosemary, and ruda was deeply symbolic, each chosen for their unique protection, prosperity, and purification properties.

Culturally significant and deeply emotional music accompanied this aromatic ritual. "La Llorona," with its poignant and haunting melody, seemed the perfect backdrop for reflecting on the past and the transformative process of being in a new space. In contrast, "Son de la Negra," vibrant and celebratory, helped seal the ritual with joy and a sense of anticipation for the moments ahead in Buenavista.

This poem captures my journey—using traditional practices to cleanse and sanctify the space while embracing our heritage. It's about creating a harmonious environment where the past's shadows give way to bright beginnings, and music and tradition blend to bless and protect the space. This ritual and the subsequent poem celebrate new chapters and the continuous thread of cultural rituals that enrich our lives.

Voices in the Chamber

In the hallowed halls where liberty's echoed,
I walked, absorbing the fervor for an ally held dear.
'We Stand with Israel'—the signs boldly declared,
a testament in Congress, strong and clear.

President Biden, at the helm of our nation,
navigates the tumultuous seas of foreign ties.

His course with Israel, fraught with hesitation,
draws my critique, though his aim might be wise.

It's not just one man steering this mighty ship,
but many hands, across aisles, with vigor they grip.
Republicans, Senators—diverse voices resound,
in their unwavering support, their stances profound.

Yet, as I venture past the grand Capitol's steps,
I urge those who question, who harbor dissent:
Let not your grievances simmer, unvoiced,
in the digital scrolls of Facebook's vast void.

Write, speak, and stand—let your congressmen hear
that accountability's demanded, year after year.
From pen to paper, let your words flow,
pushing our leaders where they're slow to go.

For while the administration may strive and succeed
in guarding our freedoms, in planting democracy's seed,
there lies a realm where they falter, where their efforts
could mend
the fragile threads of foreign policies that bend.

So let us not retreat to mere online banter,
but act with intent, our convictions to charter.
Through letters, through calls, in the civic dance,
we uphold our values, give our allies a chance.

Two truths can coexist, complex and profound:
We can champion our homeland's ground
while demanding more in the realms afar,
where the echoes of conflict are never far.

Let this be our call, from the East to the West,
in every action, may our purpose be blessed.
For in the strength of our unity, and the power of the pen,
lies the promise of peace, time and again.

Inspiration behind "Voices in the Chamber"
Emotion: Determination and Civic Responsibility

This poem is my reflection on President Biden's State of the Union address, particularly his approach toward Israel and the broader dynamics of U.S. foreign policy. As I listened to the address and thought about the reactions it provoked, I was struck by the complexity and nuance that characterize our political landscape. This poem is a reminder that understanding civic duties and the mechanics of our government is essential for effective participation in democracy.

I strongly believe that it is possible to support an administration while also holding it accountable. The poem emphasizes that life and politics are not black and white, and issues often require us to understand and appreciate nuanced perspectives. During a recent visit to the halls of Congress, I saw that the overwhelming support for Israel was evident and was reminded of the importance of advocacy and active engagement in our political processes.

Through this poem, I aim to convey that engaging with our elected officials through traditional methods like writing letters is still a powerful way to influence governance. Social media can often simplify complex issues, which is why I advocate for a more informed and direct approach to political activism. We need to educate ourselves about the structure of our government and actively participate to ensure that our democracy reflects our values and operates effectively. I encourage others to explore these complexities and engage in meaningful actions that support our democratic framework.

A Year Older, A Bit Wiser

Another year, another candle on the cake,
reflecting on a note, only a grandma could make.

Touched to the core by her heartfelt prose,
I find gratitude that continually grows.

To grandparents, parents, and sister dear,
to family and friends, both far and near.
You've shaped me, loved me, been my guide,
through every journey, you're by my side.

From global trips to savoring strange eats,
discussing politics on cobblestone streets.
Every culture, every taste, each friendly face,
has left its mark, a treasured place.

Lucky and honored, that's how I feel,
standing at this crossroad, so surreal.
Ready to forge ahead with a heart full of zeal,
excited for what the future will reveal.

Grandma's words spoke of my determined youth,
choosing knowledge over shiny truth.
A captain steering our family ship,
with pride and love on every trip.

Tonight in Mexico, with friends, I'll dine,
though life's been hectic, I won't whine.
Grateful for these "first world problems" galore,
for a full life, who could ask for more?

Here's to the future, vast and bright,
with hearts open wide, taking flight.
To the bonds that bind us, let's keep them tight,
voyaging together into the night.

Inspiration Behind "A Year Older, A Bit Wiser"
Emotion: Gratitude and Hopeful Reflection

As I celebrated another year of life, I found myself
reflecting deeply on a touching note from my
grandmother. Her words resonated with me, reminding
me of the unwavering support and love that have shaped

my journey. This reflection filled me with overwhelming gratitude and excitement for the future. I wanted to honor not just my grandparents, but also my parents, sister, and everyone who has been part of my life's voyage.

I've been incredibly fortunate to explore the world, experience diverse cultures, savor local cuisines, engage in global politics, and form lasting friendships across continents. Each person I've met and every experience I've embraced have enriched my life in ways I could never have imagined. Standing at this juncture, I feel both lucky and honored, eager to continue on this unique path.

My grandmother's note, which reflected on my childhood determination, my choice of education over material desires, and my natural leadership, inspired this poem. Her words painted a vivid picture of my life, celebrating my achievements and expressing unconditional love and pride in what lies ahead. The note was a powerful reminder of the importance of recognizing and appreciating the love and support from those around us.

On my birthday, I found myself in Mexico City, celebrating with close friends. Life had been busy—tax season, work, and various commitments had postponed my trip—but being busy is a blessing. I'm grateful for these "first world problems" and the privilege of having a packed schedule, as they are reminders of the abundant life I lead.

The poem "A Year Older, A Bit Wiser" emerged from this blend of gratitude and reflection. It captures the joy of celebrating life's milestones, the appreciation for the people who have supported me, and the excitement for the journey ahead. It is a tribute to the ongoing adventure of life and the connections that make it meaningful.

Voyage of Gratitude

In the quiet of another year's crest,
a note from my grandmother rests in my chest,
Her words, like soft linen, wrap my soul,
reminding me of the love that makes me whole.

To the elders, my pillars, my mom and my dad,
my sister, my kin, the journey we've had—
To every soul that's touched my life's frame,
I send my thanks, for you fan my flame.

Across the world, in distant lands,
I've tasted life with open hands.
Local flavors, friendships' brew,
each experience vivid, each perspective new.

I stand here now at life's sweet bend,
grateful for the past, on dreams I ascend.
The path has been rich, with tales untold,
and the future gleams like morning's gold.

Here's to the roads yet to explore,
to the bonds we've forged and the ones in store.
Thank you for being part of my verse,
as we venture ahead, the universe to traverse.

In grandma's note, a captain's tale,
of childhood dreams that set sail.
Her pride a beacon, her love a pier,
guiding my ship as new horizons near.

Tonight, amidst friends in Mexico's heart,
we'll celebrate life, a fresh start.
Though life's busy tides keep plans at bay,
I cherish the bustle, in my own way.

For each "first world problem," a badge I wear,
of a life abundant, beyond compare.
As candles flicker on this festive night,
I'm thankful for every spark, every light.

Inspiration behind "Voyage of Gratitude"
Emotion: Thankfulness and Reflection

"Voyage of Gratitude" comes from a deeply personal space, reflecting the many experiences and deep connections that have shaped my life. As I celebrated my birthday on March 9, 2024, I was struck by the overwhelming love and support I've received over the years. This support was particularly clear in a touching note from my grandmother, who recounted my childhood resilience and leadership and painted my life's journey with pride and affection, likening me to a captain steering our family ship through the vast seas of life.

This poem is a celebration of gratitude for everyone who has been a part of my story—from my beloved grandparents, parents, and sister, to the many friends and acquaintances I've made across the globe. It echoes my adventures and the cultural richness I've been privileged to experience, from savoring local cuisines to engaging in global dialogues. Each stanza is a testament to the bonds formed and the lessons learned along the way.

On this birthday, surrounded by close friends in Mexico City, I found myself postponing my original travel plans due to a hectic tax season and other life responsibilities. Yet, even in the whirlwind of a busy schedule, I felt an immense appreciation for the life I lead. The poem is not just a reflection of past journeys but also an eager look toward future adventures, emphasizing my readiness to continue exploring the world with an open heart and insatiable curiosity. This piece is an homage to the love and legacy of my grandmother's note, celebrating both the milestones achieved and the exciting prospects that lie ahead.

Ode to The Ladies of The View

To the dazzling dames of "The View,"
my daily dose of wisdom and hue.
Joy Behar, oh how you spark laughter and light,
with every quip and witty insight.

Whoopi Goldberg, creative spirits soar,
when you're in your element, who could ask for more?
A presence so commanding, yet subtly sweet,
in your groove, you make every interview a treat.

Sarah Haines, with your smile so bright,
your reasoned views make every wrong feel right.
A balance in your words, a nuance in your tone,
your clarity like icing, sweetly sown.

Sunny Hostin, in fashion and flair,
your legal eagle eye is beyond compare.
A vision of the future in your passionate plea,
reflecting dreams for my kids and me.

Ana Navarro, with sass in your stride,
never too shy to call out the tide.
Your snarky, smart quips are a joyful spark,
in the mess of the world, you leave a mark.

Alyssa, the panel's newest voice,
fair and bright, making sound choice.
A republican seat, yet controversy-free,
your respectful banter is a joy to see.

Together, you all bring diversity and age,
gluing me to every word, every stage.
A bri-guy, loyal to your podcast's flow,
"Behind the Table" has me in the know.

As I pen my life in poems, a dream ignites,
To join you there under those bright lights.
Malcolm, maybe a bestseller soon,
endorsed by The View, oh what a boon!

From viewer to guest, what a tale it'd be,
with you, dear ladies, in your company.
Here's to hopes, to dreams, to glee,
to one day sharing my story on your TV.

Inspiration behind "Ode to The Ladies of The View"
Emotion: Admiration and Aspiration

This poem springs from my deep-seated admiration
and affection for the show and its dynamic cast. I've
watched "The View" almost religiously since around 2013,
drawn in by the engaging discussions that blend politics
with the pulse of the day. What strikes me most is the
balance the show maintains; it's political, yes, but it also
weaves through the spectrum of social issues,
entertainment, and personal stories, making it richly
layered and engaging.

My fondness doesn't stop with the hosts; it extends to
the incredible crew behind the scenes. Their seamless
production and the supportive atmosphere they create
both in front of and behind the camera are nothing short of
inspiring. It's this admiration that has led me to become a
Bri-guy, a loyal follower of Brian and the delightful
"Behind the Table" podcast, where I soak up every episode,
relishing the deeper dives into the hosts' viewpoints and
the expanded discussions on hot topics.

My connection to the show is punctuated by my visits
to the studio in New York. Each visit cements my love for
this televised roundtable, even though I've yet to snag a
book or theater ticket during these outings. Yet, these
experiences have only heightened my dream—a dream
that feels like a tangible possibility as I write my
autobiography through poetry.

This creative journey has filled me with an exhilarating
sense of wholeness and an anticipation that borders on
electric. The thought of potentially sharing my work, my

story, on "The View," discussing life's verses alongside these women whom I've grown to admire from afar, thrills me. It represents not just achieving a personal milestone but also an opportunity to engage in the very conversations that have sparked my imagination and fueled my aspirations for so many years.

Sweet addiction

Oh, I'm the drug you just can't kick,
a sweet addiction, thick and slick.
Exes circle like bees to honey,
finding my charm just too sunny.

They dial up, drop texts, "Hey, Mac, I miss u,"

All longing for another blissful kiss.
A date, a glance, they pine for more,
can't help but worship what they adore.

One declared I'm top of the list,
makes all feel like they can't resist.
But here's the rub, it's plain to see,
it's tough when you're the "must-have" bee.

So here I stand, a gem so rare,
too nice to say, "Please, just don't dare."
How does one manage this loving spree?
An object of desire, reluctantly.

Inspiration behind "Sweet Addiction"
Emotion: Playful Confidence

This poem captures a moment of introspection sparked by a simple, yet loaded, text message: "I miss your kisses. Can I see you today?" Like many others, this message reflects the complex dance of desire and distance that characterizes my interactions with past lovers. Despite my straightforward approach and busy life, these individuals often struggle to accept the boundaries I set, circling back with hopes rekindled by memories of intimacy.

This poem is a playful yet poignant reflection on my allure, which seems to act like a sweet, inescapable drug. My life is a whirlwind of activities—I run a business, manage an Airbnb, lead my job's union, and have recently gone on a significant health journey, losing 55 pounds. I also dedicate time to hobbies and self-improvement, like playing tennis and studying Spanish. Amidst this, maintaining clear, casual relationships becomes challenging when others perceive our connection as deeper or more promising than intended.

"Sweet Addiction" is about being an unintentional heartthrob—the person who makes others feel extraordinarily special, even when no deep commitment is intended. My ex, Kyle, pointed out that my affable and generous nature might lead others to fall too hard and fast, becoming "addicted" to the affection and perceived lifestyle I offer. This poem explores the irony of being both cherished and burdened by the adoration that follows me despite clear communications of my intentions and capacities.

It is a reflection on the boundaries of love and the complexities of being highly desired—a sweet, sometimes overwhelming addiction for those entwined in my life's vibrant but demanding rhythm.

Legacy in Lines

Under Savannah's fatherly skies,
June blooms whispered her first breath—
Joan Millicent, a legacy begun,
woven through the warp and weft of days.

Father's lectures, a childhood compass,
guided her through halls of learning.
From Talladega's cherished gates

to the grand halls of Heidelberg's embrace.

A scholar's heart, a teacher's soul,
across continents, her wisdom flowed.
In classrooms where young minds awoke,
Joan wrote her story, hope she stoked.

Her life—a tapestry rich and vast,
from Savannah's roots to foreign paths.
In her children's laughs, in every task,
her spirit's touch—a lasting grasp.

And though today we mourn her parting,
her journey's end, her peaceful sleep.
In words, we cast her story's arc—
Joan, forever a guiding spark.

With Cherry Blossoms' brief delight,
We're reminded of her brilliant light.
Though her form has left our side,
in our hearts, she'll always abide.

In memory's garden, we meet and talk,
with every blossom, down each walk.
Joan lives on in the stories we share—
A mother, a mentor, forever there.

Living's Light

In this house where laughter once lived,
echoes of you dance in the daylight,
Each creak a whisper, each shadow a story.
Today's sun tells me, "Child, your time is a fleeting song."

Grief visits like an old friend,
some days, we sit in silence,
others, we sift through the joy you left behind—
a patchwork quilt of moments, warm and well-worn.

I'm hanging in there, mama,

prepping your home, preserving our hymns.
The road ahead whispers of work and worries,
but this breath, this brilliant now, is a battlefield of beauty.

Yes, today is exceptionally beautiful,
a stark reminder—my own clock ticks onward.
So I pledge to paint my days with purpose,
to live loud, live proud, in the echo of your enduring song.

For though we no longer share this walk,
in my heart, your spirit stirs—unseen, yet ever strong.
Your love—a beacon, no night can steal,
your wisdom—a guide, no distance can dull.

Let us live, let us remember,
for as long as the sun dares to rise,
You, me—we are forever woven into the fabric of this
finite dance,
no goodbye can erase, no shadow can dim our shared
light.

Inspiration behind "Living's Light"
Emotion: Grief and Reverence

The poems "Legacy in Lines" and "Living's Light" are
composed in heartfelt memory of Joan Millicent Bryan
Wilcox, the mother of Shannon Schmidt. Though I never
had the privilege of meeting Joan personally, her daughter
Shannon has been a beacon of inspiration in my life,
serving as an unofficial mentor whose influence has
profoundly shaped me. The news of Joan's passing deeply
affected me, stirring feelings of helplessness, as all I could
offer from a distance was my sympathy and support.

To provide comfort during this difficult time, I sent
Shannon a 24" Cherry Blossom wreath and a Cherry
Blossom tree in a vase, along with a message expressing
my condolences. I selected the cherry blossoms for their
delicate beauty and symbolism, reflecting the transient

nature of life—reminding us to cherish every moment with those we love.

The poems honor Joan's remarkable life but also celebrate the unbreakable bond between her and Shannon. They bring together memory, legacy, and the enduring spirit of love that transcends even death. "Legacy in Lines" draws upon Joan's rich life journey, from her roots in Savannah, Georgia, to her significant educational and professional achievements, capturing a life well-lived and deeply impactful. "Living's Light" addresses personal reflections on grief and the ongoing journey of living, inspired by the days I spent thinking about Shannon's loss and the universal truth that our time is finite.

Both poems are a tribute to Joan's enduring influence and a testament to the connections that continue to shape us, even in absence. They show the importance of living fully and remembering deeply, a message I hope resonates with all who read them, providing a source of solace and inspiration.

Reconnection

Hi Julie,

I've been away, yet close to all we've shared,
reflecting on our sessions, how deeply you cared.
Back in '20, you were my steady ground,
through election storms, where peace was found.

I drifted, not due to a lack of need,
but travels to Mexico took the lead.
Admitting now, I dodged, avoided our space,
hiding from issues I wasn't ready to face.

There was a moment, a crack in our mirror,
on LGBT+ paths, the reflection wasn't clear.
It stung, felt like support had thinned,
yet, avoidance was me, cloaked in wind.

Your guidance was a beacon that once shone so bright.
Can we find that light again, bring these shadows to light?
I'm reaching out, hopeful, ready to mend,
to talk, to grow, in trust, our blend.

Julie, if you're open, let's clear the slate,
discuss, understand, and navigate.
This connection—our journey—I wish to renew,
for in this therapeutic dance, there's much to view.

Your response, a welcome, a door ajar,
validating feelings, healing scars.
It's grounding to have you guide me once more,
in this space we share, to explore, restore.

Warm regards, a path re-tread,
with open hearts, let's move ahead.
In therapy, as in life, it's clear,
We grow, we learn, we hold this dear.

Inspiration behind "Reconnection"
Emotion: Vulnerability and Hope

This poem sprang from a period of introspection and renewal in my relationship with my therapist, Julie. Back in 2021, while I was dating Nico, our discussions ventured into the territory of open relationships. I shared my desires and thoughts about why I wanted such an arrangement. Julie's response, questioning the need for an open relationship and relating it to her son's experiences, felt dismissive and somewhat judgmental. It seemed like my feelings and desires weren't fully grasped or respected. This experience, unfortunately, made me feel undervalued and misunderstood.

At that time, leaning into avoidance became convenient. I was already feeling a bit exhausted from years of continuous therapy, and with the added pressures of adapting to frequent visits to Mexico, busy work schedules, and frequent travels, it was easy to find excuses not to address these feelings. I used these circumstances to justify stepping away from therapy, avoiding confronting both my feelings about the relationship dynamics I sought and the discomfort from our therapy sessions.

Reaching out to resume therapy with Julie was a significant step toward mending this aspect of my journey. Our recent conversations, where she validated my feelings and emphasized that therapy, like any relationship, requires open communication and mutual understanding, inspired me to reconnect. It reminded me of the grounding presence she once was and could be again, prompting a desire to rebuild our therapeutic relationship and explore these nuanced parts of my life with her guidance. This poem captures the essence of seeking understanding and growth, acknowledging past avoidance, and striving for a deeper, more authentic connection.

Steadfast

In the quiet hours of now,
whispered worries fade and bow.
You, a fortress strong and true,
hold the power in all you do.

Shame has no home here, nor doubt,
your spirit's light will cast them out.
For in your heart, a truth does sing,
of love profound and nurturing.

With each step, the path grows clear,
the now will shift, and skies will clear.
Your journey marked by love's embrace,
each challenge met, you'll surely face.

The boy who holds your heart so tight,
will know your love, both day and night.
For all your children feel your care,
in every moment, you are there.

Smart, beautiful, a soul so kind,
success and joy, you're sure to find.
Speak to truth, speak to power,
manifest your finest hour.

Work hard, stay true, your dreams align,
as life, work, home, sweetly entwine.
Remember, always, to take part
in caring for your noble heart.

Be who you are, so brave, so free,
for all you seek, is meant to be.
In this vast world of endless blue,
remember this: you are enough, it's true.

Queen

Legacy of Ink

In pages bound by quiet resolve,
words spill, tracing silent grooves,
Each line a thread, a gentle pulse
of a heart's undying truth.

Here, in the stillness of ink on paper,
a soul's whispers take shape and form,
revealing the depths of trials weathered,
a spirit's storm transformed.

These words, a bridge across the chasms
of time and misunderstanding's tide,
crafted not in haste, but with the rhythm
of a heart's earnest guide.

A mother pens each heartfelt chapter,
her love, her pain, distinctly scribed,
for her child, a future reader,
where her reasons and dreams reside.

With every mark, she lays a foundation,
hoping as years unfurl and weave,
the pages will speak of her devotion,
and in this legacy, he'll believe.

So one day, when time has softened,
and questions rise like morning dew,
these journal entries, tender and open,
will forge a bond, steadfast and true.

Through ink, she reaches beyond her presence,
a future where her child might see,
the depth of her love, her quiet strength,
in these words, "I did this for you and me."

Let each page be a step towards healing,
a path to understand, to embrace,
for within these written memories lies
a love that time cannot erase.

Inspiration behind "Steadfast" and "Legacy in Ink"
Emotion: Supportive Encouragement and Heartfelt Empathy

I engaged in an extensive three-hour conversation with
my coworker Kiana, discussing a spectrum of topics from
the intricacies of our work environment to our deeply
personal life journeys. Throughout our discussion, we
explored change and personal growth, which inspired me
to create artistic expressions that would both celebrate
Kiana's resilience and provide comfort during her
challenging times.

Kiana, with her boundless positivity and infectious joy,
has always brightened the lives of those around her,
myself included. In our conversation, it was important for
me to affirm her value as a coworker and a remarkable and
impactful Black queen. I reassured her that she has a
steadfast friend in me—a safe space to openly share her
thoughts and feelings. More importantly, I wanted to
remind her that she is deeply valued, that her life has

immense significance, and that she should embrace her current life's chapter with courage, as it does not define her enduring journey.

"Steadfast" emerged from this heartfelt dialogue coupled with a supportive affirmation and an uplifting quote. These pieces were crafted to remind Kiana of her inherent strength and ability to navigate life's adversities with grace and triumph. The content reflects the luminous spirit she carries, which deserves all the wonder and beauty the world can offer.

Our conversation also revealed a special connection I felt with her middle child, whose behaviors and energy resonated deeply with me. This inspired elements of the poem that highlight Kiana's unwavering love and dedication to her children, offering her solace and strength as she moves forward.

A significant piece of advice I shared with Kiana was the practice of journaling. This suggestion was not only a coping strategy but also a tool for her son to later understand his mother's thoughts and decisions during his upbringing. Recording personal experiences and emotions can serve as a bridge of understanding between Kiana and her son, particularly if she ever faces the tough decision to pause her custody battle. This is not a sign of defeat but a strategic pause for self-care, ensuring her mental well-being so she can continue to be a strong presence for her family.

Inspired by this, I crafted "Legacy of Ink." This piece explores journaling as a means of leaving behind a legacy of understanding and connection. Through the metaphor of ink and paper, the poem encapsulates the idea that a mother's written words can provide her children with insight into her life choices and emotions, fostering a future of understanding, acceptance, and strengthened bonds.

Both "Steadfast" and "Legacy of Ink" come from the threads of real conversations and genuine intentions. They serve as reminders and affirmations of strength, resilience, and the enduring power of expressed love and understanding. These creations aim to bolster Kiana's spirit, reminding her and her children of her indomitable nature and the bright future that lies ahead, underscored by the hope and belief that through understanding, all challenges can be transcended.

Clapback in the Capitol

In the halls of power where echoes form,
a t-shirt clash stirs the storm.
"Bleach Blonde Bad Built Butch," it read,
words thrown where angels fear to tread.

Oh, Crockett, with your alliterative flair,
a bold clapback in the heated air.
A merchandise line born from debate,
funds for the blue, to navigate fate.

Yet here I stand, amidst the fray,
wishing truth would lead the way.
Facts, not fiction, should guide our hand,
not the whims of a wayward band.

How I long for the days so clear,
where policy talks bring us near.
Discussions deep that bridge the split,
not insults that make the heart quit.

For when we label, call them dumb,
we lose the chance to overcome.
Listen, learn, let empathy guide,
only then can we turn the tide.

So shout out to Crockett in this verse,
her fight for respect in the universe.
But let's not forget the higher call:

to mend the divide, once and for all.

Roots of the Rhetoric

Born from the chaos of a committee clash,
where words as weapons lash and thrash.
May 17, a spectacle unwound,
in the halls where justice should be found.

Crockett's voice rose, fierce and clear,
her alliteration a spear,
"Black Blonde Bad Built Butch," she cried,
a remark that could not hide.

But this wasn't just about that day,
or the sharp words leaders say.
It's about a deeper, darker divide,
that has settled far and wide.

The USA, torn by strife,
each side brandishing a knife.
No empathy to bridge the gap,
just bitter words that trap and sap.

In Congress, where they should debate,
ideas are lost, overwhelmed by hate.
Trump era's shadow, long and grim,
where truth's light grows ever dim.

MAGA crowds and parties split,
on falsehoods many seem to sit.
But my longing, strong and true,
is for discourse that's due and new.

I dream of dialogues that heal,
where facts lead, and all can feel.
A land where listening is the key,
to understand, to set us free.

So, this poem's roots are in this plea:

For a nation where we can truly see.
Not just a fight, not alienation,
but a united, empathetic nation.

Inspiration behind "Clapback in the Capitol" and "Roots of the Rhetoric"
Emotion: Frustration and Longing for Change

These poems are inspired by a real and tumultuous incident that unfolded during a House Oversight Committee meeting on May 17, 2024. The session was meant to discuss the serious legislative matter of whether Attorney General Merrick Garland should be held in contempt of Congress, yet it quickly devolved into a series of personal attacks. The spotlight of this conflict was the heated exchange between Rep. Jasmine Crockett and Rep. Marjorie Taylor Greene, marked by Crockett's striking use of alliteration in her retort: "Bleach Blonde Bad Built Butch Body."

These poems explore the broader implications of such conflicts. They reflect a deep frustration with American politics and highlight the divisive and often disrespectful discourse that has become all too common. This division is not just a spectacle of individual disagreements but symptomatic of a larger, deeper rift within the country, exacerbated by the polarizing years of the Trump presidency and its aftermath.

Through these verses, I yearn to return to politics rooted in empathy, understanding, and factual debate rather than personal attacks and entrenched partisanship. The poems criticize the ongoing strategy of both political sides to further deepen the divide by demonizing each other, making genuine dialogue nearly impossible.

The ultimate hope I express in these poems is for a shift from this combative norm to a more constructive and uniting form of political engagement. It's a call for leaders and citizens alike to listen to one another, to debate honestly, and to foster an environment where political discourse can lead to real solutions rather than further conflict.

"Clapback in the Capitol" and "Roots of the Rhetoric" aim to reach those who feel alienated by current politics and desire a more mature and respectful governing body. They serve as a poetic commentary on the need for change in American politics and the potential for healing.

A Nation's Wake-Up Call

Suddenly, they rise, aware of a bill,
yet blind to the broader legislative hill.
Do they see the votes, the laws, the track?
Or just a snippet, a narrow-minded crack?

Joe and Clinton, apologies sincere,
for a crime bill passed, a shadowy year.
Repercussions felt, lessons learned,
promises now, with wisdom earned.

Look beyond the surface, hear their pledge,
see their past deeds, upon the edge.
Misinformation, parroted with ease,
by those who don't grasp the forest for trees.

A landslide awaits for those who see,
the broader picture, the civic decree.
Wake up, awaken, to the nation's call,
Trump's track is clear, a self-serving sprawl.

A history of disdain for the hue of our skin,
against people of color, his record is thin.
Yet some are swayed by whispers and lies,
blind to the truth, deaf to the cries.

So learn the civics, know the past.
Choose the future, one that will last.
For it's not just about one crime bill's stain,

but the promise of progress, the hope through the pain.

A nation in balance, a choice to be made,
not by whispers of fear, but a truth unafraid.
Vote for the future, the justice, the light.
Awake, stand together, and join in the fight.

Inspiration Behind "A Nation's Wake-Up Call"
Emotion: Urgency and Frustration

While scrolling through Instagram one afternoon, I noticed a growing trend among Black Instagram users expressing frustration and skepticism towards Joe Biden. The sentiment centered around the belief that Biden has done nothing for the Black community and has, in fact, contributed to mass incarceration with the 1994 crime bill. This narrative spread like wildfire, often repeated without understanding the broader political landscape.

My frustration quickly grew. It's both amusing and exasperating that people are suddenly citing a single bill, spoon-fed to them like lemmings following a script, without applying the same scrutiny to the entire realm of civics and legislation. They focus narrowly on this one piece of history while ignoring the multitude of bills introduced for or against Black people over the years.

To make an informed decision, we need to look at the bills introduced in the last four years and the four years prior. Which party blocked what? What laws could have been enacted based on proposed bills from either party in the last eight years? My frustration lies in knowing that the analysis would overwhelmingly support one side, yet many people don't grasp the basics of civics or understand how the country is run. They get stuck in the past, losing sight of the complexities of the full story.

This poem, "A Nation's Wake-Up Call," is my attempt to urge my community to see beyond the simplified narratives spread on social media. It's a call to learn, to wake up, and to understand the full context before making decisions that impact our future.

Finding My Authentic Self

I've sailed through love's tempestuous seas,
from one heart's harbor to the next with ease.
Yet, in quiet reflection, truth rings clear—
alone, unbound, I face my deepest fear.

A parade of faces, a blur of hearts,
in each, a lesson, as one departs.
But now I pause, amid life's swift dance,
to ask, not who with, but in which stance.

For love, though rich, was never quite enough.
My list of traits, though long, revealed as bluff.
It wasn't merely about avoiding past mistakes,
but uncovering what each bond forsakes.

Nico's love, a chapter bittersweet,
showed me paths where hearts and desires meet.
Yet, in our love, I saw my own reflection—
A quest for self, not mere affection.

I yearn for balance, where independence thrives,
within a love where my true self survives.
And if our paths diverge, I'll still be whole,
for the journey's mine, a solo role.

Now, with time's wisdom gently bestowed,
I forge ahead on this personal road.
in therapy's grasp, I dissect each part,
What fulfills me—core of my heart?

Honesty, respect, a power shared,
a partner's support, deeply ensnared
in mutual growth, freedom's sweet song—
these are the notes to which I belong.

So, as I tread softly in love's domain,
not seeking to bind, nor to be chained,
I explore, I question, I learn to discern
the essence of love for which I yearn.

Inspiration Behind "Finding My Authentic Self"
Emotion: Self-reflection and Empowerment

This poem draws from an introspective look at my personal journey toward understanding what truly fulfills me in life and love. Over the years, I've moved from one relationship to another, each time believing that I was searching for something meaningful, yet often finding myself running from the red flags of the past rather than understanding what I truly needed.

The realization that merely having a partner or being in a relationship wasn't the pinnacle of fulfillment came as a revelation. It prompted me to reflect on what makes a relationship truly enriching. The core of this reflection is my understanding that a healthy relationship involves honesty, trust, respect, and open communication and that both partners should contribute equally, respecting each other's independence and decisions.

In this poem, I begin to question not only what I want from a partner but also what I need from myself to be fulfilled. Through therapy and personal reflection, I've come to understand that my needs weren't just about avoiding previous mistakes but about building something fundamentally strong and balanced. I wrote this poem as a declaration of my ongoing journey to find that balance, and as a reminder that my happiness and fulfillment come from understanding and nurturing my needs before I can truly share my life with someone else.

A Brother's Love: A Poem for My Sister

Dear sister, your journey's echo reaches me,
deep in the chambers of a brother's steadfast heart.
From our first moments together, a promise made silently,
to nurture, to guard, to encourage your start.

You've blossomed, oh how brightly you've unfurled,
into a woman of grace, a mother, a guide,
a keeper of faith in this ever-spinning world.
Your strength, a silent anthem, cannot hide.

Your doubts may dance like shadows in the night,
yet in your steps, I see a path of light.
Success isn't just a destination but a view,
in every moment, love, you've triumphed anew.

I celebrate you, not just today, but every day.
In you, I see the colors of life's vibrant play.
Your love paints your children's skies a brilliant blue,
Camden's laughter, Landon's smiles, pure and true.

And Braden, though not of our blood but bond,
feels like a brother, of whom I am so fond.
Our family, a tapestry of love and grace,
in this world's vast gallery holds a special place.

So hear this, my sister, from a heart that knows,
you are cherished and admired, and it shows.
You are strong, you are beautiful, beyond all,
together, we'll catch each other should we fall.

From your brother, with love that time only grows,
a bond sealed by the sweetest rose.
Your story, a beacon for what's to come,
in the Book of Life, our pages hum.

A brother's love, eternal, deep, and vast,
in the quiet moments, in memories that last.
Forever here, in laughter or in strife,

for you, dear sister, a promise for life.

Inspiration behind "A Brother's Love"
Emotion: Love and Admiration

This poem came to me while I was sitting on a runway, my flight delayed due to weather. As I waited, my thoughts naturally drifted to my sister. I sent her a simple text, "Te Amo," a small gesture that carries the weight of my deep affection for her. Over the years, we've shared countless conversations, but a recurring theme has been her battle with anxiety.

Anxiety is a pervasive feeling of worry and fear that can distort one's perception of their capabilities and future. It's a common struggle, yet each person's experience is deeply personal. Techniques like mindfulness, therapy, and sometimes medication can help manage these feelings, empowering one to lead a fulfilling life despite the challenges.

My sister often doubts her effectiveness as a mother, her career choices, and her future. This poem is my affirmation to her that she is indeed loved, that she is more than enough, and that success is not a one-size-fits-all scenario. She has already achieved remarkable things at her age—raising children, nurturing love, and persevering through her doubts. Her story doesn't need to mirror anyone else's to be valid or celebrated.

This poem is my way of reminding her of the solid, unwavering support she has from her brother. It's reassuring that I see her struggles and strengths, and I am here to celebrate both with her. In crafting these lines, I remind her that her brother's love is a constant, ready to uplift her during moments of doubt and cheer her on through every victory, big or small.

My Guy Wish List

I dream of someone patient, calm,
who travels with ease, shares my balm.
Adventurous heart, seeking new,
entrepreneurial spirit, ever true.

Career-oriented, success in sight,
affectionate, warm in the night.
Empathetic soul, culturally aware,
nice and kind, a perfect pair.

Finds me sexy, sensual flame,
respectful of others, never in vain.
Honest words, clear and bright,
communicative, shares the light.

Open and vulnerable, without disguise,
beliefs and values, in sync, we rise.
Raised with hardship, solid and strong,
truth teller always, right or wrong.

Family bonds, deeply felt,
independent, with wealth self-built.
Mental health, a spoken theme,
handles pressure, calm and serene.

Family ties, well embraced,
compatibility charts, high placed.
Tidy and clean, organized space,
growth from past, no jaded trace.

Open to talk of love's wide scope,
discussing dreams, full of hope.
Communicates well, feelings and needs,
Independent soul, where happiness breeds.

In this wish list, my heart does lie,
seeking love that soars, touching the sky.
A partner true, in life's grand quest,
together we'll flourish, together we'll rest.

Inspiration behind "My Guy Wish List"
Emotion: Hopeful Longing and Aspiration

This poem emerges from my ongoing journey of healing and intentional living, shaped by my experiences and therapeutic exercises that guide me toward better, more fulfilling relationships. Initially, after my divorce from Darren, my therapist encouraged me to take stock of my past love choices and be intentional about what I truly seek in a partner. I crafted my original "guy wish list" as a guidepost, intending to break free from the patterns that no longer served me.

However, I didn't fully adhere to this intention when I left Darren and entered a relationship with Bax. In retrospect, that relationship was one born out of convenience, not alignment with my values. When Bax and I broke up, I revisited the list, determined to be more deliberate this time. I even used the list as a guide during dates, but my relationship with Nico revealed that some key qualities were still missing.

Through my experiences with Nico, I realized I had grown better at recognizing half-truths and hidden intentions. With that clarity, I updated my list, adding the crucial need for an interdependent relationship— something I hadn't fully understood until then. The co-dependence I had experienced before was draining me, and I knew I needed someone who could be independent but still show up fully in a partnership.

Then, I met Rafa. He checked every box on my list, including the ones I didn't know I needed. He brings a deep, genuine love and a sense of interdependence that I had been longing for.

Intentionality is about being deliberate and purposeful in actions and decisions. In the context of relationships, it means knowing exactly what you seek in a partner, thereby allowing you to recognize and avoid those who don't align with your core needs and values.

Manifestation involves bringing your desires and goals into reality through focused thought, belief, and action. By clearly articulating the qualities you want in a partner, you actively work toward attracting that person into your life.

Therapeutic Exercises help in understanding and prioritizing your needs, fostering self-awareness, and setting healthy boundaries. Knowing what you want ensures you don't waste time on individuals who don't meet your fundamental criteria for a fulfilling relationship.

The penning of this poem was born from the intersection of these concepts. It emphasizes the importance of interdependence, where partners are independent yet bring their whole selves into the relationship. It highlights the value of continuous self-improvement and growth, ensuring both partners contribute positively to each other's lives.

By leaning on these principles, the poem guides one toward relationships that are nurturing, balanced, and deeply fulfilling.

Circular Relationships

Round and round, we go,
tracing paths that never change.
Stuck in cycles, tethered tight,
to a love that's just out of range.

Promises that loop back,
echoes of what's been said.
We're dancing in a circle,
on a floor that's worn and dead.

Each step feels so familiar,
yet it leads us nowhere new.
Caught in a spinning whirlpool,
where dreams dissolve like dew.

Hope rekindles, fades again,
as seasons shift and spin,
but circular relationships,
won't let new chapters begin.

Stagnant waters can't refresh,
nor can cycles break the mold,
for growth demands new pathways,
not the comfort of the old.

So let's unbind these circles,
and seek a line that's straight and true,
for only in forward motion,
can we find what's meant for you.

Inspiration Behind "Circular Relationships"
Emotion: Frustration and Yearning for Change

In May of 2017, during a period marked by friendship turmoil, I found myself reflecting on the nature of relationships and the patterns that often trap us in cycles of unproductivity. It was a time when certain friendships seemed stuck in a loop, repeating the same mistakes and behaviors without any forward movement. This stagnation stifled growth, both individually and within the relationships themselves.

The quote, "Circular relationships are not productive," emerged from this realization. It expressed my frustration with these repetitive interactions and the need for a decisive break from these cycles to foster true growth and progress.

"Circular Relationships" draws from that moment of clarity. It explores the futility of staying in the same patterns and emphasizes the importance of seeking new paths to achieve genuine personal and relational development. The poem is rooted in the desire to break

free from unproductive cycles and to find a direction
leading to positive change and fulfillment.

Progression of Therapy Series

These poems were inspired by a series of six transformative
therapy sessions with Julie that guided me through various
stages of self-discovery, self-awareness, and healing. Each
part reflects key insights into my relationships, both past
and present, and the central themes of communication,
boundaries, and personal growth.

The six sessions are explored in two parts, each followed by
an inspiration piece that ties together the insights from three
poems

Part 1

Therapy's Light

In the therapist's chair, my tales I unfold,
discomfort and frustration, the feelings I've told.
Julie nods wisely, her insights a beacon,
addressing my issues, no room for the weaken.

Nico on pins and needles, tiptoeing around,
my need for closure, where solutions are found.
In San Diego, I'll speak, set the expectations,
clear paths ahead, no more hesitations.

Avoidance and ghosting, my old trusty friends,
confronting them now, the cycle to end.
Drafting my messages, with honesty and care,
ghosts of my past, to transparency, fare.

The 80/20 rule, a revelation bright,
family origins cast 80% of the light.

493

Reflecting on patterns, my upbringing's sway,
navigating my actions, the new adult way.

Overloaded and annoyed, I pause and I think,
communicate feelings, before on the brink.
Writing down grievances, with roommates in tow,
patterns revealed, the areas to grow.

Honeymoon with Rafa, but mindful I stay,
navigating discomfort, come what may.
Ghosting leaves gaps, a lost, lonely space,
feedback brings growth, a new kind of grace.

Childhood coping, running away,
now through communication, I choose to stay.
Anger and hurt, I face them head-on,
constructive solutions, old patterns gone.

Conversations with Nico, open and clear,
messages to ghosts, I'll send without fear.
Reflecting on childhood, behavior now seen,
self-awareness my guide, a future serene.

So here's to progression, in therapy's light,
a journey of growth, from darkness to bright.
With Julie's wisdom, and actions in tow,
a path of self-discovery, onward I go.

Communication and Trust

In reflection's gentle light, truths emerge,
clear, honest words, a vital urge.
With Rafa and Nico, I must be true,
communication's key, for me and you.

Boundaries drawn, with careful hand,
for all involved, they firmly stand.
In love and life, they shape our way,
ensuring respect, day by day.

Trust, a fragile seed to sow.
Past experiences, we both know.
Rafa and I, with hearts laid bare,
building trust, with tender care.

Defensive walls, when hurt takes flight,
I'll work to soften, seek the light.
Effective words, to bridge the pain,
in open dialogue, we'll find our gain.

Awareness grows, in every stride.
Through honest talk, we'll gently guide.
In love's embrace, and trust's sweet glow,
together strong, we'll learn and grow.

Boundaries and Balance

In reflection's quiet space, clarity blooms,
boundaries with Nico, essential to groom.
Respect and peace, a manageable sphere,
a living situation, no longer unclear.

With Rafa, open words, my reasons laid bare,
boundaries explained, with tender care.
Communication's bridge, strong and wide,
in love and trust, together we stride.

Bax's condition, a challenge to face,
Sasha's well-being, proactive embrace.
Steps taken with thought, compassion's guide,
ensuring her safety, by Bax's side.

Open communication, expectations set,
vital threads, in relationships met.
Honesty and clarity, the fabric we weave,
in healthy bonds, we learn to believe.

Through reflection's lens, the path is shown,
boundaries and balance, in love we've grown.

With open hearts and minds aligned,
in each connection, true peace we find.

Inspiration Behind Part 1: Evolution of three therapy sessions
Emotion: Self-discovery, Self-awareness, and Healing

Session: Addressing Discomfort and Moving Forward (May 28, 2024)

This session focused on recognizing and addressing feelings of discomfort and frustration, particularly with Nico. Julie emphasized the importance of open communication to set expectations and find closure. The main themes revolved around confronting avoidance, ghosting, and understanding behavioral patterns influenced by family origins. This session was about acknowledging past coping mechanisms and working towards healthier communication and self-awareness.

"Therapy's Light" emerged from this session as a reflection on addressing deep-seated discomfort and frustration. The poem highlights the need for honest communication and setting clear boundaries to navigate relationships effectively. It encapsulates the idea of moving from darkness to light, with therapy providing the necessary guidance and wisdom to foster growth and clarity.

Session: Navigating Relationships and Communication (June 4, 2024)

This session focused on the intricate dynamics between Rafa and Nico, emphasizing the importance of clear communication, setting boundaries, and building trust. Julie guided the conversation toward managing expectations and addressing hurt feelings constructively. The session was about balancing trust and openness, understanding the baggage both partners bring into the relationship, and fostering a supportive dialogue.

"Communication and Trust" was inspired by this session, reflecting the ongoing effort to maintain clear and honest communication with both Rafa and Nico. The poem delves into the challenges of setting boundaries, building trust gradually, and managing past experiences that impact the current relationship. It underscores the significance of effective communication in navigating emotional complexities and fostering a healthy, trusting relationship.

Session: Boundaries, Communication, and Managing Relationships (June 10, 2024)

This session continued focusing onsetting and maintaining consistent boundaries, addressing jealousy, and improving communication. Julie emphasized the need for respect, especially considering cultural and language barriers. The session also touched on taking proactive steps to ensure the well-being of Sasha, reflecting on Bax's situation, and maintaining an open dialogue with Rafa to address insecurities and build trust.

"Boundaries and Balance" evolved from the discussions about boundaries in this session, and reflects the necessity of balancing personal needs with respect for others and the ongoing process of improving communication to foster healthy relationships. It illustrates the importance of proactive measures, trust, and open conversations in achieving a harmonious balance in life.

Part 2

Clarifying Mixed Messages

In therapy's light, clarity sought,
boundaries and mixed messages, deeply thought.
With Julie's guidance, reflections profound
on relationships and the peace to be found.

Nico, understand, romance is not our path.
Friendship's the lane, no need for wrath.
My help's unconditional, that's who I am.
Friendship's pure, without a hidden scam.

Rafa's my choice, respect this stand.
Co-dependency, let's understand.
Find your therapist, seek your way,
independence in your journey, day by day.

Am I unclear? Let's reflect and see.
"And" not "but," in conversations be.
Rafa and Nico, tell me straight
if mixed messages make you hesitate.

Triggers and reactions, why do they ignite?
Helping hands, leading to dependency's plight.
Feedback clear, is it truth or projection?
Seeking clarity, with each introspection.

Interdependence, not a co-dependent bind,
with Rafa, a healthy balance, I find.
Helping Nico, yet his problems remain,
responsibility's his, not my chain.

Rafa's desires, a topic ahead,
boundaries maintained, communication spread.
In therapy's embrace, I'll explore
healthy relationships, forevermore.

Boundaries set, with clarity and care,
helping friends, without burdens to bear.
Mixed messages avoided, clear communication's role,
understanding triggers, self-awareness the goal.

In therapy's light, I navigate
boundaries clear, no room for debate.
Relationships healthy, interdependence in sight,
with Julie's wisdom, I embrace the night.

Self-Reflection and Caretaking

In quiet moments, I reflect,
on the care I give, with self-neglect.
Tending to others, even when it's not wise,
seeking their comfort, ignoring my cries.

Caretaker's role, a mantle I bear.
But at what cost? I stop and stare.
This journey's for me, growth to find,
no blame to place, just peace of mind.

In my reflection, truth I see,
balancing care, for them and me.
Acknowledging needs, my own embrace,
finding my way, at a steady pace.

Growth is a path, not always straight,
learning to nurture, not suffocate.
In self-reflection, strength I find,
caretaking gently, with a mindful mind.

Breaking the Cycle

In the mirror of my mind, reflections deep,
caretaker tendencies, promises to keep.
A journey unfolds, with steps I take,
to break the cycle, for my own sake.
Self-Awareness

First, I see the pattern's start,
in family dynamics, a tender heart.
Seeking approval, avoiding strife,
people-pleasing habits, shaping my life.

Awareness dawns, a light so bright,
understanding fears that take flight.
The need for love, to feel secure,
acknowledge these roots, to find a cure.

Setting Boundaries
Boundaries drawn, with courage and care,
saying "no" without despair.
Self-care isn't selfish, it's respect defined,
protecting my space, my peace of mind.

Communicate clearly, with firm resolve,
in boundaries set, problems dissolve.
Standing strong, though pushback may come,
in self-respect, my heart finds home.

Self-Validation
No longer seeking others' praise,
self-worth I nurture, in countless ways.
Validating feelings, my own voice heard,
in self-acceptance, I find the word.

I recognize my own true worth,
independent of others, a profound rebirth.
Building esteem, from within,
a strong foundation, where I begin.

Learning to Say No
The word "no" becomes my shield,
protecting needs, my own field.
Assertive yet kind, I hold my ground,
in this strength, my voice is found.

Evaluating requests, with careful thought,
prioritizing myself, no longer caught.
In guiltless "no's," I find my way,
to live authentically, day by day.

Cultivating Self-Care
Engaging in joy, hobbies anew,
in self-care practices, my spirit grew.
Exercise, nature, and moments of peace,
from stress and anxiety, a sweet release.

In nurturing self, I find the key,

to better care for others, naturally.
Replenished and whole, I stand tall,
balanced and steady, through it all.

Seeking Support
Surrounded by those who truly see,
encouragement in their company.
Trusted friends, a circle tight,
guiding me through, to the light.

Sharing struggles, gaining strength,
in supportive bonds, at any length.
Perspective gained, through their eyes,
in collective wisdom, I rise.
Embracing Imperfection

Perfection's hold, I gently release,
in self-compassion, I find peace.
Mistakes are lessons, growth's sweet song,
in imperfection, I belong.

Breaking free, with steps profound,
in self-care's embrace, I am found.
Boundaries set, validation clear,
a journey of healing, year by year.

Inspiration Behind Part 2: Evolution of three therapy sessions
Emotion: Self-discovery, Self-awareness, and Healing

Session: Clarifying Mixed Messages (June 26, 2024)

In addition to continuing to discuss boundaries, we focused on the importance of communicating openly and understanding the difference between friendship and romantic expectations. We also reflected on my behavior to help avoid sending mixed messages and foster interdependent rather than co-dependent relationships.

"Clarifying Mixed Messages" is inspired by the need to set boundaries and communicate effectively to avoid misunderstandings. The poem reflects the process of establishing clear expectations in relationships and the importance of consistent, honest communication.

Session: Self-Reflection and Caretaking (July 23, 2024)

This session focused on the importance of self-awareness and self-care, especially in the context of caretaker tendencies. Julie and I discussed my propensity to prioritize others' needs over my own, often to my detriment.

These behaviors stem from early family dynamics where harmony and approval were closely linked to self-worth and care. We discussed the necessity of setting boundaries to ensure personal growth and mental health, without placing blame on others. We focused on self-validation, which includes building a foundation of self-worth independent of others' approval, helping assert one's needs and desires. Finally, we talked about the role of balancing caretaking, prioritizing self-care and understanding triggers.

The poem "Self-Reflection and Caretaking" draws on these psychological principles and reflects the balance between supporting others and taking care of oneself, promoting a healthier, more authentic way of life.

Session: Breaking the Cycle (July 23, 2024)

In this session, Julie and I discussed the steps necessary to overcome people-pleasing behaviors and establish a healthier sense of self. The session emphasized the role of professional help in breaking my ingrained patterns and how therapy can provide a safe space to develop healthier ways to cope and interact.

"Breaking the Cycle" reflects the steps needed to overcome people-pleasing behaviors. The poem captures

the journey from self-awareness to self-validation,
emphasizing the importance of setting boundaries,
practicing self-care, and seeking supportive relationships.

Sweet Karma's Gavel

Oh, sweet karma, justice served on a golden plate,
Trump convicted on 34 counts, isn't fate great?
Fraud and hush money, the mighty fall,
from his tower of deceit, heed justice's call.

He once cried, "Lock her up!" with fervor and glee,
dragging Hillary through the mud, irony we now see.
For years, he dodged, never faced the law,
today's sweet reckoning leaves us in awe.

Be mindful, these cases came to light
through power and means to fight the fight.
Many left unpaid, their services rendered,
injustice prevails, their cries untendered.

So wake up, people, see the fraud revealed,
a man for himself, his fate now sealed.
Sweet justice, sweet karma, how grand the day,
for the one who thought he'd never pay.

Inspiration Behind "Sweet Karma's Gavel"
Emotion: Vindication and Satisfaction

The inspiration behind "Sweet Karma's Gavel" comes from a sense of justice and irony in the face of Donald Trump's long history of legal and moral transgressions. Recently, Trump was found guilty on 34 felony counts of falsifying business records to conceal a $130,000 hush money payment to adult film star Stormy Daniels, aiming to influence the outcome of the 2016 election. This verdict marks a historic moment as it is the first time a former or sitting U.S. president has been convicted of criminal charges.

The irony is palpable: during his 2016 presidential campaign, Trump vehemently chanted "Lock her up!" against Hillary Clinton, vilifying her without substantial legal grounds. Today, the roles are reversed, and Trump finds himself on the receiving end of the justice system he once so fervently weaponized. This sweet irony and karmic justice inspired the poem.

Trump's legal history is extensive and troubling:
In the 1970s, Trump and his father faced a lawsuit from the Department of Justice for racial discrimination, refusing to rent apartments to Black tenants. They settled without admitting guilt but faced further scrutiny for not fully complying with the consent decree.

The Trump University lawsuits from 2013 to 2016 highlighted fraudulent practices and misleading promises to students, resulting in a $25 million settlement.

In 2018, the New York Attorney General sued Trump for misusing funds in the Trump Foundation, leading to a $2 million settlement and the foundation's dissolution.

Numerous breach of contract lawsuits have seen Trump failing to pay contractors and vendors, resulting in multiple settlements.

Allegations of sexual harassment and defamation have led to various settlements, often with undisclosed terms.

The Trump SoHo condo sales lawsuit in 2011 accused him of misleading buyers about sales figures, settled without admitting wrongdoing.

Multiple bankruptcies of his Atlantic City casinos led to lawsuits from bondholders and contractors, often ending in settlements.

These cases reveal a pattern of self-serving behavior and legal evasion, contradicting the image of a law-abiding citizen that Trump often projected.

Despite this extensive history of criminal behavior, it is bewildering to see some in the Black community, especially Black men, supporting him. This support often lacks a rational basis, given the documented evidence of Trump's discriminatory practices and unethical behavior. The blind allegiance to a figure who has historically shown disregard for marginalized communities, including the Black community, is both shocking and disheartening.

This contradiction fuels a mixture of glee and frustration. On one hand, there is satisfaction in seeing Trump finally held accountable for his actions. On the other hand, there is deep sorrow and confusion over why anyone, particularly within the Black community, would support a man who has consistently prioritized his self-interest over the well-being of the country and its citizens.

Black men, people, wake up. This felon has always been about himself, not the country, and certainly not the Black community. It is a mystery why anyone would support someone who has shown such disregard for justice and fairness. This verdict is a reminder that no one is above the law and is a call to recognize the truth behind the facade.

Though I am overjoyed by this verdict, I also fear it may be perceived as politically motivated, potentially making the upcoming election even more contentious. This situation raises concerns for the future of democracy, the global standing of the USA, and the broader implications for justice and equity worldwide. The poem "Sweet Karma's Gavel" reflects these complex emotions and calls for a collective awakening to the reality of Trump's long-standing malfeasance.

Liquid Courage

In the quiet aftermath of our uncoupling,
I've observed a division,
not just between us, but within myself—
my relationship with the amber allure,
once a companion on fun-filled nights,
now a rare guest in my tempered life.

I reminisced on times when laughter filled glasses,
when nights slipped into forgetful dawns.
Yet, my solitude redefined the norms—
I craved clarity more than the buzz,
sought tranquility over the tumult.
My social sips never turned into daily dances,
the bottle's call, a whisper I could easily ignore.

With each new encounter, each potential heart to hold,
I search for those who favor a glass sparingly filled,
for whom the wine is a splash of color
on the canvas of our conversations,
not the palette from which all tones are drawn.

Curious, I've become of the colorful glass—
a rare indulgence in a restaurant's glow,
a toast to curiosity rather than necessity.
No more than two, never frequently within a month,
and at home, just a yearly guest—
my disdain for dependence quietly deepening.

Observing others, I see the invisible chains that bind
many,
recognizing the quiet epidemic that sweeps unnoticed.
Yet, I stand firm in my resolve,
armed with a will that's ironclad,
I politely decline,
"No, thank you," with ease, no tremor in my voice.

I've grown wary of the spirit that seduces many,
learning its dance of joy and oblivion—
alcohol, a lover to some, a fiend to others.

I fear for the unguarded,
and in rare moments, I send prayers into the void,
a silent whisper for those lost to their drink.

Thank you, for this unintended gift,
the strength to say no,
to hold my ground,
not needing the false bravery from a bottle
to face the world or speak my heart.
In this clarity, I find my courage,
a sober strength that sustains.

Inspiration Behind "Liquid Courage"
Emotion: Self-awareness and Empowerment

This poem stems from the changes in my relationship with alcohol following the end of a significant relationship. I've noticed a distinct shift in how I interact with drinking—moving from social indulgence to a more cautious, controlled approach. My encounters with alcohol have become infrequent and deliberate, focusing on quality over quantity and ensuring that it doesn't control my social interactions or personal well-being.

In the aftermath of our split, I found myself reevaluating the role that alcohol played in our lives together and how it often served as a bandage over deeper issues. This poem encapsulates my journey towards self-awareness and moderation, celebrating the strength found in choosing sobriety and the clarity it brings. It also reflects on the broader social context, recognizing how prevalent unacknowledged alcohol dependence is in society and expressing a newfound empathy for those struggling with addiction.

This shift has not only affected how I view alcohol but also how I interact with potential partners, preferring those who share my perspective on drinking as an occasional pleasure rather than a necessity. This poem is a thank you to my past experiences, which taught me the

importance of maintaining control and finding strength in
sobriety. It's a personal declaration of independence from
the need to find courage in a bottle, embracing a clearer,
more present way of living.

The Sagittarius Dilemma

Why give her Chanel, and you don't rebox,
fight her for that damn alimony.
Sagittarius, with your scattered thoughts,
Blocking the path to harmony.

Them Sagittarians, wild and free,
restless hearts that never flee,
bold and blunt, truth in their eyes,
but in this fight, they compromise.

They chase horizons, dreams untamed,
injustice here, yet they're unclaimed.
Optimism blinds their sight,
in this battle, they lose the fight.

Why give her Chanel, and you don't rebox,
fight her for that damn alimony.
Sagittarius mind in paradox,
missing the chance at matrimony.

Adventurous souls, always on the run,
seeking answers under the sun.
But in the courtroom, they hesitate,
letting go of what's at stake.

Hardworking hands, yet minds adrift,
in life's puzzle, the pieces shift.
Sagittarius, missing the mark,
in this dark maze, they embark.

Why give her Chanel and you don't rebox,
Fight her for that damn alimony.
Uncle Evan, break the locks,

find the path to your destiny.

Inspiration Behind "The Sagittarius Dilemma"
Emotion: Frustration and Confusion

Uncle Evan, this poem, "The Sagittarius Dilemma," comes from a place of deep frustration and concern. When I found out that you were going to pay alimony to your wife, it struck a nerve. From my uneducated and admittedly biased perspective, she doesn't deserve it. She's a capable woman who can take care of herself. This woman started the relationship demanding Chanel, while you, on the other hand, barely even wear Rebox.

How dare she have such materialistic expectations and now expect to be set for life on the back of your hard work? It feels like she's just collecting money without lifting a finger. She could easily get back into a salon and start doing nails or something to support herself.

Please understand, this is raw for me. My heart aches because I want everyone in our family to be happy, to enjoy life, and not be taken advantage of by anyone. I don't know all the details of your marriage, so maybe I'm speaking out of turn. I recognize the importance of understanding the boundaries of not being directly involved in your relationship. This sentiment aligns with the principle of staying out of others' personal affairs, often emphasized in therapeutic settings. As cited in various therapeutic approaches, particularly in family systems theory, it's crucial to respect the autonomy of others while managing our own emotions and reactions.

Reading over what I wrote, I realized this concern is personal. I chose my lawyers because I wanted to make sure my ex-husband didn't get a dime. He was out of work due to his alcoholism. He is smart, willing, and able to work, and I can't forget that feeling. It was a trigger, a knee-jerk reaction to hearing about alimony. I truly understand it isn't my place, and it was therapeutic to write out how I felt. Maybe it shouldn't even see the light of day, but it is honest, it is raw, and even after realizing it's personal for me, I still feel that way. No one should have to be responsible for someone capable. He does not come from money; what I see is an opportunist, and I can't respect that.

But I close with this: I am crossing a boundary, and you should understand that you should avoid this. Therapeutic settings often emphasize this principle of staying out of others' personal affairs. For instance, in the book Boundaries: When to Say Yes, How to Say No to Take Control of Your Life by Dr. Henry Cloud and Dr. John Townsend, it's highlighted that "we can't make others' decisions for them or interfere in their lives without their consent. Respecting boundaries is about acknowledging the limits of our control and influence" (Cloud & Townsend, 1992).

So, while my words come from a place of love, concern, and hope for the best for you, I acknowledge that they also come from my personal experiences and biases. Ultimately, you must make the decisions that reflect what's best for you.

A Mother's Tribute

In your eyes, I see the strength of dreams,
A journey carved by love, it seems.
Touched and honored, words fall short,
For you, my son, are my heart's fort.

Against all odds, defying stats,
You rise above, despite the past.
Part of me, part of Eli too,
A blend of greatness, through and through.

Amazing soul, you light the way,
Running the world, come what may.
A king in spirit, heart so true,

The man you are, I'm proud of you.

Grateful am I, a young mom's chance,
To see your life, your triumphs dance.
Witnessing greatness, pure delight,
Your star shines brilliantly, day and night.

A Son's Tribute

Mom, your words touch my soul so deep,
In my heart, your love I keep.
Honored and blessed, I stand so tall,
Part of you, I am, through it all.

Against the odds, we proved them wrong,
In your strength, I've grown so strong.
Half your DNA, it's plain to see,
Your courage, your love, live in me.

A great man, yes, because of you,
With a heart that's honest and true.
Running the world, just as you dreamed,
Living the life that you deemed.

Grateful am I for every chance,
To make you proud with each advance.
I love you, Mom, with all my might,
Your guiding star, my shining light.

Inspiration Behind "Mother's & Son's Tribute"
Emotion: Love, Gratitude, and Pride

Recently, my mom sent me a deeply touching text
message expressing her gratitude and pride in me. Her
words were a reflection of her emotions and the journey
we've been on together. She wrote, "Hey son, thank you so
much for being my son, a great man, knowing who you
are and what you want, a beautiful heart and a real man.

You're out here running the world like a king!! I'm so grateful I took the chance being a young mom to be able to witness this greatness."

This heartfelt message came after she spent several weeks with her best friend, a trip that I had organized for her. I purchased her flight tickets and sent her some money to help with bills. This act of support and love seemed to resonate deeply with her, leading her to reflect on our past and how far we've come.

My mom had me when she was just 14 years old, which brought its own set of challenges and hardships. Despite the odds and the statistics that often predict a less fortunate outcome for children born to teenage mothers, we have defied those expectations. Her strength, resilience, and unwavering support have played a significant role in shaping who I am today. I have managed to achieve a level of success that is often considered unlikely given our background, and my mom's message was a poignant reminder of the sacrifices and love that fueled our journey.

"A Mother's Tribute" captures my mom's perspective. It celebrates my achievements and her pride in witnessing my growth and success. This poem is an acknowledgment of her reflections on being a young mother and seeing her child thrive against all odds. It is a testament to the love and strength she has always provided, making her journey and sacrifices worthwhile.

"A Son's Tribute" is my response to her message. In this poem, I express my deep love and gratitude for my mom. It is a recognition of the integral role she has played in my life, shaping me into the person I am today. This poem acknowledges the pride I feel in being her son and carrying forward the legacy of resilience and love she has instilled in me. It is a heartfelt thank you for her unwavering support, her strength, and her belief in me, despite the challenges we faced together.

These poems are more than just words; they are an emotional reflection of our journey. They encapsulate the bond between a mother and her son, forged through adversity and strengthened by love. They highlight the triumphs over challenges and the deep sense of pride and gratitude that comes from overcoming the odds together. Writing these poems allowed me to express my appreciation for my mom's sacrifices and her role in my life, while also celebrating the achievements that we, as a family, have accomplished.

In summary, the poems "A Mother's Tribute" and "A Son's Tribute" are heartfelt expressions of the love, pride, and gratitude that define our relationship. They are a celebration of our journey, our resilience, and the unwavering bond that has guided us through life's challenges and successes.

A Union Leader's Plea

In the paper, my words were found,
a union leader's voice renowned.
In ink, my fears and hopes did blend,
of Trump's return, a chilling end.

The article, a stark reminder,
of policies that drift no kinder,
Schedule F, a threat anew,
to civil servants' work so true.

In a land of laws and liberty,
where truth should reign, and people free,
the danger looms of tyranny,
a Trump reprise, a grave decree.

My heart trembles at the thought,
of battles past, so dearly fought,
for rights, for justice, equity,
all at risk in his decree.

Yet honored was I to be heard,
to voice the truth in every word.
As Union President, I stood tall,
quoted in the journal's hall.

An interview, a chance to sway,
to hope that people, on voting day,
would choose with wisdom, clear and bright,
not swayed by falsehoods, fear, or spite.

I dream of votes based on the real,
on facts, on truths that they reveal.
Not led astray by lies' allure,
but grounded firm, intentions pure.

So here's my plea, my fervent call,
to every voter, great or small.
May your choices shape our fate,
for justice, truth, a better state.

Inspiration Behind "A Union Leader's Plea"
Emotion: Concern and Determination

The inspiration for "A Union Leader's Plea" began when
I was approached by Matt Shuham, a reporter from
HuffPost, to discuss the potential impact of "Schedule F"
on federal employees, particularly those in Chapter 337.
This policy, introduced by Donald Trump in 2020, seeks to
reclassify federal workers involved in policy-making
positions as "at-will" employees, effectively stripping them
of their civil service protections. Such a shift could lead to
job insecurity and the politicization of federal agencies.

During our conversation, I expressed my deep concerns
about the dangers of Schedule F, highlighting how it could
undermine the merit-based system that governs federal
employment and pave the way for increased political
interference in public service. My role as the Union
President allowed me to provide a unique perspective on

the potential risks and challenges federal employees might face under this policy.

The interview evolved into a comprehensive HuffPost article that included quotes from myself and others. The article shed light on the critical issues surrounding Schedule F and its implications for the federal workforce.

I felt honored to be quoted and to have my voice included in such an important discussion. The poem "A Union Leader's Plea" captures my fears of a potential return to a Trump presidency and the detrimental impact of Schedule F on dedicated civil servants. It also serves as a heartfelt plea for voters to make informed decisions based on facts and self-interest rather than being swayed by misleading rhetoric. Ultimately, the poem is a call to action, urging the public to recognize the profound consequences of their votes and to uphold the values of justice, truth, and democracy.

Whispers from Beirut: A Tribute to Salam's Mother

In the mountain shadows of Beirut,
A woman of grace and light,
Salam's mother, a beauty profound,
Now rests beyond our sight.

Salam, in this time of sorrow,
Know I stand beside you.
With every dawn, a new tomorrow,
Her love will guide you through.

Oh, Salam, your mother's love,
Blossomed in the mountain air.
Her kindness, a gentle dove,
Her spirit, ever fair.

In this hour of grief and pain,
Remember the joy she gave.
Her lessons, never in vain,

Will keep your heart brave.

Ya Salam, in these moments fraught,
Recall the love she sowed.
Her wisdom, deeply taught,
Will lighten your heavy load.

Ma fi hadā kāmilo bkhayr illa li rāḥ
("No one is complete and at peace, except the one who has
left.")

Salam, dear friend, hold fast,
Her legacy will endure.
In every mountain breeze that's cast,
Her love remains pure.

In Arabic whispers, let her be,
A song of strength and grace.
With every tear, we set her free,
In Allah's tender embrace.

Nahna hon dayman
("We are always here.")

Be strong, my friend, as you grieve,
Her light forever near.
In every heart she did weave,
We find her presence clear.

Farewell, dear mother of Salam,
Your journey now begun.
In every prayer and loving calm,
You are our shining sun.

"Rest in peace" "ترقد بسلام" (tir'od bisalam).

Inspiration Behind "Whispers from Beirut"
Emotion: compassion and remembrance

On June 19, 2024, I reached out to my dear friend Salam via Instagram to check in on him. When I saw the beautiful lady he had posted, I asked who she was, and Salam replied that it was his mother and that she had passed. My heart ached for him, and I was immediately transported back to our time in Beirut.

I vividly remember our visit to Chouf, the town in the mountains where Salam is from and where his mother lived. Chouf is a place of historical significance and breathtaking beauty. The landscape, with its lush greenery and majestic mountains, is a testament to the natural allure that has kept families rooted there for generations. The architecture of the homes, with their traditional Lebanese design, adds to the charm and timelessness of the town. The houses, built with stone and adorned with red-tiled roofs, stand as a symbol of strength and resilience.

During our visit, we departed from Salam's apartment in Beirut and made our way to Chouf. I recall smoking hookah and immersing myself in the rich Lebanese experience. Although Salam's mother was already sick at the time and I did not have the pleasure of meeting her, I was a room away, feeling the warmth and love that filled their home.

I wanted to quickly draft this tribute to Salam's mother for him, as it was the only way I knew to provide comfort from afar. Grief is hard, and while I have not experienced it to this extent, I have an understanding of it from supporting friends and family and reading about the stages of grief. My heart, love, and thoughts are with Salam, and I hope to visit him soon to offer my support in person.

Democracy's Choice

In the shadows of a looming threat,
where democracy hangs by a fragile thread,
Donald Trump, a name that resonates fear,
a specter of autocracy drawing near.

5,429 days of rhetoric and lies,
a menace to the system under clear skies.
If he wins, democracy's light will wane,
institutions crumbling, chaos will reign.

Biden stands, though age we can't ignore,
an elder statesman, yet a defender of more.
Leadership that's tested, not a threat but a guide,
to the core of democracy, where truth resides.

People fret about his age, a concern seen,
but deeper fears lurk in a covert scene.
A Black woman rising if he cannot serve,
a reality some still struggle to observe.

I cast my vote for Biden, a choice so clear,
for the nation's future, for what we hold dear.
If you cherish this land and its design,
choose wisely, for democracy is on the line.

A stark debate, two men, two fates,
one dodges questions, the other fumbles to articulate.
What a choice we face, a path so thin,
yet my thoughts are firm, on the side I'll pin.

Democracy or dictatorship, the crossroads we stand,
a vote that shapes the future of this land.
In the clash of ages, the decision's stark,
for a free tomorrow, I choose the light, not the dark.

Inspiration Behind "Democracy's Choice"
Emotion: Urgency and Determination

This poem was inspired by the first presidential debate of the 2024 election cycle, held between President Joe Biden and former President Donald Trump. This 90-minute debate, hosted by CNN in Atlanta with Jake Tapper and Dana Bash as moderators, was marked by muted microphones and the absence of a studio audience. The event highlighted the stark differences between the two candidates and the dire implications of the upcoming election.

President Biden, battling a cold, struggled through many of his answers early on, sounding hoarse and frequently losing his train of thought. Despite his initial stumbling, he improved as the night progressed, yet he often found it challenging to clearly communicate his position on various issues. His performance caused significant concern among his fellow Democrats, with one House Democrat describing the reaction among lawmakers as an unprecedented "freakout."

In contrast, former President Trump appeared more energetic, but his vigor was overshadowed by a barrage of lies and misstatements. He mischaracterized his record and many of Biden's positions, making false claims about topics ranging from abortion and immigration to his recent criminal conviction and the January 6 attack on the Capitol.

This poem reflects the critical choice facing the nation: preserving democracy versus the threat of autocracy. It echoes the deep concerns of many about the potential consequences if Trump were to win the election. The poem underscores the importance of voting for Biden, despite his flaws, as a leader who poses no threat to democracy. It also touches on the underlying racial anxieties some hold about the possibility of a Black woman becoming President if Biden cannot complete his term.

The debate showcased the severe contrasts between Biden's leadership and Trump's dangerous rhetoric. As a voter, I am compelled to choose democracy, with all its imperfections, over the authoritarian threat posed by Trump. The choice between maintaining our democratic principles and succumbing to dictatorship is clear. The poem serves as a call to action for those who value the liberties and freedoms that define the United States.

Silent Echoes of Solitude

Alone en mi mente, my thoughts wander,
to politics and more, a sea of ponder.
Coworkers chat, but shallow is the talk.
No family, no partner, just a solitary walk.

Nico escucha, but words often fade,
English not his forte, but a listening cascade.
Rafa, who knows the lingo, yet falls short,
in understanding politics, it's not his court.

Conversations with Rafa, a fickle dance,
sometimes deep, sometimes a fleeting glance.
Aloof he drifts, until ready to engage,
leaving me alone, en mi propio cage.

Friends vote but disengage from the fight.
Dad leans towards Trump, a troubling sight.
Mom's mind, a maze I can't traverse,
complexity lost, an unspoken curse.

In moments like these, I miss Darren's mind,
and Brandon's debate, intellectually aligned.
Not always in agreement, but ready to explore,
the answers to life's problems, the open door.

Now in a land where my Spanish falters,
communication stumbles, boundaries alter.
Even with English, desires seem light,

a weightless plea, lost in the night.

So here I am, alone en esta tierra,
seeking stimulation, a mental sierra.
A world of thoughts, unspoken and deep,
loneliness lingers, as silence weeps.

Inspiration Behind "Silent Echoes of Solitude"
Emotion: Loneliness and Frustration

This poem draws its essence from my profound sense of loneliness and isolation when discussing politics and the state of the world. Despite having people around me, I often find myself without anyone who truly engages in meaningful conversations about these topics. My partner Rafa, who speaks English, often dismisses political discussions, making me feel even more isolated. My friend Nico, though a good listener, struggles with the language barrier, limiting our interactions to surface-level exchanges.

My best friends participate in voting but are not deeply engaged in the electoral process or the broader political landscape. My family, with my dad's likely support for Trump and my mom's reluctance to delve into complex discussions, further contributes to my feelings of isolation.

I find myself longing for the intellectual stimulation and debates I once had with past partners like Darren and Brandon. We didn't always agree, but their willingness to engage in deep, thought-provoking conversations was something I cherished. Now, as I spend time in a country where my grasp of the language is limited, I feel even more disconnected and unable to communicate my feelings and needs effectively.

This poem captures my solitude, my desire for intellectual connection, and the silent weeping of my thoughts in a world that often feels indifferent to the weight of my words.

Repercussions in the Age of Misinformation

I opened up X, scrolling past the noise,
And there it was, a breaking news ploy:
"Morgan Freeman backs Trump, the nation's new choice."
A blue checkmark—a badge of deceit, not poise.

My heart sank, my trust took a hit.
How could it be? Freeman said this?
Yet, with a quick search, I saw the rift,
truth from lies, a dark abyss.

Fake news spreads like wildfire's light,
unchecked, it fuels ignorance's might.
Freeman stood with Hilary, then Biden too,
no word of Trump, no hint, no clue.

Yet here we are, in a digital maze,
where lies are truths in a social media craze.
Verified accounts, now bought and sold,
no longer a sign of trust, but of gold.

I'm sick of the noise, the untruths that flow,
of people believing without needing to know.
The First Amendment, meant to protect,
now twisted by lies, with no real effect.

We need repercussions, a call to account,
for those who spread falsehoods, to any amount.
An amendment for truth, for lies to be checked,
or we'll watch our institutions crumble, wrecked.

In this Wild West of a digital age,
let's find our way back to truth's clear page.
For without accountability, trust will fade,
and in the chaos, our society's made.

Inspiration Behind "Repercussions in the Age of Misinformation"
Emotion: Frustration, Concern, and Determination

The inspiration for this poem stems from a deep frustration with the rampant spread of fake news on social media platforms. A recent encounter with a false report about Morgan Freeman allegedly supporting a second Trump presidency was a poignant example. Despite the credibility implied by a verified account, a quick search revealed the news to be entirely fabricated, highlighting Freeman's support for Hilary Clinton in 2016 and Joe Biden in 2020.

This incident underscores a broader issue: the ease with which misinformation can be disseminated and believed without fact-checking. The poem reflects a growing disillusionment with social media and the erosion of trust in what was once considered a reliable source of information. It questions whether the protections granted by the First Amendment were intended to cover the spread of falsehoods on such a scale and calls for accountability and repercussions for those who deliberately spread lies.

The poem is a call to action, emphasizing the need for societal and legislative changes to address the unchecked spread of misinformation. Without such measures, the integrity of our institutions and the very fabric of our society are at risk of crumbling in the face of relentless digital deceit.

Justice Undone Series

Thinking Through Immunity

I didn't know what to think at first.
Supreme Court's ruling, a looming curse.
But diving in, I found some light,
relief that it didn't reach worse heights.

"Absolute immunity for official acts," they say,
a line drawn, though murky, in the fray.
Exhausted by decisions of this court,
the lowest rated, causing public retort.

Yet as I read, a nuance appeared,
accountability, it seems, not fully cleared.
This election now more critical than before,
up to three seats, stakes galore.

A conservative court could strip away,
rights we cherish, lead us astray.
Balance teeters, every vote a must,
in this democracy, we place our trust.

Feeling drained, yet still I stand,
to dive deeper, to understand.
The fight for justice, ever true,
in every decision, in all we do.

Sotomayor's Dissent

In halls where justice ought to reign,
a shadow falls, casting deep disdain.
Justice Sotomayor stands clear,
with Kagan and Jackson near.

"Disastrous for democracy," they decry,
as immunity for presidents reaches the sky.
"Reshapes the institution," brute force in play,

no law or precedent lights the way.

"Core powers" expand beyond bounds.
Official acts immune, justice confounds.
No distinction between what's right or wrong.
Motive ignored, the shield too strong.

"Law-free zone," a perilous stage,
for presidents to act without the cage.
"The President now a king above the law,"
democracy falters, freedoms withdraw.

Procedural bars, evidence denied,
criminal accountability cast aside.
Public trust shattered, the stakes laid bare,
a ruling that justice cannot bear.

Sotomayor's dissent, a clarion call,
against a decision that endangers us all.
For in this land where justice should prevail,
such immunity means our democracy may fail.

Jackson's Dissent

In halls of power, a shift now stands,
Justice Jackson's dissent, a clarion demands.
A paradigm shift, accountability's fall,
the balance of power disrupted for all.

Immunity, she writes, as "exemption" defined,
from duties and liabilities, a dangerous bind.
A system of law meant to constrain,
now leaves our democracy in disdain.

From individual accountability, we depart,
to a "Presidential model," tearing justice apart.
Core duties, official acts, immunity's veil,
with convoluted steps, justice grows frail.

No equal application, laws unequally spread.
A President freer, accountability dead.
Judiciary now a gatekeeper's role,
policing the President, taking its toll.

Congress's power, diminished, she cries,
the judiciary's reach, now touching the skies.
Ambiguity reigns, core powers unclear,
official or unofficial, distinctions disappear.

Deterrence lost, Presidents unchecked,
invited to cross lines, laws now wrecked.
An "energetic" executive, risks untold,
the American people left out in the cold.

"Seeds of absolute power," she warns with dread,
rule of law replaced, rule of judges instead.
A decision that shifts, norms redefined,
an intolerable risk, for justice, maligned.

Inspiration Behind "Justice Undone Series"
Emotion: Concern and Determination

The "Justice Undone Series" explores recent Supreme
Court decisions that have left an indelible mark on
American democracy. This series comprises three distinct
yet interwoven poems: Sotomayor's Dissent, Thinking
Through Immunity, and Jackson's Dissent. Each poem
focuses on the intricate legal and philosophical debates
sparked by the Court's rulings, particularly the contentious
issue of presidential immunity. The poems were inspired
by personal reactions to the rulings, in-depth analysis of
the dissenting opinions, and a broader contemplation of
the judiciary's role in safeguarding or eroding democratic
norms.

The first poem, Sotomayor's Dissent, draws directly
from Justice Sonia Sotomayor's passionate opposition to
the majority opinion. In her dissent, she condemns the
majority's decision as "disastrous for democracy," arguing

that it reshapes the Presidency by granting former presidents a broad shield of immunity, thus making a "mockery of the principle" that no one is above the law. This poem captures the gravity of her words and the implications of insulating a President from criminal accountability. It reflects on her critique of the majority's creation of a new category of "core constitutional powers," which dangerously blurs the line between official and unofficial acts. Sotomayor's concern is that this ruling creates a dangerous precedent, granting presidents unprecedented protection from legal scrutiny, potentially undermining the very foundation of American democracy.

The second poem, Thinking Through Immunity, conveys the ambivalence and exhaustion many feel in response to the Supreme Court's rulings. It expresses the relief that the decision, while problematic, did not go as far as it could have, acknowledging the restraint shown by a court known for its conservative leanings. The poem underscores the initial shock and concern about the decision's potential impact, juxtaposed with the cautious optimism that some accountability mechanisms remain intact. It highlights the importance of the upcoming election, which could significantly alter the Court's composition. The possibility of appointing up to three new justices increases the stakes, as a fully conservative court could lead to further erosion of rights and a dangerous imbalance in the judiciary. This poem is a deep engagement with the implications of judicial decisions and a recognition of the important nature of civic participation in shaping the country's future.

In Jackson's Dissent, the third poem, Justice Ketanji Brown Jackson's academic and measured critique of the majority's opinion is brought to life. Jackson argues that the majority's decision marks a paradigm shift, creating a "new Presidential accountability model" that fundamentally alters the traditional system of criminal accountability. She emphasizes that immunity, as applied by the Court, is fundamentally at odds with the principle that all individuals, including the President, are subject to the rule of law. Jackson's dissent warns of the dangers of concentrating too much power in the judiciary, where judges now serve as gatekeepers determining whether the law applies to presidential actions. She raises concerns about the erosion of Congress's power and the potential loss of deterrence against presidential misconduct. The poem captures Jackson's fears that this ruling could incentivize future presidents to act with impunity, posing "breathtaking risks" to the American people.

The "Justice Undone Series" reflects the current state of the American judiciary and its implications for democracy. Each poem provides a unique perspective on the Supreme Court's controversial decisions, exploring the balance of power between the branches of government, the importance of accountability, and the potential consequences of unchecked authority. This series is a call to awareness, urging readers to recognize the significance of these legal battles and their impact on the nation's democratic principles. It reflects on the evolving nature of justice in the United States, emphasizing the need for vigilance, civic engagement, and a commitment to the rule of law. Through this poetic exploration, the series aims to provoke thought, encourage discourse, and underscore the gravity of the judicial decisions that shape the nation's trajectory.

Reflections on Love

The philosopher Plato said,
"El verdadero amor es la admiración."
It's not just someone who loves you as you are
but who helps you grow with determination.

Por eso, la pareja que escojas
Debe tener cualidades que te falten.
Choose a partner who lifts you higher,
their strengths, your heart shall sweeten.

Elige como pareja a alguien mejor que tú.
For true love is in admiration found.
Someone who helps you flourish daily,
in their presence, your spirit unbound.

No necesitas a alguien que te quiera tal y como eres.
You need someone who sees your soul's desire.
Asumirán los periodos tormentosos.
Together, through the storm, they will inspire.

Si los dos están comprometidos en ayudar al otro a crecer.
In each other's growth, they will invest.
El amor según Platón.
Is finding in each other's growth, the very best.

As I ponder and search for love,
considering who will be my future and not just my now,
I turn to the lessons of therapy and the teachings of
philosophers,
as a guiding light to show me how.

Inspiration Behind "Reflections on Love"
Emotion: Hopeful Inspiration and Admiration

From ancient Greek Philosopher Plato's teachings and
therapy sessions, I've learned the value of finding a
partner who embodies the qualities I lack and supports my
personal growth.

Plato emphasized the importance of true love being based on admiration and mutual growth rather than mere acceptance. His philosophy suggests that a partner should complement and enhance our qualities, helping us reach our fullest potential.

This poem integrates therapy concepts like interdependency, where both partners support each other's growth and navigate difficult times together. It reflects on choosing a partner who not only loves us but also challenges and motivates us to be better.

It's important to look beyond surface-level affection and consider how a partner contributes to our overall happiness and fulfillment. I hope this poem encourages people to choose love thoughtfully, considering what truly makes them happy. It's essential to balance the heart's desires with rational considerations, seeking relationships that foster mutual growth and lasting contentment.

Veils of Reality: A Journey of Love and Truth Series

A Prayer for Clarity

In shadows cast by whispers low,
where facts and fiction intertwine,
A world of doubts begins to grow,
with tales that stretch beyond the line.

They speak of Masons, shrouded deep,
who pull the strings of Earth's great stage,
of Black Americans' secret keep,
lost histories from a hidden page.

They claim the Natives' rightful place
was but a guise, mere war-time shame.
Yet, truth reveals a different face,
through time and facts we see the same.

From Siberia, they crossed the land,
Nomadic souls on ice did tread.
No whispers back from that brave band,
their paths to history's pages led.

I beg the question, why believe,
in tales that shatter reason's light?
What wounds do these delusions weave,
What pain, what darkness fuels this plight?

A man who rarely bends to pray,
now sends a plea for minds adrift.
For when these myths lead hearts astray,
it's clarity that we must lift.

For truth and reason shape our fate,
in choices made at ballot's stand.
Yet falsehoods feed on fear and hate,
and grip the future in their hand.

This fall election, shadows loom,
With fears of truths that they despise,
The threads of doubt weave in the gloom,
A clearer path, a needed rise.

What mental state, what hurt they flee,
What shattered dreams, what broken trust,
In theories wild, they seek to be,
A world where lies seem more robust.

But hope remains in hearts aligned,
With facts and truth to guide the way,
And prayers for those with clouded mind,
That light will break their darkened day.
As reason's flame burns ever bright,
May clarity dispel the night.

Conspiracy's Veil

In whispers dark, conspiracies bloom,
Masons controlling from hidden rooms.
They craft a world of shadowed doom,
but facts dispel these crafted glooms.

They speak of John, a President,
a Hanson cloaked in myth's embrace.
But timelines clear, and evidence sent,
reveal the truth within his place.

Native bloodlines traced to lands,
where ancient paths from Asia span.
No prisoners here, just history's hands,
guiding migrations of early man.

Americans once Black, they say,
histories erased, stories spun.
Yet science shows a different way,
with evidence from which they run.

Why cling to tales of hidden might,

of secrets deep and powers vast?
Do these myths make their world seem right,
or heal a hurt left in the past?

As we peel back the layers thin,
each claim falls to the light of day,
and reason's voice begins to win,
dispelling shadows from our way.

The Freemasons, in open halls,
a brotherhood, not secret kings,
no hidden hand that rules or calls,
just men with hopes and human things.

And John, who led in freedom's name,
not cloaked in secrets dark and deep,
But part of history's honest frame,
a legacy that truth can keep.

The Natives, proud, their stories told,
not prisoners of a hidden lie,
Their ancestors, brave and bold,
from Asia's shores to new worlds nigh.

So, as we sift through tales and fear,
may clarity in truth prevail,
for in the light, all lies grow clear,
and truth alone can lift the veil.

I hope the truth, once and for all, prevails   ,
dispelling myths, setting minds to sail.

A Father's Veil

An hour on the phone, your voice unfolds,
conspiracies spun in tales untold.
Freemasons, shadows, secrets run,
Black rulers lost, where truth begun.

Native souls, you claim as bound,
war prisoners on stolen ground.
The USA, a corporate shell,
with figureheads in power's cell.

You won't vote, you won't partake,
blaming Biden for each mistake,
Trump admired, yet truth ignored,
in a maze of myths, your mind is stored.

No glance to see your own missteps,
no thought to take, no pause, no rest.
A man, a father, roles you shirk,
refusing to join society's work.

Seven children look to you,
a father's guide, a path to view,
a husband's strength, a provider's hand,
yet you withdraw, and take a stand.

Against a world you see as flawed,
through YouTube's lens, reality clawed.
Manipulated views you hold,
while brighter truths remain untold.

Your mind, so sharp, could pierce the veil,
if only you'd allow the sail,
to drift towards help, to seek the light,
to face the day, to end the night.

You're hurt, defeated, but you resist,
the therapy that could assist,
to heal the wounds, to find your place,
to join the world in its embrace.

We talk, we laugh, in moments rare,
yet your theories push, and we despair.
Your brilliance trapped in shadows deep,
a restless soul that cannot sleep.

At fifty-one, the time has come,

To cast aside the theories spun,
To be the man, the father true,
a member strong in life's great view.

I see the pain, I feel the strife,
the longing for a different life,
But know this, Dad, we stand by you,
in hopes the truth will guide you through.

For though the myths may cloud your mind,
a clearer path you still can find,
with love, with strength, with open heart,
to heal, to grow, to play your part.

I Call Bullshit, but Good Luck with Your Resistance to Be a Functioning Adult

You say you've studied, read the books,
before YouTube's hooks,
before the screens and online streams,
you dug through pages, found your themes.

You claim you don't blame anyone,
not Trump, not Biden, not the sun.
Yet, in your words, a different song,
the echoes of a lifetime long.

You care for me, you say it's true,
our views diverge, that's nothing new.
But still, you hold these shadows tight,
in tales of Masons, hidden might.

I call bullshit, yet wish you luck,
in resistance to the growing muck,
of responsibilities you shove away,
a functioning adult kept at bay.

You've got the books, the knowledge deep,
yet in the shallows, you choose to sleep,

avoiding work, avoiding life,
dodging roles of father, husband, strife.

I see the man you still could be,
a shining light for all to see,
if only you'd embrace the fight,
against the dark, into the light.

You brush off politics with ease,
yet live in theories, myths that freeze
your growth, your step into the now,
to stand as man, to take the vow.

No more debates, you draw the line.
Your truths are yours, and that's just fine.
But in the silence, hear this plea,
for you to join reality.

For in your mind, so sharp, so bright,
the answers lie within your sight,
if you'd but turn and face the real,
the pain, the hope, the truth, the deal.

I call bullshit, but with love entwined,
wishing you luck, in heart and mind,
to break the chains, to see the day,
where you can stand and proudly say:

"I am a man, a father true,
a husband, provider, through and through,
I face the world with open eyes,
in truth, in light, my spirit flies."

Good luck with your resistance fight,
but know there's hope in truth and light,
and as you walk this path you choose,
I pray you find the strength to lose

The myths, the fears, the shadows cast,
to live in truth, to find at last,
the peace, the joy, the love that's real,

in a world where wounds can truly heal.

Sleep on It

You are right; three hundred isn't enough.
A hard worker, indeed, but tough.
You're a product of your own demise,
choosing paths where hardship lies.

You've quit jobs on principles tight,
who you don't want to serve, who talks just right,
making work a grind so steep,
the path you've chosen, far too deep.

I told no lie; it's the truth I share.
It's good you're working, but be aware,
one must seek help to truly mend,
be honest, transparent, start to end.

You have a lot to confront and face,
to work through pain, find your place.
I hold no grudges, love remains,
our connection, despite the strains.

I've done the work; I'm not a child.
No father issues, no needs beguiled.
I can see the brilliance in you,
the empath's heart, the wisdom too.

Yet your theories, wild and vast,
hurt and insult, shadows cast,
on realities we face each day,
the dangers present, clear as day.

Your disdain for therapy and work,
the very systems you love to shirk,
threaded through my identity's core.
It's time to be victorious, soar.

You must reflect, see the mirror's truth,
on your healing journey, reclaim youth.
Feedback guides us, helps us grow;

there it is, just so you know.

Good night, I have much to do
before the morning breaks anew,
a million tasks, meetings to start.
Sleep on it, with open heart.

I understand your side, your view.
You think it's true, it's okay too.
You're not that person in my eyes,
just human, not perfect, in disguise.

You've been alone, made fast decisions,
living with past, amidst collisions.
But love yourself, and love us too,
change the past, start anew.

Working hard, fingers to bone,
peanuts earned, a heavy groan.
Support yourself, support us all.
Rise above, heed the call.

Sleep on it, and may you wake,
to do the work, for our sake.
Become the man we know you can,
In lives of those who love you, stand.

Inspiration Behind "Veils of Reality: A Journey of Love and Truth" Series
Emotion: Frustration and Sorrow

The inspiration for these five poems came from a single day filled with intense and emotional interactions with my father, Eli. The day began with a long phone call while I was at the grocery store, followed by a series of text messages. During our conversations, he passionately tried to educate me on his conspiracy theories, touching on topics such as the Freemasons secretly controlling the world, the idea that Black people were the original rulers, and the belief that Native Americans were actually war prisoners. He also mentioned his conviction that the USA is a corporation and that the president is merely a figurehead with no real power.

Eli's theories extended to his decision not to vote, influenced by his preference for Trump and his disdain for Biden, whom he blames for his life's struggles due to the crime bill, without acknowledging his own accountability. Despite having seven children and societal responsibilities, he resists working for "the man" and views the world through a distorted lens fed by YouTube and other manipulated sources.

Later in the day, our exchange continued through text messages, where he expressed his views on working hard, his struggles, and his rejection of therapy and education. This prompted me to reflect on the broader implications of his beliefs and their impact on our relationship and his life.

In one text, he stated, "I've been studying and reading before YouTube and I have books at home that say the same things we talked about. I don't blame anybody, and I don't care about Trump or any president. I do care about you, and I understand that your views are yours and that's okay. I'm not trying to get you to understand what I know to be true, and that's fine. I just don't want to have a conversation with you about politics anymore."

It's heartbreaking, because my father is incredibly intelligent and could see the truth if he chose to. He is hurting and feels defeated but refuses to seek help for his mental health or life challenges. Our conversations are often deep and meaningful, but his conspiracy beliefs push those closest to him away. My mother and others joke about him being off his meds, but the reality is more serious. I observe signs of depression, and his rejection of therapy is concerning. At nearly 51 years old, he continues to cling to these theories, pushing family away and avoiding the responsibilities he is capable of fulfilling.

These interactions inspired me to draft a series of poems that express my frustration and sadness over his conspiracy-riddled mind, the potential he has yet to fulfill, and the hope that one day he will see the truth and embrace the help he needs to live a better life. They reflect my love for him, my concerns for his well-being, and my wish for a brighter future where he can reconnect with reality and his family.

Each poem—"A Prayer for Clarity," "Conspiracy's Veil," "A Father's Veil," "Sleep on It," and "I Call Bullshit but Good Luck with Your Resistance to Be a Functioning Adult"—captures different facets of my feelings and reflections on his conspiracy beliefs, our relationship, and my hopes for his personal growth and healing. Through these poems, I express my love, frustration, and desire for him to confront his past, embrace the truth, and become a better man for himself and those who love him.

Gratitude Blooms

Gratitude blooms, a gentle art,
when we cherish bonds that touch the heart.
Connections forged with spirits kind,
weaving richness in life's design.

Navigating the world, so vast and wide,
forming links where hearts reside.
Diverse backgrounds, stories shared,
in these moments, we're ensnared.

Profound happiness, a treasure found,
in every handshake, love unbound.
Effortless interactions, pure and free,
crafting joy for you and me.

¡Buenos Dias! A call to rise,
cherish loved ones, be their prize.
Like a guardian shield, firm and strong,
in their embrace, we belong.

Affirmation, clear and bright,
in a circle of love, we find our light.
Supported by presence, unwavering, true,
with loved ones, there's nothing we can't do.

Inspiration Behind "Gratitude Blooms"
Emotion: Gratitude and Joy

"Gratitude Blooms" was inspired by a sense of thankfulness for the connections I've created with others throughout my life. Each encounter, each bond, has contributed to my growth and happiness in ways I had not fully appreciated until now.

I often find myself navigating the world with ease, connecting with people from diverse backgrounds. These interactions have broadened my perspective and brought immense joy and fulfillment into my life. The ability to connect with others so seamlessly feels like a gift, one that I hold dear and value deeply.

On one particular morning, filled with gratitude and optimism, I wrote a note to myself: "Gratitude blooms when we cherish the effortless connections we forge with kindred spirits, adding immeasurable richness to our lives' tapestry." This thought was a reminder to always appreciate these connections and the happiness they bring.

A personal affirmation has always guided me: "I am surrounded by a circle of love and supported by the unwavering presence of my loved ones." This affirmation reinforces the importance of recognizing and valuing the love and support we receive from those around us.

Gratitude Blooms" captures these reflections and sentiments. It is a celebration of the joy that comes from connecting with others, the richness these connections bring to our lives, and the strength we gain from their love and support. It serves as a reminder to always be thankful for the interactions that shape our journey, making life more beautiful and meaningful.

The Best Relationship

The best relationship, I've come to find,
is where we both have space, peace of mind.
Where each can thrive in their own right,
and come together when it feels just right.

In love, we're not two halves of one,
but whole individuals, under the sun.
We grow and change, we laugh and cry,
with room to spread our wings and fly.

We're not confined, we don't restrain,
but celebrate each other's gain.
In our own worlds, we shine so bright,
yet cherish moments shared in delight.

Independence is our core,
yet our hearts always seek for more.
Together, we create a space,
where love and freedom interlace.

So here's to us, to you and me,
in our best relationship, wild and free.
Not one person, but a beautiful blend,
of two souls thriving, till the very end.

Inspiration Behind "The Best Relationship"
Emotion: Balance and Mutual Respect

This poem was born from my reflections on what makes
a fulfilling and sustainable relationship. I've always
believed that the best relationships are those where each
person can thrive as an individual while coming together
to share their happiness. This balance allows for personal
growth and mutual support without the need to change or
compromise one's identity.

In contemplating this idea, I realized that a relationship should not be about merging into a single entity but rather about two complete individuals who choose to walk the same path. Each person brings unique strengths, passions, and dreams, creating a dynamic and enriching partnership. Such a relationship thrives in the freedom to be oneself and the joy of sharing life's journey with a like-minded companion.

I've seen many relationships where one or both partners feel the need to change to fit the other's expectations. This often leads to resentment and a loss of self. I believe that the best relationships are those where acceptance and encouragement reign. Each partner should celebrate the other's individuality and provide a space for growth and self-expression. The healthiest bonds are those where both people can pursue their interests, support each other's aspirations, and come together without losing their sense of self. They find joy in each other's company while maintaining personal autonomy.

"The Best Relationship" is a tribute to the beauty of partnerships built on mutual respect, independence, and love. It's a reminder that true happiness in a relationship comes from two whole individuals who complement each other, not complete each other. This poem captures my belief that love should enhance our lives, not redefine them.

Culture and Compassion

Culture doesn't shift with just our plea,
it morphs when transformed collectively.
A reflection of our daily stride,
where collaboration turns the tide.

It feels good to see the human whole,
even in those who've hurt our soul.
No one chooses to be bad and cruel,
but hurt and unhealed, they break the rule.

Hurt people, unhealed, they cause pain,
caught in a cycle, again and again.
Yet, in each one, there's a spark of light,
a human struggling in their fight.

So let's transform, together we'll stand,
building a culture, hand in hand.
Seeing the human, in joy and strife,
healing together, in this shared life.

Inspiration Behind "Culture and Compassion"
Emotion: Hope and Empathy

One day, while reflecting on my past relationships, I
found myself pondering a fundamental question: why do
people hurt each other? My mind wandered to my exes
and the pain they caused, and I sought to understand the
root of such behavior. On May 3, 2023, I witnessed an
interaction that gave me hope—a moment where someone
chose to be human despite the potential for hurt. This
contrast inspired me to write a note to myself: "It feels
good to see the human in everyone, even those who hurt
us the most. I don't think anyone chooses to be bad and
hurt people; hurt and unhealed people hurt people." This
reflection became a foundation for deeper contemplation.

On July 16 of the same year, I encountered a powerful
quote: "Culture does not change because we desire to
change it. Culture changes when the organization is
transformed – the culture reflects the realities of people
working together every day." Both the note from May and
this quote resonated deeply with me, particularly as I
reflected on the current state of the world. We are not only
divided in the USA but across the globe, with wars, strife,
and extreme political ideologies causing immense
suffering.

In pondering these two concepts, I realized that culture
cannot change without a collective shift, and hurt people

often perpetuate that hurt. This led me to a theory: through widespread education, accessible therapy for all, and the opportunity to travel and experience each other's cultures, the negativity in the world could significantly decrease. I wish everyone could access these privileges.

Until that day comes, I hold onto hope. I hope for the end of the war in Ukraine, where countless lives are lost and families torn apart. I hope for peace in the conflict between Israel and Palestine, where the struggle has led to a heartbreaking genocide, global divisions, and immeasurable deaths. I hope for resolution in the wars across Africa and the Middle East, and I pray for our own democracy in the USA, which faces threats from the rise of MAGA Trumpism and regressive efforts to peel back rights.

"Culture and Compassion" emerged from these reflections, blending personal insights and global observations. It underscores the idea that true cultural transformation requires a collective effort and that understanding and healing are essential to breaking the cycle of hurt.

My Skin Folk

I am sick of people putting her
to a different standard,
Holding her higher, higher still,
while past VPs coasted.
Critique so quick, so cold.
Where are the solutions,
the engagement, the informed debate?

She's done a lot, as much as Pence,
as VPs of yesteryears.
But your eyes are shut,
your ears, they turn away,
refusing to see, to hear
the work, the progress made.
So stop, my skin folk.
Stop being part of the problem.

Read more, engage more,
be the change we need.
Lift her up, our beautiful Black queen
deserves not your scorn,
but your pride, your unwavering support.
We deserve more than what we do
to each other, to ourselves.

Look at how quickly,
how easily we turn,
our own voices sharp against our kin.
When did we forget the power,
the unity we hold?
My skin folk, let's rise together,
stop tearing down,
and build up our own.

We are stronger than the doubt,
more resilient than the criticism.

Our queens, our leaders,
deserve our love, our strength.
Let's be the positive force,
the change-makers, the dreamers,
uplifting our people, our future,
with the respect and honor we deserve.

Against the Headlines

The fact that y'all run these negative headlines,
it's insane, absurd, unjust.
You don't even know, can't even see,
she's the most successful VP in history,
yet you cast her in shadow, in doubt.

She's the force behind Biden's stride,
turning policies into living laws.
Her hands, her mind, her unwavering will,
crafting change, shaping futures,
a silent architect in the halls of power.

She's the reason the first Black female
stands proud on the Supreme Court bench,
her vision, her fight, her legacy etched,
in the marble halls where justice reigns,
a symbol, a beacon for generations to come.

All the HBCU money, the lifeblood of dreams,
poured from her efforts, her tireless drive.
Yet you dismiss, overlook, erase
the milestones she's carved from her relentless path.
It's really sad, this blindness to her success.

She's been successful her entire career,
breaking barriers, shattering ceilings.
Yet you choose to see her through a tainted lens,
missing the brilliance, the triumph, the grace,
of a woman, a leader, a history-maker.

Open your eyes, your hearts, your minds,
see the truth, the impact, the undeniable light.
She deserves more than your headlines of spite.
She deserves your respect, your acknowledgment,
for she is more than you dare to write.

She is the pulse of progress, the breath of change,
a testament to perseverance, to unwavering fight.
So, let's celebrate, uplift, and honor her name,
for she is a queen, a leader, a guiding light.
In the annals of history, her legacy will remain.

Inspiration Behind "Challenging the Narrative Series"
Emotion: Frustration and Hope

In a world where headlines scream louder than truths, where social media paints pictures with broad, often biased strokes, we find ourselves at a crossroads. Our Vice President, Kamala Harris, is a testament to resilience, intelligence, and unparalleled dedication. Yet, the narrative spun around her by Instagram feeds, media outlets, and casual commentators often distorts her achievements, casting shadows where there should be light.

"My Skin Folk" speaks to a deeper frustration, a call to my fellow Black people to recognize and uplift our own. It's a plea to stop holding our leaders to impossible standards while others coast by unnoticed. It's about celebrating the beauty and power of Black queens, acknowledging their contributions, and understanding that we deserve better than the criticism we often inflict upon ourselves. This poem reminds us of our collective strength and the importance of unity.

"Against the Headlines" is a direct challenge to the negative portrayal of Kamala Harris. It highlights her significant, tangible achievements – from her role in passing crucial legislation to her instrumental part in appointing the first Black female Supreme Court Justice.

This poem contrasts the disheartening headlines with the reality of her success, urging readers to see beyond the surface and recognize her profound impact.

The "Challenging the Narrative" series is born from a place of frustration and hope. It's about pushing back against the misinformation and negativity that cloud our perceptions. and celebrating the truth, hard work, and undeniable contributions of our leaders. Through these poems, I hope you feel inspired to look deeper, to question the narratives presented to you, and to uplift those who deserve our respect and acknowledgment. This series is a call to become more engaged, informed, and positive and to stop putting down those tirelessly working for our collective betterment.

This series reminds us that we must look beyond the surface, question the negativity surrounding our leaders, and celebrate the truth of their accomplishments. It's an invitation to uplift, engage, and honor those who pave the way for a better future.

The Villain's Crown

Sometimes you have to don the villain's crown,
to cast off the chains that weigh you down.
For in the tale of living free,
a hero's quest demands liberty.

I'm learning to break away, to stand,
no longer guided by every hand.
I'm not used to wearing the villain's guise.
I've always sought joy through others' eyes.

But to walk my path, bright and true,
some will see a monster where there's just me and you.
The caretaker's heart, so tender, so kind,
now must learn to leave some tears behind.

It feels wrong, making someone upset,
but my life's not lived through regret.
Decisions for myself, a bold new dawn,
to live the life where I belong.

In another's story, I'm the dark knight,
but in mine, I'm the champion of the light.
I must choose my battles, face the fight,
for my happiness, for my right.

Let them call me the villain, if they must,
in my own tale, I'll earn my trust.
For sometimes, to live, to truly breathe,
you must be willing to let others seethe.

So here I stand, with courage found,
wearing the villain's crown, unbound.
For in my heart, I know what's true,
to be the hero, I must break through.

Inspiration behind "The Villain's Crown"
Emotion: Courage and Self-empowerment

This poem speaks to my internal struggle with being perceived as a villain while making choices for my own happiness and well-being. I have always been a caretaker, prioritizing others' happiness, often at the expense of my own. However, through therapy and personal reflection, I have come to understand that living authentically sometimes means disappointing others.

The inspiration for this poem came during a heartfelt conversation with my friend, Ilana. We were discussing the complex situation at home with Nico, who still lives with me despite our romantic relationship having ended, my deepening love for Rafa and the progress of my book. During this conversation, I mentioned a note I had written: "Sometimes you have to be the villain in someone else's eyes," a sentiment originally shared by my friend Tessa when discussing Nico and my reluctance to evict him.

This discussion reaffirmed my understanding that sometimes it's necessary to make tough decisions that others may view negatively to prioritize my own well-being. Donning the villain's crown symbolizes this difficult but necessary shift from people-pleasing to self-empowerment. My therapy sessions have focused on setting boundaries and prioritizing my own needs, even if it causes discomfort or conflict. The poem captures the bittersweet reality of personal growth and the courage it takes to live my truth, embracing the fact that sometimes, being the hero in my own story means being the villain in someone else's.

The Measure of Truth

I wish to be honest, to bare it all,
to stand unguarded, let my truths fall.
Yet honesty's a dance, a mutual art,
only as deep as you open your heart.

I long for transparency, clear as glass,
as with my circle, where truths freely pass.
But people's actions set the tone,
and I match the candor they've shown.

When a person's genuine, a pure exchange,
it frees me from the need to arrange,
no sugar-coating, just raw and real,
in those moments, I can truly feel.

At my rawest, the essence of me,
I crave acceptance, to just be free,
to not be taken wrong, or misconstrued,
in my truth, a space unfeigned and crude.

You know my truth, and in that knowing,
lies the peace where my love is growing,
in your presence, my safe space found,
with you, my heart, my love is bound.

You hold my truth, my sacred share,
my future rests within your care.
In you, I find the trust I seek,
my truth holder, in you, I speak.

Inspiration Behind "The Measure of Truth"
Emotion: Vulnerability and Trust

Inspired by my desire for complete honesty and
transparency, this poem explores the delicate balance of
being truthful in relationships while considering others'
readiness to receive such honesty.

The inspiration for this poem came during a conversation with my friend Ilana. We were catching up, discussing how similar we are in our love for truth-telling. We both believe in being forthright and honest, but we also recognize that not everyone can handle the truth. Some people do not give you the space and time to be truthful, and others make it uncomfortable, even punitive, when you try to tell them the truth. This negative reinforcement often makes me want to avoid truth-telling. Ilana and I both grapple with this challenge, shaped by our astrological signs—her Aquarian mind and my Piscean tendencies. I am an Aquarius rising, which may explain why I lean into this aspect of my personality, though I can't recall Ilana's full chart. Regardless, our shared experience in navigating the complexities of honesty inspired this poem.

From a therapeutic perspective, my sessions have highlighted the importance of genuine communication and creating safe spaces to be my raw, authentic self. True intimacy and connection are built on mutual openness, but I understand that not everyone is ready or willing to handle full transparency. This poem reflects my journey toward finding and maintaining relationships where I can be unfiltered and true to myself. It is guided by therapeutic concepts of vulnerability, trust, and setting boundaries necessary for healthy interactions.

In my therapy work, I might explore the differences between those who feel raw enough to tell the truth only when the climate is right and those who tell it regardless of the consequences. This ongoing journey highlights that while I strive for honesty, there may still be areas for growth and reflection with my therapist to better navigate these complexities in my relationships.

Eric's Law: A Beacon for the Invisible

In Montgomery County's shadowed grove,
a mother's heart, with worry wove.
Since George Floyd's breath was taken away,
her thoughts on justice found their way.

Eric, with a mind so bright,
yet hidden struggles out of sight.
Autism's cloak, unseen but real,
birthed a vision, a new ideal.

"Three logos," he did propose,
for those whose battles no one knows.
Autism, mental health, the silent ear,
a symbol for law to revere.

IDs to bear this mark of grace,
so peace can shine on every face.
A shield against the world's blind eye,
a voice for those who can't deny.

Linda, with a mother's plea,
"For Eric's safety, for him to be
known, understood, not cast aside.
This law is our family's guide."

"Invisible," the world might say,
but in this law, our hope shall stay,
for Eric's   dreams and friends alike,
deserve their peace, their future's light.

Senator Smith, a beacon too,
with pen in hand, the dream he drew,
January's dawn, or February's light,
Eric's law stands for the right.

So let us question, let us see,
the world through eyes of empathy.
For every Eric, silent yet strong,
deserves a life where they belong.

Injustice shook the earth's foundation,
sparked this flame of legislation.
A logo, simple, yet profound,
to ensure all voices safe and sound.

Montgomery's streets, from dawn till dusk,
shall echo with this call to trust.
A law for life, for love, for all,
in Eric's name, we rise, we call.

Inspiration Behind "Eric's Law: A Beacon for the Invisible"

Emotion: Hope and Advocacy

The inspiration for writing "Eric's Law: A Beacon for the Invisible" came from watching Eric Carpenter-Grantham and his mother, Linda Carpenter-Grantham, share their story on "The View." Their journey began with the tragic murder of George Floyd, which ignited a global conversation about justice and safety. For Linda, this tragedy heightened her concerns for her son Eric, who has high-functioning autism, an invisible disability that can complicate interactions with law enforcement.

Eric's idea to create logos for people with invisible disabilities—autism, mental health concerns, and hearing impairments—was born from a deep desire to ensure safety and understanding for individuals like himself. These logos, intended to be placed on items like driver's licenses and college IDs, serve as a critical tool for communication and recognition, aiming to protect those whose disabilities aren't immediately apparent.

Watching them on "The View," I was moved by their courage and entrepreneurial spirit. Their appearance on the show highlighted the importance of "Eric's ID Law" and showcased how individuals can turn personal challenges into powerful, positive change. Their story is a beautiful example of how a problem can be addressed with innovative solutions, and how these solutions can lead to broader societal benefits.

"Eric's Law: A Beacon for the Invisible" was inspired by their journey and the impactful message they shared. It reflects personal struggle and entrepreneurial drive, illustrating how love and determination can lead to significant legislative and social advancements. Watching Eric and Linda on "The View" reinforced my belief in the power of storytelling and advocacy, and how one family's efforts can inspire and protect many others.

This poem honors their initiative, celebrates their efforts, and raises awareness about recognizing and supporting individuals with invisible disabilities. It is a reminder that through empathy, innovation, and legislation, we can create a more inclusive and understanding world.

Introduction

The following heartfelt poems are written in both English and Spanish, including "On This Rainy Day / En Este Día Lluvioso" and "My Beloved Fufu / Mi Amado Fufu." These verses capture the deep love and profound loss of my cherished dog, Fufu, commemorating a significant and sorrowful day. Writing in both languages' honors not only my personal emotions but also the cultural connections shared with family and friends who also loved Fufu dearly. While earlier chapters incorporate Spanish through significant loves like Nico and Rafa, this collection blends both languages to create a bilingual tribute that bridges hearts and honors Fufu's enduring spirit. Join me on this emotional journey of love, loss, and everlasting bonds expressed beautifully in English and Spanish.

Introducción

On This Rainy Day / En Este Día Lluvioso" y "My Beloved Fufu / Mi Amado Fufu." Estos versos capturan el profundo amor y la pérdida significativa de mi querido perro, Fufu, conmemorando un día tan importante y triste. Escribir en ambos idiomas honra no solo mis emociones personales, sino también las conexiones culturales compartidas con familiares y amigos que también amaban profundamente a Fufu. Aunque capítulos anteriores incorporan el español a través de amores significativos como Nico y Rafa, esta colección mezcla ambos idiomas para crear un homenaje bilingüe que une corazones y honra el espíritu perdurable de Fufu. Acompáñenme en este viaje emocional de amor, pérdida y lazos eternos, expresado de manera hermosa en inglés y español.

On This Rainy Day

On this rainy day, I returned home,
from a journey long, yet swift as foam,
to see my loved ones, eager and bright,
especially Fufu, my heart's delight.

Seizures seized him, two days long,
we'd planned to take him, where he'd belong.
But his last breath, I watched him take,
his soul departing, my heart did break.

His tongue turned blue, his eyes so wide,
a window where his spirit sighed.
His lifeless form, so quickly cold,
a sight too painful to behold.

Nico washed him, wrapped him tight,
closed his eyes, we wept all night.
By morning's light, with tears still wet,
to El Cielo de las Mascotas, we went.

They gave us his paw print, set in stone,
his ashes in a box, beautifully known.
A picture space to keep him near,
a memento of our love, so dear.

At home, Nico arranged with care,
Bougainvillea blooms, vibrant and rare.
The paw print, portrait, ashes, and chain,
symbols of love in a flowered frame.

On this rainy day, my heart feels deep,
in pain for a love, eternal and sweet.
I've never arranged for a dog's farewell,
never felt a loss that words can't tell.

Fufu's eyes, so soulful and kind,
his puppy smile, etched in my mind.
His human-like cuddles, his constant cheer,
brought warmth and joy, year after year.

Seizures took him, month by month,
each day a battle, a daunting front.
Yet after each storm, he loved so hard,
his spirit shining, a true regard.

I love you, Fufito, now and always,
the rain mirrors my sorrowful days.
Trying to find light through friends and kin,
but questions linger deep within.

Why my Fufito, so young and pure?
Why must I endure this, why endure?
Yet in my heart, your love will stay,
forever cherished, come what may.

Inspiration Behind "On This Rainy Day"
Emotion: Grief and Remembrance

"On This Rainy Day" stems from grief that came in overwhelming waves after the sudden loss of my beloved dog, Fufu. Returning home from a trip to San Diego, I walked into my house only to witness Fufu enduring a severe seizure that led to his passing right before my eyes. The trauma of seeing his life leave him, his body stiffening, and his eyes remaining wide open, has left an indelible mark on my heart.

Grief is a complex and multifaceted emotion that can come in waves, crashing over us when we least expect it. I have spoken about grief in various forms before, but in grieving the loss of a pet for the first time, I found myself at a loss for how to navigate this new and intense sorrow. One month after Fufu passed, I could mostly block out the pain, but there were moments when the floodgates would open. When I thought of him, I was in tears. When home alone, I was in tears. Walking paths we once walked together burdened me with sadness. All I could do was ask, "Why?" It made no sense. He was so innocent, so young, so happy, and brought so much love into our lives.

I wished I could give him another kiss and tell him it would be okay. I wished I had never gone to San Diego so I could have been home with him in his final moments.

Grieving a pet can feel different from grieving a human, but the pain is just as real and profound. The stages of grief—denial, anger, bargaining, depression, and acceptance—apply to both kinds of loss, yet the experience is uniquely personal. For me, denial came in the form of disbelief that such a vibrant life could be extinguished so suddenly. Anger surged as I questioned why it had to happen to Fufu, someone so full of love and joy. Bargaining took the shape of wishing I had been there for him, hoping that my presence could have made a difference. Depression settled in as I walked through our shared spaces, feeling his absence acutely. Acceptance is a distant goal, one that feels out of reach as I continue to grapple with his loss.

Coping with grief requires time and patience. We must allow ourselves to feel the pain rather than suppress it. Finding ways to honor and remember Fufu, like creating a memorial with his ashes and mementos, helped keep his memory alive. Talking to loved ones and sharing stories about Fufu also provided comfort. Seeking support from others who experienced similar losses was invaluable to gaining empathy and understanding.

For those navigating their grief, know that it's okay to feel lost and overwhelmed. Each person's journey through grief is unique, and there is no right or wrong way to cope. Be gentle with yourself and allow the healing process to unfold naturally. In time, the waves of grief may become less frequent and less intense, but the love and memories will always remain.

When offering comfort to someone else, be present and listen without judgment. Sometimes, just being there and acknowledging their pain can provide immense relief. Encourage them to express their feelings and reassure them that it's okay to grieve. Sharing your own experiences with grief, if appropriate, can also help them feel less alone.

Grief is a testament to the love we have for those we've lost, whether they are human or fur babies. It reminds us of the deep bonds we form and their impact on our lives. Finding ways to honor that love and cherish those memories can help us navigate the grief journey with compassion and resilience.

Fufu was born on September 23, 2019, and passed away on July 1, 2024 at 1:25 am. He weighed 19.7 kilos. Your love and memory will always live on in my heart, Fufu, my Fufito, my love, my big baby who didn't know he was too big to throw his weight on me and too big to carelessly walk with his booty knocking things down as he went.

En Este Día Lluvioso

En este día lluvioso, volví a casa,
De un viaje largo, tan fugaz como brasa.
Para ver a mis seres queridos, ansiosos y brillantes,
Especialmente a Fufu, mi deleite constante.

Convulsiones lo tomaron, dos días sin cesar,
Planeábamos llevarlo, a donde debía estar.
Pero su último aliento, vi tomar,
Su alma partiendo, mi corazón quebrar.

Su lengua azul, sus ojos tan abiertos,
Una ventana donde suspiraba su espíritu.
Su forma inerte, tan rápidamente fría,
Una visión demasiado dolorosa, en mi vida.

Nico lo lavó, lo envolvió con ternura,
Cerró sus ojos, lloramos con amargura.
Con la luz de la mañana, lágrimas aún frescas,
A El Cielo de las Mascotas, fuimos en sendas.

Nos dieron su huella, grabada en piedra,

Sus cenizas en una caja, de belleza eterna.
Un espacio para su foto, para tenerlo cerca,
Un recuerdo de nuestro amor, tan tierna.

En casa, Nico arregló con esmero,
Flores de bugambilia, vibrantes y sinceras.
La huella, el retrato, las cenizas, la cadena,
Símbolos de amor, en un marco con pena.

En este día lluvioso, mi corazón siente hondo,
El dolor por un amor, eterno y redondo.
Nunca había despedido a un perro así,
Nunca había sentido una pérdida que palabras no describí.

Los ojos de Fufu, tan llenos de alma y bondad,
Su sonrisa de cachorro, grabada en mi eternidad.
Sus abrazos humanos, su constante alegría,
Trajeron calor y gozo, día tras día.

Las convulsiones lo tomaron, mes tras mes,
Cada día una batalla, una dura vez.
Pero tras cada tormenta, amaba con fervor,
Su espíritu brillando, un verdadero ardor.

Te amo, Fufito, ahora y siempre,
La lluvia refleja mis días dolientes.
Tratando de hallar luz en amigos y familia,
Pero las preguntas persisten, una vigilia.

¿Por qué mi Fufito, tan joven y puro?
¿Por qué debo soportar esto, por qué lo aseguro?
Sin embargo, en mi corazón, tu amor se quedará,
Siempre apreciado, pase lo que pase, ahí estará.

Inspiración Detrás de "En Este Día Lluvioso"
Emoción: Duelo y Recuerdo

"En Este Día Lluvioso" surge del duelo que me invadió
en olas abrumadoras tras la pérdida repentina de mi
amado perro, Fufu. Al regresar de un viaje a San Diego,

llegué a casa solo para presenciar a Fufu sufriendo una grave convulsión que lo llevó a su fallecimiento justo delante de mis ojos. El trauma de ver cómo su vida se iba, su cuerpo endureciéndose y sus ojos permaneciendo abiertos, ha dejado una marca imborrable en mi corazón.

El duelo es una emoción compleja y multifacética que puede llegar como olas, golpeándonos cuando menos lo esperamos. He hablado sobre el duelo en diversas formas antes, pero al llorar la pérdida de una mascota por primera vez, me encontré sin saber cómo navegar este nuevo y profundo dolor. Un mes después de que Fufu falleciera, podía en su mayoría bloquear el dolor, pero había momentos en que las puertas se abrían de par en par. Cuando pensaba en él, lloraba. Cuando estaba solo en casa, lloraba. Caminando por los mismos senderos que recorríamos juntos, me invadía la tristeza. Todo lo que podía hacer era preguntar, "¿Por qué?" No tenía sentido. Era tan inocente, tan joven, tan feliz, y trajo tanto amor a nuestras vidas. Deseaba poder darle otro beso y decirle que todo estaría bien. Deseaba no haber ido a San Diego para haber estado en casa con él en sus últimos momentos.

Llorar la pérdida de una mascota puede sentirse diferente de llorar la pérdida de un ser humano, pero el dolor es igual de real y profundo. Las etapas del duelo—negación, ira, negociación, depresión y aceptación—se aplican a ambos tipos de pérdida, pero la experiencia es única para cada persona. Para mí, la negación se presentó en forma de incredulidad de que una vida tan vibrante pudiera extinguirse tan repentinamente. La ira surgió al cuestionar por qué tuvo que pasarle a Fufu, alguien tan lleno de amor y alegría. La negociación tomó la forma de desear haber estado ahí para él, esperando que mi presencia hubiera hecho una diferencia. La depresión se instaló al caminar por los espacios que compartimos, sintiendo su ausencia de manera aguda. La aceptación es una meta distante, una que parece fuera de alcance mientras sigo lidiando con su pérdida.

Afrontar el duelo requiere tiempo y paciencia. Debemos permitirnos sentir el dolor en lugar de suprimirlo. Encontrar formas de honrar y recordar a Fufu, como crear un memorial con sus cenizas y recuerdos, ayudó a mantener viva su memoria. Hablar con seres queridos y compartir historias sobre Fufu también me brindó consuelo. Buscar apoyo de otros que han experimentado pérdidas similares fue invaluable para ganar empatía y comprensión.

Para aquellos que están navegando por su duelo, sepan que está bien sentirse perdidos y abrumados. El viaje de cada persona a través del duelo es único, y no hay una manera correcta o incorrecta de afrontarlo. Sé amable contigo mismo y permite que el proceso de sanación se desarrolle de manera natural. Con el tiempo, las olas del duelo pueden volverse menos frecuentes y menos intensas, pero el amor y los recuerdos siempre permanecerán.

Cuando ofrezcas consuelo a otra persona, está presente y escucha sin juzgar. A veces, solo estar allí y reconocer su dolor puede proporcionar un inmenso alivio. Anímales a expresar sus sentimientos y asegúrales que está bien llorar. Compartir tus propias experiencias con el duelo, si es apropiado, también puede ayudarles a sentirse menos solos.

El duelo es un testimonio del amor que sentimos por aquellos que hemos perdido, ya sean humanos o mascotas. Nos recuerda los lazos profundos que formamos y su impacto en nuestras vidas. Encontrar formas de honrar ese amor y atesorar esos recuerdos puede ayudarnos a navegar el viaje del duelo con compasión y resiliencia.

Fufu nació el 23 de septiembre de 2019 y falleció el 1 de julio de 2024 a la 1:25 am. Pesaba 19.7 kilos. Tu amor y tu recuerdo siempre vivirán en mi corazón, Fufu, mi Fufito, mi amor, mi bebé grandote que no sabía que era demasiado grande para lanzarse sobre mí ni para caminar despreocupado con su trasero tirando cosas al pasar.

My Beloved Fufu / Mi Amado Fufu

Life goes on, but I'm trapped in your memory,
La vida sigue, pero yo, atrapado en tu recuerdo,

Of those playful moments on my chest, your eternal story.
De aquellos juegos en mi pecho, tus momentos eternos.

Tell me, Fufu, how to go on without your canine laughter?
Dime, Fufu, ¿cómo seguir sin tu risa canina?

Tell me, my dear dog, how to start a new chapter?
Dime, mi querido perro, ¿cómo empezar una nueva rutina?

How to create adventures without you, my Fufito, my Chubby?
¿Cómo crear aventuras sin ti, mi Fufito, mi Gordito?

Where are the dreams and laughs without your lovely?
¿Dónde están los sueños, las risas, sin tu amorcito?

To dream and continue, without your boundless energy,
Soñar y continuar, sin tu energía inagotable,

Feels impossible, like a story with no happy ending.
Se siente imposible, como un cuento sin final feliz.

Walking will be a challenge, without your playful pauses,
Salir a caminar será un reto, sin tus pausas juguetonas,

Waiting behind, running to me, with back rubs in doses.
Esperarte detrás, correr hacia mí, con caricias en las zonas.

How to go on without you, my loyal and dear friend?
¿Cómo seguir sin ti, mi amigo leal y querido?

Seeing life without your shine, my Fufito, is hard to comprehend.
Ver la vida sin tu brillo, mi Fufito, es un gran descuido.

You took a part of me, my faithful dog,
Te llevaste una parte de mí, mi perro fiel,

With your big paws, thinking you were small, what a log!
Con tus patitas grandes, creyéndote pequeño, ¡qué nivel!

I'll always remember your moments of madness,
Recordaré siempre tus momentos de locura,

My unique friend, your antics pure and gladness.
Mi único amigo, tus travesuras siempre puras.

Who will accompany me in loneliness, who will bother
Max,
¿Quién me acompañará en soledad, quién molestará a Max,

Play with Dula, fill the void with your relaxed acts?
Jugará con Dula, llenará el vacío con tus actos lax?

Now that you're in such a wonderful place,
Ahora que estás en un lugar tan maravilloso,

Bon voyage, friend, keep being the beautiful face.
Buen viaje, amigo, sigue siendo el perrito hermoso.

Silly, intelligent, and loving, as only you can be,
Loquillo, inteligente y cariñoso, como solo tú puedes ser,

Bon voyage, my friend, in memory, you'll always be with
me.
Buen viaje, amigo mío, en mi memoria, seguiré mi querer.

Never stop being the charming dog,
No dejes de ser el perro encantador,

That lit up my life with pure love's fog.
Que iluminó mi vida con su puro amor.

Bon voyage, Fufu, I wish you peace and joy,
Buen viaje, Fufu, te deseo paz y alegría,

In the doggy heaven, remain my beloved boy.
En el cielo perruno, sigue siendo mi compañía.

I'll always remember your mischief and infinite love,
Siempre recordaré tus travesuras y tu amor infinito,

My beloved Fufu, my faithful friend, my blessing from above.
Mi amado Fufu, mi amigo fiel, mi amor bendito.

Inspiration Behind "My Beloved Fufu"
Inspiración Detrás de "Mi Amado Fufu"
Emotion: Grief and Remembrance
Emoción: Duelo y Recuerdo

This bilingual approach not only celebrates Fufu's life but also acknowledges
Este enfoque bilingüe no solo celebra la vida de Fufu, sino que también reconoce

the cultural and emotional richness of the relationship.
la riqueza cultural y emocional de la relación.

The inspiration behind this poem, "My Beloved Fufu,"
La inspiración detrás de este poema, "Mi Amado Fufu,"

stems from the profound bond and deep love shared between a pet owner and their cherished dog, Fufu.
proviene del profundo vínculo y amor compartido entre un dueño de mascota y su querido perro, Fufu.

It captures the essence of the sorrow and longing that follows the loss of a beloved companion,
Captura la esencia del dolor y la añoranza que sigue a la pérdida de un compañero amado,

who brought joy, comfort, and unconditional love into their life.
quien trajo alegría, consuelo y amor incondicional a su vida.

The poem seeks to honor Fufu's memory by reflecting on
the playful moments,
El poema busca honrar la memoria de Fufu al reflejar los
momentos de juego,

the affectionate gestures, and the unique personality traits
that made Fufu irreplaceable.
los gestos cariñosos y los rasgos de personalidad únicos que
hicieron a Fufu insustituible.

The alternating lines in English and Spanish serve to
bridge the emotions felt by the owner,
Las líneas alternas en inglés y español sirven para unir las
emociones sentidas por el dueño,

making the tribute accessible to both English and Spanish
readers.
haciendo que el tributo sea accesible tanto para lectores en inglés
como en español.

Through colorful, witty, and heartfelt verses, the poem
paints a vivid picture of Fufu's impact
A través de versos coloridos, ingeniosos y conmovedores, el
poema pinta una vívida imagen del impacto de Fufu

and the void left behind, conveying the universal theme of
love and loss in a personal and relatable way.
y el vacío dejado atrás, transmitiendo el tema universal del amor
y la pérdida de una manera personal y relatable.

Project 2025: A Witty Rhyme

In twenty-twenty-five, a plan contrived,
with aims so grand, but goals deprive.
The "Unitary Executive Theory" stands tall,
to give the President power, to have it all.

HHS, renamed to "Life's Department,"
policies shifted, an ardent statement.
Medicaid now comes with strings,
Work to earn what health care brings.

Justice Department, under new guise,
restructured, repurposed, a strategic prize.
Single moms and same-sex vows,
condemned by policy, here and now.

Education Department meets its end,
schools no longer in government's trend.
"Sexual orientation" erased from speech,
"diversity, equity" just out of reach.

Career feds replaced with chosen few,
loyalists in charge, the old adieu.
Gender equality, rights to abort,
gone from laws, courts to court.

FDA's nod for mifepristone,
reversed, in a harsh tone.
Reproductive rights, cast away,
in Project 2025's bold play.

A coalition, a hundred strong,
grows in prep, won't take long,
for the next President, this plan to wield,
a future in flux, a nation revealed.

Inspiration Behind "Project 2025: A Witty Rhyme"
Emotion: Criticism and Concern

This poem was inspired by a comprehensive political plan proposed by conservative organizations to drastically reshape the federal government and its policies. This plan, known as Project 2025, outlines several key elements to consolidate power within the executive branch and impose a specific ideological framework on various aspects of American governance and society. Below is an exploration of each element of the poem and the context of Project 2025:

Unitary Executive Theory: The plan seeks to expand presidential power, allowing the President to control the executive branch with minimal checks. This theory posits that all executive authority should be centralized under the President, potentially undermining the balance of power and checks and balances fundamental to the U.S. Constitution.

Renaming HHS: Project 2025 proposes renaming the Department of Health and Human Services (HHS) to the "Department of Life." This change likely emphasizes policies against abortion and focuses on traditional family structures, reflecting a shift towards more conservative social policies.

Medicaid Work Requirements: The plan includes adding work requirements for Medicaid recipients, potentially limiting access to healthcare for those unable to work. This could significantly impact low-income individuals and families who rely on Medicaid for essential health services.

Restructuring the DOJ: The Department of Justice (DOJ) would be restructured to align more closely with conservative values and objectives. This could involve changes in how laws are enforced and which cases are prioritized, affecting the administration of justice in the country.

Condemning Single Motherhood and Same-Sex Marriage: Policies under Project 2025 would discourage single-parent families and same-sex marriages. This reflects a return to more traditional family values and a rejection of the progress made in recent years toward inclusivity and acceptance of diverse family structures.

Dismantling the Department of Education: The federal role in education would be minimized or eliminated, potentially shifting more control to state and local governments. This could result in significant changes in how education is funded and administered, with wide-ranging effects on students and educators.

Eliminating Terms and Concepts: Words and concepts such as "sexual orientation," "diversity, equity, and inclusion," "gender equality," and "abortion rights" would be removed from federal language and regulations. This could lead to a rollback of protections and advancements made in civil rights and social justice.

Reversing FDA Approval of Mifepristone: The FDA's approval of the abortion pill mifepristone would be overturned, reducing access to abortion services. This reflects a broader effort to restrict reproductive rights and limit women's access to healthcare.

Replacing Federal Employees: Career federal employees would be replaced with loyalists chosen for their alignment with the administration's views. This could undermine the neutrality and professionalism of the federal workforce, leading to a more politicized and less independent civil service.

Project 2025's Growing Support: The plan has garnered support from numerous conservative organizations, preparing for the next presidential administration to implement these sweeping changes. This coordinated effort underscores the significance and potential impact of Project 2025 on American governance and society.

A Plea to the Public: It is crucial to understand the importance of the upcoming election and what the authors and the Trump administration plan to do with Project 2025 starting day one in office. It is imperative for the public to read, understand, and actively engage with the implications of these proposed changes. The plan represents a fundamental shift in the direction of the country, affecting everything from healthcare and education to civil rights and the balance of power within the government.

This poem serves as both an educational and a cautionary piece, highlighting the far-reaching consequences of the proposed policies. By understanding the details and potential impacts of Project 2025, citizens can make informed decisions and participate in the democratic process to shape the future of our nation.

Ode to a Trailblazing Vice President

In the annals of history, her name stands tall,
Kamala Harris, a beacon for us all.
First woman, first Black, first South Asian descent,
her presence in the White House, a landmark event.

Through pandemic shadows, she led with might,
championing vaccines, turning wrongs to right.
Economic revival in her hands she held,
with the American Rescue Plan, despair dispelled.

Bridges and roads, the lifeblood she restores,
the Bipartisan Law, modernizing our shores.
Jobs she creates, infrastructure renewed,
her efforts in steel and broadband construed.

For the sacred right to vote, she stands,
combating suppression with determined hands.
Legislative battles, she fiercely fights,
to safeguard our democracy, our voting rights.

In lands afar, where roots of migration lie,
she seeks to heal, with a diplomat's eye.
Economic growth, corruption's fall,
in Central America, she answers the call.

Justice reformed, through her guiding light,
reducing cells, promoting what's right.
Systemic inequities, she aims to sever,
rehabilitation and fairness, her endeavor.

Climate change warriors, she joins in force,
clean energy paths, she charts the course.
Carbon reduction, environmental justice she seeks,
in vulnerable communities, her voice speaks.

Gender equality, her banner high,
Paycheck fairness, rights that amplify.
Against violence, she stands, for choice, she fights,
Reproductive freedoms, she ignites.

A vice presidency marked by milestones grand,
A testament to progress in this land.
Advocate, diplomat, leader in strife,
Kamala Harris, a dynamic life.

Her work embodies the administration's will,
Every challenge faced with determined skill.
Equity and justice in every stride,
For a better nation, with her as guide.

Inspiration Behind "Ode to a Trailblazing Vice President"
Emotion: Admiration and Inspiration

This poem stems from a deep frustration with the pervasive misinformation and ignorance surrounding Vice President Kamala Harris's record. I am tired of hearing the constant refrain from media outlets and individuals claiming, "What did she do?" or "She has been quiet." This poem is a clarion call to educate readers and the American public about Kamala Harris's active and impactful tenure.

We live in an era where the media is obsessed with covering every trivial detail of certain controversial figures, particularly Donald Trump. Every action, every word, every moment is dissected, leaving little room for substantive discussion about the important work being done by others. As a result, many people remain unaware of the significant contributions Kamala Harris has made.

Her time as Vice President has been as successful, if not more so, than her predecessors. From leading the charge on the COVID-19 pandemic response and economic recovery to advocating for voting rights and addressing climate change, Kamala Harris has been a dynamic and influential figure in the administration.

This poem serves as a reminder and a challenge to everyone: get informed and stop parroting misinformation or ignorant, disengaged opinions. If you haven't followed Vice President Harris' work, admit it and take the time to educate yourself. Saying she has done nothing is not only absurd but also a gross misrepresentation of her efforts and achievements. I hope this poem, along with a detailed outline of her key accomplishments, will enlighten readers and correct the narrative, highlighting the substantial and commendable work Vice President Kamala Harris has accomplished during her tenure.

Key Areas of Focus and Accomplishments:

1. **COVID-19 Pandemic Response:**
   Harris actively promoted the administration's COVID-19 response, including vaccination efforts and public health initiatives. She traveled extensively to advocate for vaccine uptake and address pandemic-related challenges.

2. **Economic Recovery:**
   Harris supported efforts to bolster the economy, including advocating for the American Rescue Plan, which provided economic relief to individuals, families, and businesses affected by the pandemic.

3. **Infrastructure and Jobs:**
   She the Bipartisan Infrastructure Law, emphasizing investments in transportation, broadband, clean water, and resilience. Her focus included creating jobs and modernizing infrastructure.

4. **Voting Rights:**
   Harris is a vocal advocate for protecting and expanding voting rights. She worked to highlight the importance of combating voter suppression and supporting federal legislation to ensure fair access to the ballot.

5. **Immigration:**
She was tasked with addressing the root causes of migration from Central America. Her efforts included diplomatic engagement and promoting economic development and anti-corruption measures in the region.

6. **Criminal Justice Reform:**
Harris continued her long-standing advocacy for criminal justice reform, supporting initiatives to reduce incarceration rates, promote rehabilitation, and address systemic inequalities in the justice system.

7. **Climate Change:**
Harris supported the administration's climate agenda, advocating for clean energy initiatives, reducing carbon emissions, and addressing environmental justice issues affecting vulnerable communities.

8. **Women's Rights and Gender Equality:**
She championed issues related to gender equality, including supporting the Paycheck Fairness Act and advocating for policies to address gender-based violence and support reproductive rights.

Defining Characteristics of Kamala Harris's Vice Presidency:

1. **Historic Milestones:**
As the first woman, the first Black person, and the first person of South Asian descent to hold the office, Harris's vice presidency is historically significant and symbolizes progress and representation.

2. **Advocacy and Diplomacy:**
Harris is a key advocate for the administration's policies domestically and has represented the

U.S. on the international stage, engaging in diplomatic efforts to strengthen alliances and address global challenges.

3. **Focus on Equity and Inclusion:**
   Throughout her tenure, Harris emphasized the importance of equity and inclusion, advocating for policies addressing systemic inequalities and uplifting marginalized communities.

4. **Collaboration and Leadership:**
   Harris worked closely with President Joe Biden, providing counsel and supporting his agenda while taking on specific leadership roles in areas like voting rights, immigration, and small business support.

Kamala Harris's vice presidency is defined by her trailblazing role, her advocacy for key policy areas, and her efforts to address immediate crises and long-term structural issues. Her tenure is marked by a commitment to equity, justice, and effective governance.

Ballots of Honor: A Civic Hymn

Every ballot cast, a reverent hymn,
echoes of a power both vast and grim.
A duty borne from battles fought,
for every voice that freedom sought.

From the caucus fires to November's test,
each vote a stitch in democracy's vest.
Not merely a right, but a sacred call,
for the one, the many, encompassing all.

Remember the marches, the struggle, the tears,
women and warriors, through arduous years.
Voting, a tribute to those who dared
to demand the vote, and never despaired.

In local alleys, in grand halls amassed,
our choices ripple through futures vast.
From school board benches to the president's seat,
each decision shapes the world we'll meet.

Let facts be your guide, your compass, your map,
in a sea of discourse, a potential trap.
Seek truth in the clutter, find light in the dim,
an informed electorate—democracy's limb.

Across this nation, let unity bloom,
from bustling cities to quiet rooms.
Vote not just for self, but for community's weave,
for the tapestry of America that we believe.

So wield this power with solemn pride,
from sea-washed shores to mountainside.
In every act of voting, let it be said,
"Here lies the heart of the republic," widespread.

Arise, engage in this civic scene,
for your vote can chase what might have been.
Cast it with foresight, cast it with care,

in the hallowed halls of the free and the fair.

For progress, for change, take this to heart,
every election is a fresh start.
Vote for tomorrow, vote for today,
in each sacred ballot, the people's sway.

Inspiration Behind "Ballots of Honor: A Civic Hymn"
Emotion: Inspiration and Reverence

"Ballots of Honor: A Civic Hymn" is inspired by the deep history and personal relevance of voting as a foundational act of democracy, particularly through the lens of my identity as a Black, gay male. This poem is a culmination of reflection on the immense struggles and sacrifices made to secure voting rights for all, especially for those within my community.

The historical gravity of being Black in America, where my ancestors were enslaved and stripped of any rights, amplifies the significance of each vote I cast. The long and painful journey toward civil rights, marked by bloodshed, protests, and relentless advocacy, underscores the fact that voting is not merely a right but a hard-won privilege. Similarly, as a gay man, I stand on the shoulders of those who fought for visibility and equality, often in the face of overwhelming hostility.

This poem also emerges from a period of intense national turmoil, where the very fabric of democracy seems threatened by misinformation, the rise of extremist ideologies, and the erosion of factual discourse. Witnessing the distortion of truths and the spread of disinformation, especially through unregulated social media platforms, reinforces my resolve to advocate for a well-informed electorate.

Understanding the interplay of local, state, and federal governments—how policies shaped at every level affect us directly—compels me to participate actively in every election. We must re-engage with the basics of civics to appreciate the interconnected roles of the legislative, executive, and judicial branches.

This poem is a call to action, born from a combination of historical consciousness, personal identity, and the urgent need to protect the integrity of our democratic processes. It is a reminder to honor the past struggles by participating in the present, ensuring our voices contribute to a fair and equitable future. Voting, in every election, is a reaffirmation of our commitment to democracy—a duty that is both personal and universal, embodying our hopes for a society that values and uplifts every individual.

Evolving Truths: The Kamala Series

Let the Record Reflect

Let the record reflect, it's time to get wise.
Californians and Black folks, open your eyes.
White Republicans spin a deceitful tale,
about Kamala Harris, but truth will prevail.

They say she locked us up, painted her mean,
but let's break down the stats, understand what they glean.
Conviction rates rose, yes, fifty-two to sixty-seven,
but focused on violent crimes, not a prisoner's heaven.

Back on Track for first offenders, mainly our kin,
education, jobs over jail, a new life to begin.
1,900 marijuana cases, but no jail spree,
records wiped clean, a chance to stay free.

Prison overcrowding, she tackled head-on,
released 33,000, many Black, now gone.
Wrongful convictions? She stepped in with might,
correcting the system, ensuring what's right.

Her record as AG was about reform,
bail reform, ending private prisons, new norms.
Don't let them fool you, don't be misled,
get educated on facts, not lies you're fed.

So stop being fooled, don't be swayed
by narratives spun to keep us afraid.
Hear but verify, get the stats straight,
Kamala's work was to reform, not incarcerate.

Context

In the halls where justice weighs,
Kamala stands, amidst the fray.
With each decision, she learns and sways,

evolving truths to light the way.

Marijuana Prosecutions:
Laws once harsh, ensnaring souls,
yet she listened, changed her goals.
Supported freedom, cleaned the scrolls,
expunging pasts, she made them whole.

Death Penalty Stance:
No death's hand, she firmly stood,
even when the cries for blood.
Progressive views misunderstood,
she chose reform, where few would.

Cash Bail System:
Once supported, then she saw,
the impact harsh on those in thrall.
She changed, she fought, she altered law,
for justice fair, for one and all.

Prison Labor Controversy:
Critics spoke of labor's use,
yet Kamala, hearing the abuse,
stood apart, expressed her views,
for humane paths, she did choose.

Withholding Exculpatory Evidence:
Mistakes were made, the critics cried,
yet she turned, with honor tried.
Policies new, she rectified,
truth and justice, amplified.

"Back on Track" Initiative:
In her vision, second chances,
paths of light where hope advances.
Education, work, life's new dances,
a future built on firm stances.

Anti-Truancy Policy:
With intent to mend school days,
she faced backlash, many ways.

Yet, she heard, refined her gaze,
learning, growing through the haze.

Facts Matter, Narratives Are Dangerous

Before you lean in so hard, my friends,
pause, and hear this plea:
Truth, beyond the echo's bend,
calls for clarity.

Kamala's record, complex and broad,
not just a tale of woe.
From prosecutor's esteemed nod
to Senate's steady glow.

1,560 souls for weed,
state prison saw them go,
yet some now tout her pro-pot creed,
the contradictions show.

She opposed the deathly noose,
yet faced a harsh retort,
for when a cop was slain, no truce,
law enforcement's last resort.

She fought the bail that kept the poor
locked in cells of sham.
Yet cash bail stayed a rugged door,
her stance ignites the flame.

Lab tech scandal, drug cases— **1,000** tossed,
her office held the blame.
Withholding truth, lives were lost,
her leadership's marked with shame.

"Back on Track" was a beacon bright,
for first-time non-violent men.
Education, work—a hopeful light,
rehabilitation's pen.

Prison labor, a dark chapter told,
non-violent inmates stayed,
arguments that seemed too cold,
against the light, she swayed.

Anti-truancy's heavy hand
fell hard on parents' plea.
Low-income, minorities stand,
injustice plain to see.

Friends, within our Black community,
and all who heed this call,
consider facts, in unity,
and truth before the fall.

Kamala's tale is not all bleak,
nor simply pure and bright.
In complexity, we must seek,
the shadows and the light.

So, as you lean, remember well,
the depth of truth we crave.
Beyond the simple narrative's spell,
let wisdom be your wave.

Inspiration Behind the Series "Evolving Truths: The Kamala Series"
Emotion: Advocacy and Determination

The inspiration for **"Let the Record Reflect"**, **"Context"**, **and "Facts Matter, Narratives Are Dangerous"** comes from my deep frustration with the widespread misinformation and oversimplified narratives surrounding Kamala Harris's record as District Attorney of San Francisco and Attorney General of California. As someone who has been a strong supporter of Harris, especially as she campaigns for the 2024 presidency, I felt a responsibility to address these misconceptions and present the truth through poetry, providing a nuanced, fact-based perspective on her career.

I wanted these poems to explore the balance in her record between her tough-on-crime policies and her commitment to progressive reforms. Through these poems, I aim to educate readers and challenge them to engage critically with Harris's contributions, understanding the complex realities of her decisions rather than accepting reductive critiques.

Conviction Rates

- *Fact:*
  Kamala Harris raised the conviction rate in San Francisco from 52% to 67% during her tenure as District Attorney.

- *Context:*
  This figure is often cited to paint Harris as overly punitive, but it fails to account for her specific focus on serious and violent crimes. She achieved an 87% conviction rate for homicides and a 90% conviction rate for felony gun violations, underscoring her commitment to tackling the most dangerous offenses.

Back on Track Program

- *Fact:*
  Harris launched the Back on Track program, which provided first-time, non-violent offenders with alternatives to incarceration, such as education, job training, and community service.

- *Context:*
  This initiative primarily benefited Black and minority communities by offering rehabilitation rather than punishment, setting offenders on a path

to avoid future crime. Yet, this program is often overshadowed in discussions about her criminal justice record.

Prison Overcrowding

- *Fact:*
  As Attorney General, Harris's office oversaw the release of 33,000 inmates to address California's prison overcrowding crisis, as mandated by a Supreme Court ruling.

- *Context:*
  Though critics focus on her role in the release, many of these individuals were non-violent offenders, and the decision was necessary to comply with the court order and improve inhumane prison conditions. This move significantly reduced California's prison population, a victory for criminal justice reform.

Marijuana Prosecutions

- *Fact:*
  Harris has faced criticism for prosecuting marijuana-related offenses during her time as Attorney General, with over 1,500 people incarcerated for such offenses.

- *Context:*
  While this fact is often used to criticize her, it reflects the broader policies of the state at that time. Harris later advocated for marijuana legalization and the expungement of non-violent marijuana convictions, showing her evolution on the issue.

Death Penalty Stance

- *Fact:*
  Harris consistently opposed the death penalty, even in high-profile cases, such as the murder of a police officer.

- *Context:*
  Her opposition to the death penalty was seen as controversial, especially among law enforcement, but it aligned with her progressive vision for criminal justice reform and a more humane legal system.

Anti-Truancy Policy

- *Fact:*
  Harris's anti-truancy policy aimed to reduce absenteeism by holding parents accountable, sometimes prosecuting them for their children's school attendance issues.

- *Context:*
  This policy was intended to combat systemic educational inequities but was criticized for being too punitive, especially toward low-income and minority families. Harris's goal was to address root causes of truancy, though the execution of the policy had unintended consequences.

Police Misconduct and Brady Policy

- *Fact:*
  Harris's office was criticized for not implementing a policy requiring the disclosure of police misconduct, resulting in over 1,000 drug cases being dismissed.

- *Context:*
  While this criticism is valid, it highlights the
  systemic challenges within her office. Harris later
  implemented a "Brady policy" to ensure the
  disclosure of such misconduct, showing her
  responsiveness to issues brought to light during
  her tenure.

Evolving Toward Progressive Reforms

In **"Context"**, I wanted to delve deeper into Harris's
growth and evolution as a policymaker. The poem reflects
how she grew to support progressive reforms like
marijuana legalization and bail reform, even though her
earlier record, such as the 1,560 marijuana-related
incarcerations under her tenure as Attorney General, is
often weaponized against her. This shift is not a
contradiction but a sign of her willingness to adapt and
embrace more humane policies as societal norms and
understandings of justice evolved.

Her stance on the death penalty also exemplifies her
moral conviction. Despite public and law enforcement
pressure, she consistently opposed the death penalty, even
in high-profile cases, underscoring her commitment to
progressive criminal justice reform.

In **"Facts Matter, Narratives Are Dangerous"**, I wanted
to explore the importance of critically evaluating Harris's
record. For example, while her anti-truancy policies were
controversial, they were part of a larger strategy to reduce
educational inequities by targeting chronic absenteeism in
schools. However, as is often the case in complex policy
matters, there were unintended consequences that
disproportionately affected low-income and minority
families. These nuances are often lost in the broader public
conversation.

Combatting Dangerous Narratives

Throughout **"Facts Matter, Narratives Are Dangerous"**, I stress the importance of critically evaluating Kamala Harris's record, highlighting how nuanced her career truly is. For example, while she was criticized for not immediately implementing a policy to disclose police misconduct, which led to over 1,000 drug cases being dismissed, Harris eventually took steps to address this issue by instituting a "Brady policy" that required such disclosures.

The Bigger Picture

The poems are inspired by my desire to correct the false or oversimplified portrayals of Kamala Harris. Her career is marked by significant achievements in criminal justice reform and progressive policies, but also some controversial decisions. While the negative aspects of her record should not be ignored, they are often exaggerated or taken out of context. By examining the facts and understanding the full story, we can appreciate the breadth of her contributions and the positive changes she has championed.

The inspiration for **"Let the Record Reflect," "Context,"** and **"Facts Matter, Narratives Are Dangerous"** is rooted in my advocacy for a fair and balanced evaluation of Harris's legacy. These poems are a call to critically engage with the facts and reject dangerous narratives that distort her achievements. By providing a full, nuanced account of her record, these poems aim to inspire more thoughtful discussions around Harris's contributions to justice and reform.

I'm Exhausted

From the heights of the White House,
to the lows of a rally's shout,
Biden's caught the COVID bug,
while Trump dodges a bullet's slug.

Rhetoric flies from left to right,
words turned weapons in the night.
Fingers pointing, blame's hot breath,
a nation teeters close to death.

Pandemic woes and scandal's flair,
political strife in the summer air,
exhausted hearts and weary minds,
searching peace that no one finds.

Leaders stumble, chaos reigns,
public trust wears heavy chains.
In this circus, who's to lead?
When power fights, the people bleed.

Inspiration Behind "I'm Exhausted"
Emotion: Fatigue and Frustration

This poem emerged from a tremendous sense of fatigue and frustration with the current political climate in the United States. Tumultuous Events have added to growing instability and division. Observing these events unfold, I often feel exhausted and sometimes struggle to maintain hope.

Political turbulence as of this poem's creation

1. **President Biden's COVID-19 Diagnosis:** Biden's positive COVID-19 test reignited discussions about the pandemic and its management. Despite vaccinations and precautions, the virus continues to impact daily life and political discourse.

2. **Trump Rally Shooting:** The attack on Donald Trump at a political rally shocked the nation. Republicans seized on Biden's prior comments about putting Trump "in the bullseye" to argue that he incited the violence, despite a lack of evidence linking his words to the shooter's actions.
3. **Ongoing Divisions:** The political landscape is marked by extreme polarization. Both sides are quick to blame each other for any incident, exacerbating divisions and preventing constructive dialogue.
4. **Public Fatigue:** The continuous onslaught of political drama, public health crises, and social issues has left many Americans feeling drained and pessimistic about the future. The relentless pace of negative news and partisan conflict contributes to a widespread sense of burnout.

The constant barrage of political strife, health crises, and social unrest has left many feeling worn out and disillusioned. The constant turmoil and lack of progress can be demoralizing. The nation seems trapped in a cycle of blame and division, with little hope for resolution or unity. This poem is my attempt to articulate these feelings of exhaustion and to capture the chaotic state of the country. It reflects the overwhelm caused by the relentless turmoil and the struggle to find hope in the midst of it all. Writing this poem has been a way to process these feelings and attempt to find a semblance of clarity and expression amid the chaos. It's an effort to voice the collective weariness and the desire for a more stable and united future.

Senator Warren and the Fight for Union Rights

In the halls of power where shadows loom,
Senator Warren's voice breaks through the gloom.
With a heart of fire and a mind so keen,
she champions the cause of the unseen.

For decades, workers' voices have been drowned,
in states where right-to-work laws abound.
These laws, a shackle, a corporate delight,
stripping workers of their collective might.

From Massachusetts, she stands tall and bold,
a beacon of hope in stories untold.
Reintroducing the Nationwide Right to Unionize Act,
to counter the forces that have long attacked.

With Representative Sherman by her side,
they fight for a cause that cannot be denied.
The PRO Act, a promise, a beacon of light,
for every worker's struggle, their day and night.

Twenty-seven states, bound by these chains,
witness wages fall and workers' pains.
But Warren and Sherman call for a change,
to end this unjust, economic exchange.

"Republicans and their corporate kin,
have made it their mission, their battle to win.
To weaken unions, to silence the call,
of workers united, standing tall."

From Starbucks baristas to tech's silent servers,
this fight is for all, for the tireless workers.
"Right-to-work" laws, a deceptive name,
in truth, they play a sordid game.

A race to the bottom, a shadowy path,
where profits soar on the workers' wrath.
Warren's bill, a clarion, a shield,
for those who toil in every field.

Supported by unions, from coast to coast,
from steelworkers' strength to teachers' boast.
They stand with Warren, they stand with pride,
for the right to unionize, they will not be denied.

In solidarity, they raise their voice,
to fight for fairness, to make their choice.
For higher wages, for safer grounds,
for benefits and rights, their fight resounds.

Rebecca Dixon echoes history's cry,
against laws born from a past so wry.
Rooted in efforts to divide and control,
but today's movement has a unifying goal.

From past to present, the fight endures,
with Warren's leadership, a future ensures.
For every worker, in every state,
the right to unionize, a cause so great.

"AFGE supports this noble quest,
for workers' safety, health, and best.
AFSCME's Saunders, with a powerful call,
repeal these laws, dismantle them all."

In this moment, we witness a tide,
workers' voices, amplified and wide.
A Gallup poll, a hopeful sign,
71% in favor, a line to define.

For Starbucks, Amazon, Trader Joe's too,
Workers rise up, demand what's due.
The Worker Power Coalition stands,
24 million strong, in united hands.

Senator Warren, your courage inspires,
a future where workers achieve their desires.
With the Nationwide Right to Unionize Act,
you lead the charge, with a visionary pact.

In the Senate's halls, where futures are sealed,
your voice, a promise, a sword, a shield.
For every worker, in every land,
your fight, our fight, together we stand.

Inspiration Behind "Senator Warren and the Fight for Union Rights"
Emotion: Passion and Solidarity

"Senator Warren and the Fight for Union Rights" is inspired by the tireless efforts of Senator Elizabeth Warren and Representative Brad Sherman to reintroduce the Nationwide Right to Unionize Act. This legislation aims to counter the detrimental impact of "right-to-work" laws that have plagued workers in twenty-seven states, making it increasingly difficult for them to form unions and advocate for better wages and working conditions.

Senator Warren's dedication to workers' rights is not new. Her advocacy spans decades, consistently highlighting the importance of unions in ensuring fair treatment, adequate pay, and safe working environments for all. This poem is a tribute to her unwavering commitment to dismantling laws that favor corporate interests over the well-being of workers.

As the President of the CFTC, Chapter 337 of the National Treasury Employees Union (NTEU), I applaud Senator Warren's advocacy and work. I see the very real, everyday benefits and the critical need for unionization. Being part of a union has profoundly impacted my work environment, ensuring workplace fairness, equitable and progressive compensation, and accountability. Our union has been a powerful vehicle for advocacy and support, allowing us to stand together and fight for the rights and interests of our membership.

The Nationwide Right to Unionize Act, which Warren and Sherman champion, seeks to eliminate the legal barriers that hinder union formation and diminish workers' collective bargaining power. The poem encapsulates their shared vision of a future where every worker can exercise their right to unionize and fight for equitable labor standards regardless of their state of residence.

The inspiration also stems from the broader labor movement, which has seen significant momentum in recent years. From baristas at Starbucks to tech workers in Silicon Valley, employees across various industries are uniting to demand their rights. The poem reflects this growing solidarity and the collective power of workers who refuse to be silenced by oppressive laws.

Moreover, the support from various unions and advocacy groups underscores the widespread recognition of the need for this legislation. Organizations like AFGE, AFL-CIO, SEIU, and others have voiced their backing, reinforcing the importance of the Nationwide Right to Unionize Act in leveling the playing field for all workers.

The poem is not just a reflection of political advocacy but also a call to action. It celebrates the resilience and determination of workers and their allies, emphasizing that the fight for workers' rights is far from over. Senator Warren's leadership in this area represents hope and inspires all who believe in the power of collective action to bring about meaningful change.

6,000 Moments: The Heart of Daytime TV

In the studio's glow, where stories unfold,
a journey of seasons, in memories told,
from the very first episode's fresh delight,
to today's celebration, 6,000 in sight.

Each season a tapestry, vibrant and vast,
moments of joy, heartaches that passed,
transitions of voices, faces we knew,
Each co-host a beacon, tried and true.

Year one, a spark, new voices found,
Conversations deep, where laughter's sound,
echoed in homes, a comforting balm,
in the storm of life, a steady calm.

Season two brought change, new faces in frame,
Yet the essence remained, the heart just the same.
Through debates and fun, a family grew,
every moment shared, to the audience true.

Mid-seasons marked with tears and cheers,
big stories, bold talks, addressing fears.
Transitions seamless, like seasons blend,
a timeless bond, co-hosts as friends.

A constant light in the shifting cast,
some faces stayed, anchors steadfast,
their wisdom, humor, grace defined,
a legacy of voices, intertwined.

In these craziest times, their strength we see,
navigating change, with empathy.
Dynamic discussions, truth laid bare,
In every episode, they deeply care.

And now, at 6,000, the best cast yet,
energy vibrant, on this we bet.
A sisterhood of voices, so diverse,
in laughter, in tears, they immerse.

From the first laugh to today's embrace,
a journey of moments, we proudly trace.
For in this show, we find a part,
of our own lives, our beating heart.

Here's to the co-hosts, past and new,
to every story shared, every truth.
In these times, so wild, so vast,
what a group to have, from first to last.

So let's re-view, and celebrate,
6,000 memories, moments great.
For in this show, we find our way,
through life's crazy, come what may.

Inspiration behind "6,000 Moments: The Heart of Daytime TV"

Emotion: Nostalgia and Celebration

The 6,000th episode of The View was a milestone that I couldn't miss. It was a celebration of all the crazy, heartfelt, and unforgettable moments that have defined the show over the years. One of the highlights was Joy Behar, who is always a delight with her humor and candidness. Watching her react to old clips, especially when she didn't remember dancing with Beyoncé, was priceless. The show spiced up this special episode with the game "Let's Re-View," where Joy's reactions to resurfaced clips from the last 27 years brought laughter and nostalgia.

I wanted to honor this remarkable journey and the 6,000th episode with a poem. The poem captures the essence of "The View"—its ability to blend serious discussions with light-hearted fun, the seamless transitions of co-hosts, and the enduring presence of favorites like Joy. It's a testament to the show's impact, its resilience, and the joy it has brought to its viewers, including myself.

Writing this poem allowed me to reflect on the many seasons of the show, the big moments that have shaped its legacy, and the incredible energy of the current cast. Despite the crazy times we are living in, "The View" continues to provide a platform for dynamic conversations, making it the best group of ladies to navigate these difficult discussions.

So here's to "The View," its 6,000 episodes, and the journey we've all shared. The poem is a tribute to the laughter, the tears, the debates, and the undeniable magic that happens when these remarkable women come together on our favorite daytime TV show.

A Letter to Kamala Harris

Kamala, you were my choice in '19.
Your strength and grace, a powerful sign.
You have what it takes, to carry us through.
In these uncertain times, we look to you.

I won't add to the noise, or beg the doubt,
instead, I celebrate, I lift you up and shout.
Congratulations, Kamala, with pride I say,
you are the hope to guide our way.

To my fellow Americans, hear my plea,
stand with democracy, let's keep it free.
Help make these uncertain times a stable place,
with unity and strength, we'll set the pace.

It's still a choice, clear and binary,
one future bright, one adversary.
With age out the question, let's forge ahead,
with health and unity, let's move instead.

Congratulations, Kamala, best of luck.
In you, our faith, our future is struck.
We band together, hand in hand,
for a brighter tomorrow, for our land.

Inspiration Behind "A Letter to Kamala Harris"
Emotion: Support and Hope

My admiration and unwavering support for Kamala Harris, who was my pick during the 2020 primaries, inspired this poem. I vividly remember meeting and taking a selfie with her at the Charlotte airport, which solidified my belief in her capabilities and potential to lead our nation. I had just watched her on "The View" and loved her comments. On the show, she had expressed how Americans are "absolutely ready for a woman of color president and are looking for understanding and 'commonality' in their leaders, 'more than first looking to determine if a leader is the gender or race that we prefer.' When I saw her, I thanked her for her candor and commented on her insights on the show. She was so gracious and generous with her time.

Kamala Harris's first run in the primaries showcased her dedication, intelligence, and commitment to justice and equality. Her background as a senator and former attorney general of California demonstrated her ability to tackle complex issues and advocate for the marginalized. Seeing her step into the national spotlight filled me with hope and excitement for the future of our country.

As President Biden steps down and endorses Kamala Harris for the 2024 presidential election, I am overwhelmed with pride and excitement. This pivotal moment in history, with Kamala Harris poised to potentially become the first Black and biracial woman president, is a testament to her perseverance and the progress we've made as a nation.

In these uncertain times, Kamala Harris embodies the strength and vision we need to navigate uncharted territory. My letter to her is a heartfelt congratulations, a celebration of her achievements, and a rallying cry for all Americans to stand together, support democracy, and work toward a stable and unified future.

Kamala Harris has what it takes to lead us forward. Through this letter, I hope others will also recognize the importance of coming together and supporting a leader who can truly make a difference. Congratulations, Kamala Harris, and best of luck on this historic journey.

Uncharted Territory: A Plea to My Nation

In this land of promise, shadows now loom,
Biden steps down, in Harris, we find room.
A nation at a crossroads, history's page,
In the heart of democracy, we wage.

Kamala, a beacon in this tumultuous sea,
Presidential, able, our guiding plea.
But will the nation rise, will it embrace?
A Black, bi-racial woman, will prejudice efface?

Uncharted territory, a landscape so vast,
Our future uncertain, can we learn from our past?
From Harriet's courage to King's dream profound,
In Harris, their legacies resound.

Oh, my Black brothers and sisters, hear my call,
Together we rise, or divided we fall.
To the nation at large, to the willing ear,
Let not fear and hatred commandeer.

Just because Biden's out of the race,
We stand at a threshold, history to face.
Project 2025, a specter of dread,
Trump's return, democracy's thread.

A rally cry echoes, through valleys and peaks,
To Democrats, undecided, those the future seeks.
The question of age has now been removed,
Don't let other doubts be reproved.

Get behind Kamala, let's forge anew,
History's in our hands, what will we do?

Save our land, our world, as we know,
In unity and strength, let progress flow.

In uncharted territory, we boldly tread,
With hope as our compass, and love widespread.
For in Harris, we find not just a name,
But a symbol of progress, a path to reclaim.

Inspiration Behind "Uncharted Territory: A Plea to My Nation"

Emotion: Hope and Unity

The inspiration for "Uncharted Territory: A Plea to My Nation" arises from my unwavering support for Kamala Harris and the critical juncture we find ourselves in as a nation. While I have always believed in Kamala's capabilities and leadership, the sudden news of President Biden stepping down and endorsing her for the 2024 presidential election made me question whether the USA was truly ready for this historic change. It was not a doubt in Kamala's ability, but rather a concern about the nation's readiness to embrace a Black, bi-racial woman as president.

In this uncharted territory, my immediate response was to call on my Black brothers and sisters to stand firm against fear and hatred. This is a pivotal moment in our country's history, and we must unite to counter the divisive forces represented by Project 2025 and the potential return of Trump to the Oval Office. The poem is a rallying cry for Democrats at large and the undecided voters, emphasizing that with Kamala, the question of age is no longer relevant. We must not let other doubts cloud our judgment.

Kamala Harris is a readily presidential and highly qualified candidate, embodying the qualities we need to unify, strengthen, and progress as a nation. Despite being in uncharted territory, we must hold on to hope and get behind Harris, for she is now our symbol of progress. The poem urges all Americans to recognize the critical importance of this moment and to support Kamala Harris with unwavering determination.

"Uncharted Territory: A Plea to My Nation" reflects my plea for unity and action, highlighting the necessity of standing together to ensure a brighter future for our country. It is a testament to the belief that, even in uncertain times, we have the power to shape our destiny by supporting a leader who represents the progress and potential of our nation.

A Nation's Turning Point

The delegates are cast,
anxiety fills the air,
a nation's hope teeters,
caught off guard, I watch,
CNN's harsh glow,
Priscilla's steady voice,
but my heart pounds,
Biden's exit,
a storm brews within.

Elders' whispers,
Pelosi, the Obamas, the Clintons,
shaping destiny's path,
a turning point,
a crossroads for our time,
the party divided,
anxiety seeping through the cracks,
a nation on edge.

Who will lead this uncertain dance?
who will rise to carry the torch?
Biden's faith,
a bittersweet echo,
we are the United States,
yet unity feels distant,

a fragile dream.

Doubt and hope intermingle,
questions hang in the air,
what next in this political waltz?
a storm brews within,
as we stand at this precipice,
a nation's turning point,
anxious, divided, yet yearning for unity.

Inspiration Behind "A Nation's Turning Point"
Emotion: Anxiety and Hope.

"A Nation's Turning Point" draws from a moment of uncertainty and anxiety in American politics. The poem captures the shock and confusion felt when President Biden announced his decision to step down from the 2024 presidential race, a decision revealed during a tense CNN broadcast. This announcement, set against the backdrop of a nation already fraught with division and concern, became the catalyst for the poem's exploration of fear and hope.

The poem is influenced by the significant roles of the party's elders, including figures like Nancy Pelosi, the Obamas, and the Clintons. Their legacy and whispers of guidance shape the current political environment, creating a turning point where the future of the party and the nation hangs in the balance. The poem reflects on the achievements made during Biden's presidency, acknowledging the progress while highlighting the uncertainty that his departure brings.

The metaphor of a dance is used to depict the political maneuvering and the delicate balance of power, emphasizing the nation's anxiety about who will lead next. The poem seeks to provoke thought about the future, capturing the tension and the fragile hope that unity and strength can still prevail amidst the turmoil. It is a call to reflect on the importance of leadership and the collective

resilience of the American people during a pivotal moment
in history.

The Custodian of Light

In the corridors of my soul, there's a switch.
Not the eager flare of a constant beam,
but a sentinel's torch, selectively bright,
guarding reserves of a finite gleam.

Some beam like lighthouses, perpetual and fierce.
Waves crash, yet their light never falters or fades.
But I? I am the keeper of the flicker,
turning the handle only when the shadow invades.

My switch isn't faulty, nor rusted, nor broken—
it's cautious, reserved, rationing sparks.
For in the quiet dim, I gather the pieces
of energy spent in the light and the dark.

I pulse in the night like a star's soft blinking,
not ceaseless, but timed, with precision so rare,
Each burst of my spirit, a spectacle fleeting,
a dance with the dark, handled with care.

So, let them shine constant, those eternal beacons.
I'll toggle my switch in this shadow-play game,
illuminating corners when the moment feels fitting,
then retreating to quiet from whence I came.

Inspiration Behind "The Custodian of Light"
Emotion: Guardedness and Resilience

This poem sprang from a heartwarming and insightful
conversation with my grandmother. As we talked about
energy and the nature of our social engagements, we
recognized a shared approach to life. Both of us are
cautious about how and when we "switch on" our energy,
guarding it closely like a treasured light. We agreed on the

importance of being selective with our social interactions, not to withhold ourselves from the world, but to preserve our inner light and engage meaningfully. This poem is a reflection on being proper and self-aware custodians of our energy, ensuring we do not squander it but rather illuminate the right moments with our presence. It celebrates the wisdom of choosing when to shine brightly and when to conserve our glow for the aspects of life that truly merit our light and attention.

The Myth of the One

In the labyrinth of hearts, there's no single key,
no lone wanderer destined to unlock me.
Not one, but many could fit the cast,
it's not about finding 'the one' to last.

What matters more in the throes of fate,
is the one who resonates at a rate
that matches the rhythm of your own heart's drum,
a companion who makes the everyday hum.

The concept of "one" is a fairy tale spun,
instead, seek the one who makes life fun—
who brings you joy, who shares your sorrow,
who dreams of today and every tomorrow.

Look for the balance in the give and take,
for shared respect, that's no mistake.
A safe harbor in a storm, a confidant so true,
someone who cherishes the real you.

This is your 80/20, or perhaps 20/80.
The proportions shift, the blend plenty.
For love is a spectrum, not a fixed line,
it's the mutual dance, uniquely divine.

So let go the myth, embrace the real.
Find joy in who makes you feel.
'The one' is a myth, a fanciful dream,

but 'your one' is out there—just follow love's beam.

Inspiration Behind "The Myth of the One"
Emotion: Realism and Empowerment

This poem emerged from a conversation with my grandmother, during which we explored our shared skepticism about the notion of "the one" in romantic relationships. We discussed how love and relationships are inherently dynamic, not confined to the fairytale-like idea of a perfect match that popular culture often portrays. This poem encapsulates our belief that seeking "the one" is more about finding balance, mutual respect, and effective communication than fulfilling a predetermined romantic ideal.

The poem reflects a realistic approach to relationships, emphasizing that finding someone to spend a lifetime with involves assessing compatibility, the ability to resolve conflicts, and the capacity to grow together. It challenges the fantasy of effortless perfection in love, advocating instead for a partnership built on continuous effort and mutual understanding.

From a therapeutic perspective, this aligns with theories that emphasize the importance of healthy relationships as evolving entities where both partners contribute actively. For instance, John Gottman's research on marital stability underscores the need for deep friendship, a strong emotional connection that forms the basis for conflict resolution and long-term satisfaction. Similarly, the concept of "differentiation" in relationships, as explored by Dr. David Schnarch, stresses the importance of each partner maintaining their individuality while being emotionally connected, avoiding the merger fantasy that "the one" often suggests.

"The Myth of the One" reflects these principles, aiming to inspire a more grounded and pragmatic approach to love, where the magic comes not from fairy-tale destiny

but from the everyday work and dedication invested in
nurturing a truly compatible partnership.

Too, A Reflection on Excess

In a land where the word 'too' often falls,
on ears that barely perceive its calls.
Too extreme, too liberal, too bold,
in a narrative that's recklessly told.

America, in her tempest's roar,
becomes the very thing she swore
to stand against in days of old.
A story of courage, now untold.

Hatred blooms from seeds of fear,
too scared that someone's too near.
That they might take, or worse, transform
the familiar into a fearsome storm.

How did the hearts of many grow so cold?
Feeling too right, yet too bold.
Justifying actions without remorse,
veering far from a steady course.

The political climate, too out of hand,
dividing more than it can withstand.
America is 'too' right now, it seems,
Lost somewhere in between her dreams.

Yet, in this storm of fear and blight,
I cling to faith with all my might.
Too much has happened, yet I see,
the strength in unity, in you and me.

Because I, too, have faith, undeterred by the night,
that together, we can still make things right.
Too hopeful? Perhaps, but it's worth the fight,
for a future where 'too' finds a lighter plight.

Inspiration Behind "Too, A Reflection on Excess"
Emotion: Frustration and Hope

This poem arose from a stimulating discussion with a coworker about the current political climate in the United States. Our conversation highlighted the extreme polarization and the overwhelming nature of today's political discourse, which often feels excessively charged and divisive. This dialogue led me to ponder the necessity of moderation and the importance of returning to a focus on facts rather than fueling the fires of extremity.

This poem captures the essence of that conversation—acknowledging that the fervor of political engagement has, in many ways, exceeded healthy discourse. Both sides of the political spectrum contribute to this escalation, creating an environment where everything feels "too" charged, "too" extreme, and "too" divisive. The poem reflects a longing for a calmer, more centered approach to politics and public dialogue, prioritizing neutrality and factual integrity over emotional excess and partisan bias.

By invoking the word "too," the poem emphasizes how excessiveness can detract from meaningful conversation and progress. It advocates for stripping back to simplicity and truth, urging a collective step back to reassess and, hopefully, diminish the hyperbolic nature of current interactions. This shift is essential for healing and progressing as a society, where calmness and fact-based discussions prevail over the chaos of extreme partisanship.

My Name in the Hat

In a whirl of rage and disbelief,
upon hearing a name that spelled grief,
I found myself pacing, a mind in despair,
Donald Trump's candidacy hung in the air.

Livid and scared, feeling utterly bare,
I sought a course that might repair
this sinking ship, our democracy's test,
I Googled fiercely, my spirit possessed.

"How does one run for president?"
A question charged, my energy spent.
And soon enough, the FEC's gates,
opened a path to challenge the fates.

Registering wasn't as daunting as thought.
A principal campaign committee I sought.
More than $5,000 in hand, I could claim,
Malcolm Alexander—Neal, a presidential name.

A letter arrived, ink fresh on the page,
from citizens hopeful to set the stage.
Invitations to speak, from Wausau to Edgar,
though their earnest script seemed vague and bizarre.

Handwritten notes from Emily and Celed,
proposing a vision that they beheld.
A third-party candidate, fresh and new,
with ideas and a spirit that could pursue.

They wrote of gatherings, large and small,
farm shows, parks, a civic call.
A chance to speak, to be heard, to stand,
and offer an alternative to the land.

Yet skepticism tinged my hopeful spree,
a handwritten invite seemed fantasy.
But there it lay, my unexpected role,
a knee-jerk candidate, now on the roll.

For when the world seems beyond repair,
and leaders evoke nothing but despair,
sometimes, action is the sole cure,
to throw your name in, pure and sure.

So here I stand, perhaps naive,
in a candidacy few might believe.
But in action, I found a peculiar grace,
a presidential hopeful, entered in the race.

Inspiration Behind "My Name in the Hat"
Emotion: Determination and Defiance

This poem is from a moment of frustration and disbelief following the announcement that Donald Trump would run for president again in 2024. This news struck a deep chord within me. I felt hopeless and outraged at the prospect of such a divisive figure potentially leading the country once more. In a surge of emotion, I channeled my distress into a decisive act of defiance—I researched how to officially register as a presidential candidate.

The poem captures the spontaneous decision to throw my own name into the ring, driven by a mixture of despair and a daring challenge to the status quo. It reflects a moment when I thought, "If someone whom I see as fundamentally unfit can aspire to this office, why shouldn't I?" This wasn't just a symbolic gesture but a personal awakening to the power of proactive engagement in the face of discouraging political developments.

This poem is about understanding that sometimes you have to channel your frustration into action. While I don't actually intend to run for president, registering felt like a positive direction for my energy. It felt good to make that move, and registering as a candidate created a story to tell and sparked an interaction with a political group. I don't know where the action will ultimately lead, but it was a constructive way to direct my anger.

From Our Elders

From the halls where history whispers,
where leaders' voices blend and sway,
their echoes ring with praises bright,
for one who chose to lead, then lay
the mantle down, with grace and might.

In corridors of power's past,
they gather, elders wise and true,
to honor him who bore the weight,
and bridged the chasms, old and new.

Obama's words, a clarion call,
for futures built on hopes reformed,
a steadfast hand to guide us all,
through storms of change, through nights unformed.

And Clinton's voice, with wisdom shared,
of battles fought, of triumphs won,
he speaks of strength in unity,
of work that's done, yet just begun.

Together they, in unison,
raise high the torch, with light profound,
a testament to duty's path,
where hope and progress both are found.

Their praises weave a tapestry
of honor, strength, and futures bright,
for Biden, who, with steady hand,
has shaped the dawn, then left the night.

So, from our elders, let us take
their wisdom, strength, and guiding flame,
to forge ahead, to build, to make,
a world where justice knows no name.

A Patriot's Testament

In the halls where history's threads entwine,
a voice resounds, both deep and kind.
From a leader who has seen it all,
a testament to heed the call.

Joe Biden, a name etched in gold,
in service, brave, in courage, bold.
A friend, a partner, through thick and thin.
His legacy, where to begin?

Sixteen years and more we've seen,
a journey shared, a noble dream,
with empathy and resilience bright,
a beacon in the darkest night.

He battled storms, both near and far,
from pandemics' grip to wars' scar.
He lifted hopes, created light,
in every heart, in every fight.

Jobs flourished, drugs' costs fell,
climate's cry, he answered well.
Gun safety's dawn, a long-sought peace,
for workers' rights, he earned their lease.

He pointed us away from hate,
from chaos, lies, and bitter fate.
With honesty and kindness true,
he reminded us what we could do.

Now, he steps aside with grace,
for country's love, he leaves the race,
A torch passed on, a light held high,
for future's dawn, a brighter sky.

In uncharted waters, we now sail,
with faith in leaders, we prevail,
a vision of a land so grand,

united, strong, hand in hand.

To Joe and Jill, our thanks we send
for leading through times we can't pretend.
Your legacy, a guiding star,
forever near, no matter how far.

May we, in honor, carry forth,
the dreams you've sown, the endless worth,
of freedom, hope, and equality,
a testament for all to see.

A Historic Gamble

In Fayetteville's fervent air,
Kamala stands, her spirit bare,
a gamble takes the party's flight,
against the odds of darkest night.

With Joe's endorsement, she ascends,
a journey where the path extends,
through storms of race and gender's snare,
a Black woman's climb laid bare.

Two centuries of walls so high,
only once a Black man's sky,
never yet a woman's reign,
history's echo, sharp and plain.

LaTosha's voice, a hopeful tone,
reflects a future yet unknown.
Kamala's strength, her will, her grace,
a contrast in this fervent race.

Her tenure marked by highs and lows,
a legacy that fights and grows.
With youthful eyes on rights so dear,
she speaks to hearts both far and near.

In debates, her voice, a blade

against the past, her stance is made.
Reflecting now and future's face,
in every step, in every pace.

Challenges vast, supporters few,
yet in her stance, a courage true.
With every doubt and every cheer,
a trail she blazes, year by year.

In patriarchy's shadowed land,
She lifts her voice, she makes a stand,
With resilience born of strife,
She carves her path, she claims her life.

For every skeptic, every sneer,
A story told, both far and near,
Of dreams deferred, of battles won,
Of endless nights that greet the sun.

Kamala's path, a beacon bright,
Against the backdrop of the fight,
A gamble on a future grand,
A bet on hope, a bold command.

Inspiration Behind "Voices of Leadership Series"
Emotion: Inspiration and Solidarity

The poetic series "Voices of Leadership" is inspired by
the political events and statements following President Joe
Biden's historic decision to step down from his re-election
campaign. This series captures this pivotal moment
through three distinct poems: "From Our Elders," "A
Patriot's Testament," and "A Historic Gamble."

President Biden, recognizing the challenges ahead and
prioritizing the nation's future, announced his decision to
step aside for the good of the Democratic Party and the
country. This unprecedented move, while maintaining his
role as president for the remainder of his term, was made
to ensure the party's best chance at retaining the White

House in the upcoming election. Biden's endorsement of
Vice President Kamala Harris as the Democratic nominee
highlights his confidence in her leadership and the historic
nature of her candidacy as a Black woman in American
politics.

Former Presidents Barack Obama and Bill Clinton
publicly praised Biden's tenure and supported his decision
to endorse Harris. Obama's statement emphasized Biden's
remarkable character, empathy, and resilience, while
Clinton highlighted Biden's significant achievements and
his dedication to democratic values. These endorsements
reaffirm Biden's legacy and underscore the importance of
unity and continuity within the Democratic Party.

Kamala Harris's potential candidacy represents a
monumental step forward in American politics,
challenging centuries of racial and gender biases. Her
selection by Biden as his preferred successor reflects a bold
move to embrace diversity and progress. Harris faces the
daunting task of overcoming deeply entrenched sexism
and racism. However, her advocacy for reproductive
rights, strong support among Black voters, and sharp
political acumen position her as a formidable contender
against Donald Trump. The historical context is significant,
as Harris's campaign will not only confront Trump's
legacy but also seek to break through the barriers that have
historically excluded women and people of color from the
highest office in the land.

"From Our Elders" is inspired by the collective wisdom
and praise from former Presidents Obama and Clinton,
who highlight Biden's legacy and endorse Harris's historic
candidacy. Their words provide a foundation of support
and guidance for the future.

"A Patriot's Testament" reflects on President Biden's
selfless decision, capturing his dedication to the country
and his belief in the greater good. It emphasizes the values
of empathy, resilience, and democratic principles Biden
embodies.

"A Historic Gamble" explores the significance of Kamala Harris's candidacy, the challenges she faces, and the hope she represents for a more inclusive and progressive future. It acknowledges the hurdles of racism and sexism while celebrating the groundbreaking nature of her potential presidency.

President Biden's decision to step down and endorse signifies a shift towards embracing diversity and addressing systemic issues of racism and sexism. With the support of Democratic elders and the party's unified vision, this bold move aims to defeat Donald Trump and pave the way for a more equitable and just society. As the nation navigates this transformative period, the collective strength and resilience of the Democratic Party, as well as the unwavering support from its leaders, provide hope. The upcoming election will undoubtedly test these ideals, but with determination and solidarity, there is a renewed belief that progress and victory are within reach.

"Voices of Leadership" is a testament to leadership's enduring spirit and the unwavering commitment to a brighter future for all.

The Prosecutor and the Felon

Kamala Harris, our new Democratic star,
whipped the delegates, left them in awe.
The Phoenix of the night, she soared so high,
transforming election season in the blink of an eye.

Fifty million raised, a feat unmatched,
a wave of hope, the promise newly hatched.
No longer a rematch of two old foes,
a fresh dawn breaks, where excitement grows.

The prosecutor, fierce and bright,
against a felon, stripped of might.
Her battles fought in courtrooms grand,
against the crimes that plagued our land.

Financial fraud, assault's dark stain,
she stood tall, with justice's reign.
Now, the nation looks to her with pride,
a beacon of change, our steadfast guide.

Campaigns buzzing, streets alive,
voters ready, democracy revived.
No more debates of old, tired tales,
the contrast clear, our choice prevails.

Oh, how I'm driven for November's race,
to see the prosecutor take her place.
A renewed spirit, a chance to vote,
for justice, progress, hope's bright coat.

Kamala Harris, lead us through,
the nation turns its eyes to you.
In this battle, fierce and grand,
the prosecutor will firmly stand.

Inspiration Behind" The Prosecutor and the Felon"
Emotion: Hope and Admiration

"The Prosecutor and the Felon" draws inspiration from the historic political events of July 21, 2024. On this day, Kamala Harris announced her presidential candidacy after President Joe Biden decided to step down from the 2024 presidential race and endorse her as his successor. This announcement marked a significant turning point in the election season, transforming the political landscape almost overnight.

Harris's candidacy quickly garnered substantial support, securing enough delegate endorsements to become the presumptive Democratic nominee by the following day. The tagline of her presidency, "The Prosecutor versus the Felon," captures the stark contrast between her legal and ethical background and that of her opponent, Donald Trump, who faces numerous criminal charges.

The atmosphere on July 21 was initially fraught with worry and panic as the nation grappled with Biden's unexpected decision. However, as the day progressed and news of Harris's swift and strategic mobilization spread, a wave of excitement and hope began to build. Her campaign's record-breaking fundraising, amassing over $50 million in just 24 hours, further fueled this newfound optimism.

The poem reflects my awe and happiness at this pivotal moment. It captures my excitement about Kamala Harris's leadership and my belief in her ability to guide us to victory and preserve our democracy. Despite facing fierce attacks and baseless claims from Trump, Harris's campaign demonstrated resilience and effectiveness, solidifying her position as a formidable contender in the upcoming election.

This poem is a tribute to the remarkable events of July 21 and the renewed hope that Kamala Harris's candidacy has brought to our nation.

A New Dawn for K

In the twilight of her years, K sat,
an Irish heart, American dream at risk.
Four winters under a shadow, she muttered,
"I'll die with Trump as my final witness, how terrible."
Election night, states turning red,
a daughter's embrace, a mother's dread.

But time, a relentless river, flowed.
Through a pandemic's fog, hope barely glowed,
And then, a whisper of change, a light,
Biden's name echoed, soul of the nation in flight.
A breath, a sigh, four years now past,
a promise renewed, a future cast.

"Mom," said Mary, joy in her eyes,
"You won't leave us with that shadow in the skies.
Biden's hand on the helm, guiding us right,
economy blooming, world's envy in sight."
But shadows loom again, a rematch near,
K's heart wavers, caught in fear.

Ireland's shores, a distant call,
yet here, in America, she'd seen it all.
The highs, the lows, the battles fought,
a nation's soul, with tears, she'd sought.
Then Kamala's name, a beacon bright,
a promise of history, a radiant light.

"Mary," she whispered, hope intertwined,
"Will I see our first female president, so kind?
An African-Indian star to light our way,
a testament to progress, a brighter day."
Mary nodded, determination in her stance,

"We'll fight, Mom, for this precious chance."

Fox's lies, a web so tight,
yet truth and hope shine through the night,
Divisiveness crumbles, love prevails,
in every heart, this hope regales.
K smiled, the weight of years released,
In this promise, her soul found peace.

"Mary, I'll stay, through struggle and strife,
For this vision, this future, this life.
And when my day comes, far from now,
I'll rest, knowing we rose somehow,
witness to glory, to a nation's rise,
with you, my daughter, under these skies."

So let's march, with K in our hearts,
to a future where every soul imparts,
a legacy of love, of unity grand,
an America renewed, hand in hand.
For K, for Mary, for history's grace,
Let's build a world, a sacred space.

Inspiration Behind "A New Dawn for K"
Emotion: Hope and Resilience

This poem was inspired by a conversation with my coworker, Mary Connelly. Mary shared the poignant story of her elderly Irish American mother, K, who was deeply affected by the political climate during President Trump's tenure. As each battleground state was called on election night, K remarked to Mary, "I will have to die with Trump being my last president I witness; how terrible."

Four difficult years and a pandemic later, the election of President Biden brought renewed hope, and Mary reassured her mother, "Mom, you won't have to die under Trump; we have Biden." However, with the possibility of a Trump rematch, K feared leaving this earth with Trump as president again or the prospect of returning to Ireland.

The recent announcement of Kamala Harris as the new Democratic nominee rekindled hope for K, envisioning the possibility of witnessing the first African/Indian American female president of the United States. This poem captures K's journey through political despair to newfound hope, reflecting the resilience and aspirations shared by Mary and her mother.

After sharing "A New Dawn for K" with Mary, she was deeply moved and immediately sent it to her mother. K expressed deep appreciation for the poem, comparing its impact to that of renowned poet Seamus Heaney. She conveyed her admiration through Mary, who relayed that K would like to know more about me and intended to send a personal thank you note.

K later sent a heartfelt message directly to me, expressing how the poem captured her story so accurately and resonated deeply with her experiences and emotions. She shared her hope for the future, inspired by Kamala Harris's candidacy, and expressed her desire to meet me someday.

Mary sent a beautiful photograph of her mother. The picture, filled with warmth and familial love, showed K sitting in her cozy living room, surrounded by soft, warm light filtering through the windows. K was seated on a comfortable couch with her husband, Mary's dad, beside her. He exuded a gentle strength, his presence a testament to their enduring partnership. The family's pair of adorable dogs lay contentedly at their side, adding to the warm and inviting atmosphere.

K's face reflected a mixture of wisdom, resilience, and newfound hope. In her gentle smile and bright eyes, one could see the strength that carried her through challenging times and the anticipation of witnessing a historic moment. The entire scene was a portrait of familial love, heritage, and hope, capturing the essence of the home they had built together.

This exchange filled me with immense happiness and fulfillment in the ability to touch someone's heart and provide comfort through my poetry. Hearing K's reaction and knowing that my words brought her hope and joy during such a pivotal time is deeply rewarding. This experience reinforces my belief in the power of storytelling and poetry to connect us, bridge our experiences, and inspire resilience and optimism. It also strengthens my determination to continue sharing stories and weaving the lives, dreams, and hopes of people around me into my work. Thank you, Mary and K, for allowing me to be a part of this beautiful journey.

In Memory of Melissa

In the heart's quiet chambers, where sorrow softly treads,
we remember Melissa, a beacon, a friend.
Her smile, a sunrise, warm and bright,
guiding us through the darkest night.

Caring and kind, she stood by our side,
a ride-or-die spirit, with unyielding pride.
On the court, she soared, both basketball and volley,
her laughter echoed, always jolly.

In these pictures, her light remains,
captured moments, easing the pains.
Her arms around friends, love in her eyes,
a testament to bonds that never dies.

Though tears fall, a body's weapon against pain,
we find solace in her memory's gentle rain.
At just forty-two, so young, so dear,
her spirit whispers, forever near.

Four young hearts she leaves behind,
in their laughter, her soul we find.
We hold them close, through each passing day,
guided by the love she shared in every way.

Melissa, in our hearts, you'll always stay,
a guiding star, never far away.
In every act of kindness, in every game we play,
your spirit lives on, lighting our way.

Inspiration Behind "In Memory of Melissa"
Emotion: Grief and Remembrance

My dear friend Jason Gould's beloved friend Melissa
Minnfield passed away on July 18, 2024. I had the privilege
of meeting Melissa when she sat at my table at Jason and
Ron's wedding. Although our conversations have faded
from my memory, her vibrant spirit, uplifting vibes, and
beautiful, bright smile left an indelible mark on me. One
cannot forget such radiant energy.

To honor her memory and offer Jason and her family a
lasting tribute, I reached out to Jason for more insights
about Melissa. Despite his pain, he shared a few heartfelt
words about her, describing her as caring, kind, a "ride-or-
die" friend, and an enthusiastic basketball and volleyball
player. Jason mentioned, "Tears are the body's weapon
against pain" and added, "Let's just say I shed a few today.
Rest peacefully, my friend. We will take care of your
family!"

Using Jason's sentiments, I crafted a poem to capture
Melissa's essence, celebrate her life, and ensure her spirit
lives on in our hearts. The poem aims to provide comfort
to those grieving, reflecting the love and memories that
continue to connect us all to Melissa.

A Shadow Looms: The Mandate's Grip

In halls where power's whispers blend,
A vision dark begins to mend,
They craft a future, bold yet grim,
A mandate sung in shadows dim.

The banner waves of Project's might,
Their dream to lead, to mold the night,
Yet hidden 'neath the guiding hand,
A threat to freedom stains the land.

They speak of families, values old,
But in their tales, a heart grows cold,
For rights they slice with sharpened edge,
A warning clear upon the ledge.

They rally troops, an army's call,
To break the state, to let it fall,
Yet voices lost in echo's keep,
Cry out for freedoms they will weep.

In classrooms where young minds should grow,
They plant their seeds, a narrow row,
Diversity, they seek to bind,
A single path, a single mind.

Our nation's heart, so richly hued,
Is brushed with shades of narrow views,
The rainbow dims, a monochrome,
As freedoms slip from hearth and home.

Beware the siren's call, so sweet,
That lures the steps of freedom's feet,
For in the guise of order's gain,
Lie chains that forge a silent pain.

Rise up, dear voices, speak the truth,
Defend the light for every youth,
For in our hands, the power stays,
To guard the dawn of brighter days.

Resist the shadow's creeping tend,
And hold the line, our rights defend,
For freedom's song must ever ring,
In hearts where hope and justice sing.

Inspiration Behind "A Shadow Looms: The Mandate's Grip"
Emotion: Concern and Resistance

The poem "A Shadow Looms: The Mandate's Grip" was inspired by a deep concern for the implications of the Project 2025 Mandate for Leadership. This document, created by The Heritage Foundation, outlines a comprehensive plan for a potential future conservative administration. It has generated polarized reactions, with liberals decrying its potential harms and conservatives praising it as a groundbreaking initiative. However, a closer examination reveals significant threats to democratic principles and individual freedoms, particularly for those who do not subscribe to ultra-conservative values.

Summary of Project 2025

Project 2025 is a concerted effort by over 50 conservative organizations to prepare for a future conservative administration. It involves detailed policy recommendations across various sectors of government, intending to reshape federal agencies and policies according to conservative ideologies. The project is built on four main pillars:

1. **Policy Recommendations:** A comprehensive view of how major federal agencies should be governed.

2. **Personnel Database:** A system to identify and recommend individuals for positions within the administration.

3. **Presidential Administration Academy:** Training for individuals on how to function effectively within the government.

4. **Agency Teams and Transition Plans:** Detailed plans to implement policy changes swiftly upon taking office.

Key Points and Their Implications

1. **Restoring the Family:**

- Emphasis on traditional family structures.
- Elimination of marriage penalties in welfare programs and the tax code.
- Introduction of work requirements for food stamps.
- Implications: These policies could marginalize non-traditional families and overlook the diverse family structures present in modern society.

2. **Dismantling the Administrative State:**

- Reducing the size and power of federal agencies.
- Returning more control to the people.
- Implications: This could lead to decreased regulation and oversight, potentially harming public welfare and safety.

3. **Defending National Sovereignty:**

- Strengthening borders and national security.
- Implications: Policies might include stringent immigration controls, which could affect refugees and immigrants seeking a better life in the United States.

4. **Securing Individual Rights:**

- Emphasis on protecting individual freedoms as outlined in the Constitution.
- Implications: Certain rights, especially those related to LGBTQ+ individuals and other minority groups, may be threatened. For example, the removal of terms and programs related to sexual orientation, gender identity, and diversity from federal rules could lead to increased discrimination.

5. **Cultural and Educational Reforms:**

- Removing progressive terms and programs from federal policies.
- Outlawing pornography and imposing strict penalties on its distribution.
- Promoting universal school choice.
- Implications: These measures could lead to a reduction in academic freedom and an increase in censorship, affecting the quality and inclusivity of education.

Specific Concerns

- **LGBTQ+ Rights:** The project proposes removing protections and recognition for LGBTQ+ individuals, which could lead to increased discrimination and reduced rights.
- **Federal Workforce:** The plan aims to make federal workers easily fireable and shift the workforce towards Trump loyalists. This undermines the principles of merit-based employment and impartiality in the civil service, moving towards a more authoritarian structure.
- **Educational Policies:** By removing diversity and inclusion programs, the project threatens the

progress made towards creating inclusive educational environments.

Conclusion

This poem and summary aim to educate the public about the true nature of Project 2025. While it is heralded by some as a significant conservative achievement, the reality is that it poses serious threats to individual freedoms and democratic principles. It is crucial for people to be well-informed, critically evaluate the facts, and understand what is at stake during this election cycle. As a federal worker, I am particularly concerned about the potential impacts on the federal workforce and the pivot away from democracy towards a more authoritarian regime. I believe in the power of truth and facts to prevail, and I hope this effort will help people make informed decisions.

Buenos Días

First thoughts bloom with dawn, setting the day's bright way,
Guard your mind with care, let in light, chase shadows far away.
In the quiet morning hush, plant seeds of hope and cheer,
for what you welcome now will shape the path you steer.

Let not the noise of doubt intrude, nor the whispers of fear.
Stand firm, be mindful of what you hold dear.
Rise with purpose, breathe in strength, let positivity sway,
for the first thoughts you embrace will guide your entire day.

Inspiration Behind "Buenos Días"
Emotion: Hope and Encouragement

For about six years, I sent out "Buenos Días" inspirational quotes every weekday morning to a growing circle of close family and friends. Eventually reaching 125 recipients, this practice brought a sense of connection and positivity to our mornings. However, during the turbulent times of my divorce in 2019 and the subsequent onset of the pandemic in 2020, my consistency wavered. As we emerged from lockdown in 2020, I briefly resumed the practice, but technical difficulties with the application I used led to another hiatus. After visiting a Van Gogh exhibit in Mexico City with Rafa and his mom, I felt a renewed inspiration to restart my morning "Buenos Días" quotes. This time, I have incorporated affirmations, a practice I began in 2020, to further enhance the positive impact of these messages.

One unique aspect of my quotes is the special focus during Black History Month, where I exclusively share quotes from African Americans, highlighting lesser-known figures alongside the traditional icons. Instead of affirmations, I briefly describe each individual's significance and contributions to African American and American history. The feedback I receive is heartwarming; people often tell me the quotes resonate deeply with them, making them feel heard and connected. This beautiful feedback motivates me to continue this practice, as it not only allows me to share my journey but also supports the mental and spiritual well-being of those I love. Starting the day with these positive messages has become my form of meditation, preparing me for the challenges of the workday and strengthening our collective spiritual souls. Buenos Días!

Pillars of My Heart Series

Found Family

Sometimes, company's the finest cure,
a lively crowd can reassure.
With friends around, we'll not forget,
the joys of life are not a threat!

So here's to those who wrote of peace,
found in solitude's sweet release.
But I'll argue, with a cheeky tone,
that in good company, we're truly at home.

Cornerstones of My Being

In the tapestry of my life, threads woven tight,
Shayna and Charmaine, your presence, a light.
Through shadows of doubt and whispers of fear,
your voices, a balm, always drawing me near.

When the world feels heavy, and burdens press down,
your laughter lifts me, turns sorrows around.
In moments of silence, your understanding glance,
brings comfort and warmth, a soul-soothing dance.

You see me in ways few ever could,
in the quiet of night or the bright daylight flood.
Your unwavering support, like a fortress of grace,
holds me steady, a strong, sacred place.

Through highs and lows, through joy and despair,
your friendship, a constant, always there.
In the echoes of your love, I find my song,
with you by my side, I always belong.

Your laughter is music, your words a sweet hymn.
In your eyes, I see the best parts within.
In your embrace, I find peace and release,
your friendship, a gift, a boundless increase.

In this world so vast, so often unknown,
with you, I've found my truest home.
Through every storm and every clear day,
you light up my path, show me the way.

Gratitude fills me, too deep to express,
for friends like you, who bring out my best.
In the heart of our bond, I find my true self,
with you, I am rich, in love's greatest wealth.

Shayna and Charmaine, your names I hold dear.
In the fabric of my being, you are ever near.
Thank you for seeing, for knowing, for being,
the cornerstone of my heart, in this life, worth living.

Inspiration Behind "Pillars of My Heart Series"
Emotion: Gratitude and Love

The poems "Found Family" and "Cornerstones of My Being" are rooted in the profound appreciation for the chosen family that sustains me through life's challenges. These friends—Charmaine and Shayna, —are more than just companions. They are the lifeblood of my emotional well-being, the steadying forces that uplift my spirit, soothe my soul, and provide an unshakable sense of belonging.

Both poems were born from moments of introspection during personal transitions, notably in navigating the end of a significant relationship. During these times of change, it became clear how vital the support of my closest friends has been. Their presence, even from afar, is a source of comfort and joy, reminding me that while solitude can be peaceful, the bonds we choose bring light and life to our days. Whether through laughter, words of comfort, or silent understanding, they help me feel seen, understood, and deeply valued.

These friendships—more than just relationships—are the cornerstones of who I am, shaping my sense of self and reminding me of the power of connection. The poems serve as heartfelt tributes to these essential bonds, celebrating the love, gratitude, and profound happiness that come from the family we find and choose for ourselves.

The Comments Section Series

The Comments Section

In the digital agora, voices rise,
Kamala Harris, a spark in the skies.
From prosecutor's bench to D.C.'s dance,
She's the queen of the chance, the circumstance.

"She's fierce, she's fire," one comment declared,
"A beacon of hope, someone who cared."
"Is she enough?" another one pried,
In the labyrinth of opinions, the truth is tried.

A heart emoji, a thumbs down here,
The spectrum of feelings, from cheer to jeer.
"She stands for us," "She's not our voice,"
The chorus of democracy, each has their choice.

Dynamic, rhythmic, the pulse of the feed,
In every word, a hope, a need.
Witty retorts, sharp as a knife,
The comments a reflection, a slice of life.

Who is She?

In the glare of lights, the question posed,
"Is she Indian, is she Black?"—he froze.
No answer, no grace, just silence stark,
A dance of avoidance, leaving a mark.

"Why should Black voters trust you?" pressed,
The query hung, unanswered, undressed.
A thousand voices, unified and clear,
Echoed in the silence, the truth we fear.

"She cooked him," they laughed, the sharp retorts,
As calmness wielded like a sword in courts.
"Her voice, steady, respectful, yet bold,"
A leader's test, the truth unfolds.

"Get him!" they cheered, "Oh, how she shone,"
Not letting the madness become the norm.
"We can't grow numb to this endless storm,"
As he fell silent, a signal forlorn.

"Has anyone ever confronted him so?"
The shock, the awe, the voices grow.
"Give her a raise," "What's her Venmo, please?"
In admiration, the calls to appease.

"Can he handle the heat of foreign strife,
When a simple question cuts like a knife?"
The crowd, united, questioned his stance,
As he wavered, unsteady, lost in a trance.

"She stood tall," they said, "in the face of might,"
A beacon of truth in the darkest night.
"Protect her, love her, this woman of steel,"
For she wields the truth, making leaders kneel.

In the aftermath, the echoes remain,
Of questions unanswered, a leader's disdain.
"Who is she?" they ask, with voices bold,
A champion of truth, her story unfolds.

100 Days to Go

Fox News, a curious tale unfolds,
Favorability rising, the numbers bold.
"Keep the momentum," they cry, "don't stop!"
A surge of hope, the fear to drop.

"Ever since 2016, I don't trust the polls,"
Yet whispers of change, a bell that tolls.

"Met die-hard Republicans, now Harris-bound,"
In swing states, new voices found.

"Mango Mussolini, inconsolable," they jest,
A symbol of chaos, put to the test.
"NO complacency," the warning clear,
As November draws ever near.

"We are not going back," they firmly state,
"Stop Trump, vote!" before it's too late.
"Don't let complacency set in, act now,"
"Do our part, Vote!" the rallying vow.

"Harris 2024," a hopeful cheer,
"Great news, but vote, make it clear!"
"Never believe the polls, go out and cast,"
"Vote blue, everyone, make it last!"

"Oh yes!!!! Go Kamala!" they declare,
"America will vote for democracy, fair!"
"Just donated to Kamala," the support flows,
A tide of change, as the momentum grows.

"It's going to happen!!!" the optimism bright,
"People who never cared, now see the light!"
"Can't believe a Fox poll," they caution,
"Yet, we must vote, with passion and caution."

"Keep helping, we must fight," they call,
"Get rid of fascism, once and for all."
Even as numbers dance, confusion in the fray,
"We know it's Fox, but the stakes are high today."

100 days to go, the path still long,
A chorus united, resilient, and strong.
"Let's go," they chant, a nation awake,
For democracy's future, their stand they take.

Raeshanda's Reel

"Raeshanda, you may not be an archer,
But you keep hitting that target, for sure."
She draws on her board, wisdom in jest,
With humor and truth, she brings out the best.

"Trump won't share a stage, won't share a room,
His fears laid bare, as she seals his doom."
Misogyny, racism, without constraint,
"Raeshanda's reel," the truth so quaint.

"The 'No Lies Detected' button," they laugh,
"Kamala's got them shook, on her path."
"Historically, he fails with prosecutors," they say,
"And Kamala's ready to slay, come what may."

"Somebody scream, 'turn 'em loose,'" the cry,
As the popcorn's ready, anticipation high.
"He won't want to lose to a woman, no less,
A Black woman, oh, what a mess."

"He called her names," a scandal, they claim,
"His small vocabulary, just part of the game."
"He's scared, can't compete with her smarts,"
Her words cut deep, leaving lasting marks.

"DonOLD is done, Kamala is in!"
The chorus grows louder, the excitement within.
"He talks like a toddler, deflects, and whines,
But she's got the poise, the wit, the lines."

"Raeshanda, you are not Michael Myers,
But you stay killing them, with your fires."
"Raeshanda, you may not run for blue,
But you give us hope, and for that, we thank you."

As the debate looms, the stage set to blaze,

The nation waits, in a popcorn craze.
For the showdown of wits, the clash of minds,
Raeshanda's humor, a guiding light, so kind.

Qualified and Overqualified

Let's be VERY honest, let's draw the line,
Kamala Harris, a star, overqualified, she shines.
Former President Trump, a product of privilege,
White as the snow, his rise, an easy bridge.

"Trump's been president, how's he not fit?"
A puzzled voice asks, in a debating wit.
But what qualifies, beyond a failed term,
When substance is lost, and scandals confirm?

"Pure idiocy," they cry, "he held the throne,"
But Harris never earned a delegate of her own.
A reality star, a realtor, his claim,
No political background, just a famous name.

"White privilege got him to the highest seat,
Just like Kavanaugh, Supreme Court elite."
America's fear, an educated Black woman,
Kamala, poised, with qualifications uncommon.

"Just because he held the position," they declare,
"Doesn't mean he's fit, doesn't mean he's there."
A man of real estate, of TV fame,
Versus a woman with justice in her name.

"His team works overtime, creating a scandal's heat,
But this isn't Hillary, they can't repeat."
"Trump barely qualified for a cashier's role,"
Yet he led the nation, a staggering toll.

So, hold on, did they just say,
Kamala's more qualified, in every way?
The truth stings for some, but it's clear as day,
Education and experience pave the right way.

In this election, the stakes are high,
Qualifications matter, no need to lie.
Kamala Harris, overqualified, a beacon bright,
Versus a past of privilege, fading into night.

Mics and Misinformation

Dr. Umar speaks, a claim bold and wide,
"Kamala doesn't like Black men," his words glide.
But the facts, they tell a different tale,
A prosecutor's past, the justice scale.

"I'm sick of the talk," one voice resounds,
"Check the numbers, stop being clowns.
It's sad, unfortunate, a Black man's disdain,
For a Black woman's rise, her efforts in vain."

"Put the mics away," another cries,
"We need background checks for these lies."
"Umar, a tool of white supremacy's scheme,"
Inopportune times, the truth does gleam.

"The Jasmine Brand, you have a duty,"
"Be careful with your voice, your community."
"Shame on spreading disinformation's fire,
There's an appetite for truth, let's aspire."

"We have bigger fish to fry," they say,
"In the fight for democracy, we cannot sway."
"Not today, not ever, we're pushing through,
Together, united, in the red, white, and blue."

"Why do we turn against our own?"
"Can't we celebrate success, let it be shown?"
"Kamala's history, her past loves clear,
Married to a white man, the hate, the sneer."

"His words, a conspiracy's echo,

Pointless chatter, a shallow show."
"He speaks just to hear his own voice,"
An agent of chaos, not the people's choice.

"Cut off his mic, enough of the hate,"
"We can't come together at this rate."
"Umar's opinion, a grift in disguise,
Let's not let this distract from the prize."

In the end, the call is clear,
For unity, truth, a future dear.
"Kamala, overqualified, a leader bright,
In this battle, we stand, ready to fight."

The Staged Spectacle

BREAKING: Trump rushed offstage,
A noise, a moment, a scripted rage.
They've made him a victim, time and again,
From lost elections to failed coup plans.

He's played the martyr, the narrative spins,
Justice barely touched him, the privilege wins.
"What will they do now?" the fear expressed,
"A living martyr, the stage is set."

"Trump needs an award," the sarcasm flows,
"Worried about shoes, the show must go."
"Empathy never his trait," they say,
"He incites violence, then acts in a play."

"An episode of Scandal," the crowd chimes in,
"Was it staged?" the questions begin.
"They missed, so it's all fake," they cry,
"No evacuation, just chants of 'USA.'"

"Aaaaand CUT! Good job everyone,"
The crowd stayed, as if for fun.
"Directed by Smollett," the jokes abound,

"Trump with his fist raised, grabbing the crown."

"A shooter aimed, but no one behind?"
"Questions arise, the truth confined."
"A publicity stunt, the narrative clear,
A staged event, the crowd to cheer."

"His followers, a cult-like crew,
Eating up lies, believing the new."
"The setup, the drama, the acting seen,
A spectacle crafted, a political scene."

"He's a felon now, a shot at fame,
From rally stage to a criminal's name."
"The pity votes, the narrative tight,
A master class in propaganda's might."

"And scene..." the curtain falls,
On a staged spectacle, the crowd appalled.
"We about to live in wild times," they say,
"Will surviving gunfire win him the day?"

The skepticism, the disbelief,
In a staged world, where truth is brief.
"A plot, a play, a script so tight,
Trump's theatrics, the endless night."

Inspiration Behind "The Comments Section Series"
Emotion: Frustration and Introspection

The "Comments Section Series" emerged from the often tumultuous, yet captivating world of Instagram comments. Each poem in this series was inspired by the collective voice and diverse perspectives expressed in the comment sections of various posts, especially those related to political events and figures like Kamala Harris. As someone who frequently finds themselves scrolling through these comments, I've experienced the dichotomy of comfort and distress that comes with reading people's reactions. On one hand, seeing support for sanity and reason amidst the chaos can be reassuring; on the other hand, the prevalence of negativity, rudeness, and cyberbullying can be deeply unsettling.

The comment sections often serve as a microcosm of society, reflecting a broad spectrum of opinions and emotions. They can be both a source of solace and a breeding ground for negativity. This duality inspired me to capture the essence of these voices through poetry, distilling the collective energy and sentiments into cohesive pieces that reflect the psychological and emotional landscapes of those engaging in these digital dialogues.

The Comments Section

This poem captures the chaos and diversity of opinions found in Instagram comment sections. It reflects the mixture of support, criticism, humor, and frustration expressed by users reacting to political events and figures. The inspiration came from the overwhelming flood of reactions that follow every significant political update, highlighting both the positive and negative aspects of public discourse.

Who is She?

Inspired by comments reacting to Kamala Harris's identity and qualifications, this poem explores the public's perception of her as both a trailblazer and a polarizing figure. The comments often centered around her race and gender, with supporters celebrating her accomplishments and detractors questioning her legitimacy. The poem encapsulates the admiration and criticism she faces, reflecting the complex intersection of race, gender, and politics in the public eye.

100 Days to Go

This poem emerged from the anticipation and urgency expressed in the comments as the election approached.

Users voiced their hopes and fears, the need for vigilance, and the importance of voting. The poem captures the collective anxiety and determination, highlighting the critical nature of the upcoming election and the stakes involved. The inspiration came from the palpable energy and rallying cries for action seen in the comments.

Raeshanda's Reel

Raeshanda, a popular social media influencer known for her humorous takes on serious issues, inspired this poem. Her posts often include sharp, witty commentary on current events, which resonated with many users. The poem reflects on her ability to distill complex political and social issues into accessible, entertaining content, and the way her perspective offers a refreshing take amidst the often grim political landscape. The comments expressed both admiration for her insight and the recognition of her influence.

Qualified and Overqualified

This poem was inspired by the comparisons between Kamala Harris's qualifications and those of her political opponents, particularly Donald Trump. The comments often highlighted the disparity in experience and competence, with many users emphasizing Harris's overqualification in contrast to Trump's perceived lack of fitness for office. The poem reflects the frustration and disbelief of those who struggle to understand the continued support for Trump despite his controversial tenure.

Mics and Misinformation

Inspired by comments reacting to the spread of misinformation and the reckless use of public platforms, this poem addresses the dangers of unchecked rhetoric and the impact of irresponsible statements. The inspiration came from the frustration expressed by users who lamented the pervasive nature of false information and the individuals who perpetuate it. The poem emphasizes the need for accountability and critical thinking in an era of rampant misinformation.

The Staged Spectacle

This poem was inspired by reactions to what many perceived as a staged event involving Donald Trump. The comments were filled with skepticism and disbelief, with users questioning the authenticity of the incident and expressing cynicism about its motives. The poem captures the sense of disillusionment and distrust that often accompanies political theatrics, highlighting the public's growing fatigue with manipulative displays.

The "Comments Section Series" not only explores political themes but also delves into the psychological and emotional impact of social media use. The comment sections, while providing a platform for expression, can also be a source of stress and negativity. The constant exposure to polarized opinions and the prevalence of cyberbullying can take a toll on mental health. The contrast between supportive comments and vitriolic attacks can be jarring, often leaving users feeling overwhelmed or disheartened.

Excessive screen time, especially on social media, can exacerbate feelings of anxiety and stress. The constant stream of information and the pressure to stay updated can create a mental overload. It's important to recognize the signs of social media fatigue and take proactive steps to manage screen time.

One of the unique aspects of spending time in comment sections is the creation and reinforcement of echo chambers. On platforms like Instagram, algorithms often curate content based on users' interactions, leading to a self-reinforcing cycle of exposure to similar opinions. This can create a distorted sense of consensus or amplify negative sentiments, leaving individuals with a skewed perception of public opinion. This environment can cause heightened stress or anxiety, particularly when users encounter aggressive or hateful comments that clash with their own beliefs or values.

The anonymity or pseudonymity offered by comment sections often emboldens users to express opinions they might otherwise keep private. This can lead to a proliferation of harsh, unfiltered comments that can be particularly distressing to read. For those who are targets of these comments, the experience can be akin to faceless bullying, intensifying feelings of vulnerability and helplessness. This anonymity can also lead to a dehumanization of individuals, as users may forget that there are real people behind the screen, further contributing to a toxic environment.

For those who manage or moderate social media accounts, there is an additional layer of mental health considerations. Moderators often face the challenging task of sifting through a large volume of comments, many of which may be negative or abusive. This constant exposure can lead to emotional exhaustion, burnout, and even secondary trauma, as moderators must continually engage with distressing content.

Online disinhibition refers to the tendency for individuals to behave more aggressively or openly online than they would in face-to-face interactions. This phenomenon can lead to an escalation of negative comments and interactions in comment sections. The lack of immediate real-world consequences allows users to express anger, frustration, or hostility in ways they might not otherwise. For those who read these comments, witnessing such unrestrained negativity can be disheartening and can contribute to a cynical view of human nature.

Comment sections can evoke a wide range of emotions, from joy and amusement to anger and sadness. The unpredictability of these reactions can be mentally exhausting. For instance, while supportive comments can provide a sense of community and validation, negative or hateful remarks can trigger self-doubt and insecurity. This emotional rollercoaster can be particularly challenging for individuals with existing mental health conditions, as it can exacerbate symptoms of anxiety or depression.

Therapists often suggest practicing mindfulness when engaging with social media, especially in comment sections. This involves being aware of one's emotional reactions to what is read and recognizing when it might be time to take a break. Mindful consumption can help users manage their exposure to potentially harmful content and maintain a balanced perspective.

It's important to set clear boundaries around social media use. This can include limiting time spent reading comments, avoiding engaging in heated debates, and unfollowing accounts that consistently post distressing content. For some, it may also involve completely avoiding comment sections to protect their mental health.

If negative comments or online interactions are affecting one's mental well-being, it can be helpful to seek support from friends, family, or a mental health professional. Talking about one's experiences can provide relief and help develop strategies to cope with the impact of online negativity.

Users can also contribute to a healthier online community by promoting positive interactions. Leaving supportive comments, reporting abusive content, and engaging in constructive discussions can help counterbalance the negativity often found in comment sections.

Finally, practicing self-compassion is crucial. Recognizing that one's worth is not determined by online comments and being kind to oneself in the face of negativity can help mitigate the impact of harsh words.

Navigating the digital landscape of comment sections requires a careful balance of engagement and self-care. While these spaces can offer a glimpse into the collective psyche and provide a platform for expression, they can also be sources of stress and negativity. By approaching these interactions mindfully and setting healthy boundaries, individuals can protect their mental health while staying informed and connected. Remember, it's okay to step away, prioritize self-care, and focus on real-world relationships and experiences.

Condemning the Darkness

A statement from President Joe Biden,
briefed on a night where shadows hidin'.
The news of a shooting, a rally turned dire,
but thankful, Trump safe from the fire.

"I'm grateful," he says, with a prayer in his voice,
for Trump and his family, a nation's choice.
"We await further news, as the tension unfolds,
grateful to the Secret Service, brave and bold."

"No place for violence," a clear call to all,
"We must unite, prevent the fall."
In this land of freedom, diverse and wide,
violence has no place, must be cast aside.

Nancy Pelosi echoes, a voice of pain,
her family touched by violence's stain.
"Political violence, a blight on our land,
no room in society for this hand."

"Thank God Trump is safe," her words sincere,
a prayer for all, for calm to steer.
"Let us pray for those who attended, unscathed,
as we learn more details, the truth to pave."

In this moment, a quote we recall,
from Martin Luther King Jr., a message for all:
"Returning violence for violence, a deeper dark,
a night devoid of stars, a harsh remark."

"Hate cannot drive out hate," a truth so bright,
"Only love can do that, a guiding light."
Let this be our beacon, in times so fraught,
To rise above the chaos, in peace, we're taught.

A rally turned wrong, a call to unite,

to condemn the violence, to stand for what's right.
For in this land, under the same sky,
we must find our common ground, to soar and fly.

A Moment of Clarity

The name Thomas O Crooks, a tale unfolds,
a 20-year-old, Republican, the story told.
America, a land where guns outnumber men,
it was only a matter of time, the refrain.

"No one wants to hear her speak," they say,
but democracy's voice can't be cast away.
"I'm still voting Biden," another stands tall,
in the face of chaos, refusing to fall.

An attack on a candidate, a strike at the core,
violence in democracy, something to abhor.
"How did you miss?" a cruel jest laid bare,
a nation's wound, exposed, raw in the air.

"We may never know the full truth," they sigh,
as theories swirl, the facts to defy.
"Moronic ways, attacking each other,"
In a thread of words, chaos smothers.

"No conspiracy theory, but strange indeed,"
Trump supporters' stance, a confusing creed.
Inciting violence, yet fearing the same,
a double standard in a twisted game.

"Staged AF," some claim with doubt,
"Not one person ran, no panic throughout."
"A teleprompter's glass, a cut to his ear,
a fist pump, no fear, the scene unclear."

"It wasn't a Democrat, not an immigrant,
not LGBTQ, nor African descent."
He was young, white, Republican, it's true,
a moment stark, a historical view.

One of those moments, clear yet obscure,
when everything shifts, but the future's unsure.
A nation watches, holds its breath tight,
as the narrative twists, in the dimming light.

An AP photo, a rally's scene,
in Butler, Pennsylvania, the chaos seen.
A chilling clarity, a nation's sigh,
in the aftermath, a collective cry.

The Weight of Principles

In Ohio, a man burdened by his creed,
overcame the weight of his own beliefs.
Past comments on Trump, sharp and clear,
"America's Hitler," "Cynical," "Noxious" in the rear.

Once a "Never Trump," his stance was bold,
"Terrible candidate," "Never liked him," told.
"A fraudster, insurrectionist, threat to democracy,"
The convictions strong, a clear philosophy.

Fox News Democracy, the stage is set,
contenders for VP, the stakes higher yet.
JD Vance, a name among the rest,
was it just a phase, "Never Trump November's" jest?

"Project 2025," the plan revealed,
a doomsday scenario, the future sealed.
A convicted felon, still a felon indeed,
a sexual abuser, still facing the deed.

A promise to ship jobs, 100,000 out of D.C.
Another 50,000 reclassified, a political decree.
Stripping protections, a power grab clear,
federal workers' fate, now tied to fear.

The American Federation, their voices raised,

500,000 at risk, a future dazed.
Trump's executive order, once repealed,
now a looming threat, potentially revealed.

A guide, "Project 2025," to fast-track the aim.
Conservative values, policies to reclaim.
In the first 180 days, a swift, aggressive course,
a nation divided, democracy's force.

The Ohio man, once principled and true,
now stands at a crossroad, a decision to pursue.
The burden of principles, a heavy load,
in the face of change, a new story unfolds.

For in the land where freedom's torch shines bright,
the weight of principles must guide the fight.
To stand for truth, to uphold the right,
in the face of power, to resist the night.

The Cost of Four More Years

Eight years past, Trump posed a dare,
"What the hell do you have to lose?"—a question laid bare.
Fast-forward to 2024, and we answer with clarity,
we've lost much, and the stakes grow heavy.

Under a conservative reign, the losses are stark,
from Supreme Court shifts to shadows that mark
the federal bench with judges so few,
diverse voices silenced, a narrow view.

Trump's picks, Gorsuch, Kavanaugh, Barrett in tow,
a conservative bench, decades to grow.
"Politics is local," they often proclaim,
but the Court's reach extends, none can remain the same.

From Detroit's streets to the nation's span,
the decisions made affect every woman and man.
Racial equity, civil rights, the environment, and more.

Federal judges' rulings shape the core.

Project 2025, a chilling blueprint,
authoritarian leanings, no subtle hint.
From ending free meals to controlling the law,
a vision of power, a chilling draw.

In Detroit, we feel the weight of this shift,
With food insecurity and policies adrift.
His visit to 180 Church, a performative play,
seeking Black votes in a manipulative way.

We, daughters of Detroit, stand firm and true,
Cass and Renaissance graduates, our roots renew.
Educated in D.C., yet back home we came,
to the city we love, where we stake our claim.

Our passions united in art, culture, and health,
in family, community, and the city's wealth.
We see through the facade, the opportunists' guise,
for another four years, we cannot compromise.

For Detroit and beyond, the choice is clear,
to protect our future, we must steer.
In this critical moment, we raise our voice,
for equity, justice, and a different choice.

The Real Stakes

We need to stop acting as if voting for Biden
is a gift or a favor, a duty to be bidden.
Joe Biden will be fine, he'll find his way,
but there are others who won't be okay.

It's the women, standing tall, fighting for rights,
who will face the darkness in the absence of lights.
Visible minorities, under the gaze of disdain,
their hopes and dreams caught in a conservative chain.

It's the LGBTQ+ community, seeking a place,
to live, love, and flourish without hiding their face.
Non-Christian faiths, in a land of the free,
seeking respect, seeking dignity.

It's the disabled, the unions, the middle class, too,
struggling for fairness, for what's just and true.
The working poor, with dreams yet to find,
in a system that often leaves them behind.

The health of the planet, a pressing call,
in the face of neglect, we risk it all.
Project 2025, a shadowy plan,
threatens the progress, the work we've begun.

So, let's be clear, let's make it plain,
this vote is more than just a name.
It's for the future, for justice, for care,
for those who need it, who need us to be there.

In this election, the stakes are high,
beyond one man, it's about the sky—
the earth, the air, the rights we hold,
for every person, young and old.

We vote not just for a leader's crown,
but for the everyday lives, the joy, the frown.
For the love and the freedom, the truth and the right,
for the light in the darkness, the hope in the fight.

Draining the Orange of His Pulp Fiction

Let's drain the orange, peel back the lies,
the $1,200 "Trump Check," a grand disguise.
A topic of talk, a myth to unfold,

in the story of relief, the truth is bold.

The CARES Act's gift, a grant so clear,
$1,200 per adult, $500 for children near.
For households making less than $99k alone,
or $198k for couples, as shown.

Some credit Trump, but let's set it straight,
the House Democrats were the ones to create.
In the age of misinformation, we must debunk,
for the truth, in the face of myths, cannot be shrunk.

The "stimmy" helped, a temporary reprieve,
but long-term benefits? Hard to perceive.
It eased the strain, but did not heal,
the deeper issues, the systemic deal.

Ask yourself, is your vote worth a mere check,
or an all-inclusive trip, a brief fleck?
In a rainbow not read, a book not seen,
the deeper truths, the hidden mean.

For real change, we need more than a sum,
more than a moment, more than a crumb.
It's about the future, the long-term view,
pushing our needs to the top, breaking through.

So, let's not be fooled by the orange pulp's tale,
for a brighter future, we must prevail.
Read beyond the headlines, the easy facade,
for the truth lies deeper, in the details broad.

The Reapplication

HR: Let's lay out the facts, let's set the scene.
You were once at the top, in charge, so keen.
But your performance? Lacking, a poor show,
the company swiftly hired someone new, you know.

Angry, you couldn't handle the shift,
refused to leave, caused quite the rift.
Called your friends, caused chaos and strife,
vandalized the workplace, disrupted life.

When finally you left, on your way out the door,
you took confidential documents, much more.
Caught red-handed, refused to return,
holding on tight, watching the bridges burn.

And now, here you are, reapplying for the post,
the same job, the same company, the same coast.
But your record speaks loud, clear as a bell.
The situation? "Dumb as hell."

For who would trust a return to that seat,
after such actions, deceit, and defeat?
The unqualified, the reckless display,
seeking a comeback, hoping for the same pay.

But lessons are learned, trust once broken,
cannot be mended with mere words spoken.
So here's the truth, as clear as can be.
This reapplication? A far-fetched plea.

A Vision Beyond Delusion

Tonight, Trump stood before the crowd,
words stumbled, faiths insulted, lies allowed.
The election, again, twisted in his tale,
bragging, repealing rights, a dark veil.

He proposed cuts, billions from schools,
appointing extremists, disregarding rules.
Announced plans for a second term's spree,
filling ranks with criminals, like a twisted spree.

Attacked lawful voting, a democracy's core,
rambled on, leaving many bored.

Sounded like someone, at best, you'd avoid,
at worst, a leader you can't afford.

Harris for President, a voice clear and true,
offers a future, fresh and new.
Focused on freedom, opportunity, and grace,
a vision of security for the American race.

America deserves more than bitterness and scorn,
more than the delusions of a past forlorn.
Kamala Harris, a beacon, a guiding light,
for a better tomorrow, for what's right.

Inspiration behind "Voices from the Feed Series"
Emotion: Reflection and Urgency

The "Voices from the Feed Series" is a collection of poems inspired by political discourse and social reflections captured through Instagram posts. These posts, sourced from various blog pages and a personal connection, encapsulate the diverse and often intense reactions to current politics. The series explores the intersection of politics, misinformation, and the power dynamics at play, all while emphasizing the impact of social media on public perception and mental health.

Condemning the Darkness

Instagram posts reacting to statements from President Joe Biden and Speaker Nancy Pelosi in the wake of a shooting incident at a Trump rally inspired this poem. The posts were a bipartisan call for unity and a condemnation of violence. I was inspired by the shared sentiment that political violence, regardless of affiliation, has no place in American society. The poem reflects on the broader implications of political rhetoric and the need for peace, drawing parallels to historical moments of violence and the lessons learned. The reference to Martin Luther King Jr. calls for love and unity over hatred and division.

A Moment of Clarity

This piece was inspired by posts stating the Trump rally shooting incident was seemingly staged. The posts were filled with skepticism and speculation, questioning the disturbance's authenticity and the motivations behind it. The inspiration for the poem came from the public's fatigue with misinformation and staged political spectacles. The poem captures the collective disbelief and the realization that such incidents, whether genuine or orchestrated, contribute to the erosion of trust in political narratives. It focuses on the broader impact of staged events on public perception and the importance of discerning truth from manipulation.

The Weight of Principles

This poem was inspired by an Instagram post outlining JD Vance's past and present comments, particularly his critical remarks about Donald Trump before aligning with him. The post showed past descriptions of Trump as potentially "America's Hitler," a "cynical asshole," "cultural heroin," and "noxious" and "reprehensible," which contrast with his current political stance. The poem explores the internal conflict and moral dilemmas individuals in the political arena face when their values are tested. It reflects on integrity and the consequences of compromising one's principles for political gain. The poem emphasizes the importance of staying true to oneself amidst external pressures and the long-term repercussions of abandoning core beliefs.

The Cost of Four More Years

This poem was crafted from a post shared by Aminata B. Sow, a fellow Cass Technician, discussing the potential consequences of another Trump presidency, especially for marginalized communities. The post expressed fears about the erosion of civil rights, the rollback of environmental protections, and the exacerbation of societal divisions. The inspiration came from the collective anxiety and concern for the future, particularly among those most vulnerable to policy changes. The poem discusses the tangible and intangible costs of political decisions and how they often disproportionately affect overlooked groups. It underscores the importance of considering the societal implications of political leadership and the stakes involved in elections.

The Real Stakes

"The Real Stakes" drew inspiration from posts questioning the effectiveness of short-term relief measures like the $1,200 stimulus checks provided during the pandemic. The discussion centered on the disparity between immediate financial relief and the need for long-term systemic change. The poem reflects on the superficial nature of these one-time payments and the deeper issues they fail to address, such as systemic inequality and the lack of meaningful support for those in need. It critiques the narrative that such measures are sufficient and calls for a more comprehensive approach to addressing socioeconomic disparities.

Draining the Orange of His Pulp Fiction

This poem was inspired by posts critically examining the narrative surrounding Trump's role in distributing pandemic relief funds. The inspiration came from the need to dispel misinformation and clarify the role of House Democrats in passing the CARES Act. The poem focuses on manipulating public perception and the importance of accurate information in understanding political actions. It also critiques the tendency to oversimplify complex issues and the dangers of attributing credit or blame without a thorough understanding of the facts.

The Reapplication

"The Reapplication" was inspired by posts drawing analogies between Trump's attempt to return to the presidency and an employee reapplying for a job after a series of egregious actions. The inspiration came from the disbelief and outrage expressed by those who viewed his re-election bid as audacious, given his previous term's controversies. The poem uses the metaphor of a job application process to highlight the situation's absurdity, emphasizing the serious consequences of allowing someone with a problematic track record to return to a position of power.

A Vision Beyond Delusion

This final poem in the series was inspired by posts contrasting the visions of Trump and Vice President Kamala Harris for America's future. The inspiration came from the stark differences in their proposed policies and leadership styles, as discussed by users reacting to Trump's speech at a TPUSA event. The poem reflects on the dissatisfaction with Trump's divisive rhetoric and the hope for a more inclusive and forward-looking leadership under Harris. It captures the yearning for a leader who prioritizes freedom, opportunity, and security, starkly contrasting the bitterness and backward-looking delusions in Trump's remarks.

Mental Health and Social Media: A Reflection

These poems, while rooted in political discourse, also reflect broader concerns about the role of social media in shaping public opinion. While powerful communication and information dissemination tools, social media platforms can also be sources of misinformation and stress. The constant exposure to political debates and often polarizing content can lead to mental fatigue and anxiety, particularly during intense election cycles.

Studies have shown that excessive social media use is linked to increased levels of anxiety, depression, and loneliness. For instance, a report by the Pew Research Center indicated that a significant portion of adults feel worn out by the political content they encounter online.

It's important to practice mindfulness and set boundaries around social media use. Parents also must monitor and guide their children's interactions with these platforms, recognizing that younger generations experience social media differently than adults.

We must prioritize mental health and well-being as we navigate the complexities of this election cycle and social media's pervasive presence. Taking breaks, engaging in self-care, and being critical of the content we consume are vital steps in maintaining a healthy balance. Remember to care for your mind, body, and soul. Stay informed, but also stay grounded and compassionate toward yourself and others.

A Unity of Voices

In the heartland's whisper and the city's hum,
Tim and Kamala rise, a powerful drum.
From Minnesota's lakes to California's coast,
a unity of voices for those who need it most.

A teacher's heart and a prosecutor's gaze,
they bring their stories in diverse arrays.
Tim, with roots deep in rural soil,
Kamala, a fighter with relentless toil.

Together, they stand as an unlikely pair,
yet bound by a vision to lead with care.
In blue-collar towns and bustling streets,
their message of hope, where every heart beats.

For justice, for freedom, for every soul,
they march together toward a common goal.
In their hands, a promise, in their eyes, a fire,
to uplift a nation, to inspire and aspire.

With every step, they break new ground
in the halls of power, where truth is found.
A ticket of change in a pivotal year,
Tim and Kamala, in a partnership clear.

A journey begins, with courage and grace,
as they face the future, united in this race.
For all who believe in a brighter day,
Tim and Kamala, leading the way.

Inspiration Behind "A Unity of Voices"
Emotion: Hope and Collaboration

This poem was inspired by Kamala Harris' powerful
and strategic decision to select Tim Walz as her running
mate for the 2024 presidential election. This choice
symbolizes a partnership of hope, resilience, and a shared
commitment to saving the nation from divisive forces.

Kamala Harris's campaign, characterized by its full-steam-ahead momentum, finds in Walz, a partner who embodies the values of Midwestern humility and a plain-spoken approach that resonates with everyday Americans. His small-town roots and experience as a high school teacher and National Guard member bring an authentic, relatable appeal to the ticket. This authenticity is crucial at a time when the country needs leaders who can bridge divides and connect with both urban and rural communities.

The poem reflects the significance of this partnership, highlighting Walz's liberal policies and willingness to take on Donald Trump with sharp, buzzy critiques that have made him an unexpected yet fitting choice. By selecting Walz, Harris underscores her commitment to a campaign that focuses on fundamentally transforming the nation, ensuring that the voices of working families, the marginalized, and those often left behind are heard and uplifted.

The inspiration also draws from the idea that Walz, though not a typical top-tier pick, represents a new hope—a leader who can help carry forward the vision of a united, progressive America. His selection as vice president matters deeply in this pivotal election, not just for the electoral strategy but for what it symbolizes: a partnership aimed at healing the nation and driving it toward a more inclusive, compassionate future

Intentional Ignorance

You don't have to intend the wound
for the blade to cut deep.
Missteps, they say—
but when the foot falls twice,
Is it still a stumble, or is it a dance?

Kamala. Kamala. **Kamala.**
Not just a name, but a rhythm,
a heartbeat of history.
Mispronounce it, twist it,
and you twist the story of all who came before.

Yet, here she stands,
smirking in defiance,
"You can call her whatever you want,"
as if the syllables don't matter,
as if the meaning can be molded
to fit the shape of her ignorance.

Intentions are whispers in the wind,
but impact—
that's the stone that shatters glass.
She doubles down,
entitlement heavy in her voice,
as if misjudgment is her birthright,
as if she can rewrite the legacy of disregard
with a flick of her tongue.

"You don't have to intend racism to accomplish it,"
a truth spoken,
powerful as thunder,
yet lost on ears
tuned to Privilege's tune.
When you refuse to see humanity
you build walls with your words,
brick by brick,
syllable by syllable.

Kamala. Kamala. **Kamala.**
Say it with care,
say it with respect,
or don't say it at all.
For the history in her name
is not yours to diminish,
not yours to reshape
to fit the smallness of your intent.

Inspiration behind "Intentional Ignorance"
Emotion: Anger and Defiance

This poem stems from a recent incident where Rep. Nancy Mace, R-S.C., repeatedly mispronounced Vice President Kamala Harris' name during a CNN panel, despite being corrected multiple times. This act, whether intentional or not, highlights a deeper issue of disregard and disrespect that is often rooted in racial bias. The poem seeks to explore the idea that racism and disrespect do not always require malicious intent to be harmful; rather, they can manifest through repeated acts of ignorance and entitlement.

The poem draws on the powerful statement, "You don't have to intend racism to accomplish it," made during the heated exchange on the panel. It reflects on how something as seemingly simple as mispronouncing a name can carry the weight of history, legacy, and identity, particularly for marginalized communities. By focusing on the deliberate nature of Mace's actions and the subsequent defense of her behavior, the poem underscores the importance of recognizing the impact of our words and actions, regardless of intent.

The repetition of Kamala Harris' name within the poem serves as a reminder of the respect and care that should be given to every individual's identity, particularly when that identity is tied to a history of struggle and resilience. The poem challenges the reader to consider the broader implications of their actions and to understand that true

respect comes from acknowledging and valuing the
humanity in each person, starting with something as
fundamental as pronouncing their name correctly.

The Party of Progress

In the hands of those who build, not break,
where values guide the path they take,
a legacy of jobs, they weave, they sew,
a nation's heart, in work, they grow.

From Clinton's era, tech did rise,
twenty-two million jobs beneath clear skies.
With balanced books and futures bright,
a boom of promise, in the softest light.

Then came the storm, a recession's wrath,
but Obama steered us back on path.
Eleven million jobs, like seeds in spring,
from crisis came a blossoming.

And now, with Biden, as we heal,
thirteen million strong, the numbers real.
A pandemic's grip, we did defy,
and saw the workforce touch the sky.

But contrast this with what we've seen,
a different tale, a harsher sheen.
For Trump, with boasts so grand and tall,
saw millions lost, a bitter fall.

Before the plague, jobs did grow,
yet reckless winds began to blow.
And as the virus claimed its due,
a net loss marked the red and blue.

In Reagan's time, jobs bloomed as well,
but Bush's years were less to tell.
With wars and crises, growth was slow,
a struggle in the ebb and flow.

So now, when choice is yours to make,
remember what's at stake.
The party that creates, that lifts the weight,
is one that values love, not hate.

For in the numbers, truth is clear,
a future bright, without the fear.
To build a nation strong and fair,
choose those who work with care.

The Democrats, with steady hand,
have grown the jobs across the land.
It makes good sense to cast your vote
for those who keep this ship afloat.

For values matter, this we know,
in every job, in every row.
A party that believes in you,
will help your dreams, and future too.

Inspiration Behind "The Party of Progress
Emotion: Confidence and Pride

This poem was inspired by the stark contrast in job
creation records between Democratic and Republican
administrations over the past few decades. The numbers
tell a compelling story that reflects each party's values and
priorities and highlights the impact of their economic
policies on the lives of millions of Americans.

Democratic Administrations: A Record of Growth

Bill Clinton (1993-2001)

Under President Bill Clinton, the U.S. economy
experienced one of its most robust periods of growth.
Twenty-two million jobs were created during his
administration, with an average annual job growth of
2.9%. Clinton's tenure was marked by the tech boom and a

strong economic expansion, which contributed to widespread prosperity and a balanced federal budget.

Barack Obama (2009-2017)

President Barack Obama inherited the Great Recession, one of the worst economic downturns in U.S. history. Despite the initial challenges, Obama's administration oversaw the creation of 11.6 million jobs with an average annual job growth of 1.6%. The economic recovery was gradual but steady, and by the end of his presidency, the nation had regained its footing and was on a path to sustained growth.

Joe Biden (2021-present)

President Joe Biden took office during the height of the COVID-19 pandemic, facing an unprecedented public health and economic crisis. Under his leadership, the U.S. economy has added 13 million jobs as of mid-2024, with an average annual job growth of 5.6%. This surge in job creation reflects the rapid recovery and reopening of the economy, coupled with substantial investments in infrastructure and innovation.

Republican Administrations: A Mixed Record

Ronald Reagan (1981-1989)

President Ronald Reagan's administration saw the creation of 16.5 million jobs, driven by economic recovery in the mid-1980s. While this was a significant achievement, it came after a deep recession accompanied by rising income inequality.

George W. Bush (2001-2009)

President George W. Bush's tenure was less successful in job creation, with only 1.3 million jobs added. The early 2000s recession and the financial crisis of 2008 severely hampered job growth, leading to a sluggish economy by the end of his term.

Donald Trump (2017-2021)

President Donald Trump's administration initially saw job growth driven by tax cuts and deregulation, with approximately 6.5 million jobs created before the pandemic. However, the COVID-19 crisis led to the loss of over 20 million jobs, resulting in a net loss of around 2.9 million jobs by the end of his term. This marked the first time since the Great Depression that a president left office with fewer jobs than when they took office.

The Math is Clear: It Just Makes Sense

When comparing the job creation records of Democratic and Republican administrations, the differences are striking. Over the past few decades, Democratic presidents—Clinton, Obama, and Biden—have collectively added approximately 46.6 million jobs to the U.S. economy. In contrast, Republican presidents—Reagan, Bush, and Trump—have seen about 23.7 million jobs, with Trump's term ending in a net job loss.

These numbers are not just statistics; they reflect the lived experiences of millions of Americans who have benefited from policies that prioritize job creation, economic stability, and growth. The Democratic approach, rooted in values of inclusivity, investment in innovation, and support for working families, has consistently delivered stronger job growth and economic resilience.

In a time when economic stability is more crucial than ever, the math is clear: It just makes sense to support the party with a proven track record of creating jobs and building a stronger, more equitable economy.

<h1 style="text-align:center">A 2024 DNC Poetry Journey</h1>

A Night of New Beginnings

In the heart of Chicago, where history is made,
we gathered together, unafraid,
to witness the dawn of a new era's light,
as Democrats stood strong on the first DNC night.

Joe Biden took a bow, his legacy clear,
with words of wisdom, steady and sincere.
He passed the torch to Kamala's hand,
a beacon of hope for this great land.

She'll be the leader our children admire,
a president who'll lift us higher.
From the depths of struggle, she will rise,
with justice, compassion, and fearless eyes.

Hillary spoke of ceilings shattered,
of dreams that once were bruised and battered.
But now, the future's in our grasp,
as we break through, we'll not unclasp.

Raphael Warnock's prayer was bold,
a call for unity, a story told.
That when we vote, we shape our fate,
and for our children, it's never too late.

Abortion rights, a rallying cry
for freedom's fight, we will not shy.
Amanda, Kaitlyn, Hadley, too,
their stories remind us of what we must do.

The war in Gaza, a solemn note,
but on this night, we still took vote.
For peace, for justice, for every life,
in every struggle, in every strife.

Mallory McMorrow took the stage

with Project 2025's dark page.
A warning clear, a fight we face
to protect democracy, in every place.

This night was more than speeches made,
it was a promise, a pledge conveyed.
That in the face of every fight,
we'll stand together, united in might.

For in this room, with hearts aligned,
We felt the power of a shared mind.
The future's here, within our reach,
and on this night, we found our speech.

So, let us march with heads held high.
With Kamala leading, we'll touch the sky.
For this is our time, our sacred call,
to build a nation, just for all.

A Night of Hope and Fire

On the second night in Chicago's gleam,
the stage was set for a powerful dream.
Michelle stepped up, her words a spark,
in the darkest night, she left her mark.
"Hope is making a comeback," she proclaimed,
and with those words, our spirits flamed.

She spoke of Kamala, so strong, so wise,
a leader to trust, a future to prize.
With dignity and grace, she stands tall,
for every American, she fights for all.

Yet warnings came, sharp and clear,
from the voices we hold dear.
Avoid the "foolishness," Michelle did say,
for action is needed, now more than yesterday.

Then Barack took the stage, with humor and pride,
"Following Michelle is tough," he sighed.

But with grace and strength, he spoke his mind,
reminding us all, we cannot be blind.

"This convention," he said with pride,
"has always welcomed those who stride,
with funny names and hopeful hearts,
in this land where every dream starts."

No more division, no more despair,
for in unity's light, we find our repair.
Barack urged us forward to reject the disgrace,
No more of the chaos we've had to face.

Doug Emhoff shared a tender side,
the love for his wife, a joy he can't hide.
In every story, every laugh, every cheer,
we saw the woman who's led with no fear.

Republicans joined, their voices strong.
In this fight, they, too, belong.
For truth, for justice, they made their plea,
for a future where all can be free.

Bernie stood, his vision clear
for the working people he holds dear.
"This is not a radical dream," he spoke,
but a path to lift the common folk.

The night was filled with songs and pride
as states cast votes with spirits wide.
From Georgia's beats to California's vibe,
the roll call echoed far and wide.

And as Kamala and Walz took the stage,
we felt the turning of a new page.
For this is the moment, the time is now,
to rise together and take our vow.

In this night of hope, of fire, of grace,
we found our purpose, our rightful place.
With Kamala at the helm, we'll soar high,

for in unity and hope, we touch the sky.

A Night of Joy and Resolve

On the third night, joy took the stage,
in Chicago's heart, where history's made.
A shift from fear to hope's embrace,
Kamala's journey, a nation's grace.

Bill Clinton, the explainer-in-chief,
spoke of Kamala with firm belief.
"For the people," she stands tall
against a man who'd see us fall.
"Count the I's," he said with wit.
A warning clear, we won't forget.

Tim Walz, with humble might,
spoke of freedom, what's just, what's right.
A coach, a teacher, a voice so strong,
in every heart, his words belong.
For his children, he shed a tear,
and in that moment, we all drew near.

Oprah, the voice of history's thread,
told of paths that heroes tread.
From New Orleans to Berkeley's halls,
Kamala's rise, the story calls.
"Choose joy," she urged us all,
for in that choice, we rise, we fall.

The night was filled with melodies sweet.
John Legend, Stevie, set the beat.
But in the music, the message clear,
Kamala's moment, drawing near.

The parents of a hostage spoke
of pain, of hope, a world bespoke.
A nation watched, a world held breath,
in their words, the weight of death.
But even in the darkest fight,

they called for peace, for what is right.

Aquilino, with a soldier's pride,
told of wounds that won't subside.
From January's cold attack,
to this night, he had our back.
A call to guard democracy's flame,
in Kamala's hands, we stake our claim.

The night was not just speeches spun,
but a battle cry, a race begun.
With every word, with every song,
we felt the pull, the purpose strong.

So, as the third night's lights did fade,
a resolve was born, a future laid.
For joy, for freedom, for the fight,
we march together into the night.
Kamala leads, the future bright,
in her, we trust, our guiding light.

The Final Night's Call

In the heart of Chicago, under bright lights' gleam,
Kamala Harris took the stage, a patriot's dream.
With the weight of history in her every word,
she spoke for the people, every voice heard.

"Democracy or tyranny," she made it clear.
In this fight, there's no place for fear.
Against the chaos, she stood tall,
a promise of justice, for one and for all.

"We're not going back," she said with might,
to the days of division, the endless fight.
In her voice, a call to be free,
from violence, from hate, from tyranny.

Her mother's wisdom, her father's grace,

in Kamala's story, we found our place.
A life lived with purpose, with passion, with pride,
in her journey, we all confide.

For every life lost to the gun's cruel hand,
she stood with the fallen, took a stand.
From Sandy Hook to Uvalde's pain,
she vowed, "We won't let this be in vain."

The Central Park Five, they spoke with fire,
of a man who fueled a nation's ire.
But in Kamala, they found hope anew,
a leader who stands for what is true.

With her family beside her, the stage was set,
a future we're proud of, one we won't forget.
For freedom, for justice, for the land we adore,
Kamala leads us to a brighter shore.

So, as the balloons fell, the cheers rang out,
in Kamala Harris, there is no doubt.
A new dawn rising, a new chapter to write,
led by a president who'll carry the light.

Inspiration Behind "A 2024 DNC Poetic Journey"
Emotion: Hope and Empowerment

The series, "A 2024 DNC Poetic Journey," was born from the historic moments that defined the Democratic National Convention of 2024. Each poem in this collection captures the pivotal night and the collective spirit, challenges, and hopes of a nation on the brink of transformative change.

A Night of New Beginnings sets the stage with Kamala Harris emerging as the Democratic nominee, symbolizing a departure from the tumultuous past and an embrace of fresh possibilities. This poem draws from the powerful speeches of Michelle and Barack Obama, who electrified the convention by urging the nation to reject divisiveness and rally around a future defined by unity, integrity, and hope. Their words echoed through the convention hall, reminding everyone that "hope is making a comeback" and that the journey ahead demands courage, resilience, and a commitment to the values that truly make America great.

A Night of Hope and Fire explores the raw emotions and determination that characterized the convention's third night. The focus shifts to the "joy strategy" that Kamala Harris and her running mate, Minnesota Governor Tim Walz, convey as the candidates who can restore the nation's spirit. The poem reflects the joy and optimism of Harris' candidacy, contrasting it with the darkness and despair that the previous administration had sown. The night celebrated resilience, with voices like Oprah Winfrey connecting the historical dots, highlighting how Harris embodies the best of America, and Tim Walz energized the crowd with his heartfelt speech, culminating in a rousing football-themed pep talk.

A Night of Joy and Resolve captures the emotional depth and unwavering resolve that marked the convention's final night. Kamala Harris delivered a speech that was as personal as it was political, weaving her life story into her vision for America. This poem reflects the powerful testimonies of those affected by gun violence, the poignant presence of the Central Park Five, and the rallying cries for freedom and justice that reverberated throughout the convention hall. It was a night where Harris not only laid out her plans but also reminded the nation that this election is about choosing between democracy and tyranny, freedom and oppression.

The Final Night's Call brings the series to a crescendo, drawing on the emotions, speeches, and moments that defined the convention's closing night. This poem encapsulates the sense of urgency and the call to action that permeated the atmosphere. Now fully in her element, Kamala Harris rallied the nation around patriotism, freedom, and the enduring struggle for democracy. The poem echoes her clarion call that "we are not going back," capturing the collective resolve to move forward, rebuild, and reclaim the nation's promise.

This series reflects the hope, fire, joy, and resolve that the 2024 Democratic National Convention inspired in millions. It is a tribute to the power of words, the strength of the human spirit, and the belief in a better tomorrow. Each poem celebrates the resilience of a nation that, despite its struggles, continues to strive for unity, justice, and progress.

A Promise for All Americans

In the heart of this great land, where the rivers flow free,
where mountains touch the sky, and plains stretch to the
sea.
We stand united, not by color or creed,
but by the spirit of a nation, where dreams take the lead.

From the bustling cities to the quiet country lanes,
in the laughter of our children and the work of our hands,
we find our strength in diversity's embrace,
a patchwork of people, one united face.

Today, we turn the page, a new chapter unfolds,
with a vision for the future where every voice is bold.
Where Democrats, Republicans, and those in between
join hands in a promise to keep our nation's dream.

We come from different walks, yet our paths converge,
in the love of freedom, where our passions surge.
For justice, for peace, for the common good,
we strive together, as one people should.

In the echo of the past, we hear a call
to rise above division, to bridge every wall.
With Kamala at the helm and Walz by her side,
we sail toward a future where all hopes abide.

Let us honor the veterans, who've fought for our right
to speak, to assemble, to stand and to fight.
Let us cherish the workers, who build and who care,
for the dignity of labor, for the burdens they bear.

In the eyes of the farmer, the teacher, the nurse,
we see the soul of America, diverse and immersed.
In the dreams of the youth, in the wisdom of age,
we write a new story on history's page.

From the middle class that fuels our might,
to those struggling to find the light,

We pledge to lift each other high,
for in our unity, we reach the sky.

We are the heirs of a promise, born in liberty's name,
to build a nation where all can claim
their place at the table, where all voices are heard,
in a land where freedom is not just a word.

So let us move forward, with hope as our guide,
with compassion, with courage, standing side by side.
For America's strength lies not in division,
but in the unity of purpose, in a shared vision.

Today, we pledge to be worthy of this time,
to climb every mountain, to rise and to shine.
Together, we forge a path that is clear,
a future for all, where there's nothing to fear.

In this land of the free, where every dream can soar,
let us work for a better tomorrow, and so much more.
For the promise of America, for the land that we adore,
we stand together, as one people, forevermore.

Inspiration Behind "A Promise for All Americans"
Emotion: Unity and Optimism.

The inspiration behind this poem is deeply rooted in the powerful message Kamala Harris delivered during her historic acceptance speech at the Democratic National Convention. Her words were a call to action and a symbol of hope, unity, and determination for all Americans, regardless of their background or political affiliation. She spoke to the heart of what it means to be an American, emphasizing the strength in our diversity, the importance of common sense, and the belief in the promise of a better future.

Listening to her, I was struck by her ability to thread together the struggles and aspirations of everyday people with the larger vision of our nation's future. She spoke with a clarity and purpose that resonated deeply with me, making it clear that her leadership is not just about politics but about restoring faith in the American dream. Her message inspired me to craft a poem that would capture her vision—a vision that I believe will guide us through the challenges ahead and help us to build a brighter, more inclusive future.

A dream would be to deliver the inaugural poem–the thought of which feels like an incredible honor that would be both thrilling and daunting. I am calling this inaugural poem Kamala Harris is going to win this election, and with her leadership, she will restore hope in our nation. I want to ensure that every word reflects the depth of her commitment to the American people and the transformative power of her leadership. This poem is a tribute to her victory and reflection of the hope she embodies for all of us as we embark on this new chapter in our country's history.

Who is Tim Walz?

He's a voice from the heartland, where the sky meets the soil.
A man of small towns, where neighbors toil
in fields of care with hands that mend.
A life built on service, a patriot to the end.

Born in Butte, where the streets are few,
he learned early the power of what we do.
In a town of 400, he grew up strong
in a place where you don't leave folks behind for long.

He wore the uniform, stood tall in the Guard,
a son of the soil who worked hard.
From the cornfields of Nebraska to Congress's halls,
he stood for the people, answered the calls.

He's a teacher at heart, a coach on the field,
guiding young minds, showing what's real.

In Mankato's halls, his lessons were clear,
respect, hard work, and holding loved ones dear.

As Governor, he fought for the middle class,
cutting taxes, pushing forward, no need to ask.
He gave kids meals, banished hunger from the schools,
while others banned books, he followed different rules.

In Minnesota, he fought for reproductive rights,
"Mind your own damn business," he'd say with might.
He shared his own story, the struggle and pain
of IVF battles, hope born from the rain.

A hunter, a veteran, a father with pride,
he knows the cost when loved ones have died.
But he also knows that freedom means more
than just a right to bear arms, it's a call to do more.

He's here to protect, to build, to defend,
to ensure that this nation, on its future depends.
With Kamala Harris, he stands side by side
to take on the challenges, to turn the tide.

So, who is Tim Walz? He's a man with a plan,
a fighter, a leader, who knows where he stands.
In the trenches, he'll battle, in the fields, he'll sow
for the future of America, together we'll grow.

Inspiration Behind "Who is Tim Walz"
Emotion: Admiration and Pride

The inspiration for this poem comes from the
significance of introducing Tim Walz to the American
people at a critical moment in our nation's history. With
the unexpected shift in the Democratic ticket, it became
essential to highlight who our vice-presidential nominee
is—someone who embodies the values, resilience, and
commitment that resonate with everyday Americans.

This poem paints a vivid picture of Tim Walz beyond being a political figure as a person shaped by his roots in small-town America, his service in the military, and his deep connection to teaching and public service. It draws on the powerful moments from his 2024 DNC speech, where he shared his personal journey, his passion for protecting freedoms, and his dedication to building a better future for all.

In a time of rapid change and uncertainty, the poem aims to reassure and inspire Americans by showing the qualities of a leader who understands the challenges we face and who stands ready to fight for the values that unite us. Tim Walz is a symbol of hope, integrity, and the pursuit of a better tomorrow—a vice president who will stand shoulder-to-shoulder with Kamala Harris to lead our nation forward.

Down to the Thread

We're down to the thread, with everything on the line,
in the final stretch, where the stakes intertwine.
Kamala and Trump, the last leg in sight,
a race for the ages, a battle of might.

Politics churn in the heat of the day,
as SCOTUS looms large in the fray.
Congress, the stage where futures are set,
every move, every word—a calculated bet.

RFK Jr., with a twist in the plot,
endorses the man once thought to be not.
Harris, undeterred, with momentum to claim,
eyes on the debate where she'll stake her name.

The polls they swing, a dance on a wire,
as the nation watches, fueled by desire.
For a leader, for change, for a future that's bright,
each vote is a voice in the looming fight.

Facts first, they say, but who holds the truth?
In a world where news spins and the lines are aloof.
Watch, listen, and live in this hour of trial,
as the fate of a nation is hung in the dial.

The crowds, they gather in battleground states,
Every handshake, every rally, the weight of our fates.
From Michigan to Georgia, the buses roll on,
With hopes that November brings a new dawn.

We're down to the thread, with all on the line,
A decision awaits that will echo through time.
The clock, it ticks, as the campaigns collide,
In the final moments, where history resides.

Inspiration Behind "Down to the Thread
Emotion: Urgency and Anticipation

This poem captures the intense and unpredictable 2024 presidential race as it enters its final, critical moments. This election is unlike any other, with a dynamic shift on the Democratic ticket and a fierce contest against a former president. The poem is inspired by the high stakes and the urgency that now pervades the political landscape.

Kamala Harris, having stepped into the role of the Democratic presidential nominee, brings a historic and powerful presence to the race. Her campaign is fueled by the energy generated at the Democratic National Convention, where she rallied the nation with a message of hope, freedom, and resilience. In contrast, Donald Trump continues to galvanize his base, now unexpectedly bolstered by the endorsement of RFK Jr., adding another twist to an already complex race.

The poem reflects the gravity of the situation, where every decision, every poll, and every debate carries significant weight. It touches on the broader political context, including the influence of the Supreme Court, the role of Congress, and the media's portrayal of events, all of which contribute to shaping the final outcome.

"Down to the Thread" symbolizes the fine line on which the nation's future hangs. It emphasizes the importance of every vote, the importance of the battleground states, and the tension surrounding this historic election. The inspiration for this poem lies in the recognition that this moment in history will define the country's trajectory for years to come.

The Fence Walkers' Call

Kamala, we've seen the dance,
The glitter, glam, the grand romance.
But now we ask, with earnest plea,
Show us the path, let us see.

The lights were bright, the words were strong,
But somewhere, somehow, something's wrong.
We need more than just the song,
We need the map to bring us along.

For those who cheer, you've won their hearts,
But what about the ones apart?
The fence is high, the ground unsure,
They need the plan, the solid cure.

We don't need gloss, don't need the show,
We need the facts, the hows, the go.
Lay out the steps, the nuts, the bolts,
Win over minds, secure the votes.

How will you lift, how will you mend?
How will you bring this fight to end?
For every promise that you make,
Show us the hands that shape the stake.

Tell us how you'll bridge the gap,

From dreams and words to actions mapped.
Convince the ones who hesitate,
That you're the one to navigate.

The time is now, the stakes are high,
To win the house, to clear the sky.
Bring the meat, the bread, the wine,
Turn that doubt into a line.

Kamala, we're close, but not yet there,
You've lit the spark, now fan the air.
For democracy's fragile thread,
Give us the plan to move ahead.

Inspiration Behind "The Fence Walkers' Call
Emotion: Uncertainty and Expectation

This poem was born out of a reflection on the 2024 Democratic National Convention, particularly Kamala Harris's keynote speech. While the DNC was heralded by many Democrats as a great success—full of energy, hope, and a powerful narrative—the reception beyond the party's base told a more nuanced story. Independents, never-Trumpers, and those who once supported Trump but are now disillusioned, watched the spectacle with a critical eye. They were drawn in by the emotions and the promise of change but found themselves yearning for something more tangible.

Kamala's speech, while rousing and full of passion, left some crucial questions unanswered for these voters. They wanted to know how her administration would achieve the ambitious goals she laid out. They sought details, concrete policies, and a clear path forward—how would she balance the budget, protect freedoms, and heal the nation's divides? This poem was written to echo their concerns and to serve as a plea, a call to action, for the campaign to not take the election for granted.

"The Fence Walkers' Call" speaks directly to the
dynamic of this election—a race too close to leave anything
to chance. It urges Kamala Harris and her team to shift
their strategy in the final stretch, to provide the substance
that these undecided voters crave. It's a reminder that
while hope and inspiration are powerful, they must be
backed by clear plans and actionable steps if they are to
win over those who remain on the fence.

This poem is more than just a reflection; it's a rallying
cry to ensure that the Democratic campaign doesn't just
win the hearts of those already convinced but also secures
the minds of those who are still weighing their options. It
acknowledges the excitement within the Democratic Party
while recognizing that the road to victory in November
requires a broader, more detailed conversation with the
American people.

Threads Unraveled

Kamala spoke with fire and grace
but left some folks still in their place.
Bob and Sharon, on their farm,
felt a tug, but kept their calm.

"Could be worse," they both agreed,
but Trump's shadow still sewed seed.
Craig, with pizza, shrugged and scoffed,
"Promises, sure, but what's the cost?"

Ryan felt a flicker, brief,
but doubts hung heavy like a thief.
Tim rolled eyes at glittered praise,
"Where's the meat in all these plays?"

Kamala's pitch, a thread too thin
for hearts that cling to where they've been.
The stage was set, the lights were bright,
but some saw shadow in her light.

They're not all in, they're not all sold,
wary of the tales she told.
A game of wit, a dance of chance,
in the end, it's still a stance.

For every stitch she tried to mend,
there's a thread left loose in the end.
Can she sew a quilt that holds,
or will it fray in folds?

Inspiration Behind "Threads Unraveled
Emotion: Skepticism and Doubt

This poem was inspired by the complex and tense atmosphere surrounding the final stretch of the 2024 presidential race, as highlighted in a detailed CNN article. The article painted a vivid picture of the current political landscape, emphasizing the precariousness of this election—where every move, every word, and every decision could tip the scales. The race is down to the thread, with Vice President Kamala Harris and former President Donald Trump fighting for voters' hearts and minds in a contest that could define the nation's future.

The CNN article provided information that fed directly into the poem's creation. It discussed key elements like the significance of post-DNC poll bumps, the unpredictable impact of RFK Jr.'s endorsement of Trump, and the energized Democratic campaign that seeks to maintain its momentum. It also explored Harris's challenges in appealing to undecided voters and the ongoing tug-of-war in battleground states that could determine the election outcome.

These themes resonated deeply and formed the backbone of the poem. "Threads Unraveled" captures the urgency and the delicate balance that defines this moment in American politics. The poem reflects on the intense emotions and the high stakes of the race, where the nation's future hangs by a thread. It speaks to the pressures faced by both campaigns, the unpredictable nature of voter sentiment, and the need for clear, decisive action to secure victory.

The significance of the article lies in its ability to convey the gravity of the situation. It is a reminder that despite the fanfare and excitement of the DNC, there is still much work to be done. The article emphasized that while the Democratic Party might feel confident, they cannot afford to be complacent. It's a call to remain vigilant, address the concerns of all voters—especially those on the fence—and ensure that the electorate hears and feels the campaign's message.

"Threads Unraveled" is a poetic expression of these ideas. It unpacks the tension, the hope, and the fear that characterize this election. The poem explores the delicate threads that hold the fabric of this campaign together, acknowledging the possibility of those threads unraveling if not carefully managed. It's a reflection on the fragility of the moment and a plea for attention to detail, strategy, and substance as the race reaches its critical final phase.

Ghetto

From Venice's canals, the word took flight,
a place where Jews were hidden from sight.
"Ghèto," they called it, near the foundry's flame,
a neighborhood born from iron's name.

Yet, in the shadows of history's stage,
the word transformed, took on new rage.
In America's streets, it found a new home
where my people were left to roam.

Urban neighbors, we build our lives
in places where struggle and hardship thrive.
But they call it "ghetto" with a sneer,
a word now soaked in bias and fear.

They see us as danger, they see us as plight,
ignoring the systems that birthed this fight.
The red lines drawn, the homes denied,
the dreams deferred, the tears we've cried.

Systemic racism, it carved the walls,
But they blame our culture for the fall.
They overlook the root, the deep-set pain,
And pass off our lives as society's stain.

How sad, how unjust, how deeply untrue
to see only the surface, not the view
of a community rich with love and pride
in a world that too often turns a blind eye.

But still, we rise, in spite of the name,
in spite of the burden, the hurt, the shame.
For "ghetto" is not who we are,
We are strength, we are hope, we are stars.

Inspiration Behind "Ghetto"
Emotion: Resilience and Frustration

"Ghetto" was born from my reflection on the word's
origins and how it has evolved into something that carries
heavy connotations of prejudice, exclusion, and systemic
injustice. The word "ghetto" originated in 16th-century
Venice, Italy, and likely comes from "ghèto," meaning a
foundry or slag, referring to the segregated area where the
Jewish quarter was located. Even then, the word carried
the weight of segregation and social exclusion.

Over time, the word "ghetto" found its way into
American vernacular, becoming a label for urban
neighborhoods predominantly inhabited by marginalized
or minority groups. Over the last 30 years, the concept of
the "ghetto" in the United States has been closely tied to
the effects of systemic racism and economic inequality.
Urban neighborhoods predominantly inhabited by African
Americans and other minorities have often been labeled as

"ghettos," a term that carries with it negative assumptions about the people who live there. It frustrates me to see how the term "ghetto" has been used to unfairly label these neighborhoods, especially those where Black Americans and other minorities live. This label perpetuates negative stereotypes and obscures the root causes of our struggles, like systemic racism, discriminatory housing practices, and social exclusion.

These neighborhoods often suffer from a lack of investment, inadequate access to quality education, healthcare, and employment opportunities, and are frequently targeted by discriminatory housing practices. Redlining, where banks and insurers refused services to residents of certain areas based on racial or ethnic composition, played a significant role in the creation and perpetuation of these ghettos. Even though redlining was officially outlawed in the 1960s, its legacy still looms large over these communities today.

In the last few decades, policies like mass incarceration and the War on Drugs have disproportionately targeted minority communities, entrenching poverty and limiting opportunities for upward mobility. This systemic imbalance has led to persistent racial disparities in wealth, education, and health outcomes.

Some urban areas have seen revitalization and gentrification, but these developments often displace long-term residents rather than benefit them. Investments in infrastructure, businesses, and housing tend to favor newcomers, leaving the original residents marginalized and excluded from the benefits of economic growth. This has deepened the racial imbalance, as wealthier, often white, populations move into these neighborhoods, pushing minority populations further into poverty.

This poem resonates deeply with me as I've personally experienced the impact of redlining and systemic barriers. As a successful gay, Black man in the USA, born to parents who were just 14 years old, I've beaten many of the statistics stacked against me. But despite my successes, I've still faced significant obstacles. One of my most financially painful experiences was when I tried to refinance my home. I was denied because of the color of my skin, and my home was valued far below its worth—yet my white boyfriend at the time received a fair valuation. To this day, I still carry the financial burden of that discrimination. The system needs to be fixed so that my community can also access generational wealth, equal lending, healthcare, and all the economic opportunities that white communities have enjoyed for centuries.

In this poem, I shed light on the historical and ongoing injustices that have led to the marginalization of our communities. I challenge the narrative that blames the residents of these neighborhoods for their conditions, rather than recognizing the decades of systemic oppression that have shaped their realities. It saddens and angers me how often the truth is overlooked, and I believe we must break this cycle of generational burden by addressing these systemic issues, and by educating others to change mindsets and environments.

The hope for the future lies in breaking these systemic chains by addressing the root causes of inequality. We must invest in education, healthcare, and economic opportunities within our communities—not just for show, but to truly empower our people.

Education and awareness are key to this transformation. By educating others about the history and realities of systemic racism, and by advocating for policies that promote equity, we can break the cycle of generational burden. This burden shouldn't be ours to carry from generation to generation; it's a collective responsibility to ensure that future generations inherit a world where all people, regardless of race or background, have the opportunity to thrive.

The poem "Ghetto" is not just a lament—it's a call to action. It's a reminder that while the strength, hope, and

brilliance of our communities continue to shine, true
justice will only come when the systemic chains are
broken, and mindsets shift from blame to understanding,
and from exclusion to inclusion.

The Childless Cat Lady's Voting Guide

Gather 'round, childless cat lady's here,
With a head full of facts and a message clear:
Voting's no TikTok, don't play it like a game,
Misinformation? Pfft, it's always the same.

Swipe left on vibes, and right on truth,
Get off the 'Gram, stop wasting your youth.
Read some bills, dig deep in the files,
Not just cute memes, or their polished smiles.

These candidates out here? They're selling their wares,
But do their votes align with the values you care?
They promise, they dance, they give you a wink,
But what did they really do? Let's stop and think.

Research, dear friend, is where you must start,
Pull back the curtain, get to the heart.
What did they vote for? What did they shun?
Who's fighting for you when the day is done?

So gather your cats, brew your tea,
Sit with the news and read thoroughly.
Make your own choice—be astute, be wise,
And let your vote reflect the truth, not lies.

At the booth, be bold, don't just go with the flow,
The country's your house—make sure you know!
Childless, cat lady, or anything in between,
Your voice is the loudest it's ever been seen.

So read up, speak out, and raise a fierce paw,
Vote for the future, and the world you saw!

Inspiration Behind "The Childless Cat Lady's Voting Guide"

Emotion: Empowerment and Wit

After watching the first debate between Kamala Harris and Donald Trump, I was buzzing with energy. Harris did exactly what I hoped: She stayed calm, steady, and delivered the facts, not drama. A CNN poll showed what I already knew—63% of registered voters agreed she outperformed Trump. And it wasn't just me; the numbers spoke for themselves! Harris's confidence and clarity left Trump's chaos in the dust.

And guess what? 96% of Harris supporters believed she had a better night. I was beaming! It was a pivotal moment, not just for the election, but for our country. Harris had the edge on key issues like abortion and democracy. Plus, her favorability among independent voters rose to 48%, up from 30% before. It was clear—she didn't just win the night; she won hearts and minds.

The debate proved that she could stand up to Trump, who still held some ground on the economy, immigration, and his role as commander-in-chief. But honestly, who do you want protecting democracy and your rights? The answer was clear to me: Kamala Harris. She has the wisdom and composure that we need in these times.

And just when the debate couldn't have made me happier, Taylor Swift herself dropped an Instagram post endorsing Kamala Harris and Tim Walz for 2024. It was like the cherry on top! Swift urged her fans to do their own homework, echoing what I've been thinking: Don't get your news from TikTok alone. Do your research, dive into the issues, and make an informed choice. Her post drove nearly 406,000 people to visit vote.gov in just one day. That's the Swift effect—real action, real change.

Swift's words hit home: "I've done my research, and I've made my choice. Your research is all yours to do, and the choice is yours to make." Wise advice, right? So

whether you're a cat lady or not, it's time to dig deep.
Read up on policies, understand what's at stake, and most
importantly—VOTE! The future of this country depends
on it.

So, gather your facts, put on your reading glasses, and
let's do this. Together, we can keep calm and Swift on.

Embarrassment

Oh, the audacity draped in gold,
A swagger of arrogance, confidence bold,
While world leaders chuckled, shaking their heads,
At policies spun like tangled threads.

Trump, you claimed respect in every glance,
But some saw chaos in your dance,
A disruption, a rupture, not grace or tact,
Global relations straining under the fact.

Macron with his treaties torn in two,
Merkel stood tall, your words untrue,
Trudeau clashed, and May gave her sigh,
While you tweeted storms under the sky.

Fox called you out without a care,
A Mexican voice in the open air,
Tusk spoke softly, but his words did sting,
The world watched you, their reluctant king.

And now, in debates, you twist and turn,
Facts fall like ashes as your words burn,
Eighty-one million stood tall and said no,
To a man the world saw as a show.

Lies unravel, your fabric frayed,
As truth emerges, undismayed.
An embarrassment you became, not the crown,
As leaders around you watched you drown.

Still, you persist, with head held high,
But the world leaders laugh, no need to deny.

Inspiration Behind "Embarrassment"
Emotion: Disapproval and Shame

The poem "Embarrassment" was inspired by the 2024 presidential debate between Vice President Kamala Harris and former President Donald Trump, where the stark differences in their leadership styles were on full display. Harris presented herself with poise and precision, debunking many of Trump's false claims, while Trump leaned heavily on divisive rhetoric, misinformation, and personal attacks.

Trump's behavior during the debate was emblematic of the vulgar and tactless approach he often takes, which many world leaders and political analysts have described as not only inappropriate but also damaging to international relations. His remarks about Harris, particularly the crude insinuation that she had "put out," were an example of the disrespectful and sexist language that has characterized much of his rhetoric, leaving many viewers—myself included—shocked and disgusted. This moment in the debate exemplified Trump's tendency to undermine serious political discourse with offensive, attention-grabbing remarks, further alienating global leaders and the American public.

Kamala Harris, on the other hand, stood firm against Trump's barrage of misinformation. She fact-checked his misleading statements on topics like the economy, immigration, and abortion. For example, Trump falsely claimed that Harris and Biden had caused the highest inflation in U.S. history and allowed migrants to overrun American towns, spreading baseless accusations like immigrants eating pets in Springfield, Ohio. NPR's fact-checkers debunked many of these assertions in real-time, clarifying that inflation was largely driven by global events, including the pandemic and the war in Ukraine, and that violent crime had, in fact, decreased.

The contrast in their debate styles reflected a larger narrative: Trump's divisive and crude behavior versus Harris's composed and fact-based leadership. Harris's calm dismantling of Trump's claims was seen as a masterclass in debate performance, highlighting her vision for America's future while pushing back against Trump's legacy of chaos and division. As the debate ended, it was clear that Harris had shown herself to be a capable, resilient leader, and Trump, once again, had revealed his tendency to rely on gaudy, vulgar tactics rather than substance.

This poem was written to encapsulate the feeling shared by many who watched the debate: that Trump's words and actions have not only embarrassed him but have also embarrassed the country on the global stage. Despite his claims of being respected by world leaders, it is clear that many of them, along with American voters, view his leadership as tacky, divisive, and detrimental to both domestic and international progress.

Index

The Emotions of the Verses of Life:
Through Chapters of Love

Preface

The emotion label for the "Preface" of *Verses of
Life* is **introspection**. The preface of the book highlights
deep self-reflection, personal growth, and a thoughtful
exploration of love, relationships, and the process of
transformation through lived experiences and therapy.

Intro Chapter

The emotion label for the "Intro Chapter" is **anticipation**.
The poems invite you onto a journey of self-discovery,
filled with reflection, optimism, and emotional
exploration, setting the tone for the meaningful and
personal themes to follow.

1. *Veress of Life: An Emotional Prelude*

The emotion label for " Verses of Life: An Emotional
Prelude" is **introspection**. The poem invites deep reflection
on the full spectrum of human emotions, guiding you
through a personal and emotional journey that explores
the complexities of love, life, and self-discovery.

2. *Meet Malcolm*

The emotion label for "Meet Malcolm" is **resilience**. The
poem reflects strength and determination through the
journey of overcoming challenges, acknowledging the
influence of upbringing, and celebrating personal growth
shaped by love, discipline, and self-discovery.

3. *My Name Is Malcolm Elajuwon, Alexander Neal*

The emotion label for "My Name Is Malcolm Elajuwon, Alexander Neal" is **pride**. The poem reflects a deep sense of honor and connection to heritage, identity, and family, celebrating the meaning and significance behind each part of the name and the cultural legacy it carries.

4. *I am a Pisces*

The emotion label for "I am a Pisces" is **contemplation**. The poem emphasizes thoughtful reflection on personal identity, the complexities of the Pisces sign, and the interplay of astrological traits with life experiences, therapy, and cultural influences.

5. *My Chart*

The emotion label for "My Chart" is **self-awareness**. The poem reflects deep introspection and understanding of personal identity, as the poem delves into the complexities of astrology and how each element of the natal chart shapes my multifaceted personality.

6. *Love and Legacy*

The emotion label for "Love and Legacy" is **purpose**. The poem reflects a deep sense of intention, driven by a desire to make a meaningful impact through love, advocacy, and breaking barriers, while leaving a lasting legacy rooted in both personal and communal growth.

7. *Boundless Becoming*

The emotion label for "Boundless Becoming" is **optimism**. The poem radiates positivity, celebrating growth, exploration, and the limitless potential of life, while reflecting a joyful embrace of self-discovery and continuous evolution.

8. *Wanderlust Symphony*

The emotion label for "Wanderlust Symphony" is **freedom**. The poem reflects the liberating and transformative experience of travel, celebrating the joy of exploration, cultural immersion, and self-discovery through a nomadic lifestyle.

9. *Breaking the Silence*

The emotion label for "Breaking the Silence" is **empowerment**. The poem reflects a strong call to action, challenging stigmas around mental health in minority communities, and advocating for healing and growth through therapy, while offering hope and strength for future generations.

10. *Three Truths Inspired by Oprah*

The emotion label for "Three Truths Inspired by Oprah" is **gratitude**. The poem reflects deep appreciation and admiration for Oprah's influence, acknowledging her as a guiding force in storytelling, purpose, and uplifting others.

11. *Echoes of Open and Close*

The emotion label for "Inspiration for 'Echoes of Open and Close'" is **reflection**. The poem delves into the cyclical nature of life, exploring how beginnings and endings shape personal growth and understanding, with a focus on lessons learned from love, transitions, and self-discovery.

12. *Turning Thoughts to Gold*

The emotion label for "Turning Thoughts to Gold'" is **creativity**. The poem celebrates the transformative process of turning raw thoughts and emotions into meaningful art, highlighting the challenges, joys, and fulfillment that come from creative expression.

13. Journey's Verse

The emotion label for "Journey's Verse" is **evolution**. The poem reflects a continuous process of personal growth and self-discovery, shaped by relationships and life transitions, as it explores identity, love, and the pursuit of emotional fulfillment.

14. Unwritten Chapters: A Mosaic of Me

The emotion label for "Unwritten Chapters: A Mosaic of Me" is **introspection**. The poem reflects deep self-reflection, as it weaves together past experiences, love, loss, and personal growth, while exploring the ongoing journey of life and the evolving narrative of my identity.

Childhood Chapter

The emotion label for the "Childhood" chapter is **nostalgia**. The poems reflect a deep sense of reflection on my formative experiences, blending the emotions of anticipation, fear, love, and revelation, while exploring the profound impact of those early years in shaping my identity and resilience.

15. Rooted in Detroit

The emotion label for "Rooted in Detroit" is **nostalgia**. The poem reflects a deep connection to childhood, family, and the city of Detroit, evoking fond memories of love, resilience, and the foundational experiences that shaped my identity.

16. New Beginnings in a Family Mosaic

The emotion label for "New Beginnings in a Family Mosaic" is **belonging**. The poem reflects the warmth and connection felt in embracing new family members, celebrating the unity, love, and shared experiences that create lasting memories and a sense of home.

17. *Echoes of East Side Vicariate*

The emotion label for "Echoes of East Side Vicariate" is **nostalgia**. The poem reflects a fond remembrance of formative years, friendships, and pivotal experiences that shaped my personal growth and identity during middle school, evoking warmth and reflection on the past.

18. *Journey to Cass: A Prelude*

The emotion label for "Journey to Cass: A Prelude" is **growth**. The poems reflect a journey of personal development, capturing the apprehension, excitement, and transformation experienced during my transition from middle school to high school, highlighting themes of resilience, self-discovery, and newfound confidence.

19. *First Steps at Cass Tech*

The emotion label for "First Steps at Cass Tech" is **exhilaration**. The poems capture the excitement, anticipation, and personal growth experienced during my transition into high school, highlighting new challenges, friendships, and self-discovery in a dynamic and transformative environment.

20. *Winter Reflections at Cass Tech*

The emotion label for "'Winter Reflections at Cass Tech'" is **contemplation**. The poems reflect a thoughtful examination of personal growth, academic challenges, social experiences, and the complexities of adolescence, capturing the transformative moments that shaped my teenage years.

21. *Sophomore Year Shifts*

The emotion label for 'Sophomore Year Shifts'" is **self-discovery**. The poems reflect my journey through personal exploration, evolving identity, budding relationships, and newfound leadership, capturing the excitement,

challenges, and growth experienced during this pivotal
year.

22. *Summer School Silhouettes at Harvard*

The emotion label for "Summer School Silhouettes at
Harvard" is **inspiration**. The poem reflects the sense of
excitement, personal growth, and motivation that came
from a transformative experience at Harvard, filled with
intellectual challenges and the realization of vast future
possibilities.

23. *11th Grade Confessions*

The emotion label for "'11th Grade Confessions'"
is **yearning**. The poem encapsulates deep longing,
unrequited love, and the emotional complexity of
navigating identity, affection, and self-discovery.

24. *The Summer of Revelation*

The emotion label for "The Summer of Revelation"
is **liberation**. The poem reflects the profound emotional
and psychological freedom that comes from embracing my
true identity, stepping out of societal constraints, and
finding relief in authenticity.

25. *First Day of Senior Year*

The emotion label for "First Day of Senior Year'"
is **empowerment**. The poem conveys a sense of bold self-
expression, confidence, and the decision to embrace my
identity without fear, symbolizing personal strength and
the power of authenticity.

26. *The Orbit of Unrequited Love*

The emotion label for "The Orbit of Unrequited Love"
is **yearning**. The poem reflects the deep intensity of
unrequited love, capturing the emotional complexity of

desire, pain, and personal growth that arises from navigating the overwhelming feelings of a first love.

27. *Unspoken Acceptance*

The emotion label for "Unspoken Acceptance" is **gratitude**. The poem highlights a deep appreciation for the subtle, unspoken support and understanding from my father, conveying the warmth and emotional depth of acceptance that requires no words.

Kyle Chapter

The emotion label for the "Kyle" chapter is **introspection and growth**. It reflects on my emotional journey through a significant romantic relationship, highlighting lessons learned about love, trust, and self-discovery, and the lasting impact of these experiences on personal development.

28. *How We Met*

The emotion label for "How We Met" is **camaraderie**. The poem reflects the deep bond of friendship and mutual support formed through shared experiences, capturing the trust and connection that blossomed between two friends navigating the challenges of life and love together.

29. *Journal Entry: A Love Beyond the Reefs*

The emotion label for "Journal Entry: A Love Beyond the Reefs" is **reflection**. The poem conveys introspection on the complexities of friendship, love, and past mistakes, set against the backdrop of nature's beauty, capturing the lessons learned about relationships and emotional growth.

30. *A Trust Unraveled*

The emotion label for "A Trust Unraveled" is **betrayal**. The poem reflects the pain and heartbreak of a relationship built on mistrust, secrets, and unrequited love, capturing the emotional complexity of friendship, love, and the lessons learned from a broken bond

31. *Reflections on Kyle*

The emotion label for "Reflections on Kyle" is **affection**. The poem expresses deep feelings of warmth, connection, and love, capturing the evolving bond between friendship and romantic love, along with the vulnerability and joy that come with it.

32. *Endless Love: A Valentine's Memory*

The emotion label for "Endless Love: A Valentine's Memory" is **romantic nostalgia**. The poem reflects a fond remembrance of a first love and Valentine's Day, filled with warmth, tenderness, and a reflection on how that experience shaped my approach to love and affection.

33. *NYC Ambulance*

The emotion label for "NYC Ambulance" is **resilience**. The poem reflects the strength found in a challenging moment, where love and protection prevailed in the midst of chaos, capturing the intensity of the experience and the bond it forged between us.

34. *Betrayal's Edge*

The emotion labels for "Betrayal's Edge" is **betrayal** and **despair**. The poem captures the intense feelings of heartbreak, confusion, and hurt following the discovery of infidelity, while also reflecting on the emotional toll and the eventual healing that comes from navigating trust broken by betrayal.

35. *Through with Love*

The emotion label for "Through with Love" is **empowerment**. The poem reflects a journey of emotional release, finding strength in letting go of a toxic relationship, and embracing self-worth through the cathartic power of music.

36. Jace and Kyle Night

The emotion label for "Jace and Kyle Night" is **turmoil**. The poem reflects the intense emotions of jealousy, betrayal, and conflict, while also capturing the eventual growth, healing, and resolution that followed the chaotic and emotionally charged events of that night.

37. Reflections on a Broken Mirror

The emotion label for "Reflections on a Broken Mirror" is **regret**. The poem reflects a deep sense of reflection on past misunderstandings and missed opportunities for healing, capturing the sorrow of not being able to guide someone through their struggles and the lessons learned from the emotional conflict.

38. Missing You, Finding Me

The emotion label for "Missing You, Finding Me" is **longing**. The poem reflects a deep sense of missing someone dear, while also capturing the bittersweet process of personal growth, self-discovery, and navigating emotional challenges during their absence.

39. A Summer of Transition

The emotion label for "A Summer of Transition" is **anticipation**. The poem reflects the excitement and emotional intensity of transitioning from one relationship to another, capturing the long-held desire and the culmination of feelings that lead to a new beginning filled with hope and possibilities.

Jace Chapter
The emotion label for the "Jace" chapter is **passion and heartache**. The poems convey the intense love and emotional struggles of a hidden relationship, highlighting the pain of being unseen and the personal growth that arises from enduring such challenges.

40. The Love That Spanned Years

The emotion label for "The Love That Spanned Years" is **nostalgia**. The poem reflects a deep reminiscence of a love that evolved over time, filled with longing, joy, and emotional intensity, capturing the bittersweet memories of a relationship that shaped my heart and soul.

41. Our First Kiss

The emotion label for "Our First Kiss" is **euphoria**. The poem captures the intense joy, anticipation, and passion of a long-awaited romantic moment, filled with emotional release and the thrill of deep connection, marking the beginning of a meaningful journey.

42. Lust in the Concrete Jungle

The emotion label for "Lust in the Concrete Jungle" is **intensity**. The poem reflects the powerful and passionate connection between us two lovers, filled with unrestrained desire, excitement, and the reckless abandon of our relationship, capturing the overwhelming and consuming nature of lust.

43. Unspoken Truths

The emotion label for "Unspoken Truths" is **vulnerability**. The poem expresses deep emotional honesty, capturing the fear, longing, and uncertainty of unaddressed feelings in a relationship, while seeking clarity, communication, and mutual connection.

44. *2009's Missing Memory*

The emotion label for "2009's Missing Memory" is **hurt**. The poem expresses deep feelings of pain, frustration, and unacknowledged love, capturing the sense of being hidden and undervalued in a relationship that lacked visibility and recognition.

45. *A Plea for Us*

The emotion label for "A Plea for Us" is **desperation**. The poem expresses a deep yearning for reconnection and honesty, capturing my vulnerability as I reflect on the lost bond. There's a sense of longing for the past, mixed with a desire to mend the relationship, and hope that the friendship within the relationship can be rebuilt despite the emotional distance that has grown between us.

46. *The Structure of Trust*

The emotion label for "The Structure of Trust" is **reflective**. The poem conveys a thoughtful meditation on the importance of trust, integrity, and fidelity in both personal relationships and life. It reflects on the teachings of Gary Pavela and emphasizes the value of honesty and trustworthiness in building meaningful connections, while also warning against the dangers of deceit and ambition. The overall tone is one of contemplation and moral insight.

47. *Sasha's Swipe: A Christmas Surprise*

The emotion label for "Sasha's Swipe: A Christmas Surprise" is **amused frustration.** The poem humorously expresses my frustration at an unexpected financial hit, paired with the surprise and eventual affection for Sasha, the Pomeranian. While the situation is frustrating—discovering a large charge without consent—it is softened by humor and my eventual love for the dog, turning a moment of exasperation into one of fond reflection.

48. In the Shadows of Love

The emotion label for "In the Shadows of
Love" is **heartache** and **self-realization.** The poem reflects
deep feelings of pain, sadness, and frustration from being
hidden in a relationship, but it also captures my journey
toward self-worth and understanding. The emotional
weight of unreciprocated love and being kept in the
shadows is palpable, yet the poem ends with a sense of
empowerment and self-prioritization.

49. The Grad School Realization

The emotion label for "The Grad School
Realization" is **disappointment and awakening.** The poem
conveys my deep sense of disillusionment with a love that
remains hidden, accompanied by the growing realization
that I deserve more. The tone is marked by the pain of
unfulfilled expectations, but it also signals an emerging
self-awareness and the strength to seek a love that is open
and fully embracing.

50. Betrayal Unveiled

The emotion label for "Betrayal Unveiled" is **betrayal**. The
poem reflects the deep pain and hurt caused by
discovering infidelity, with a focus on the broken trust and
emotional aftermath that follows.

51. The Last Test

The emotion label for "The Last Test" is **resignation**. The
poem reflects an acceptance of the end of a relationship,
with the acknowledgment that long-distance didn't cause
the breakup but revealed deeper truths, leading to the
realization that letting go was necessary for my personal
growth.

52. To My Soulmate, Departed

The emotion label for "To My Soulmate, Departed" and "Jace's Response" is **introspection and emotional growth**. The poems are inspired by a reflective moment in the my relationship with Jace, leading to self-awareness about my own co-dependence and a deeper understanding of Jace's need for individuality. The process of turning this exchange into poetry reveals a cathartic journey of balancing love and personal space, fostering emotional maturation.

53. *The Love I Closed Down*

The emotion label for "The Love I Closed Down" is **self-awareness.** The poem reflects a deep realization about past relationships, where love was constrained by fear, logic, and self-protection. Through personal growth and therapy, I gain insight into my emotional journey and find a safe space to fully embrace love once again.

Mark Chapter

The emotion label for the "Mark" chapter is **passion and nostalgia.** The poems convey the intense love and complex emotions of a long-term, passionate relationship, highlighting both the thrilling moments and the bittersweet lessons learned from a connection that left a lasting impact despite its end.

54. *The Night at the Conrad: Meeting Mark*

The emotion label for "The Night at the Conrad: Meeting Mark" is **passion and longing.** The poem vividly recounts the intense emotions of desire, connection, and the thrill of a love affair that spanned years. It captures the depth of physical attraction, the momentary doubts, and the overwhelming passion that defined the relationship, all underlined by a sense of longing for something more than a fleeting connection.

55. *From Digital Sparks to Miami Nights*

The emotion label for "From Digital Sparks to Miami Nights" is **nostalgia**. The poem reflects a deep sense of fondness and longing for the vibrant love affair with Mark and the enchanting connection to Miami. There's a bittersweet tone, recalling the thrill and beauty of those moments, but also acknowledging that it has faded, leaving only memories. The love for both myself and the city is wrapped in a wistful reflection of past joy, passion, and the warmth of Miami nights.

56. *A Birthday in Miami*

The emotion label for "A Birthday in Miami" is **affectionate nostalgia.** The poem fondly reflects on the joy, love, and cherished memories of a special trip with Mark and friends. While there's a hint of reflection on missed red flags, the overall tone is one of warmth, affection, and gratitude for the experiences shared during that time. The love for Mark and Miami's magic shines through, creating a nostalgic reminiscence of the bond and carefree happiness of those moments.

57. *The Night I Let Go*

The emotion label for "The Night I Let Go" is **heartbreak and realization.** The poem captures the moment of emotional release and the quiet acceptance of a love that was fading. There is a bittersweet reflection on the joy of the relationship juxtaposed with the painful acknowledgment of its inevitable end. The feelings of longing, unspoken words, and the quiet heartbreak of letting go create a poignant sense of loss, but also the beginning of emotional clarity.

58. *When Darren Called*

The emotion label for "When Darren Called" is **transition and reflection.** The poem expresses a sense of moving on from past relationships, reflecting on patterns of love, and the difficult process of letting go while stepping into something new. It's filled with the weight of decisions, the bittersweet recognition of love's end, and the hope and complexity of beginning anew with Darren. The undertone of reflection, mixed with the courage to face emotions and confront past loves, shapes the emotional landscape of this piece.

59. A Love Affair That Lingered

The emotion label for "A Love Affair That Lingered" is **conflicted**. The poem captures the tension between my desire for Mark and the internal struggle with the choices made. While the love and attraction for Mark is strong, there's an underlying conflict stemming from the betrayal and rationalization of infidelity, creating a push-and-pull dynamic within my emotions.

60. Two lovers

The emotion label for "Two Lovers" is **entangled**. The poem reflects the complex web of emotions that arise from managing two relationships at once, highlighting the internal and external complications of love, lust, and loyalty. I am caught in the intertwining dynamics of affection, temptation, and the consequences of my actions, creating a sense of emotional and relational entanglement throughout the narrative.

61. The Fork in the Road: A Poem on Decisions and Destiny

The emotion label for "The Fork in the Road: A Poem on Decisions and Destiny" is **reflective**. The poem conveys a deep sense of introspection, where I look back on pivotal choices and my consequences. There is a tone of acceptance and understanding, highlighting how decisions, both big and small, shape my journey, without dwelling on regret.

Darren Chapter

The emotion label for "Darren" is **heartache and personal growth**. The poems convey the sorrow of separation and loss, alongside the journey of self-discovery and the lessons learned from the end of a significant relationship.

62. Cocktails and Beginnings

The emotion label for "Cocktails and Beginnings" is **nostalgic** with a hint of caution. The poem reflects a sense of fondness for the early stages of a connection, coupled with an awareness of red flags that were overlooked at the time. There's a wistfulness in remembering the simplicity and excitement of the first meeting, mixed with a subtle acknowledgment of the complexities that would later surface.

63. Support Through Law School Series

The emotion label for the "Support Through Law School Series" is dedication with a sense of **bittersweet reflection.** The inspiration for this series is rooted in a deep commitment to partnership, underscored by the shared dreams and sacrifices made along the way. While the poems celebrate the strength of the bond and the achievements accomplished together, there's a bittersweet undertone, acknowledging both the fulfillment of their goals and the eventual end of the relationship. It captures the duality of pride and wistfulness.

64. The Proposal

The emotion label for "The Proposal" is romantic **anticipation with fulfillment.** The poem captures the build-up of excitement, love, and thoughtfulness in planning the proposal, alongside the deep emotional connection between the two of us. The sense of anticipation is strong throughout the preparation, culminating in the moment of asking for a lifelong commitment, and the fulfillment of that love is realized when the proposal is accepted. It conveys love, joy, and a sense of destiny intertwined with the couple's journey.

65. *4435 S Indiana Series*

The emotion label for the "4435 S Indiana Series" is **nostalgic pride.** The reflection carries a deep sense of pride in the accomplishments, love, and shared dreams that were realized through hard work and dedication. There is also a layer of nostalgia, as the poems revisit a time of hope, partnership, and the creation of something lasting, despite the eventual end of the relationship. The overall tone blends accomplishment with a bittersweet remembrance of the journey and the love that built a home, even as it acknowledges the complexities of the past.

66. *The Graduation Trip*

The emotion label for "The Graduation Trip" is **joyful nostalgia.** The poem reflects on a deeply meaningful and joyful journey, filled with love, exploration, and the fulfillment of dreams. The sense of pride in the relationship and the sacrifices made is palpable, as is the nostalgia for a time when everything felt hopeful and connected. It's a celebration of shared experiences, while acknowledging the passage of time and the lasting impact of those moments.

67. *When I Bought a Bike*

The emotion label for "When I Bought a Bike" is **betrayal and self-realization.** The poem expresses deep feelings of betrayal, confusion, and frustration, but ultimately leads to a powerful moment of self-discovery and empowerment. It captures the unraveling of my relationship, the pain of infidelity, and the realization that choosing oneself is the path forward amidst the wreckage of the past.

68. *Thresholds Crossed*

The emotion label for "Thresholds Crossed" is **betrayal and emotional devastation.** The poem conveys a deep sense of betrayal, heartbreak, and the collapse of trust within a relationship. It explores the pain of infidelity, the emotional toll of broken promises, and the eventual journey toward healing and reclaiming personal strength amidst the ruins of love.

69. *Therapy Series*

The emotion label for "The Therapy Series" is **self-reflection and emotional growth.** The series captures a profound journey through relational struggles, personal vulnerability, and self-discovery. It highlights the emotional toll of navigating therapy, both as a couple and individually, while ultimately leading to clarity, empowerment, and the realization that healing sometimes requires letting go. The poems reflect the turbulence of trying to mend a fractured relationship and the parallel path of internal growth and self-understanding.

70. *Therapeutic Gratitude Series*

The emotion label for "Elegy for Peace" and "Therapist Farewell" is **closure and self-acceptance.** These poems reflect a journey of emotional growth, highlighting the acceptance of personal peace after relational turmoil and the role therapy played in fostering self-understanding and communication. The inspiration stems from both the bittersweet end of a relationship and the therapeutic process that led to deeper self-awareness, advocating for personal needs, and finding serenity in solitude.

71. *Our Last Words Series*

The emotion label for the poem series "Our Last Words Series" is **grief and acceptance.** The series captures the emotional weight of final exchanges, blending sorrow, unresolved tension, and the realization that my relationship has reached its end. While the poems explore the complexities of apology, farewell, and reflection, the overarching emotional tone centers on the grief of letting go and the gradual acceptance of separation and closure.

72. *Ashes of Yesterday*

The emotion label for "Ashes of Yesterday" is **empowerment** through loss. The poem captures my emotional journey from heartbreak and the physical destruction of my past to a profound sense of personal liberation and inner strength. While the imagery evokes sadness and destruction, the dominant emotion is the empowerment that comes from reclaiming peace and freedom in the face of loss.

73. *The Planner in Me Series*

The emotion label for the "The Planner in Me Series" is **nostalgic reflection.** The series stems from a deep sense of looking back on the shared experiences, joy, and love that came with meticulously planning and embarking on travels with Darren. It evokes a bittersweet remembrance of the beauty, bonding, and eventual unraveling of a relationship, while honoring the personal growth and shared passion for exploration that defined that chapter of life. The reflection is filled with both gratitude for the memories and a lingering sense of loss for what once was.

74. *The Final Verse of Us*

The emotion label for "The Final Verse of Us" is **somber acceptance**. The poem expresses a deep sense of closure, marked by the formal dissolution of a marriage in a court setting. It carries the weight of loss, regret, and reflection, yet it also conveys a sense of peaceful resignation to the end of a shared journey. I acknowledge the love and life that once flourished, while accepting the need to part ways and move forward, wishing my former partner well in a bittersweet farewell.

75. Dissolution of Marriage

The emotion label for "Dissolution of Marriage" is **resigned reflection.** The poem captures the quiet, somber mood of finality as the two of us individuals end our marriage, dividing my shared life with a sense of acceptance. There is a reflective tone, acknowledging the memories and past love, but also a sense of detachment as we move toward separate futures. The poem carries an undercurrent of melancholy, with an acceptance of the new reality and the weight of the history they leave behind.

Brandon Chapter

The emotion label for the "Brandon" chapter is **resilience and self-discovery.** The chapter explores the journey of moving on, overcoming challenges, and finding personal strength and growth through love and loss.

76. Meet Me in the Middle (East)

The emotion label for "Meet Me in the Middle (East)" is **hopeful patience.** The poem reflects a sense of calm anticipation and a thoughtful, measured approach to love. It balances the excitement of new connections with the wisdom of patience, highlighting a journey of self-awareness, slow-building romance, and the lessons learned from past experiences. There's optimism in the careful progression of feelings, with an undercurrent of reflection on boundaries and self-discovery.

77. *Taste of Chicago, Last Taste of Home*

The emotion label for "Taste of Chicago, Last Taste of Home" is **reflective clarity**. The poem expresses a mix of nostalgia, introspection, and personal realization, as I navigate through moments of joy, connection, and emotional highs, ultimately arriving at a deeper understanding of love, friendship, and boundaries. There's a sense of learning from past experiences, both pleasurable and challenging, with an underlying tone of growth and acceptance.

78. *Cancún Confessions*

The emotion label for "Cancún Confessions" is **regretful realization**. I express a sense of fun and adventure overshadowed by ignored red flags and emotional turbulence. In the poem, I reflect on the reckless choices I made in the moment, the tension between joy and underlying issues, and the eventual realization that I overlooked important boundaries and warnings. There's a blend of longing for clarity, acknowledgment of my mistakes, and a deeper understanding of the emotional toll these decisions had on me.

79. *We Moved onto Ashland*

The emotion label for "We Moved onto Ashland" is **nostalgic resilience.** I reflect on the joy and excitement of moving into a new home with Bax, savoring the moments of fresh beginnings and love. However, the tone shifts as I recount the challenges of the COVID-19 lockdown, with an underlying sense of uncertainty and confinement. Despite the external chaos, the poem expresses warmth, gratitude, and a resilient bond, finding comfort in togetherness during trying times, all while looking back with a fond, reflective lens.

80. San Diego: The Sunny Move

The emotion label for "San Diego: The Sunny Move" is **disillusioned hope.** The excitement and optimism of moving to San Diego, chasing dreams under sunny skies, gradually give way to the harsh realities of a struggling relationship. Beneath the surface of California's beauty, there is a sense of disappointment and sadness as I confront the challenges of Bax's mental health and substance use. While the poem begins with hopeful energy, it ultimately reflects the painful recognition that love alone isn't enough to sustain a dream that's falling apart.

81. Echoes of Reflection: A Journey Through Shadows and...

The emotion label for the "Echoes of Reflection: A Journey Through Shadows and Light" is **introspective clarity.** The series emerges from deep self-reflection, grappling with complex themes of racial identity, personal growth, relationship dynamics, and a pivotal moment of choice regarding drug use. Through this process, I navigate the shadows of past experiences and step into the light of renewed understanding and alignment with my true self. The poems reflect a journey of insight, acceptance, and transformation.

82. Italy, a Verb

The emotion label for "Italy, a Verb" is **resigned liberation.** The poem reflects the journey from hope and effort in a relationship to the eventual realization of its end. While the experience of traveling through Italy brings about disappointment and emotional weight, it also serves as the catalyst for personal freedom and rebirth. The sadness of the relationship's demise is paired with a sense of relief and newfound clarity, marking the emotional shift from burden to liberation.

83. In Tandem: Poems of Love and the Mind's Maze

The emotion label for the "In Tandem: Poems of Love and the Mind's Maze" is **reflective compassion**. This series is driven by deep introspection and empathy, exploring the complexities of navigating love alongside the challenges of mental health. It embodies both the tenderness of understanding and the weight of emotional negotiation, blending love, struggle, and growth in a compassionate and introspective way. The reflection on therapy, personal growth, and support in the face of mental illness emphasizes care, resilience, and profound connection.

84. Winds of Mexico

The emotion label for *"Winds of Mexico"* is **liberation**. The poem reflects the emotional release and freedom experienced after making the decision to leave behind a relationship that no longer served me. It carries the weight of self-discovery, breaking free from emotional burdens, and embracing a new chapter in life. The winds of change in Mexico represent the liberation from past ties and the beginning of personal rebirth.

85. Not Quite Friends

The emotion label for *"Not Quite Friends"* is **compassion**. The poem captures a sense of ongoing care and empathy for someone from the past, despite the distance and the end of our closer relationship. There's a quiet, enduring concern for Bax's well-being, a willingness to forgive, and a deep-seated desire for him to find peace and stability. Compassion permeates every line, reflecting my struggle to let go while still hoping for the other's healing and growth.

Nico Chapter

The emotion label for the "Nico" chapter is **growth and resilience.** The chapter explores the complexities of friendship and love, emphasizing personal development, healing, and the strength to set boundaries.

86. Self-Discovery in Mexico City

The emotion label for "Self-Discovery in Mexico City" is **liberation**. The poem captures my journey of breaking free from old ties, seeking independence, and exploring new possibilities. There's a sense of empowerment and freedom in navigating love, self-awareness, and the excitement of a new environment. While I acknowledge the tension between love and a desire for spontaneity, the overarching feeling is one of personal liberation and discovery.

87. How We Met

The emotion label for "How We Met" is **serendipity**. The poem captures the unexpected and organic way that Nico and I connected, despite initial hesitations. There's a feeling of chance and surprise in how love unfolded, leading to a deeper bond that neither anticipated. The tone reflects a sense of gratitude and appreciation for the way events transpired, even with the ups and downs along the journey.

88. Our Journey in Two Worlds

The emotion label for "Our Journey in Two Worlds" is **bittersweet reflection**. The poem captures a sense of gratitude for the shared experiences and growth while acknowledging the complexities of love and friendship. There's an undercurrent of fondness for the good times and acceptance that not all relationships are meant to last, evoking both appreciation and melancholy as I look back on the journey with Nico.

89. *Our Language of Love*

The emotion label for "Our Language of Love" is **nostalgic understanding**. The poem reflects on the beauty and complexity of communication in a relationship, with a deep appreciation for the shared journey and the unique ways love was expressed. There's a sense of fondness and acceptance, acknowledging that while language brought us closer, it was ultimately the deeper differences that caused us to part.

90. *Seasons of Us*

The emotion label for "Seasons of Us" is **bittersweet reflection.** The poem conveys a mix of gratitude and sadness, recognizing the depth of a friendship and connection that ultimately couldn't last. While there's no regret, there's a sense of mourning for the loss of both love and friendship, balanced by an appreciation for the experiences shared.

91. *Confesiones y Comprensiones*

The emotion label for "Confesiones y Comprensiones" series of poems is **introspective connection.** The explanation reflects deep thought about communication, emotional vulnerability, and the ways in which love and understanding are built through linguistic and cultural bridges. There's a focus on the complexities of connection and the tenderness required to navigate differences, making the tone reflective and emotionally nuanced.

92. *Growth Beyond the Garden*

The emotion label for "Growth Beyond the Garden" is **self-realization.** The poem reflects a deep internal awareness, acknowledging the delicate balance between helping others and maintaining my own boundaries. There's a sense of introspective growth, where I realize the need for self-care and the importance of allowing others to stand on my own. This journey of understanding my role in fostering independence in relationships carries a tone of reflection and empowerment.

93. Beyond the Changes

The emotion label for "Beyond the Changes" is **acceptance with hope.** The poem expresses a sense of coming to terms with the evolution of a relationship, recognizing the shifts without losing the deep connection and love that remain. There's a clear acceptance of the changes while holding on to hope for the future, whether in friendship or something more. The tone is one of positivity, embracing the ongoing journey with mutual support and care, and focusing on growth, love, and maintaining a meaningful bond.

94. Con Amor, Pero Solo Amigos

The emotion label for "Con Amor, Pero Solo Amigos" is **compassionate detachment.** The poem conveys a gentle yet firm expression of love with the clear intention of transitioning from romantic love to friendship. There's a tender recognition of the bond that remains, but also a compassionate request to let go of expectations for now, allowing for personal growth and openness to what the future may hold. It expresses care and understanding, while encouraging acceptance of the present situation.

95. Mt. Helix

The emotion label for "Mt. Helix" series is **reflective reconciliation**. The poems conveys a deep sense of reflection on the personal growth and evolving relationship between Nico and I. It highlights the reconciliation of emotions, the healing of past misunderstandings, and the journey toward accepting an uncertain future. The shared experiences at Mt. Helix, and the meaningful conversations about growth and gratitude, reflect a sense of closure and peace, balanced with openness to continued friendship and connection.

96. *Boundaries and Bridges*

The emotion label for "Beyond the Changes" is **acceptance with affection.** The poem reflects a calm, grounded acknowledgment of the evolving dynamics in the relationship, paired with a deep sense of care and commitment to maintaining a meaningful connection. There's a balance between letting go of romantic expectations while embracing the bond of friendship and mutual support, making acceptance and affection the dominant emotional tones.

97. *Shadows and Light*

The emotion label for "Shadows and Light" is sorrow with **compassion**. The poem reflects a deep sense of sadness and loss over the dissolution of trust, combined with a strong thread of compassion for Nico's pain and struggles. I acknowledge the hurt caused but choose to approach it with empathy and a broader understanding of mental health and healing, intertwining sorrow with a caring, compassionate perspective.

Rafa Chapter

The emotion label for the "Rafa" chapter is **love and emotional intimacy**. This chapter reflects the depth of a growing connection, highlighting the passionate, thoughtful, and enduring nature of the relationship while capturing the emotional bond and shared experiences that define their journey.

98. *First Date Series*

The emotion label for the "First Date Series" is **nostalgia and anticipation**. The reflection on

early dates and the growing romantic connection
evokes fondness and a sense of excitement for the evolving
relationship. The recollection of significant moments, like
shared activities and honest conversations, conveys a
feeling of emotional depth and trust. The themes
of vulnerability, openness, and honesty bring in elements
of serenity and hope, as the series captures both the thrill
of new love and the desire to build something lasting.

99. Distance in Love

The emotion label for "Distance in Love" is **longing with
hope.** The poem captures a deep yearning for a loved one
who is far away, while simultaneously expressing
optimism and joy about the strength of the connection. I
reflect on memories and anticipates future moments with
excitement, finding comfort and hope in the distance as
love continues to grow.

100.   In the Beginning Days

The emotion label for "In the Beginning Days" is **joyful
anticipation and tender affection.** The poem radiates
feelings of excitement and delight as a new connection
blossoms, marked by care and thoughtfulness. There is a
deep sense of gratitude, mutual admiration, and hope for
the unfolding future, while moments
of vulnerability and intimacy highlight the emotional bond
taking root. Love and possibility are felt throughout, with
a subtle undercurrent of trust and security building
between two people.

101.   Portrait of Rafa: Lines and Light

The emotion label for "Portrait of Rafa: Lines and
Light" is **admiration and affectionate reverence**. The
poem expresses deep appreciation for Rafa's physical
presence, personality, and the beauty he embodies, both
inside and out. There is a sense of wonder and awe at his
attributes, mixed with tenderness and love, as the I reflect

on his qualities with a poetic reverence. The admiration is not just for his appearance but for his character, as his smile, voice, and essence are painted with warmth, respect, and adoration.

102.   *Chasing the Contradictory Unicorn*

The emotion label for "Chasing the Contradictory Unicorn" is **conflicted yearning and hopeful introspection**. I am wrestling with internal contradictions—a desire for both closeness and distance, admiration and frustration, seeking a balance between independence and connection. There's an undertone of self-awareness and vulnerability as I reflect on my complex emotional landscape, coupled with a hopeful desire for the person who can understand and navigate these contradictions. The concept of the unicorn represents my hope for finding someone rare and unique who can align with my dualities, transforming my contradictions into harmony.

103.   *A Tale of Two Hearts*

The emotion label for "A Tale of Two Hearts" is **love** with mutual understanding and growth. The poem reflects a deep emotional connection between two individuals who are navigating the complexities of our relationship with honesty, vulnerability, and support. It highlights the challenges we face, our commitment to one another, and the mutual effort to grow together through love, communication, and healing.

104.   *In the House of the Queen*

The emotion label for "In the House of the Queen" is **awe and admiration.** The poem captures a sense of reverence and admiration for Rafa's mother, highlighting her elegance, grace, and the warmth she exudes. I feel both enchanted and inspired by her presence, reflecting a deep appreciation for the encounter and its lasting impact.

105.   Echoes of Intimacy: Poems of Love and Self-Reflection

The emotion label for *the Poems* "Embrace of the True Self,"
"Hotel Quiet Currents," and "Distance and Connection"
is **introspection and clarity.** Each poem stems from
moments of deep self-reflection, prompted by relationship
dynamics and personal experiences. I reflect on my own
needs, boundaries, and growth while navigating a
relationship, embracing authenticity, solitude, and the
ways we maintain connection despite physical distance.
The overall tone conveys a thoughtful exploration of self-
awareness and the complexities of love.

106.   Layers of Us

The emotion label for "Layers of Us" is **vulnerability and
discovery**. It expresses my journey of uncovering
emotional layers within a relationship, exploring the
nuances of communication, cultural differences, and the
unfolding understanding between us. There's a tender
acknowledgment of the complexity in revealing our true
selves, mixed with the excitement and nervousness that
come with that vulnerability. It reflects my introspective
process of learning, peeling back layers, and embracing the
beauty of this shared experience.

107.   Baggage Claim

The emotion label for "Baggage Claim" is **reassurance and
humor.** It reflects my effort to clarify misunderstandings
about my relationship status while maintaining a
lighthearted tone. There's a sense of confidence in
addressing doubts, mixed with playful humor to ease
tension. At its core, the poem reassures that despite the
complexities and "baggage" from past relationships, my
current relationship is strong and full of love. It's a mix of
honesty, acceptance, and a focus on the future, with an
undercurrent of warmth and commitment.

108.   *Pride in the City*

The emotion label for "Pride in the City: A Colorful Symphony" is **joyful celebration and pride.** The poem reflects the vibrant, exuberant energy of Mexico City's Pride parade, capturing the joy, love, and unity experienced while celebrating both personal and collective identity. There is also a strong sense of confidence and pride in the relationship, as well as optimism about the future, with themes of fun, acceptance, and togetherness woven throughout the celebration of love and self-expression.

109.   *You Have Me Intoxicated*

The emotion label for "You Have Me Intoxicated" is **playful infatuation and passion.** The poem captures the lighthearted, intoxicating energy of falling deeply for someone, with a sense of joy and excitement. The use of Britney Spears' lyrics adds a playful, fun element to the expression of strong romantic attraction and the blending of cultures. There is also an undertone of longing and desire after spending time with the partner, creating a vivid sense of emotional intoxication and connection.

110.   *Friendship's Voice*

The emotion label for "Friendship's Voice" is **vulnerability and emotional struggle with isolation.** I navigate feelings of loneliness despite the outward appearance of happiness and shared moments with others. There's a deep sense of disconnect in my relationship, leading to self-reflection and an internal battle with conflicting emotions. The connection with Shayna offers comfort and understanding, creating a balance between my feelings of isolation and the solace found in friendship. There's a strong undercurrent of seeking validation and yearning for emotional connection while simultaneously feeling the weight of internal conflict.

111.   Echoes of Understanding

The emotion label for "Echoes of Understanding" is **vulnerability and emotional reconciliation**. I express feelings of isolation and disconnection, while also revealing a deep need to be heard and acknowledged. There's a shift towards healing and growth as Rafa listens and validates the my emotions, leading to a sense of reassurance and mutual respect. This poem captures the comfort found in honest communication and the strengthening bond as we navigate emotional complexities together. The underlying emotions are gratitude, understanding, and renewed hope.

112.   This Is Me: El Amor a Través de la Acción

The emotion label for "This Is Me: El Amor a Través de la Acción" is **gratitude and connection**. The poem reflects deep appreciation for the experiences shared, the bonds formed, and the way love is expressed through actions. There's also a sense of personal growth, overcoming language barriers, and finding comfort in friendship, all wrapped in the warmth of shared moments and care.

113.   Between the Lines

The emotion label for "Between the Lines" is **frustration and longing for authenticity.** I express discontent with the surface-level joking that masks deeper truths, revealing a desire for honesty and emotional intimacy. There's a feeling of yearning for a connection where both humor and vulnerability coexist without avoidance. The underlying emotions are hope for a genuine relationship, disappointment in the evasiveness, and a desire for clarity and openness.

114.   *A Partner I Must Have*

The emotion label for "A Partner I Must Have" is **yearning for protection and companionship.** The poem expresses a deep desire for a balanced, strong, and loving partner who provides emotional security, support, and defense, while also complementing my giving nature. There is a clear longing for a relationship built on trust, protection, and mutual care.

115.   *He Put It on My Calendar*

The emotion label for "He Put It on My Calendar" is **gratitude and affectionate love.** The poem conveys a deep sense of appreciation for the thoughtful actions that strengthen the relationship. It highlights the comfort and security found in shared planning and being aligned in daily life, fostering a strong emotional connection. There's a warm acknowledgment of Rafa's care and attentiveness, which enhances my feelings of love and admiration.

116.   *Un Amor Como el Primer Beso*

The emotion label for "Un Amor Como el Primer Beso" is **youthful passion.** The poem captures the feelings of excitement, nervousness, and rediscovery of love that feels fresh and reminiscent of a first love. There's a mixture of joy and fear, with me experiencing a deep emotional connection that rekindles sensations of youthful exuberance and timeless romance. This love is described as both thrilling and tender, evoking a sense of wonder and vulnerability.

117.   *In the Garden of Butterflies*

The emotion label for "In the Garden of Butterflies" is **hopeful vulnerability and evolving love.** The poem captures the delicate balance of embracing new love while acknowledging past wounds. There's a tender vulnerability in recognizing the scars of previous heartbreaks, yet the hope of trust and growth shines through in Rafa's nurturing presence. The feelings of love is fresh, like new blooms, and there's a quiet courage in allowing the heart to open again, trusting in the process of love and healing.

118.   Love's Gentle Remedy

The emotion label for "Love's Gentle Remedy" is **comfort and solace in love.** The poem expresses the calming and healing power of love during difficult and stressful times. I find peace, safety, and warmth in Rafa's presence, with love acting as a remedy for life's challenges. There's a deep sense of gratitude and relief, highlighting the soothing impact of a supportive and loving relationship.

119.   What a Difference Time Makes

The emotion label for "What a Difference Time Makes" is **love's deepening progression.** The poem reflects on the growth of love over time, from initial feelings of affection to a profound and enduring connection. There's a sense of reflection, joy, and gratitude for how love has evolved, moving from cautious beginnings to a strong, committed bond. I feel fulfilled and complete, cherishing the shared memories and looking forward to the future.

120.   Mi Amor, Mi Compañero

The emotion label for "Mi Amor, Mi Compañero" is **joyful anticipation and love.** The poem expresses excitement, love, and eagerness for a deeper commitment, filled with warmth, care, and enthusiasm for shared experiences and future plans. There's a sense of affectionate hope and celebration of the bond growing between the two partners.

121.   *Our Love in Words*

The emotion label for "Our Love in Words" is **deep love and intimacy**. The poem reflects a heartfelt connection between Rafa and I, emphasizing mutual support, shared dreams, and the comfort found in communication. It conveys the tenderness and trust in our relationship, highlighting both the simplicity and depth of our love.

122.   *Who is This? A metaphorical Revelation*

The emotion label for "Who is This? A Metaphorical Revelation" is **joyful transformation and love.** The poem reflects a sense of newfound happiness, personal growth, and the joy of being in a relationship that brings out a fresh, radiant side of myself. It conveys light-heartedness, contentment, and a celebration of love's positive influence on my life.

123.   *All In, Forever Yours*

The emotion label for "All In, Forever Yours" is **devotion**. The poem expresses deep love, commitment, and a heartfelt plea for reassurance and renewal in the relationship. It. conveys passion and determination to mend past mistakes and build a future together, highlighting vulnerability, hope, and an unwavering bond. I am dedicated to the relationship, willing to work through challenges, and committed to moving forward in love.

124.   *Our Equation of Forever*

The emotion label for "Our Equation of Forever" is **love and commitment.** The poem expresses deep affection, admiration, and a sense of certainty about the future with Rafa. It conveys hope, joy, and confidence in the relationship, celebrating the strong foundation we've built together. The themes of partnership, mutual growth, and shared dreams highlight the sense of trust and stability I feel, with an overarching tone of excitement for the future.

125.   *Bésame, Mi Amor*

The emotion label for "Bésame, Mi Amor" is **deep love and devotion.** The poem reflects a profound emotional connection, passion, and tenderness between myself and Rafa. It conveys feelings of love, intimacy, commitment, and a sense of eternal bond. The language expresses romantic affection, admiration, and a promise of lasting devotion.

126.   *Love, Green Cards, and Entrepreneurial Hearts*

The emotion label for "Love, Green Cards, and Entrepreneurial Hearts" is **playful resilience and confident love**. The poem expresses a lighthearted yet determined approach to navigating love amidst external doubts, blending humor with a deep sense of partnership and shared ambitions. It reflects both a loving commitment and a confident defiance of societal judgments, showcasing the strength of the relationship through entrepreneurial spirit and mutual dreams.

127.   *Quiet Love*

The emotion label for "Quiet Love" is **profound affection and introspective tenderness.** The poem conveys a deep, quiet love that overwhelms me, evoking feelings of contentment, awe, and an internal struggle to express the magnitude of the emotion in words. It reflects a quiet reverence for the depth of connection and the weight of love shared between partners.

128.   *Navigating the Lows with You, Mi Cielo*

The emotion label for "Navigating the Lows with You, Mi Cielo" is **resilient love and deep commitment.** The poem expresses the strength of enduring love through challenges, highlighting the growth and communication necessary to weather difficult moments. It conveys feelings of perseverance, dedication, and mutual support, reflecting a mature and grounded relationship built on understanding and trust.

129.   *A Promise in Córdoba*

The emotion label for "A Promise in Córdoba" is **anticipation and deep devotion.** The poem radiates a sense of excitement and heartfelt love as it builds toward a significant life moment—proposing marriage. The emotions conveyed include commitment, joy, and the tenderness of planning a future together, set against the backdrop of a meaningful journey.

Perspectives on a Shared World Chapter
The emotion label for the "Perspectives of a Shared World" chapter is **empathy and reflection**. The collection conveys a deep understanding of diverse experiences and encourages thoughtful consideration of personal and societal issues.

130.   *Under Flushing Lights: Coco's Victory, A Poem*

The emotion label for "Under Flushing Lights: Coco's Victory, A Poem" is **exhilaration and gratitude**. The poem captures the joy, excitement, and sense of triumph experienced during Coco's victory, combined with feelings of deep appreciation for friendship, shared moments, and the memorable adventure that unfolded in New York.

131.   *To Latoya, on the Passing of Johnny O*

The emotion label for "To Latoya, on the Passing of Jerry" is **grief and solace**. The poem expresses deep sorrow for the loss of a loved one while simultaneously offering comfort, hope, and gratitude. It balances the pain of mourning with the light of healing, focusing on the enduring love and positive legacy Jerry leaves behind.

132.   *New Year's Eve Resolutions Series*

The emotion label for "New Year's Resolutions Series" is **reflection and cultural appreciation.** The series reflects a deep sense of introspection influenced by contrasting cultural traditions, along with an appreciation for the communal, spiritual, and personal significance derived from the experiences in Puebla. The emotions conveyed include a thoughtful blend of gratitude, hope, and a desire for growth, all deeply rooted in the merging of cultural practices and personal aspirations.

133.   *Poems Inspired by an Australia and New Zealand Trip*

The emotion label for "Poems Inspired by an Australia and New Zealand Trip" is **wonder and connection**. The description reflects a deep sense of awe, joy, and fulfillment derived from the diverse and vibrant experiences during the trip. The poems are inspired by the beauty of cultural diversity, human interaction, and personal reflection, blending the excitement of new discoveries with meaningful conversations and shared moments. There's a strong emotional undercurrent of curiosity, gratitude, and a desire for deeper understanding.

134.   *Bali on Two Wheels*

The emotion label for "Bali on Two Wheels" is **adventure and freedom**. The poem reflects the exhilaration and liberation of exploring Bali on a motorbike, capturing the joy of discovery, personal growth, and connection to the island's vibrant beauty.

135.   *Ode to a Shero on The View*

The emotion label for "Ode to a Shero on The View" is **admiration and resolve.** The poem conveys deep respect for Liz Cheney's courage, her commitment to truth, and her stand against political challenges, while also emphasizing a determined call for justice and democratic ideals.

136.   Cleansing Chants

The emotion label for "Cleansing Chants" is **renewal and serenity**. The poem reflects a sense of spiritual cleansing, peace, and rejuvenation, as well as a hopeful embrace of new beginnings filled with positivity and protection.

137.   Voices in the Chamber

The emotion label for "Voices in the Chamber" is **determination and civic responsibility**. The poem expresses a strong sense of purpose, urging action, engagement, and accountability in the political sphere. It conveys a commitment to both supporting key allies and holding leaders accountable, with a focus on taking meaningful, proactive steps beyond passive discourse.

138.   A Year Older, A Bit Wiser

The emotion label for "A Year Older, A Bit Wiser" is **gratitude and hopeful reflection.** The poem conveys a deep sense of appreciation for family, friends, and past experiences while looking forward with optimism and excitement for the future. It blends heartfelt thankfulness with introspective thoughts, celebrating growth, cherished relationships, and the anticipation of new adventures and continued bonds.

139.   Voyage of Gratitude

The emotion label for "Voyage of Gratitude" is **thankfulness and reflection.** The poem expresses deep appreciation for family, life experiences, and the journey of growth, while embracing both the past and future with a sense of gratitude and warmth.

140.   *Ode to the Ladies of The View*

The emotion label for "Ode to The Ladies of The View" is **admiration and aspiration**. The poem expresses deep respect and appreciation for the hosts of "The View," acknowledging their unique personalities and contributions. It also conveys a hopeful yearning to one day join them in conversation, celebrating the possibility of shared success and dreams.

141.   *Sweet Addiction*

The emotion label for "Sweet Addiction" is **playful confidence**. The poem exudes a sense of lighthearted self-assurance, with a playful tone about being the irresistible focus of others' affection. There's an undertone of amusement at the attention received, balanced with a hint of reluctant responsibility.

142.   *Living's Light and Legacy in Lines*

The emotion label for "Legacy in Lines" and "Living's Light" is **grief and reverence**. These poems express a deep sense of sorrow for the passing of Joan Millicent Bryan Wilcox while also honoring her life and legacy with profound respect and admiration. The poems reflect the bond between Joan and her daughter, Shannon, and aim to provide comfort through thoughtful reflection on the beauty and fragility of life.

143.   *Reconnection*

The emotion label for "Reconnection" is **vulnerability and hope**. The poem expresses a heartfelt desire to renew a meaningful therapeutic relationship while acknowledging past avoidance and personal growth. It conveys a mix of vulnerability in admitting struggles and mistakes, and hope for healing, understanding, and reestablishing trust.

144. *Steadfast*

The emotion label for " 'Steadfast' and 'Legacy in
Ink'" is **supportive encouragement and heartfelt empathy.**
These poems are inspired by a deep desire to uplift and
affirm Kiana's resilience during challenging times,
providing both emotional solace and a reminder of her
inherent strength. The emotions conveyed reflect a mix of
compassion, admiration, and the commitment to help her
navigate life's struggles with grace and optimism.

145. *Clapback in the Capitol*

The emotion label for "Clapback in the Capitol" and "Roots
of the Rhetoric" is **frustration and longing for change**.
These poems reflect deep dissatisfaction with the divisive
and disrespectful nature of modern American politics,
while also expressing a strong desire for a return to
empathetic, constructive discourse that fosters unity and
meaningful debate. The frustration is rooted in the current
political climate, and the longing is for a shift toward a
more respectful, solution-focused dialogue.

146. *A Nation's Wake-Up Call*

The emotion label for "A Nation's Wake-Up
Call" is **urgency and frustration**. The poem expresses a
sense of urgency for people to recognize the broader issues
in politics, beyond narrow perspectives, and to understand
the importance of civic engagement. It also conveys
frustration at misinformation and the failure to grasp the
larger implications of political choices, while urging for
informed action and justice.

147. *Finding My Authentic Self*

The emotion label for "Finding My Authentic Self" is **self-
reflection and empowerment.** The poem expresses a deep
introspection on past relationships and personal growth,
coupled with a growing sense of empowerment as I seek

balance, independence, and authenticity in love and life. It conveys both vulnerability in the face of fear and strength in the pursuit of self-discovery.

148. *A Brother's Love: A Poem for My Sister*

The emotion label for "A Brother's Love: A Poem for My Sister" is **love and admiration.** The poem conveys deep affection, unwavering support, and a heartfelt appreciation for the sister's strength, beauty, and journey through life, while also expressing the enduring bond between siblings.

149. *My Guy Wish List*

The emotion label for "My Guy Wish List" is **hopeful longing and aspiration.** The poem expresses a heartfelt desire for a loving, compatible partner with specific qualities, reflecting an optimistic and idealistic vision of a fulfilling, balanced relationship.

150. *Circular Relationships*

The emotion label for "Circular Relationships" is **frustration and yearning for change.** The poem conveys a sense of being stuck in repetitive cycles, coupled with a desire for growth and new beginnings, reflecting both weariness and the hope for breaking free.

151. *Progression of Therapy*

The emotion label for "Progression of Therapy" is **self-discovery, self-awareness, and healing.** This comprehensive label encapsulates the emotional journey of introspection, confronting discomfort, and improving communication. It reflects a deep sense of vulnerability and determination as you work towards healthier relationship dynamics and emotional clarity. Through self-discovery and heightened self-awareness, you break free from old habits and establish clear boundaries, fostering personal growth and well-being. The poems inspired by these therapy sessions illustrate the ongoing process of navigating complex relationships, building trust, and prioritizing self-care, ultimately leading to a more authentic and balanced life.

152.   *Sweet Karma's Gavel*

The emotion label for "Sweet Karma's Gavel" is **vindication and satisfaction.** The poem conveys a strong sense of justice and poetic irony, celebrating the fall of someone who once wielded power with impunity. There's a clear tone of triumph as karma delivers its reckoning, reflecting satisfaction in seeing accountability finally prevail after years of perceived injustice.

153.   *Liquid Courage*

The emotion label for "Liquid Courage" is **self-awareness and empowerment.** The poem reflects a deep sense of introspection and personal growth, highlighting the journey from indulgence to clarity. There's a strong feeling of empowerment in choosing sobriety and finding courage within oneself, rather than relying on external substances. It conveys a quiet strength and resolve, with a compassionate acknowledgment of the struggles others face.

154.   *The Sagittarius Dilemma*

The emotion label for "The Sagittarius Dilemma" is **frustration and confusion.** The poem conveys a sense of exasperation towards the indecisiveness and paradoxical behavior of a Sagittarius, particularly in the context of personal and financial conflicts. It reflects a mix of bewilderment at their actions, as well as a call for clarity and resolution, highlighting the inner conflict and missed opportunities.

155.   *A Mother's & Son's Tribute*

The emotion label for " *A Mother's & Son's Tribute*" is **love, gratitude, and pride.** It expresses a profound appreciation for the bond between a mother and son, capturing the shared journey of resilience, growth, and mutual pride. Both the message from my mom and my poetic response reflects deep feelings of admiration, heartfelt acknowledgment of past challenges, and an overwhelming sense of gratitude for the strength and love that have shaped our lives.

156. A Union Leader's Plea

The emotion label for "A Union Leader's Plea" is **concern and determination.** The poem conveys a deep sense of worry over potential political changes, particularly a return of Trump and the threat to civil servants through Schedule F. At the same time, there is a strong sense of resolve, I am using my platform to inspire voters to act with wisdom and integrity, hoping to influence a future grounded in justice and truth.

157. Whispers from Beirut: A Tribute to Salam's Mother

The emotion label for "Whispers from Beirut: A Tribute to Salam's Mother" is **compassion and remembrance**. The poem conveys deep sympathy and support for Salam during his time of loss, while honoring and celebrating the memory and legacy of his mother. It reflects feelings of empathy, sorrow, and a heartfelt tribute to a beloved family member, emphasizing enduring love and the lasting impact of her spirit.

158. Democracy's Choice

The emotion label for "Democracy's Choice" is **urgency and determination**. The poem conveys a strong sense of urgency regarding the state of democracy, highlighting the looming threat of autocracy and the critical importance of voting decisions. It reflects determination in advocating for the preservation of democratic institutions and values, emphasizing the pivotal role of informed and decisive voting in shaping the nation's future. The tone is both cautionary and resolute, urging readers to recognize the gravity of their choices and act to uphold democratic principles.

159.   *Silent Echoes of Solitude*

The emotion label for "Silent Echoes of Solitude" is **loneliness and frustration.** The poem conveys feelings of isolation and a yearning for deeper, more meaningful connections. It highlights the struggle with superficial interactions, communication barriers, and the longing for intellectual and emotional engagement, reflecting a profound sense of solitude and the desire for understanding.

160.   *Repercussions in the Age of Misinformation*

The emotion label for "Repercussions in the Age of Misinformation" is **frustration, concern, and determination**. The poem conveys a deep sense of exasperation with the pervasive spread of fake news and misinformation, highlighting the erosion of trust and the challenges it poses to societal institutions. It expresses profound worry about the potential downfall of democratic values and the integrity of information systems. Simultaneously, the poem embodies a resolute commitment to seeking accountability and advocating for truth, emphasizing the urgent need for proactive measures to combat deceit and restore credibility. These emotions reflect both the emotional strain caused by misinformation and the steadfast resolve to uphold and strengthen democratic principles.

161.   *Justice Undone Series*

The emotion label for " Justice Undone Series'" is **concern and determination.** This reflection conveys a deep-seated worry about the integrity of American democracy in light of recent Supreme Court decisions. It highlights frustration with divisive and potentially harmful judicial rulings that threaten foundational democratic principles. Simultaneously, it embodies a strong sense of determination to advocate for accountability, truth, and the preservation of democratic norms. The series serves as a passionate call to awareness and civic engagement, urging readers to recognize the critical impact of judicial actions and to actively participate in safeguarding the nation's democratic future.

162.   Reflections on Love

The emotion label for "Reflections on Love" is **hopeful inspiration and admiration.** The poem conveys a deep sense of philosophical reflection on the true nature of love, emphasizing the importance of mutual growth and admiration in a relationship. It highlights the desire for a partner who not only loves you as you are but also helps you to grow and flourish, reflecting a commitment to personal development and the nurturing of each other's strengths. By blending insights from Plato and lessons from therapy, the poem underscores a hopeful and determined approach to finding a meaningful, growth-oriented partnership, celebrating the transformative power of love that inspires both individuals to reach our fullest potential.

163.   Series: 'Veils of Reality: A Journey of Love and Truth'

The emotion label for "Veils of Reality: A Journey of Love and Truth" is **frustration and sorrow**. This series of poems expresses deep emotional conflict, reflecting my love and concern for my father while grappling with feelings of sadness, frustration, and helplessness in response to his conspiracy theories and mental health struggles. There is also an underlying tone of hope for clarity and healing.

164.   Gratitude Blooms

The emotion label for "Gratitude Blooms" is **gratitude and joy.** The poem conveys a deep appreciation for meaningful connections and relationships, highlighting the importance of cherishing bonds that enrich life. It reflects feelings of happiness and fulfillment derived from diverse backgrounds, shared stories, and supportive interactions, emphasizing the beauty of love and unity.

165.   *The Best Relationship*

The emotion label for "The Best Relationship" is **balance and mutual respect.** The poem conveys a harmonious blend of individual independence and shared connection, emphasizing the importance of personal growth alongside a supportive partnership. It highlights feelings of freedom, joy, and fulfillment that come from both partners thriving individually and celebrating our togetherness. The poem reflects a deep appreciation for a relationship where love and autonomy coexist, fostering a dynamic and enduring bond.

166.   *Culture and Compassion*

The emotion label for "Culture and Compassion" is **hope and empathy.** The poem conveys a sense of optimism for collective transformation and the importance of compassion in shifting cultural norms. It highlights the belief that understanding and healing those who cause pain can lead to a more unified and compassionate society. The emphasis on collaboration, recognizing the humanity in everyone, and the shared journey of healing reflect a profound sense of empathy and hopeful determination for positive change.

167.   *Challenging the Narrative Series*

The emotion label for "Challenging the Narrative: An Inspiration" is **frustration and hope**. The series conveys a deep sense of exasperation with the negative portrayals and misinformation surrounding leaders like Kamala Harris, highlighting the need to counteract biased narratives. Simultaneously, it embodies a strong sense of hope and determination to uplift and celebrate the true achievements and resilience of Black leaders. The reflection emphasizes the importance of unity, collective strength, and positive recognition, blending feelings of resistance against negativity with an optimistic vision for empowerment and acknowledgment within the community.

168.   The Villain's Crown

The emotion label for "The Villain's Crown" is **courage and self-empowerment.** The poem conveys the bravery and determination required to break free from restrictive roles and assert my own path to happiness. It highlights the internal struggle of choosing personal freedom over others' expectations, reflecting a strong sense of self-determination and resilience in the face of potential criticism or misunderstanding.

169.   The Measure of Truth

The emotion label for "The Measure of Truth" is **vulnerability and trust.** The poem conveys a deep longing for honesty and transparency in relationships, highlighting the desire for genuine connections and mutual understanding. It reflects feelings of vulnerability in being open and the hope for trust and acceptance from others, emphasizing the importance of authentic communication and emotional safety.

170.   Eric's Law: A Beacon for the Invisible

The emotion label for "Eric's Law: A Beacon for the Invisible" is **hope and advocacy**. The poem expresses a strong desire for justice and recognition for individuals with hidden struggles, highlighting the push for a more inclusive and compassionate society.

171. *On This Rainy Day/En Este Día Lluvioso*

The emotion label for "On This Rainy Day" is **grief and remembrance**. The poem expresses deep sorrow over the loss of a beloved pet, highlighting cherished memories and the enduring love that remains.

172. *My Beloved Fufu / Mi Amado Fufu*

The emotion label for "My Beloved Fufu / Mi Amado Fufu" is **grief and remembrance.** The poem conveys deep sorrow and longing for a lost beloved pet, highlighting cherished memories and the enduring love that remains. It reflects the emotional struggle of moving forward while honoring Fufu's joyful presence and the lasting impact he had on the my life.

173. *Project 2025: A Witty Rhyme*

The emotion label for "Project 2025: A Witty Rhyme" is **criticism and concern.** The poem conveys a strong sense of disapproval toward the proposed political changes, highlighting apprehensions about shifts in policies and the potential impact on various social and governmental institutions. It reflects a wary outlook on the future, emphasizing my unease with the direction outlined in Project 2025.

174. *Ode to a Trailblazing Vice President*

The emotion label for "Ode to a Trailblazing Vice President" is **admiration and inspiration.** The poem celebrates Kamala Harris's groundbreaking achievements and leadership, highlighting her role as a beacon of progress and equity. It conveys deep respect and motivation, emphasizing her contributions to justice, equality, and the betterment of society.

175.   *Ballots of Honor: A Civic Hymn*

The emotion label for "Ballots of Honor: A Civic Hymn" is **inspiration and reverence.** The poem honors the importance of voting and democratic participation, evoking a deep respect for civic duty and encouraging active engagement in shaping the future.

176.   *Evolving Truths: The Kamala Chronicles*

The emotion label for "Inspiration Behind the Series 'Evolving Truths'" is **advocacy and determination**. The text conveys a strong commitment to supporting Kamala Harris by addressing misinformation and promoting a nuanced understanding of her record. It highlights my dedication to fostering informed and fair discourse.

177.   *I'm Exhausted*

The emotion label for "I'm Exhausted" is **fatigue and frustration.** The poem captures a profound sense of weariness and irritation with the ongoing political turmoil, leadership challenges, and the nation's state of chaos, reflecting the emotional toll these issues take on individuals.

178.   *Senator Warren and the Fight for Union Rights*

The emotion label for "Senator Warren and the Fight for Union Rights" is **passion and solidarity.** The poem passionately advocates for workers' rights and unionization, highlighting a strong sense of unity and determination in the fight against oppressive laws.

179.   *6,000 Moments: The Heart of Daytime TV*

The emotion label for "6,000 Moments: The Heart of Daytime TV" is **nostalgia and celebration**. The poem evokes a sentimental longing for cherished memories while celebrating the enduring legacy and meaningful connections forged through the daytime TV show's journey.

180. *A Letter to Kamala Harris*

The emotion label for "A Letter to Kamala Harris" is **support and hope.** The poem expresses strong encouragement and optimism for Kamala Harris's leadership, emphasizing unity and a collective aspiration for a brighter future under her guidance.

181. *Uncharted Territory: A Plea to My Nation*

The emotion label for "Uncharted Territory: A Plea to My Nation" is **hope and unity.** The poem conveys a strong sense of optimism and calls for collective solidarity in supporting Kamala Harris during a pivotal moment in the nation's history. It emphasizes the importance of coming together to overcome challenges and forge a better future.

182. *A Nation's Turning Point*

The emotion label for "A Nation's Turning Point" is **anxiety and hope.** The poem captures the tension and uncertainty of a pivotal political moment, reflecting the nation's fears and divisions while also conveying a deep yearning for unity and a brighter future.

183. *The Custodian of Light*

The emotion label for "The Custodian of Light" is **guardedness and resilience.** The poem portrays a deliberate and selective approach to sharing my inner light, highlighting my cautiousness in preserving my energy for moments of true need. It reflects a strong sense of endurance and the ability to maintain balance between illumination and restraint, emphasizing the strength required to navigate and protect against darkness.

184.   The Myth of the One

The emotion label for "The Myth of the One" is **realism and empowerment.** The poem encourages a practical and liberating perspective on love, challenging the traditional notion of finding a single destined partner and promoting the value of compatibility and mutual respect in relationships.

185.   Too, A Reflection on Excess

The emotion label for "Too, A Reflection on Excess" is **frustration and hope.** The poem expresses frustration with the pervasive negativity and divisiveness fueled by the overuse of the word "too," highlighting the challenges it poses to unity and understanding. Despite these frustrations, the concluding verses convey a sense of hope and faith in the power of collective strength and optimism to overcome adversity and foster a brighter future.

186.   My Name in the Hat

The emotion label for "My Name in the Hat" is **determination and defiance.** The poem reflects a bold, spontaneous decision to challenge the status quo in response to feelings of disbelief and frustration. It embodies a sense of courage in taking action, even when the odds seem uncertain or improbable, driven by a desire to effect change.

187.   Voices of Leadership Series

The emotion label for "The inspiration for 'Voices of Leadership Series'" is **inspiration and solidarity**. The text conveys a strong sense of motivation and unity in response to significant political changes, emphasizing support for leadership, diversity, and the collective effort to build a more inclusive and progressive future.

188.   *The Prosecutor and the Felon*

The emotion label for "The Prosecutor and the Felon" is **hope and admiration.** The poem celebrates Kamala Harris's achievements and her role as a transformative leader, conveying optimism for positive change and expressing deep respect for her commitment to justice and progress.

189.   *A New Dawn for K*

The emotion label for "A New Dawn for K" is **hope and resilience**. The poem captures a journey from fear and uncertainty to renewed optimism, emphasizing the strength and perseverance of individuals as they strive for a brighter and more inclusive future.

190.   *In Memory of Melissa*

The emotion label for "In Memory of Melissa" is **grief and remembrance**. The poem poignantly honors Melissa's memory, capturing the deep sorrow of her loss while celebrating the lasting impact of her kindness, joy, and the love she shared with those around her.

191.   *A Shadow Looms: The Mandate's Grip*

The emotion label for "A Shadow Looms: The Mandate's Grip" is **concern and resistance**. The poem conveys deep apprehension about emerging threats to freedom and diversity, while also expressing a strong determination to defend and uphold democratic values. It emphasizes the urgency to speak out against oppressive forces and to protect the nation's cherished rights and liberties.

192.   *Buenos Días*

The emotion label for "Buenos Días" is **hope and encouragement**. The poem inspires a positive and mindful start to the day, emphasizing the importance of nurturing hopeful thoughts and resilience against doubt and fear.

193.   Pillars of My Heart Series

The emotion label for "Pillars of My Heart" series is **Gratitude and Warmth.** This label captures the deep appreciation, love, comfort, and joy that permeate both poems, reflecting the foundational and supportive role these relationships play in your life.

194.   The Comments Section Series

The emotion label for "The Comments Section Series" is **frustration and introspection.** The series captures the chaotic and often polarized nature of online discourse, particularly in comment sections, while reflecting on the emotional and psychological impact of engaging in these digital spaces. It explores the tension between support and negativity, as well as the broader implications for public perception and mental health.

195.   Voices from the Feed Series

The emotion label for 'Voices from the Feed Series'" is **reflection and urgency.** The series is inspired by the dynamic political discourse and its impact on society, emphasizing the critical need to address misinformation and the power of social media in shaping perceptions. It conveys a reflective tone about the current political landscape while urging thoughtful engagement and mental well-being in the midst of intense political and social challenges.

196.   A Unity of Voices

The emotion label for "A Unity of Voices" is **hope and collaboration.** The poem celebrates the partnership of Tim and Kamala, highlighting their shared vision and determination to bring about positive change. It conveys a sense of optimism and unity as they work together to inspire and uplift the nation.

197.   *Intentional Ignorance*

The emotion label for "Intentional Ignorance" is **anger and defiance**. The poem conveys strong frustration towards the intentional disrespect of Kamala Harris's name, highlighting the impact of such actions and asserting the need for respect and recognition.

198.   *The Party of Progress*

The emotion label for "The Party of Progress" is **confidence and pride**. The poem highlights the achievements of Democratic leadership in fostering economic growth and job creation, contrasting them with other administrations. It conveys a sense of optimism and assurance in choosing a path that values progress, care, and unity for the future.

199.   *A 2024 DNC Poetic Journey*

The emotion label for "A 2024 DNC Poetic Journey" is **hope and empowerment**. The series conveys a sense of optimism and determination, capturing the transformative energy and emotional depth of the 2024 Democratic National Convention. It emphasizes themes of unity, resilience, and the collective will to pursue a better future, driven by a deep belief in progress and justice.

200.   *A Promise for All Americans*

The emotion label for "A Promise for All Americans" is **unity and optimism.** The poem evokes a sense of national solidarity and hope for the future, emphasizing collective effort, diversity, and shared aspirations. It celebrates the strength found in unity and the promise of a better tomorrow for all.

201.   *Who is Tim Walz?*

The emotion label for "Who is Tim Walz?" is **admiration and pride**. The poem highlights Tim Walz's qualities as a dedicated leader, teacher, and veteran, emphasizing his strong values, service to others, and commitment to protecting and uplifting the American people. It conveys a sense of respect and confidence in his ability to lead.

202.   *Down to the Thread*

The emotion label for "Down to the Thread" is **urgency and anticipation**. The poem captures the high-stakes nature of the final stretch in a political race, filled with tension and the weight of decisions that will shape the future. It conveys a sense of anxious excitement and the critical importance of the moment.

203.   *The Fence Walkers' Call*

The emotion label for "The Fence Walkers' Call" is **uncertainty and expectation.** The poem reflects a call for clarity and substance in political leadership, expressing the need for a detailed plan to win over undecided voters. It conveys a sense of urgency for action and concrete solutions in a time of high stakes.

204.   *Threads Unraveled*

The emotion label for "Threads Unraveled" is **skepticism and doubt**. The poem conveys the uncertainty and hesitation of those who remain unconvinced by Kamala Harris's message, despite her passionate delivery. It reflects a lingering wariness and the challenge of winning over those still on the fence.

205.   *Ghetto*

The emotion label for "Ghetto" is **resilience and frustration**. The poem highlights the deep injustices faced by marginalized communities, expressing frustration at the misrepresentation and systemic racism that fuel the negative connotations of the word "ghetto." At the same time, it celebrates the strength, pride, and perseverance of those living in these communities.

206.   *The Childless Cat Lady's Voting Guide*

The emotion label for "The Childless Cat Lady's Voting Guide" is **empowerment and wit**. The poem encourages responsible, informed voting with a humorous and playful tone, emphasizing the importance of critical thinking and research in the political process. It delivers a lighthearted yet meaningful call to action.

207.   *Embarrassment*

The emotion label for "Embarrassment" is **disapproval and shame**. The poem critiques the arrogance and chaotic leadership of Donald Trump on the global stage, expressing a sense of national and international embarrassment while highlighting the disconnect between his self-perception and the reality of his reception by world leaders.